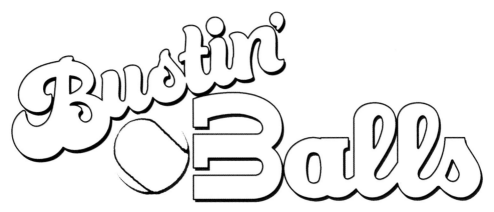

WORLD TEAM TENNIS 1974–1978
PRO SPORTS, POP CULTURE AND PROGRESSIVE POLITICS
BY STEVEN BLUSH

BUSTIN' BALLS
World Team Tennis 1974–1978
Pro Sports, Pop Culture, and Progressive Politics

ISBN: 9781627310994
©2020 Steven Blush
Blush Books · www.StevenBlush.com

Designed by Ron Kretsch
Cover photo by Elliott Curson

Printed in Korea
10 9 8 7 6 5 4 3 2 1

Feral House
1240 W Sims Way #124
Port Townsend WA 98368

www.FeralHouse.com

Contents

Chapter 1

World Team Tennis

CULTURAL REVOLUTION THROUGH SPORTS

Billie Jean King, Philadelphia Freedoms, 1974
"Mother Freedom" fought for on-court equality

> ## *"For too long, tennis has been a rich, white country club game. It's time for a change."*
> **—BILLIE JEAN KING, Philadelphia Freedoms, 1973**

World Team Tennis wasn't just a new sports league: it was a new sport. The tennis boom of the '60s and '70s inspired it, as did the era's social progress—particularly the emphasis on gender equality, and leveling the playing field for women. It was a left-leaning pro sport, a business venture to change the world through a new sports construct.

Team tennis made perfect sense in the '70s because it captured the era's look and feel. The WTT mindset was stealthy and subversive in a mainstream athletic realm, with its overlap of pro sports, pop culture and proto-woke politics. It was a bold social experiment promoting a cultural revolution through sports.

You have to go back to what tennis was: a sport of the rich, played in gated enclaves—the epitome of civility. WTT took on a stuffy, white, upper-crust country-club pursuit, and took aim at its "quiet, please" staging.

Tennis had changed greatly since its 1874 roots in Major Walter Clopton Wingfield's gardens (though lawn tennis variations went back to the 1100s). Especially after WWII, with the popularity of indoor courts, and better equipment by the '60s, like larger racquets and easier-to-follow yellow balls. But everyone still wore white, and was generally well behaved.

World Team Tennis tried to transform a popular sport accentuating the achievements of the individual into a team sport, rooted by loud crowds. To the core audience of tennis purists committed to church-mouse silence, this concept bordered on heresy, but WTT aimed to strip the finest old-world leisure activity of its most pompous aspects and deliver it to working-class American sports audiences, and casual tennis fans.

Many of the players were rowdier than the heckling fans. Women wore shorter dresses and tighter blouses than ever dared at Wimbledon or Roland Garros. There were plenty of sexy players, salty backstories and circus-like sideshows to follow.

WTT's most radical concept was men and women on the same court together—with women's scores worth equal value to men's. Aside from economic success, the league's ultimate goal was a heartfelt effort to open sports fans' minds to gender equality. It was like a sports re-education camp, promoting tolerance through athletics.

"Woman and men are equal in World Team Tennis. That's because we've always had to fight for everything we've gotten. Women definitely get the respect."

—ROSIE CASALS, Detroit Loves, 1974

Billie Jean King officially introduced World Team Tennis to the media in the weeks leading up to her epic "Battle of the Sexes" with Bobby Riggs. She practiced for that match at the home of her WTT team owner. We now understand September 20, 1973's match at the Houston Astrodome as that socio-political moment which redefined gender equality in sports and male primacy in the workplace.

WTT was in fact a version of King-Riggs: with men and women facing each other on the court. Billie saw the future of sports as men and women competing together, and team tennis was a fulfillment of her commitment to the feminist struggle—with an equal number of men and women on each roster, working to achieve a common goal.

Hers was a daring vision, and a radical departure. No one had tried such a thing in sports, and nobody could've attempted such a feat other than a renegade like King.

"Just say I'm here because I'm part of the women's lib movement. Billie Jean King is my idol. She proved that women really aren't all that inferior in sports."

—PAM AUSTIN, Denver Racquets, 1974

WTT connected to the rise of the pro women's circuit, and the inequities addressed by "The Original 9." That's when King, Rosie Casals, Kerry Melville, Nancy Richey, Peaches Bartkowicz, Kristy Pigeon, Judy Dalton, Valerie Ziegenfuss and Julie Heldman signed $1 contracts with *World Tennis* publisher Gladys Heldman to launch a series of women's tournaments in 1970 that became the Virginia Slims Tour. The ladies' work inspired 1972's Title IX legislation, the benchmark for women's equality in school sports.

Before that moment, women's tennis was viewed as a sideshow or an exhibition. On average, men winners made $50,000, while women got $7,500. In late 1972, Slims netter Shari Barman discussed the inequality with her Hollywood agent father—and Fred Barman became a league co-founder. Each of "The Original 9" partook except for Judy Dalton (Julie Heldman worked as WTT color commentator for an embryonic HBO).

Billie Jean's husband Larry King played a key role in WTT, as co-founder, president, commissioner, marketing chief, and franchise owner/GM. Larry saw the league as an effective way to showcase Billie Jean as her career wound down.

Larry King and Billie Jean Moffitt met at Cal State LA where he was a star on one of coach Scotty Deeds' famed college teams. The two married in 1965 and split up in the late '70s, long before their 1987 divorce. Their relationship may make little sense today, but they lived in a very different world.

WTT took place during the swinging '70s. The unisex rosters consisted of brothers and sisters, husbands and wives, and friends and lovers. The milieu made for marriages, divorces, affairs, quickies and other perfidies.

Three members of the Austin and Amritraj families played WTT, as did siblings with surnames Richey, Holladay and Gerulaitis. Kerry Melville and Raz Reid fell in love as teammates, and are still married. Clark Graebner traded the mother of his children for a younger blonde. Betty Ann Grubb had an affair with her coach before she married her second husband—and for a while the three awkwardly traveled together in the team van.

> ## "In Philadelphia, Billie Jean got up onstage with us. While she was dancing, I was hitting tennis balls into the crowd in a Freedoms jacket. That was the roots of writing 'Philadelphia Freedom.'"
> —ELTON JOHN, 1975

WTT overlapped with rock and roll culture. Elton John wrote "Philadelphia Freedom" in tribute to his friend Billie Jean King and her team, the Philadelphia Freedoms. The band Bread penned the Billie Jean paean "Mother Freedom" that played before Freedoms games.

Vitas Gerulaitis of the New York Apples made the scene at Studio 54, Regine's and Le Jardin. Kenny Rogers, the Pittsburgh Triangles' most famous season ticketholder, regaled crowds singing his sordid 1967 hit, "Ruby, Don't Take Your Love To Town." Phoenix Racquets star Dean Martin Jr. had a famed pop star past as a celebrity-son member of Dino, Desi and Billy (1968's "I'm a Fool"). Miami journalists dubbed Florida Flamingos player-coach Frank Froehling's roster "The Froehling Stones." The Denver Racquets and Boston Lobsters made as much news for their co-ed locker rooms.

WTT was born of a subversive spirit, at the height of the Cold War, when Americans still loathed the communist Soviet Union. So the league shocked the world in 1976 when the top netters of WTT and the USSR competed in a "friendly" series played under WTT rules, with well-received games from Moscow to Indianapolis. In 1977— one year after the patriotic American Bicentennial—the league fielded the Soviet national team in their ten-team circuit. It's difficult to explain how subversive and disconcerting it all was.

Team sports reigned supreme in the early '70s. So WTT's planned success formula was to pull from the millions of American weekend tennis players. The league also felt that as a team sport, it could push a specific roster every night, immune to tournament upsets.

The era's "sports league boom" was based on the mistaken belief that fans craved something new and different. In 1973, former Buena Park, CA mayor Dennis Murphy, behind the American Basketball Association (ABA), World Hockey Association (WHA) and World Football League (WFL), joined with Larry and Billie Jean King, Fred Barman and Chicago indoor tennis club mogul Jordon Kaiser to form World Team Tennis.

Murphy was able to align 16 owners, many he either knew or worked with in the other upstart circuits. What all the "renegade sports leagues" shared were hard-charging

Tennis

World Team Tennis

WTT's no-line court, as seen on a 1977 trading card

entrepreneurs with little to no experience running sports franchises. Those unable to scout tennis talent lost their shirts as fly-by-night ventures. None of these owners were mega-rich in need of seven-figure tax write-offs.

As tennis' answer to the ABA's red, white and blue basketball, WTT introduced in 1976 their multicolored court. Service boxes were blue and green, backcourts brown, sidelines red, and the alleys maroon. League officials said the lineless court made it easier to follow the ball. But the players found it difficult, especially off the green. Larry King invented the multicolored court—and the man was colorblind! The playing surface, first used at the Soviet series, was "Sporteze" or "Sport-Face," a thin portable rug-like floor. It was a fast surface that when wrongly applied made for erratic bounces.

Team monikers reflected the city and region or an aspect of tennis. So there were the New York Sets, Chicago Aces, Denver Racquets, Detroit Loves, and L.A. Strings; there were the Baltimore Banners (for Francis Scott Key's "Star-Spangled Banner"), Golden Gaters (for the Bay Area's Golden Gate Bridge), Pittsburgh Triangles (the city of Three Rivers), Philadelphia Freedoms (as in Independence Hall), San Diego Swingers (later the Hawaii Leis), and Houston E-Z Riders (for owner E.Z. Jones and the film *Easy Rider*).

WTT received news coverage, from sporadic TV broadcasts to beat reporters in the *New York Times, Los Angeles Times, Boston Globe*, and *Sports Illustrated*. Wire services ran team standings and player transactions, for papers nationwide. News copyrighters wrote headlines like: Freedoms Curtailed, Banners Furled, Triangles Bisected, Strings Tied, Lobsters Extinct.

Most teams had few American stars, but rather a smattering of Aussies, Indians, Brits, Dutch, Swedes and French. Tennis insiders derided the league for its retread players. But when WTT took its midseason break for Wimbledon, its players won many of the titles.

"I've gotten a lot out of tennis. But I've tried to think of the feminine and feminist parts too."
—EVONNE GOOLAGONG, Pittsburgh Triangles, 1974

The league offered all the trappings of the team-sports experience. The players—each team of three men and three women—sat on benches in uniforms with their names and numbers on the back. Each team had a coach or a player-coach, who set the lineups and argued line calls like a baseball manager. League bylaws allowed for substitutions, player shuffling in the middle of a game, like a manager bringing in a relief pitcher. There were 15-minute intermissions (that could last an hour). Many netters enjoyed the camaraderie, but every squad had to rid itself of members who could not adapt to the team game.

The league tweaked tennis' rules to attract non-tennis fans. Everything was geared to speed up the game and prevent painfully long matches. Rhode Island tennis promoter James H. Van Allen even reinvented the scoring system. Roman numerals replaced Anglicized French words like "love" and "deuce." Each match consisted of five events: women's singles, women's doubles, men's singles, men's doubles, and mixed doubles. The player or doubles pair earned one point for every game victory so accumulated games decided the matches, not sets.

A big innovation was the "super-tiebreaker," to avoid long matches of "deuce." If a match remained deadlocked after five sets, each team picked a mixed doubles duo, and whichever squad first scored five points was declared the winner. To add to the action, when the sudden death point reached three-all, the server had a choice of sides to serve.

> **"The short sets create interesting tennis; you have to pay attention to each point. We should adopt it for all play—it's so much more exciting!"**
> —MONA GUERRANT, New York Sets, 1977

The referees made for quite a sight. WTT matches in 1974 included up to 12 officials, between in-chair and on the floor. Things got streamlined down to four linemen, with fit young men not wearing stiff suits but blue shirts with numbers, gray slacks and sneakers, running around the court. Two linesmen in fixed positions crouched to watch the baseline and one sideline at the server's edge, as the other two fixed linemen watched service line and centerline at the receiver's end. When the receiver returned serve, the two movable men darted into place between rallies to watch the other sideline and baseline.

All the linesmen attended one of the league's officials' training schools, and all 144 graduates earned $25 a match, unlike most linesmen back then, who worked for free. Not like country club tourneys, linespersons included blacks, women, and refs of other sports, like retired MLB umpire Al Forman. A few became local celebs, like Nancy Lewis (L.A. Strings), Dick Roberson (San Diego Friars) and Warren Wertheimer (Golden Gaters).

From the start, the league's primary problem was that attendance never approached the break-even point necessary to pay the salaries needed to attract marquee players. Turnout figures were vastly inflated—yet those bogus numbers still told the story.

In 1974, the 16-team league drew an alleged 833,966, averaging 2,369 fans per match. In 1975, 10 teams drew 503,858 for an average crowd of 3,053. Business boomed in 1976 with the arrival of Chris Evert (her Phoenix franchise made up 40% of league business) luring 843,144 or 3,850 per. In 1977, the league predicted a million fans but reached just 850,000. In 1978, the final season, WTT broke the million-fan mark with two weeks. No franchise made money.

The league took on tennis' power elites, and lost handily. They fought the law and the law won. Part of the move to play pro tennis indoors was to break free of the promoters. But in the end, all the big tournaments, sanctioning bodies, and industry gatekeepers did their utmost to kill the league or to shake it down. They diverted major advertisers and likely allies with power plays and legal wrangling designed to vex WTT at every turn.

> **"The owners ran the league as though they weren't working for the same corporation, and the players treated it like it had as much money as baseball or football. They fought each other instead of working together to keep the league going."**
> —LARRY KING, World Team Tennis president, 1978

1975 MEDIA BROCHURE

WORLD TEAM TENNIS

WTT Media Guide, 1975
Athletics and activism in action

The owners were like the gang that couldn't shoot straight. Proprietors with authoritarian surnames like Fuhrer, Kaiser, and King were undone by infighting. There was little sense of unity, and owners regularly spoke of acquiring others' players under contract.

The players displayed a similar lack of loyalty, taking leave from their teams to partake in second-tier Opens and never pushing the overall product. Tennis fans cared little for WTT's mixed-gender doubles focus, and resisted changes to the game and culture. Any league's success depends upon its teams' ability to build a fanbase, and few delivered.

Today, the original WTT reads like other grand failed experiments too far ahead of their time, yet many of its constructs endure. Born of activism—progressive in a most positive sense—this sports league not fueled by patriarchy foretold our future.

Along with gender justice came a tacit focus on the taboos of sexual equality, LGBTQ long before meat-&-potatoes America was ready. The league also reached out to African-American netters—WTT's most offbeat offshoot was 1978's mixed-doubles tandem of NBA star John Lucas and transgender sports legend Renée Richards. So WTT's greatest challenge as the first sexually integrated league was to successfully position sports equality into a saleable package.

Too bad its promised racial integration never materialized. Neither players like Margot Tiff, Lenny Simpson and John Lucas nor involved stars like Reggie Jackson and Bill Cosby sparked an inner-city tennis uprising. Yet in other ways, the league literally changed the world—for instance, the rise of Eastern European tennis connects back to its WTT ties.

> **"My aim is to be a good tennis player, not a good black tennis player. But I've seen what pressures —especially racial—can do to athletes, and I don't want that to happen to me."**
>
> **—MARGOT TIFF, Cleveland Nets, 1975**

Because of WTT, tennis loosened up. Traditional rules evolved. It was the dawn of the athlete as performer, and the league provided colorful stages, resulting in flashy clothing, screaming fans, and increased prize money and TV opportunities. The league was into modern street marketing and corporate tie-ins long before anyone else. Because of WTT, tennis became less about who you knew and more about what you could do.

The league impacted modern pro sports, as the breeding ground for future team owners and sportscasters, be it Robert Kraft (New England Patriots) and Jerry Buss (L.A. Lakers) or reporters like Lesley Visser, Mary Carillo, Mike Lupica, Skip Bayless, Dave Sims, John Clayton, Dan Shaughnessy, and Tony Kornheiser. Most notably, gender equality on the playing field started with Billie Jean King's efforts with WTT. Much credit rightly goes to Virginia Slims Tour and Title IX—but WTT was the social laboratory where such integration began.

Today, the WTT brand has been reinvented, as a corporate-based exhibition of rising talents and retired pros: a club sport, on par with pro lacrosse or semi-pro soccer. Most everyone in attendance gets tickets through or distributed by some financial services firm.

Margot Tiff, Cleveland Nets, 1975
WTT's first African-American star

For various cultural reasons, no Great American Tennis Revolution ever materialized. At the time of this writing, tennis is less popular in the USA than at any time in the past 50 years—a trend few could have foreseen.

"It was of an earlier time when tennis was exploding, and there were people with new ideas trying to find ways of making money. The initial concept of Team Tennis as it started was a great idea."
—GEOFF MASTERS, Indiana Loves, 2019

"World Team Tennis opened up with a pop and now sounds like a bowl of soggy Rice Krispies."
—BILL COSBY, 1974

Chapter 2
WTT 1974-1978
THE HISTORY

Phil Dent, Detroit Loves, 1974

"World Team Tennis has revolutionized professional tennis. We are ready to play!"
—BETTY JONES, Houston E-Z Riders, 1974

"White is out and love is a forbidden word," declared M. Charles "Chuck" Reichblum, a national news syndicator and former Duquesne University sports information director, in announcing the National Tennis League (NTL), modeled after the major pro circuits like football, baseball and basketball.

"We're shooting to make this a major league operation," he said. "We'll stress colorful balls and uniforms. The traditional white not only will be discouraged, it will be banned. We also aim to get away from the Victorian scoring, which has been a major drawback to the game's popularity." NTL notably planned to integrate women and men on each team.

Reichblum said at an October 4, 1972 press conference he could not release specifics about his NTL, slated to begin May 4, 1973, but that there were 32 cities under serious consideration for $250,000 franchises, with four on the verge of joining—Pittsburgh, Miami, Los Angeles and Houston.

The new league, based in Pittsburgh but incorporated in Delaware, introduced Reichblum as president, attorney William D. Sutton as secretary, and industrialist John H. Hillman III as treasurer. The founders said that they'd not yet reached out to the tennis establishment—such as the U.S. Lawn Tennis Association (USLTA), International Lawn Tennis Federation (ILTF) or World Championship Tennis (WCT)—about their plans. Chuck posited: "We are going it alone. We're confident the vast growth of tennis will make our team tennis concept successful."

Then, at March 14, 1973's Los Angeles Sportscasters Luncheon, Dennis Murphy of Fullerton, CA, who co-founded the American Basketball Association (ABA), World Hockey Association (WHA) and World Football League (WFL), announced the International Professional Tennis League (IPTL), a new league to feature matches between teams of men and women representing 12 unsold North American cities.

Murphy, with Hollywood agent Fred Barman (the two knew each other since Barman represented WHA L.A. Sharks winger Mike Byers), Billie Jean King and her husband Larry, and CFO Jim Jorgensen, said their new league planned to begin play in April 1974.

Larry King said that Billie Jean 100% favored team competition involving men and women, and the total reboot of a sport based on separate tournaments for the sexes. There was nothing new about promoters trying to turn individualistic athletics into team sports; as it had been unsuccessfully tried with bowling, boxing and golf.

Their league's uniqueness was "intersexionality"—women and men on the same court, playing mixed doubles for pay, and their singles sets counting just as much. Murphy also announced an April 28 meeting for potential franchise owners at Miami's Jockey Club.

"Both parties recognized that to have two groups trying to organize rival tennis leagues would precipitate another war."
—DENNIS MURPHY, World Team Tennis co-founder, 1973

A potential legal battle was averted between the two embryonic leagues over control of the new idea of team tennis when backers of the NTL and IPTL met at the Jockey Club the night before on April 27, and announced a merger to create what was first called the World Team Tennis League.

Murphy said franchises would be announced at a league meeting in Chicago May 21-22, though three had already been awarded to NTL founder Chuck Reichblum in Pittsburgh (awarded a franchise in exchange for dropping legal action), Jordon Kaiser in Chicago (owner of the defunct WHA Chicago Cougars), and tennis-mad oilman E.Z. Jones in Houston. Nick Mileti, owner of the WHA Cleveland Crusaders (and later the NBA Cavaliers) had just about locked up a Cleveland franchise.

A league official said 32 investors from 29 cities sought franchises. Other cities being considered included Atlanta, Boston, Buffalo, Cincinnati, Dallas, Denver, Detroit, Fort Lauderdale, L.A., Milwaukee, Minneapolis, Mexico City, New Orleans, New York, Philadelphia, Portland, St. Louis, St. Paul, San Diego, San Francisco, Tampa, Toronto, Norfolk-Richmond and Washington, D.C. The official also said that three different groups sought a Miami team. Murphy wanted a 12-team league in its first season. Reichenblum's business model showed how the league could break even with 3,000 paid fans per game.

Representatives of the 16 franchise finalists met at Chicago's Ambassador West Hotel for World Team Tennis' formal introduction. The meetings began by introducing league commissioner George MacCall—a 1965-67 U.S. Davis Cup captain who teamed with Pancho Segura—signed to a lucrative five-year deal. MacCall and Executive VP Kaiser led the confab, explaining the season would run from May to August, with all matches at air-conditioned indoor facilities. The season's timing was to curb conflict with existing tourneys, including a mid-year break for Wimbledon.

Murphy also said the 16 teams would compete in two divisions: eight in the Eastern Division, eight in the West, each broken down into two Sections: the Atlantic and Central Sections in the East, with the Gulf Plains and Pacific Sections in the West.

Murphy identified the franchises and their principal owners okayed to pay the $50,000 franchise fee as: Boston, Raymond Ciccolo; Chicago, Jordon Kaiser; Cincinnati, Brian Heekin and Bill DeWitt, Jr.; Cleveland, Nick Mileti; Denver, Frank Goldberg, Bud Fisher and Ben Press; Detroit, Seymour Brode and Marshall Greenspan; Houston, E.Z. Jones; Los Angeles, Jerry Buss, Jerry Fine, Dennis Murphy and Fred Barman; Minnesota, Len Vannelli,

BOSTON LOBSTERS

The Best Catch In New England

1978 Ticket Order Form

Martina Navratilova

Martina Navratilova, Boston Lobsters, 1978
Czech exile in the cradle of Yankee capitalism

John Finley and Lee Meade; New York, Jerry Saperstein; Philadelphia, Dick and Ken Butera; Phoenix, Gary Davidson; Pittsburgh, Chuck Reichblum, John Hillman and William Sutton; St. Louis, Ted Cohen and Earl Buchholz Jr.; San Diego, Dr. Leonard Bloom; San Francisco, Cathie Anderson and Larry King; Toronto-Buffalo, John F. Bassett and John C. Eaton.

Most WTT owners were connected to other rebel sports leagues. Frank Goldberg and Bud Fisher ran the ABA Denver Nuggets. WHA owners included Kaiser (Chicago Cougars), Mileti (Cleveland Crusaders) and Len Vannelli (Minnesota Fighting Saints). John Bassett and John Eaton owned the WHA Ottawa Nationals and the WFL Toronto Northmen/Memphis Southmen—infamous for poaching Miami Dolphins stars Larry Csonka, Jim Kiick, and Paul Warfield.

Lamar Hunt, the tennis promoter and football team owner who coined the term "Super Bowl," partook in the Chicago meeting, but decided to stay with his WCT circuit. Brian Heekin's Cincinnati Sports Inc. (CSI), behind the ABA Kentucky Colonels and WHA Cincinnati Swords, quit after banks refused to finance a downtown arena (CSI later sold the Colonels to KFC owner John Y. Brown, husband of '70s TV star Phyllis George).

ABA co-founder and WHA president Gary Davidson saw the writing on the wall and sold his Phoenix franchise to a Baltimore bloc for $300,000, six times what he paid for it. Dr. Leonard Bloom, owner of San Diego's ABA and WHA teams, sold out to a Honolulu group for $250,000. Harlem Globetrotters founder Abe Saperstein's son Jerry flipped his New York franchise to Wall Street broker Sol Berg. Nick Mileti dumped his team on his cousin, Cleveland rock & roll deejay Joe Zingale. No other WTT investor made a dime.

WTT's first league meetings took place June 1–2, 1973 in Palm Springs at the Ocotillo Lodge, run by L.A. owner Jerry Buss. There, the owners established league's bylaws—naming a Board of Directors, run by president Murphy, VP Kaiser, and administrator Larry King. To sign players, they selected a three-man recruiting committee, led by King, MacCall, and Player Personnel Director Steve Arnold (who convinced hockey star Bobby Hull to sign with WHA, and later ran Major League Volleyball). All 16 owners who paid $50,000 felt blindsided by additional levies of $10,000 needed to run the 1974 season.

Even though WTT's upcoming three-month season would take a two-week break to allow its stars to compete in Wimbledon, European tennis elites feared the league because its schedule cut directly across the French and Italian Opens.

WTT representatives met in London over the weekend of June 24 with the Association of Tennis Professionals (ATP). WTT hoped to attract major stars from the International Lawn Tennis Federation circuit. The ILTF connected to tennis' various governing bodies like the ATP and USLTA.

"This is a time when we need to be united. We need to preserve our global circuit that we have built up, and safeguard proper tennis, as we know it."
—JACK KRAMER, ATP Director, 1973

Jack Kramer, director of ATP, a union with 130 of the world's star players, warned of WTT: "This is a dangerous issue and it needs careful thinking. We've been cautious in our approach to it so far. Now that we know more, the executive board must reevaluate it and decide if our members should get involved or not."

Kramer, a 1940s star who once drew 15,000 to Madison Square Garden during a blizzard, decried "this blatant attempt by rich American businessmen to take over the sport." The agent, the epitome of the tennis establishment, saw how this renegade league could weaken ATP's control of the men's game. Kramer even floated the idea of holding $100,000 tourneys every week WTT played, to prevent his stars from being drawn away.

ATP was already at war with ILTF, with no end in sight. Kramer led a boycott of the world's top 70 men from 1973's Wimbledon, over ILTF's decision to suspend Yugoslavia's Niki Pilić for refusing play Davis Cup matches for his Communist nation.

As a battered Wimbledon entered its second day without ATP's top 70, WTT director George MacCall chatted up players and signed a few to his new inter-city league. WTT knew their success could harm the power of ILTF and ATP, and hoped to avoid friction. But those bodies were too wrapped up in the Pilić issue to close ranks and counter the WTT threat.

The 16 teams, each of three men and three women, needed 96 men and women pros. By the end of the Wimbledon boycott, 79 ATP players signed up for WTT's inaugural season. MacCall also claimed to have dozens more verbal deals from WCT and Virginia Slims players. "I think I've talked to 75 percent of the ATP players, and I'm very pleased with their response," he said. "Tennis has always been an individual sport rather than a team sport. But in WTT, we're trying to exploit team spirit in tennis for the first time."

WTT's progressive business model included terrific benefits compared to playing week-in/week-out tournaments—guaranteed pay, pension plan, medical insurance, travel expenses, full-time coaches and trainers, local endorsement forecasts, and just 22 road matches over three months.

Many netters just wanted easy money for a 13-week season: the average WTT players in 1974 made $3,900 a week at a time when NBA-ers made $3,300. Plus there was a chance to play on a team, represent a city and connect with a community, a role reversal from their usual touring mercenarism.

So, in a brief time, a radical new pro league was conceived, a unique format devised, a disastrous lawsuit avoided, a commissioner hired, organized attacks thwarted, and 16 franchises sold to vie in a grueling 44-game, 13-week slate. All they needed were stars.

Larry King said each team would obtain player services negotiation rights through a pro draft like football or basketball. He explained: "It will be each owner's responsibility to build a top team. We feel this will be an important sport of the '70s."

MacCall mused: "The concept and the league are Americana. All major sports are built on these concepts. There's no question that the concept is right, the timing is right, and the game is right."

"I strongly believe that this league is in the interest of furthering tennis players' incomes."
—JOHN NEWCOMBE, Houston E-Z Riders, 1973

In the first WTT player draft, held August 3, 1973 on the eighth floor of New York's Time-Life Building, most drafters seemed pitifully unfamiliar with the draftees. But from a grab bag of talent they pulled out prizes like Billie Jean King and John Newcombe.

King, 1973's top women's player and Wimbledon champ, signed a five-year deal with Philadelphia worth a lofty $100,000 per, primarily due to her friendship with owner Dick Butera, proprietor of Hilton Head Tennis Club, where King just happened to work as head pro. Newcombe, the mustachioed Aussie also got $100,000 from Houston, as part of his wish to live by his John Newcombe Tennis Ranch in nearby New Braunfels, TX.

The two were among WTT's ten "preferential choices"—wherein a team could cut a deal for its top pick before the draft. Many of the sport's stars got selected. But there was no sign that any were ready to join.

Selection order was decided from names picked from a hat. Miami chose first with 18-year-old Ft. Lauderdale whiz Chris Evert. When told, Evert said, "There's a 50/50 chance I'll play. If I was to be drafted by any city, I'm glad it's Miami. It's close to my home." But the two parties failed to come to terms.

Next, Boston took Australia's Kerry Melville, San Diego chose her country-mate Rod Laver, and Phoenix picked American Jimmy Connors. Pittsburgh opted for Aussie Ken Rosewall, Detroit took American Rosie Casals and the Golden Gaters went for Australian Margaret Court. Minnesota opted for New Orleans' Linda Tuero, Cleveland took Sweden's Björn Borg, and Chicago chose Illinois icon Marty Riessen, while Tom "The Flying Dutchman" Okker went to Toronto-Buffalo. Aussies rounded out Round One, with Roy Emerson to New York and Tony Roche to Denver.

In these first moments of gender equality in team sports, six women got drafted in Round One, and were 15 of the first 32 players chosen. In all, the 20-round draft of 312 players took six hours. While every player drafted felt attracted by an opportunity to earn more money for less work, they also knew that they could face ILTF bans for partaking in the renegade league.

Despite widespread disbelief WTT would acquire enough big-named stars to succeed, league officials remained upbeat. Dennis Murphy pointed out: "People were saying we wouldn't sign anybody, and already we've signed two of the world's top tennis players."

> **"World Team Tennis, when we announced it, we were the villains, let me tell you. I went to the U.S. Open with Billie, and I got attacked. I mean, Donald Dell, Arthur Ashe—that whole lily-white tennis establishment. They were furious."**
>
> **—DICK BUTERA, Philadelphia Freedoms owner, 2018**

World Team Tennis launched in the weeks leading up to September 20, 1973's $100,000 winner-takes-all "Battle of the Sexes" match at the Houston Astrodome between "The Libber" Billie Jean and "The Lobber" Bobby Riggs—a monumental sports event which

this is WORLD TEAM TENNIS

"This is World Team Tennis" brochure, 1974
The league's first season was a total blur

"The Battle of the Sexes," Astrodome, 1973
Houston-area poster for the historic King-Riggs match

redefined gender equality. Over 30,000 spectators and 50 million American TV viewers saw the 30-something King sweep the 55-year-old postwar tennis star Riggs, 6-4, 6-3, 6-3.

The "Battle" was, in fact, the second of its kind. Four months earlier, in a globally televised Mother's Day showdown, Riggs took on Australian Margaret Court—and both physically and verbally manhandled the prim-and-proper top money-winner on the women's tour, 6-2, 6-1. Billie Jean's beatdown of the women's chauvinistic critic of the women's game held a deeper meaning, for Ms. King, and her vision for WTT.

One pro netter not impressed by the King-Riggs hoopla was recent WTT signee Evonne Goolagong. The Aboriginal netter sneered at her Pittsburgh Triangles press introduction, "It seems like a circus to me. They're like performing seals." When told of that, Billie jeered, "They don't like me because I talk about money all the time. I'm a mercenary. I'm a rebel."

Margaret Court became the next to sign with WTT, coming to terms on a multi-year pact with the Golden Gaters. So by October 29, tour pros signed to WTT included, Billie Jean, Newcombe, Goolagong, Court, Owen Davidson (Minnesota Buckskins), Isabel Fernandez (Pittsburgh Triangles), John Alexander (Los Angeles Strings), Kerry Melville (Boston Lobsters), Kerry Harris (Detroit Loves), and husband-and-wife Clark and Carole Graebner (Cleveland Nets).

Mark Cox, a ranked English pro who'd moved to Canada, spoke with the Oregon Sportswriters and Sportscasters Association before the start of the Pacific Coast Indoor Tennis Tournament—and he assailed team tennis as harmful to the sport. He said, "There are so many initials in tennis, you need a dictionary to understand. It is a duty of the players to keep tennis an international sport." Yet despite his strident remarks, Cox would become one of the few netters to play in all five seasons of the original WTT.

"The last thing the game needs is internal strife. We don't need player bans. It is up to us to work with all organizations for the betterment of tennis."
—WALTER ELCOCK, USLTA, 1974

World Team Tennis—which had yet to swing a racquet—scored its biggest victory when USLTA, father of organized tennis, offered sanctioning. After long negotiations, USLTA president Walter E. Elcock sent his proposal to Jordon Kaiser on January 18, 1974 asking for $200 per match for each of 16 teams plus a TV revenue split. The projected $144,000 would "put WTT players in good standing" for USLTA events like the U.S. Open for the next five years.

The offer was to pave the way for approval by the ILTF, which had threatened to ban WTT players from all major European championships. ILTF planned a January 26 meeting in London, and Elcock was "hopeful Kaiser would accept the offer by that date."

MacCall said, "Our job now is to convince the ILTF that there are enough players for everybody... I'm not saying there isn't going to be trouble, but as long as you have communication, as we have with the ILTF, you have a strong chance of avoiding it."

In a conciliatory move to the ILTF, George MacCall and Dennis Murphy said the owners voted to allow any WTT players to play in the ILTF's big five tournaments—a move that could wreck rosters and marketing plans.

The basic issues, already clouded in a battle for control of the game, were complicated by an about-face by the ATP, who first offered support, but in a bid to quell militants who wanted a ban, did a complete policy reversal and said it would not expel members who joined WTT but it would take a neutral position in the debate. The British Lawn Tennis Association "kept open" its options about the threat WTT posed in Europe. Opposing the ban were Australia and the USLTA led by Walter Elcock.

But Italy, France and Sweden insisted on expelling any player signed to WTT. They saw WTT as a threat to their domestic tournaments and a move toward U.S. control of tennis—resulting in a complete break between the parties.

WTT received a boost after a February 14 news conference in London announcing an agreement between WTT and ILTF, in which WTT would pay ILTF $48,000 per year in sanctioning fees and arrange its schedule to not conflict with Wimbledon, U.S. Open, Davis Cup and other major national titles. George MacCall called it "an extremely positive step in the world of tennis. We've always hoped to avoid any confrontations with existing tennis entities but WTT feels that players had to have freedom of choice."

But such a deal still jeopardized top netters' appearances at major "summer circuit" Opens such as the Italian and French.

The next day, WTT took a huge PR hit when WCT player rep Arthur Ashe rebuked the league's overtures, declaring, "Cleveland owns my contractual rights, but I'm not going to play team tennis. I prefer the tournament concept."

That comment was far more restrained than his recent zinger that WTT wasn't what tennis was all about—and that if it worked, he'd eat his racquet. Regarding WCT's initial decision to bar its players, Ashe responded, "We must adopt new ideas and WTT is one of those new ideas. If players earn more money than at tournaments, that is good."

But the threat was palpable: In addition to Ashe and Stan Smith, Marty Riessen had a personal beef with WTT. Riessen said he rejected a multi-year deal with Chicago, after the team put him in ticket advertisements—during their contract negotiation!

Rod Laver said of his talks to join the L.A. Strings: "They made me an offer I could afford to refuse."

"We hope and firmly believe that continental European countries will follow us in our action to preserve traditional tennis."
—PHILLIPE CHARTIER, French Federation president, 1974

Tennis officials from France, Italy, West Germany and Sweden put an angry motion in place Wednesday, May 1 for the annual ILTF meetings. They demanded an inquiry into the ILTF's deal with WTT—namely how it certified WTT events during the French and Italian Opens, and sought a global ban on WTT for changing the basic rules of the game.

France and Italy insisted that WTT players be banned from all their contests. ILTF argued the ceasefire secured the best possible deal with the new league, which included financial inducements for players to compete in the French and Italian tournaments.

WTT stars Jimmy Connors and Evonne Goolagong became pawns in this dispute. They both won step one of the Grand Slam, the Australian Open. Then both got denied a chance to compete in the second leg, the French Open. The French Lawn Tennis Federation (FFLT), led by a Napoleonic chap named Philippe Chartier, refused their bids.

Six days later, a French Tennis Federation spokesman admitted the WTT situation was the main reason for a Connors/Goolagong ban—although the official reason given was their missed formal filing deadlines. The spokesman said, "We're sorry but that's how it is. Even if they'd filed on time, we would have refused them. That is our stated policy."

Philippe Chartier threw down the gauntlet. He denounced WTT as a "circus" while an FTF attorney labeled the league "an obnoxious, disruptive organization, not a sport, but show business like the Harlem Globetrotters." Chartier divulged he'd faced great pressure to accept the netters, yet persisted: "We have no intention at all of changing our mind."

Connors immediately flew to Rome in a final bid to play the Italian Open—where he made no headway in a meeting with Gianfranco Cameli, executive secretary of the Italian Federation. As per Cameli: "There were no grounds at all for a change in the federation's position. The WTT and its players are banned in Italy and that's it. Our position on WTT has been crystal clear: we won't budge one single inch. I am sorry for Connors. I am afraid he hasn't fully understood our position, but there is really nothing that he can do."

Connors then flew to Paris to appeal his French Open ban before Judge Pierre Regnault at the Palais de Justice. Jimmy's lawyer Robert Badinter unsuccessfully argued that the Roland Garros Stadium ban was discriminatory, unfair and prejudicial. An FTF member sniffed, "This is not a question of persons but of principle."

His agent Bill Riordan responded by suing "everyone"—including a $10 million suit naming the French and Italian Federations, and the American heads of ATP, Jack Kramer and Donald Dell, for barring WTT players. Connors joked, "I'm in the wrong court. I should be on clay."

WTT's 1974 preseason got off to a clumsy start when Billie Jean King had to exit a February 17 exhibition in the Detroit suburb of West Bloomfield, Michigan, to nurse a bruise and a cut under her left eye after getting hit in the face by a ceremonial six-foot spinning tennis racquet. Detroit Loves owner Seymour Brode explained: "We have this cute gimmick with a big racquet, which we twirl to see who starts service. King sustained her injuries by the man spinning the racquet, when one edge came down and hit the rim of her glasses." So she sat out the rest of this "test" for WTT, ready to begin play in less than 90 days.

Three days before the May 6 season opener, former U.S. Davis Cupper Ed Turville said:

"I don't see how they'll get 3,500 or 4,000 a night. It's tough to get that for any tournament final, so 22 nights per year could be impossible."

"We're a league based on men's and women's play. For a balanced team to have equal advantages, they must have equal opportunities. The time is now."
—GEORGE MACCALL, commissioner, 1974

George MacCall—who admitted his league was ready to open its first season without USLTA approval—stated from his Newport Beach, CA office: "No investor went into this thinking they'll break even right away. The owners have to be ready to lose $100,000 the first season, but crowds will come. If we pull 2,000 this year, no one will complain."

One tennis exec with inner workings of the negotiations vented: "I can't understand it. They gave one gal player $20,000, a car and an apartment for four months. And she isn't even rated in the Top 10 in our country. They're just throwing money around."

Some franchises proved overzealous. The Chicago Aces promoted an opening-night match between John Newcombe of the Houston E-Z Riders and the Aces' Marty Riessen. But Newcombe was previously committed to playing the WCT finals in Dallas, while Riessen's agent, WTT foe Donald Dell, urged his client to sue the franchise.

Tom Okker would be forced to leave the WCT finals in order to play in the Toronto-Buffalo Royals home opener. He got coerced by a "save the franchise" effort, after local media blasted team management upon learning that the Dutch star would not play opening night as advertised. So, immediately after that Royals' Toronto opener, Okker flew late that night back to Dallas to resume play. WCT officials were livid.

In his introductory essay for WTT's opening night program, MacCall extolled: "I hope our successes signal the beginning of a new era of cooperation in international tennis. The game deserves to become a full-fledged major league spectator team sport."

"This opening match means we're finally going to get tennis to the masses. There was hooting and hollering and I know how it energized my team. The players were saying later, 'The people just loved it!' And I think they did."
—BILLIE JEAN KING, 1974

WTT's opening night at The Spectrum in Philadelphia on Monday, May 6 was treated like a movie premiere, with celebs flown in from Hollywood and New York. The event starred an inter-Penn. rivalry between player/coach King's Philadelphia Freedoms and the Pittsburgh Triangles, led by Australians Ken Rosewall and Evonne Goolagong.

The evening started 30 minutes late, delayed due to a rain deluge that paralyzed much of the East Coast. Iggy Geneva and His Mummers String Band—the gaudily attired icons of Philly's infamous New Year's Day Mummer's Parade—filled the arena of the NHL Flyers and NBA 76ers with melody.

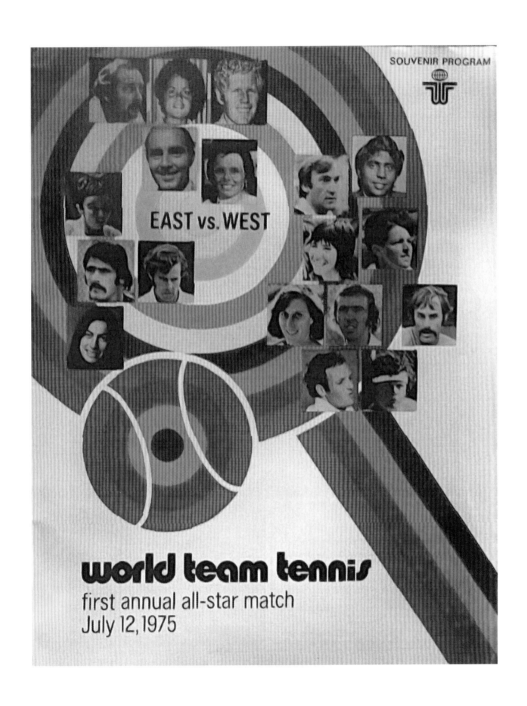

WTT First Annual All-Star Match program, 1975
Equal representation through tennis domination

The dressy crowd of 10,611 (7,324 paid) in the 17,000-seat Spectrum roared when the lights dimmed for opening ceremonies and player intros. A crescendo hit when a huge Liberty Bell replica rolled into the arena and rang. The multi-platinum group Bread's "Mother Freedom," a rockin' ode to Billie Jean King, resounded during warm-ups before her opening match with Goolagong.

The Triangles came on court in bright green-and-yellow cashmere warm-ups—with the team's emblem sewn on the uniforms by the owners' wives right before play began. Pittsburgh co-owner Frank Fuhrer joshed: "We're going in with cashmere, although we may go out in burlap." At the previous day's press conference, King snarled to Triangles GM Chuck Reichblum, "We'll beat the pants off you!"

The trash talk from the Philly bench in blue-and-white unnerved 39-year-old Triangles player-coach Ken Rosewall. Ken lost a point and got so angry at British teen Buster Mottram that he stalked off the court. He shook his racquet in King's face like a scolding teacher, and did the same to her bench. King kept Buster fairly quiet the rest of the night. Rosewall said, "It's one of the conditions we'll have to get used to. It might get worse as the season goes on."

Later it was learned that Vic Edwards—Triangles personnel director and Goolagong's coach/mentor—had a "gentleman's agreement" with King to tone down the bench noise, but she failed to obey. "That's the last time I'll enter in any agreement!" she retorted.

A balcony banner read: "From every tennis court watch the Freedoms win." King lost her opener to Goolagong, but her team prevailed in the three-hour epic 31-25—as red, white and blue balloons rained from the rafters, and Freedoms smacked balls into the crowd.

More noticeable than the tennis was the pro sports hoopla one typically encountered at baseball or basketball games. There was a 20-minute halftime with a series of giveaways, awarding season tickets, autographed racquets, a color TV and a cruise to Nassau. An electronic scoreboard flashed a replica Liberty Bell after every Freedoms point.

But other than a few leather-lunged exhortations, it was hardly the spleen-venting, catcalling, red-blooded American sports fans the league hoped to attract.

King said pre-match: "We're in show business. It's gotta be lively. We don't want people sitting on their hands. Let them scream and do anything."

King, known for habitually counting attendance between strokes, looked at WTT's first turnout and said it would "take three to five years to fill arenas." From the losing dressing room, Rosewall replied, "It's a totally new format. Younger players will find it easier to adapt than the older ones."

Fallout began the next day. Players at the WCT finals weighed in—negatively. WTT jokes replaced Linda Lovelace jokes and ethnic slurs in the hotel lobby and dinner tables.

Ilie Năstase snapped: "WTT should retain the normal scoring system. I don't like the scoring at all. I'll await judgments on the rest of it." Tom Gorman said, "It appears they are trying to cultivate a whole new body of fans and there's a great danger of turning off established fans." Rod Laver snarled, "Now that the bloom is off, it'll be interesting to see how the other matches draw." Năstase, Gorman and Laver all later joined WTT.

"We're very pleased with the crowd reaction. But we are disgusted with the length of the matches."
—LEE MEADE, Minnesota Buckskins GM, 1974

A week into the season, the big complaint was the length of these matches, some lasting four hours. Houston E-Z Riders coach Clarence Mabry, despite starting the year a perfect 4-0, pled for a shorter program. He noted that their fastest match went three hours and 23 minutes. Mabry seemed equally unnerved by the 2,167 that attended the E-Z Riders' home opener at cavernous Sam Houston Coliseum vs. the Chicago Aces.

Likewise, King loved her Freedoms' 6-0 start to the season but was angered by the length of the matches, after it took three hours to shred the Cleveland Nets. Tennis expert Dick Charnock voiced frustration after covering the L.A. Strings' home opening win over the Florida Flamingos at the L.A. Sports Arena that ran well past midnight.

By the next week, owners approved cutting the number of sets in half, to one set each of men's and women's singles, men's and women's doubles and mixed doubles. They also decided that no player could partake in more than two events. Owners also voted to keep practice nets for a substitute to warm up, as a reason ascribed to the match lengths was that substitute players were going in cold. Halftime was cut to curtail matches to the ideal two-plus hours. The league even discussed switching to a less lively ball to prolong rallies. "It all seemed too dull and repetitious," admitted a league official.

"I knew what I was in for when I signed. I support the team concept and I'm in it all the way."
— BETTY STÖVE, Baltimore Banners, 1974

Even WTT's most ardent advocates had to admit that the first month was stormy. For instance, after Game One's 10,000-plus, Philadelphia drew just 1,787 (1,396 paid) for their next home game against Boston. But the league took solace in not all early turnouts being lousy. The Golden Gaters outdrew the baseball world champion Oakland A's in their May 8 home opener. On June 1, a crowd of 9,300 at the Met Center in Bloomington, MN saw the Minnesota Buckskins fleece Billie Jean King's previously unbeaten Freedoms.

Another good sign was all the exciting court action. A "super-tiebreaker" settled every set of Tuesday June 11's game in Denver between the Racquets and Nets, in a wild 32-26 triple super-tiebreaker, to end Cleveland's ten-game win streak. In Toronto, the visiting Pittsburgh Triangles took a nine-point tiebreaker to rip the Royals 26-25. In Chicago, the Boston Lobsters overcame a 6-2 deficit in a final set super-tiebreaker to oust the Aces.

The league needed winning franchises in media capitals like New York, Los Angeles and Chicago in order to generate press and attract advertisers. But those cities' teams began 1974 terribly and drew flies, with home crowds of often less than 1,000 in large arenas.

"I'd like more attendance," said Chicago Aces owner Jordon Kaiser, whose tickets sold poorly at his Lakeshore Racquet Club. George MacCall said, "It's true we have been soft

WTT tickets
Above: Pittsburgh Triangles vs. Toronto-Buffalo Royals, Buffalo, 1974
Opposite: The Soviets vs. Los Angeles Strings, Greensboro, 1977

in some cities, but these things take time." New York Sets GM Jerry Saperstein, ruing the empty tiers at 15,000-seat Nassau Coliseum, where audiences fell from opening night's 4,999 to weeks later 457, said: "We're disappointed but not distressed. We know we can't draw fans by offering free soap bars. We must get our product to the masses, not just tennis fans. Realize over a year we don't have 15,000 seats to fill, we have 330,000."

King said, "Our team will lose money this season but we expected that. We're all optimistic but it will take four years to put WTT across." Freedoms owner Dick Butera said he sold 92,364 tickets in 22 home games—if so, 4,199 per, though all tickets sold after midseason got slashed 50%. Yet he insisted, "fan interest is definitely growing."

> *"Tennis was always really quiet. But in World Team Tennis, Billie and Larry let the fans yell, like in football and basketball. You really had to focus because you never knew when you'd get a catcall."*
> **—TRISH BOSTROM, Sea-Port Cascades, 2012**

In tennis' sanctification of silence, where a foot shuffle in the stands or the sound of a child kills players' focus, WTT crowds were urged to shout, cheer, jeer, sneer and wave signs like at a football game. Fans cast off the shackles of decorum of this hush-hush sport and gave hell to these gentlemanly jocks with timely Bronx cheers, raspberries and taunts. It was a scene that players found hard to adjust to, and purist fans saw as sacrilege.

The Baltimore Banners' Jimmy Connors dove into a Spectrum audience after drunken heckling about his fiancée Chris Evert. Detroit's Rosie Casals fired a serve into the stands in Chicago over the catcalls. Denver's Françoise Dürr, after double faulting to Marita Redondo at the L.A. Forum, drilled a rowdy male spectator with a scorcher to the chest.

> *"Hecklers don't bother me. I'm glad I've played well enough to make them mad as hell."*
> **—ROSIE CASALS, 1974**

The commissioner defended the noise, saying "fans have rights, too" but that he also empathized with Connors: "Speaking as an athlete, not as commissioner, with what was said to Jimmy, I would've gone up there with him." MacCall said all players were issued a "Code of Conduct" that "was not too specific" and he'd judge each case on its merits.

The polite and reserved Margaret Court opined: "I don't like encouraging the wrong kind of fans. Vulgar comments that break a player's concentration are in dreadful taste and destroy what the game is all about. Concentration is a strange thing. People can't get that we can ignore the railroad roaring by or planes zooming overhead at Forest Hills, and then get shaken up by some shout from the stands. But that's just the way it is."

"They got personal. Like, if they felt you weren't the most attractive person, as you were about to serve, they'd tell you to take off the mask."
—ALLAN STONE, Indiana Loves, 2019

Betty Ann Grubb had issues with it all. "The crowd is rough," said the cool Californian competing for Florida. "It was really bad in Detroit during a recent match. They were just animals. You're down on the court and you think about how there's no way out. It hits you psychologically because you're so close to the people, and they're really yelling at you. They just hate you for some reason. You've done nothing wrong, but they really hate you. I guess you expect the crowd to be against you on the road, but not that much."

John Alexander, a 23-year-old from Sydney, hated the abuse his L.A. Strings took May 22 in Pittsburgh. During a 6-4 defeat to fellow Aussie Ken Rosewall, John lost his temper over a fan yelling, "Alexander, you're a bum." So he smacked a ball across the arena, and nearly decapitated a child. He roared: "That wasn't cheering, it was heckling. The owners say that we need to get used to it. I won't and I never will." May 7 at Pittsburgh Civic Center, a chorus of fans razzed Philly's King with "Billie Jean, do you use Brut?"

Hawaii Leis player-coach Dennis Ralston ripped: "Tennis is not like baseball. I like the team concept but some places incite fans to do anything, and that's wrong. In Baltimore and Philadelphia people yell, 'Miss it' when you serve, and the announcers encourage them. And Jimmy Connors going into the stands when someone said things about Chris Evert, tennis doesn't need it. Soon people will start throwing things. Billie Jean says she loves it but all I have to do is hire goons to go heckle her. That's wrong, too." Ralston also called WTT scheduling "a joke" after his team had to play in Miami, Detroit, Houston and Oakland over four days. He said, "We feel like a bunch of zombies."

"We went into the season assuming that because tennis was booming, people would come to the games. We didn't give it the proper promotion."
—RALPH LEO, Chicago Aces publicist, 1974

Halfway through the 1974 campaign, most of WTT's attendance reports included free tickets and inflated figures. Top attendance for any given week were the markets where Billie Jean King had just played. Frank B. Fuhrer, a 49-year-old Pittsburgh insurance exec who'd taken control of the Triangles, conceded that at $50,000 per team, plus contracts, arena rental and start-up, the owners bought licenses to lose. The Minnesota Buckskins folded first, with the league assuming payroll by midseason.

Fuhrer felt that even more ominous than the poor turnout in key cities was ILTF's continued threat to blackball WTT-ers from European play. ILTF gave two reasons for its hesitancy to sanction WTT. First, it objected to the WTT rule that allowed for mid-match substitutions. Second was ILTF's claim it hadn't been paid $46,000 in sanctioning fees.

Fuhrer expressed regret over some fellow owners' failure to deliver: "An agreement is an agreement. Our players are here as a result of the ILTF, and we have a commitment to pay the fee. If we lose our sanction because we don't pay the fee, we deserve to lose it." Other owners, led by Fuhrer foe Larry King, refused to pay ILTF because they felt their sanctions proved ineffectual, and that ILTF should've interceded to fix WTT's French Open ban. Fuhrer vowed, "Four or five owners have to go. Some of them are promoters and not businessmen. But I'm not going to name names."

"What could we do? Without two women, there was no way the Nets could play women's doubles."
—CHUCK REICHBLUM, Pittsburgh Triangles GM, 1974

Another interesting night of WTT occurred in Pittsburgh between Fuhrer's Triangles and Joe Zingale's Cleveland Nets on July 25 before 2,664 at the Civic Arena. With the Nets' Peaches Bartkowicz, one of the league's top doubles players, quitting over Zingale's refusal to re-work her contract (for the seventh time since March!), and their top female Nancy Gunter in William Penn Hospital with a foot injury, Pittsburgh was awarded a 6-0 forfeit win in the opening women's doubles set, resulting in their 26-22 victory.

Cleveland violated a WTT rule saying each squad must have three men and three women players on the bench for every match. But they only dressed one woman, Laura DuPont. When the Nets signed Winnie Shaw Woodridge earlier in the week, they broke another rule: no players could be signed after July 19.

Nets player-coach Clark Graebner groused, "This was a big handicap for my players. We started the match six points down, yet we almost pulled it out." Graebner officially protested the match played with an open roof for "tennis under the stars." He harped, "Many teams have complained about the roof. This is supposed to be an indoor league."

> ## *"We were beaten by a better team tonight. The year was a very good one for us. But now it ended—and what we did before was totally washed away."*
> ### —BILLIE JEAN KING, 1974

The 1974 season ended with a shocking surprise on the court, as Tony Roche's lightly regarded Denver Racquets (30-14) swept Billie Jean King's league-leading Philadelphia Freedoms (35-9) in a best-of-three championship. Billie Jean expressed dismay watching player-coach Roche hoist the inaugural Teflon Cup and get named Coach of the Year. Roche admitted afterwards that he didn't think it would mean so much to win the first World Team Tennis championship.

> ## *"It would be a gross misstatement if I told you there were no teams with financial issues."*
> ### —FRANK FUHRER, Pittsburgh Triangles owner, 1974

WTT endured myriad problems in 1974. The unique league received scant media coverage. Players found it difficult to adjust to being part of a team, and to prepare for 20-minute games. Many were just in it for the money and did not take their obligation seriously. Because the season coincided with the big European clay court tournaments, it proved tough to find capable stand-ins whenever a player left or got hurt.

Of course, the owners erred trying to get these teams into the public eye. Handicapper Jimmy the Greek established 2-1 odds against the league's return for a second season.

Ken Rosewall offered: "This is the only country optimistic enough to start this kind of a league. The owners really went out on a limb. The players can always go back and play the tour circuit. I suppose we'll find out if it's all been worth it."

Florida Flamingos player-coach Cliff Drysdale enthused: "World Team Tennis is the best thing to happen to tennis in years. It has helped generate more publicity for tennis in four or five weeks than anything else has in four or five years." Flamingos reserve Mike Belkin echoed: "WTT gives us tennis bums a chance to get back into it. It used to be that a player was over the hill at 28 but with WTT a guy could play until he's 50."

> ## *"The World Team tennis concept is exciting. But there's a lot to be done before it leaves an imprint on American sports society."*
> ### —PAM AUSTIN, 1974

MacCall reflected on the 1974 season: "It's a wonder that we've accomplished what we have. We had problems with the sanctioning bodies. I made three trips to Europe in seven weeks. We couldn't set a schedule until two months before the season opened. That left people feeling things were up in the air." He also said of trying to sign foreign stars, "In many nations, players are not at ease to play if the governing bodies don't give an okay."

Major media dissed WTT. Curry Kirkpatrick wrote in *Sports Illustrated*: "WTT is the most unprofessional, kinky, bizarre and ridiculous sports gambit to come along. It will need fewer franchises, fewer matches, a shorter schedule and maybe another revised format to escape sinking into oblivion. But it is a living, breathing spectacular tribute to fools and their money." Tennis expert Bud Collins penned: "Nobody's gone into business with greater unfamiliarity since Laurel and Hardy joined the Foreign Legion. Anybody who ever held a racquet got drafted. If you weren't, you should quit the game in shame." As per Jeff Prugh in the *L.A. Times*, "Team tennis is the new rich kid on the block who gets teased for his short pants, speaking with a lisp and insisting on playing by his rules."

Detroit star Rosie Casals retorted: "Why are people knocking change? Yes, we're trying to attract new fans. But we're also trying to get to the common person and the underprivileged—and you just don't get them interested at the country clubs."

In the off-season, the league's front office underwent overhaul. On August 30, a Fuhrer succeeded a Kaiser when the 16 owners on the Board of Governors elected Frank Fuhrer as WTT president to succeed Jordon Kaiser—forced to resign over lawsuits amid unpaid bills from his Chicago Aces. Fuhrer proffered, "I don't know a tennis ball from a pile of manure. But I know how to keep people organized, motivated and disciplined." The next day, Fuhrer announced the formation of a four-member committee (including himself) to find a replacement for George MacCall who abruptly departed over "policy differences."

"Last year it was so bad, we couldn't get people out to see how shoddy the product was."

—SOL BERG, New York Sets owner, 1975

The lights went out before November 26, 1975's WTT Draft at New York's Americana Hotel—which may have been an omen for the league's second year. Earlier in the day, an owners' meeting proved inconclusive. WTT's biggest battle appeared to be a saturated sports market, in tight economic times.

As for the draft itself, it was to laugh, with celebrities among the draftees. Billie Jean's Freedoms took 55-year-old Bobby Riggs in the seventh round. Boston took Elton John in the tenth, Hawaii picked Bill Cosby in the 13th, and L.A. selected Johnny Carson in the 14th. Detroit spent their final pick on USLTA president Stan Malless; Denver took hoops star John Lucas in the eighth, because the owners of the champion

Racquets ran the ABA Nuggets; Denver also took Dean Martin Jr. in the 15th. None of the above signed for '75.

Neither did any of the top three draft picks sign with the league: Colin Dibley (Boston), Jeff Borowiak (Hawaii) and Julie Heldman (Chicago). Others unsigned first-rounders included Jan Kodes (Baltimore) and Chris Evert (Florida, again). The other 15 franchises also bid for players on the defunct Minnesota Buckskins, netting league coffers $22,500.

While faltering in Year One at the box office, WTT completed their season—which was more than could be said for the recently defunct World Football League. It was a season in which the 16 teams lost a collective $8 million, thrice the projected amount.

> ### *"The honeymoon is over. We paid players more than they ever made and a lot of them had a take-the-money-and-run attitude. That bothers me."*
> —RAY CICCOLO, Boston Lobsters original owner, 1974

Stacks of bills went unpaid. Thirty players, over 20% of the league, were not fully paid. A babysitter answered the league phone, situated in Hopkins, Minnesota, as the publicist kept odd hours. Buckskins GM Lee Meade joked: "We're in a contest to see who can lose the least money because nobody will make any, that's for damn sure." Loves GM Bob Love lamented, "We're like every other WTT team: we're for sale."

At January 15, 1975's league meetings, the '74 champion Denver Racquets became the Phoenix Racquets, sold to a group with Oakland A's slugger Reggie Jackson. WTT also granted the new San Diego Friars to Frank Mariani, law partner of L.A. owner Jerry Buss.

Other franchises were given six weeks to settle their debts and raise money in the form of a $50,000 letter of credit to partake in the 1975 season—an insurance policy to cover possible salary non-payments or other financial breaches. Also at these meetings, owners voted to replace Frank Fuhrer with Larry King. "Mr. Billie Jean" mused: "We've had a Kaiser, a Fuhrer and now a King. I guess we'll have a Czar next."

WTT returned for Season Two five teams short. The Boston Lobsters folded, and in a convoluted move, the Philadelphia Freedoms became a new Boston Lobsters. Billie Jean got traded to New York, to improve the flagging Sets. The Detroit Loves left Motown for cow town to play as the Indiana Loves. Franchises unable to secure credit folded, so no more Baltimore Banners, Chicago Aces, Florida Flamingos or Toronto-Buffalo Royals.

A redistribution draft resulted in Detroit's Rosie Casals joining L.A., Toronto-Buffalo's Tom Okker to the Golden Gaters, and Chicago's pick Marty Riessen to Cleveland. Of the 133 netters to partake in 1974 only 62 re-signed. For 1975, 26 first-year netters joined the scaled-back league.

Despite 1974's psychic bloodletting, Billie Jean King remained upbeat for 1975: "There are fewer teams but there's more depth and talent this year." Reluctant WTT president Larry King gushed: "A few teams will make money when you consider appreciation of value. Some will make an operating profit. Our league is in terrific shape." Sets owner Sol Berg blasted, "It's been rough, like a poker game with high stakes. Put up or get out."

WTT Magazine, 1975 debut issue
Illustrating the league's progressive vision

Larry King announced an uneven 11-team league for 1975. But when the Houston E-Z Riders shut operations one week before the season opener—unable to provide a letter of credit and facing lawsuits from unpaid players and Union Bank of Houston—the move looked genius. A scheduling fiasco was averted with a balanced two-division league.

"The league wasn't designed to destroy tennis. It was designed to enjoy good tennis."
—FREW McMILLAN, Golden Gaters, 1975

Everyone agreed there were too few spectators and too much travel. So for 1975 a bloc led by L.A.'s Jerry Buss came up with the "WTT Spectacular"—eight teams gathered over a weekend in one city, competing five times in three afternoons. It sounded like something off a circus marquee: "48 of the world's top players, eight exciting teams."

In promoting the Strings' first Spectacular, a 72-hour tennis orgy June 4-6 at the L.A. Sports Arena, team GM Bart Christensen speculated: "There's no place in the world that fans can see this many great players on the same court in just three days."

Indiana Loves GM Bill Bereman concurred: "We and the L.A. Strings people believe in the Spectacular concept, rather than shot-gunning 22 home matches against single teams and trying to promote each one. The argument you hear against the Spectacular concept is you won't be able to build city identity. I won't argue that. But the other argument is, 'Why lose a lot of money trying to build city identity?' The Spectacular decreases costs."

The Indiana Loves ended their first home Spectacular on June 15, losing the weekend's final match to Cleveland, 28-20. Officials at the 18,000-seat Indiana Convention Center estimated the crowds at seven hundred per match. For the weekend, Indiana won three of five; L.A. also won three, San Diego and Golden Gaters each won two, while Hawaii won just once.

Berenson realized "it was a disaster" as these events didn't draw, and the length, up to ten hours, "fatigued crowds." Lobsters GM Bob Mades, while standing by the grandstand watching the slim crowd May 25 at Boston U.'s Walter Brown Arena for the first night of a Spectacular, said, "Maybe I'm crazy but this is not what team tennis is about."

A young Mike Lupica in *World Tennis Magazine*, among the four hundred for that weekend's climax between Phoenix and Indiana, called it "The Marquis de Sade Invitational, like having the Chicago Cubs play the San Diego Padres in Fenway Park."

Jeff Austin of the Phoenix Racquets said, "Everything is bad about the idea of a Spectacular. Who in Boston cares about Phoenix playing Indiana?" Lobsters player-coach Ion Țiriac called Spectaculars "the worst thing to ever happen in sports."

"I was very disappointed in the crowd. I'd do anything to get even 3,000 to the games—go to rallies, ring doorbells, anything."
—VITAS GERULAITIS, Pittsburgh Triangles, 1975

Vitas Gerulaitis was not upset by Saturday, May 5's Triangles match after he got swept 6-0 by the Strings' Bob Lutz or by his team's first loss of the new season, 25-24. The 21-year-old steamed over the mere 1,437 in attendance at Pittsburgh Civic Arena. Asked if Evonne Goolagong missing the game limited the draw, Vitas voiced, "The idea Evonne's absence hurt the crowd holds no water. But if there was a turnout, we would've played harder."

Saturday, July 12, 1975 was a major moment—the first WTT All-Star Match, played before 7,112 at the L.A. Sports Arena. The spotlight event got broadcast live nationally on NBC-TV at 11:30 p.m. EST. A week prior at Wimbledon, WTT netters took 12 of 16 final spots, losing only in men's singles. The league felt like it had turned a corner.

The All-Star Match featured 16 stars, eight from the Eastern and Western Divisions. Tony Roche (Phoenix) and Fred Stolle (New York) served as coaches. The sides partook in a five-set WTT match; Marty Riessen (Cleveland) and Greer Stevens (Boston) led the East to victory, 28-21. Billie Jean King received an ovation, but lost to Françoise Dürr, 6-4—the third time Dürr defeated King in 1975. Riessen got named All-Star Male MVP and Dürr Female MVP. At this event, WTT unveiled its multicolored no-line court.

> **"The court had no lines. They were all in quadrants, divided into four colors. To serve the ball in, you had to hit it in the right square. This was not traditional tennis."**
>
> **—ALLAN STONE, 2019**

Billie Jean King had a monster season with the New York Sets, who won their first 16 games but then lost in a one-game playoff to the Boston Lobsters, a team they'd crushed all year. In the 1975 championship the Pittsburgh Triangles, led by Female MVP Goolagong, swept the Golden Gaters in a best of five.

The Gaters—with Coach of the Year Frew McMillan and Male MVP Tom Okker—played home matches at Oakland Coliseum Arena. But for the finals, they got displaced by Ringling Bros. and Barnum & Bailey Circus, and bumped to S.F.'s Cow Palace.

Playoff MVP Gerulaitis chugged bubbly from the Bancroft Cup, as he dedicated the victory to his leather-lunged "G-men," the "rudest fan club ever." Larry King called it "The greatest night in WTT history."

But despite all the high-decibel revelry, only 11,000 spectators took in the three-game title series. More than a few of the top pro men and women who were quick to jump on the WTT bandwagon in 1974 were kicking themselves for signing multi-year contracts.

The cover of August 1975's *Tennis Illustrated* had a tombstone emblazoned "World Team Tennis, 1974-1975. R.I.P." It was quite clever—however, it was incorrect. No team made money in 1975—but none lost their shirts. Attendance improved and every player got paid. WTT claimed to draw 28% more spectators than in 1974. But despite such modest increases, all the high-priced stars didn't help enough.

The L.A., San Diego and the Golden Gaters developed solid deep-pocketed ownership, as did new groups in Boston and Phoenix (where crowds doubled from

1975
SEASON
ADVERTISING
RATES

world team tennis

World Team Tennis advertising rate card, 1975
Ad rates dropped sharply after the 1974 season

1974 in Denver of 1,881 to 4,066 in 1975). Pittsburgh and New York had wealthy owners but drew poorly, even for promotions (headband night, racquet cover night, ball night, nickel beer night). Hawaii and Cleveland remained question marks.

Indiana averaged 2,300 fans per game, but signed no super-salaried stars; rather, they picked netters proper for a team setting and amassed no super debt. Bill Bereman said nobody on his six-person team earned more than $40,000, so he'd only lose a league-low $100,000.

"We knew we would grow. But I don't think we anticipated how fast we'd move."

—LARRY KING, 1976

Entering season three, WTT's main claim was surviving its first two. In 1975, Hawaii lost $180,000; Pittsburgh dropped $375,000. New York lost the most at $500,000 with the highest payroll ($400,000), while Indiana lost $100,000 with the lowest ($160,000).

When/if WTT made it, New York would be the last team to make money, after the nine other owners each put in $50,000 to fund Sol Berg after his 1974 Sets lost $850,000. Sol said: "No way in hell we'll make money this year but we can make it in the long run." A good sign was all ten teams that partook in 1975 returned for 1976 with ownership intact.

League officials emphasized a *Los Angeles Times* (3/11/76) study on the 1970s tennis boom that said: "Over 33 million Americans now play tennis. This is an increase of over 60% in a year." In a WTT promotional brochure, part of a venture with Minute Maid, Larry King wrote: "If you're hooked on tennis, you'll love World Team Tennis '76."

In February 1976, Triangles owner Frank Fuhrer got re-elected Chairman of the Board, and Larry King remained President. King claimed that those remaining 16 franchises sold in 1974 for $50,000 were now worth between $750,000 and $1,000,000. But Bill Bereman said, "If someone put up $1 million for my franchise right now, he'd have it."

Despite painful travel, limited practices, and dwindling interest, there was a cadre of players certain that team tennis was the fiery brand America was calling for. Billie Jean King did more for tennis than any other pro, sweeping the sport out of the Stone Age. But she didn't have the money to buoy WTT for a few more seasons. Bereman said, "This year could be critical. If the growth isn't as expected, some owners will decide to bail."

The teams were better financed, each with increased $100,000 letters of credit locked in Larry King's safe in Newport Beach. WTT's new standard contract assured each player to play all 44 matches, a far cry from 1974 when Jimmy Connors signed with Baltimore for 18 games—or 1975 when a player had to be available for just 33. Fuhrer said, "All systems are Go. We have good players, an expanded fan base, and small budgets. We're in a tennis boom. If we can't make it now, it's because we're too stupid to run a league."

Ticket sales were up for 1976. The Gaters reported 61,000 advance tickets, compared to 45,000 the past year. Hawaii sold 1,200 season tickets, up from just 650 in '75. Corporate sponsorship soared to $1.5M, from $14,000 in '74. But there was still no national TV deal, with just 1976's All-Star Match aired. Some teams signed local TV/radio deals.

> ## "Whenever Chris Evert came to town it was a big deal, and they'd sell out. Unfortunately, the only time they'd sell out was when Chris Evert came to town."
> —MIKE FRANCESA, sports radio host, 2018

Weekly matches premiered on the embryonic HBO; Wednesday, May 5's debut telecast starred the world's #1 woman Chris Evert's debut with her Phoenix Racquets against the Indiana Loves in Salt Lake City. WTT's first major advertisers were the official tennis ball Penn, official airline American, and official soft drink Tab. WTT also began playing all of its games on multi-colored courts. But far more had to be done to reach breakeven.

December 11, 1975's annual Player Draft addressed WTT's survival in 1976 and beyond. Nearly two hundred of tennis' biggest names got selected. The league reeled in a big fish when Ilie Năstase signed a one-year deal for $100,000 with the Hawaii Leis (after a trade involving the New York Sets, cash, and picks). Hawaii said that the colorful Romanian, his wife and daughter would reside in Honolulu for the five-month season.

Martina Navratilova, granted U.S, asylum from Communist Czechoslovakia, moved in with Fred Barman, his wife, and daughter Shari in Hollywood, before signing a $300,000 multi-year pact with the Cleveland Nets. Rod Laver inked with the San Diego Friars. The draft also held surprises, be it Hawaii's gamble on NBA star John Lucas or San Diego's failure to retain player-coach Dennis Ralston (plucked by Pittsburgh and traded to L.A.).

> ## "I always wanted to play World Team Tennis. I don't want to talk about politics. My mother and father are stuck in Czechoslovakia and I can't see them. The only reason I defected was to play tennis."
> —MARTINA NAVRATILOVA, Cleveland Nets, 1976

Notably AWOL from WTT were top men like Björn Borg, Arthur Ashe and Guillermo Vilas. According to a league official, Sweden's national idol stayed away because "every time WTT makes an offer to Borg, the King of Sweden matches it, and it's unlikely any team could match the wealth of King Carl XVI Gustav." Sets GM Bob Kain remarked, "I feel fairly certain in a year or so WTT will include most of the game's ranking stars."

In one of the first cases of sports free agency, Cliff Drysdale sued the WTT draft for anti-trust violations. The Florida Flamingos picked the South African star in 1974 but failed to pay him in full. He spent the next season in Pittsburgh, who withheld his draft rights. The league did their best to get the case thrown out of court, but on March 5, 1976,

Pittsburgh judge Louis Rosenberg rejected WTT lawyer Frank Clements (older brother of NFL QB Tom Clements) and ruled that the league had to defend its draft in a trial. The league settled out of court with Drysdale, who was free to sign with the San Diego Friars.

On March 8-9, after Larry King broached Soviet tennis officials on a goodwill tennis challenge series between the stars of the USSR and WTT, an American squad let by Billie Jean King steamrolled the awestruck Bolsheviks two nights in a row at a sold-out Lenin Stadium in Moscow. The two sides then crossed the Atlantic for three sparse turnouts in Cleveland, Philadelphia, and Indianapolis, as the Americans celebrated the first and only WTT-USSR Challenge Cup.

Right before the 1976 season opener, Frank Fuhrer demanded Larry King's removal as league president. "King and I are having a battle, and it is dynamite," fumed Fuhrer. The final straw was King's attempt to switch Pittsburgh's May 8 match in Boston against the Lobsters to May 16 so that Evonne Goolagong could partake in a televised promotion in California at La Costa Country Club. Fuhrer relented after sponsor Bristol-Myers bought $10,000 of tickets for two upcoming Triangles games. So he moved the match to May 17. Frank said, "I just don't like the way Larry King does things. We're defending champions and I'm not having King change my schedule to accommodate his interests. We're going to get all of these conflicts of interest out of this league. King will go—it will be done."

King: "As president, I'm not free to speak as an owner. But Frank has his conflict of interests backwards, which isn't unusual. He should be careful speaking to the press on internal league politics because he hurts his franchise as well as his partners. He can be strong-headed but I'm happy he goes for publicity. It's good for the league, and good for the Triangles." Goolagong got hurt in a May 7 game at Pittsburgh Civic Arena and missed May 8's event—with a private jet waiting at Pittsburgh Airport to fly her to the shoot.

"These fans don't come to see tennis. They come to have a drink, have a party; not just to boo me. It's a circus."
—ILIE NĂSTASE, Hawaii Leis, 1976

One week into the season, Ilie Năstase said he knew that it was a big mistake to sign to WTT. He said over a beer in the locker room after his Leis fell to Pittsburgh at the Civic Arena: "Oh, the money's very good. I can't complain about that. What makes it bad is the fans and how they carry on. They're way more interested in yelling than in good tennis."

Năstase's singles set against Gerulaitis got off to a rough start when he cussed about the scoreboard and the line calls. His crude gesticulations and gestures riled up the Pittsburgh crowd. More than once he incited Vitas' "G-Men" fan club; he also stuck his tongue out at a fan, and smacked a ball off the wall in front of the first row of seats. "I'll put on my best act if that's what people want. What do I care? I get paid win or lose."

"Nasty" had issues with rival players. In New York, he quit a doubles match against the Sets' Sandy Mayer over Sandy's purported stall tactics earlier in men's singles. In other games, he nearly came to blows with Pittsburgh's Mark Cox, and slammed a serve

San Diego Friars, pocket schedule, 1976
Introducing the arrival of legend Rod Laver

Kristien Kemmer Shaw, Phoenix Racquets, 1977
She and Chris Evert became WTT's "It Girls"

at the Gaters' Frew McMillan's noggin. When asked if he'd like to return to WTT in 1977, Năstase explained, "No, I won't. I mean I don't want to. I mean, please talk to my agent."

In what might've been the greatest night of Bay Area tennis, 12,581 fans at Oakland Arena at July 10, 1976's WTT Second Annual All-Star Match saw Betty Stöve and Diane Fromholtz of the Western All-Stars cap a wild women's doubles comeback to top Billie Jean King and Evonne Goolagong in a nine-point super-tiebreaker, and snag a 28-27 OT victory.

Chris Evert—the league's box office star and top singles star with a lethal .884 win-loss ratio, said afterwards, "The crowd's reaction was just great... After another two or three years I plan to cut back on tournaments and concentrate on WTT." Two days later, Arizona Governor Raul Castro proclaimed "Chris Evert Day."

By mid-July, the WTT said they drew over 350,000 fans in 103 games for an average of 3,500 per match. Phoenix was getting 6,500 per game, up 62% from 1975. Indiana claimed crowds up 80%, San Diego up 92% and L.A. up 126%. Optimism ran high.

"I'm still up in the clouds from [winning] Wimbledon. It'll probably take me a couple matches to get back into team tennis."
—CHRIS EVERT, 1976

The midseason break for Wimbledon proved another boon for WTT, with all-WTT finals in women's singles (Evert vs. Goolagong), women's doubles (Evert–Navratilova vs. Stöve–King), mixed doubles (Françoise Dürr–Tony Roche vs. Rosie Casals–Dick Stockton) and men's singles (Sandy Mayer vs. Vitas Gerulaitis).

When the league returned, a record crowd of 13,492 saw a Racquets-Triangles game in Pittsburgh, a rematch of the women's finals—this time Goolagong prevailed over Evert, 6-4. But that turnout was mostly due to Pittsburgh owner Frank Fuhrer advertising free tickets after a series of poorly attended and disappointing home losses.

In the August playoffs, four teams remained: Evert's Phoenix Racquets and Okker's Golden Gaters in the West, with King's high-flying New York Sets and the surging Pittsburgh Triangles (last place on July 19) in the East. The Gaters swept Phoenix in the best of three, while the Sets lost Game One in Pittsburgh before two wins in New York.

When all was said and done, Billie Jean King achieved the last of her stated tennis goals with a WTT title, as the New York Sets swept the Gaters over three nights before a total turnout of 14,000. The post-game party at Nassau Coliseum lasted for hours. Sandy Mayer and King got named Male and Female Playoff MVPs.

But lucrative salaries were still sinking the league, especially with attendance figures so low. The average 1976 contract was $40,000 per player with no minimum. Based on ten teams and six players per team, salaries totaled $2,500,000. The best-paid stars were Rod Laver $165,000, Evonne Goolagong $150,000, Chris Evert $140,000, Billie Jean $130,000 and Ilie Năstase $125,000—all mega-deals in its day.

Strings owner Jerry Buss, a Ph.D. who became wealthy in real estate, said: "If you think the cost of purchasing a home has increased, you should try to buy a World Team

Tennis franchise. Most people have put the value of a franchise close to a million dollars, and they deeply feel, 'Why should anyone else join WTT unless they put up comparable money?' I don't think the million-dollar price tag will be relaxed. I have no doubt at all that the price will go up." He also insisted WTT had a waiting list of franchise applicants.

Ex-Florida Flamingos player-coach Frank Froehling, still owed money from the 1974 season, said in 1976: "WTT has caught on a bit but I don't think it will make money. You have to draw 3,000 to 5,000 every match to break even. It's tough to average that many people on a regular basis for any tennis matches, even big tournaments. We played in a big arena and we got buried—we had nights with only 600–700 people. They're fighting a losing battle. I like the concept and I enjoy it all, but realistically, I don't think they'll make it."

"We look to the future and the view is spectacular. The growth is phenomenal, and it will continue. WTT has not only arrived, it is here to stay."
—BILLIE JEAN KING, 1977

One month after the 1976 season, WTT introduced new commissioner Butch Buchholz. The 36-year-old Davis Cup legend behind tennis clubs and coaching camps was player-coach of the 1974 Chicago Aces and '75-'76 Hawaii Leis. Early '76 he coached WTT All-Stars in the WTT-USSR Challenge Cup, with games from the Kremlin to Cleveland.

In his first decision, Buchholz relocated the league offices from Newport Beach to his hometown near St. Louis. Days into the job he dealt with a crisis, when the Women's Pro Council excluded WTT players from the lucrative Colgate International Series run by ILTF chief Derek Hardwick. The CIS also connected to all the world's top tournaments.

After two days of January 1977 WTT meetings in Cleveland, Buchholz and Larry King announced a 12-team league for the upcoming season. King said: "In view of the acceptance by star players of WTT's concept and the continuing growth of the league, we will accept two new franchises at $1 million apiece." He said expansion had been put off last year because "we wanted to maintain our quality of play. Now, competition in our league is better than in major tournaments." But the 1977 season still included ten teams.

"I've done everything in Europe and all over the world. So I'm excited to try World Team Tennis."
—BJÖRN BORG, Cleveland Pittsburgh Nets, 1977

Indiana Loves, illustrated promotional poster, 1976
Tennis folk art, created for Bill Estes Chevrolet

WTT emerged from hibernation February 1 with two big announcements. First was co-signing sexy Swede Björn Borg and his 19-year-old Romanian fiancée Mariana Simionescu to a three-year $1.5 million deal with the renamed Cleveland-Pittsburgh Nets.

Then, after 1976's epic WTT-USSR Challenge Series, Soviet officials approved their national team as a 1977 franchise. A new team, the Pennsylvania Keystones, wasn't ready to go, so WTT needed one more squad. But novelty aside, it was hard to see hot-blooded Americans rooting for this Big Red Machine, listed as "The Soviets" or "Soviet Union."

For 1977, the defending champion Sets changed their name to the New York Apples. The Hawaii Leis left for the Pacific Northwest as the Sea-Port Cascades. When the 1975 champion Pittsburgh Triangles disbanded, Gerulaitis signed with the Indiana Loves.

Billie Jean King spent the off-season recovering from her third knee surgery. Evert went back to Phoenix for one more season in the sun. Navratilova was miserable in Cleveland, so Buchholz finessed her trade to the floundering Boston Lobsters. Rod Laver, professional sports' oldest-ever Rookie of the Year at age 38, got a fat $150,000 per for three years to return to San Diego. L.A. owner Jerry Buss said that he offered Jimmy Connors similar money plus a pricey job for his coach, but he refused to even consider returning to WTT.

"Despite the offers, I have no plans to return to World Team Tennis. That one season in Baltimore, I played to the smallest crowds of my career."
—JIMMY CONNORS, 1977

WTT had hired San Francisco's Pacific Select Corporation to conduct a comprehensive marketing study. The owners sought new ideas, as no team had yet broken even in four seasons. They learned that their crowds were female-dominated, and 80% serious tennis players who liked the scoring system but disliked the heckling and lack of sportsmanship.

So they pledged to not alienate die-hard tennis fans, and to dissuade audience banter. An Apples exec offered, "We found people coming to our matches were real tennis people in the mainstream who felt we'd totally bastardized the game." Racquets owner Jimmy Walker stated, "We don't encourage cheering. We found out our first year we don't have to. We used to plant hecklers, but no longer. You'll always have a few of them anyway."

Larry King finally stepped down from league management, over his various conflicts of interests. In 1976 he stepped down as president of the Sets, his wife's team, to once again be WTT president. In '77 he owned pieces of the Gaters, Apples and Soviets, and ran WTT Properties, the league's marketing arm. One owner offered: "It's not as if Larry's taking money from both ends and hurting people. He protects his interests on both ends."

A new roadblock emerged for WTT, as storm clouds brewed for the league's most bitter tennis war yet. Owners ended a two-day midseason meeting June 13–14 at San Francisco Tennis Club by issuing a carefully worded release voicing concerns about the finer points of the upcoming merger of Lamar Hunt's WCT with the Grand Prix circuit. The merger would make it impossible for any top or above-average player to play WTT

Björn Borg, Cleveland-Pittsburgh Nets, 1977
Wire photo documenting the Swedish star's one WTT season.

and the top tournaments. What upset WTT was a requirement to play in 24 instead of the current 15 tournaments to qualify for post-tour bonuses.

But WTT owners weren't panicking, with most of the top women under wraps and Björn Borg and Ilie Năstase signed. Buchholz boasted, "Grand Prix considers us the competition, and we consider them the competition too." Golden Gater Frew McMillan did not see the merger as a real threat: "What good will it be if it kills the golden goose?"

"Tournaments are the meat and potatoes of tennis. World Team Tennis is just a side order to it."
—ROD LAVER, San Diego Friars, 1977

WTT players excelled again at Wimbledon, with all eight women quarterfinalists in the league, including women's titlist Virginia Wade (New York Apples). Buchholz caused a stir at Wimbledon with his June 27 announcement about the league going international in 1978 with a six-team European division.

Butch said Soviet Bloc franchises had been committed in Poland, Hungary, Romania and USSR, plus two more in England and France. Other nations under consideration included Holland, Denmark, Sweden, Italy, Austria, Czechoslovakia, and East and West Germany. Franchises reportedly sold for $1 million per, with a divisional HQ in Moscow. WTT said Europeans like Borg or Năstase could play for their own nations if desired without indemnity to their American teams. None of this came close to occurring.

At the third annual WTT All-Star Match on July 9, 1977, East beat West 23-18 in front of a sell-out crowd of 14,153 at the San Diego Sports Arena. Newly crowned Wimbledon champion Björn Borg of Cleveland-Pittsburgh, and Dutch star Betty Stöve of Seattle-Portland captured MVP honors. Debate arose when Butch Buchholz added Ilie Năstase to the 20-player squad despite his only playing three games for the L.A. Strings. To install Ilie as a "wild card" instant all-star was a dubious move, justified as promotion for WTT.

To assuage angry Billie Jean King and others, it was decided Năstase would be introduced but not partake. So he happily drove to S.D. in his new Mercedes courtesy of new owner Jerry Buss. But when Frew McMillan got injured, Năstase had to step in. The fact that King even partook, serving an ace in the final set of the East win, spoke to Butch's tact. She boasted, "The crowd here shows how far WTT has come." The Soviets' Olga Morozova never got off the bench. Chris Evert had the flu and stayed home.

The Apples went on a late-season tear to repeat as WTT champion in 1977. King, Virginia Wade, Sandy Meyer, Fred Stolle, owner Sol Berg, et al. partied on the Phoenix court after wrecking the Racquets.

After the season, Jimmy Connors re-declared skipping WTT, dashing hopes for a 1978 St. Louis team. Buchholz said a team was dependent on the local star agreeing to a three-year deal including $1 million in perks, and the installation of A/C as part of the NHL St. Louis Blues' purchase of the 18,000-seat Checkerdome. Connors and Buchholz agreed to revisit the issue in 1979. Björn Borg hurt his knee in WTT play, and never returned.

"I sensed WTT was not the success it was touted to be. The crowds were sometimes really poor. It did not catch on like basketball, baseball or football. It was more lightweight."

—TANYA HARFORD, Indiana Loves, 2012

The 1978 season provided more questions than answers. No team had yet broken even. WTT expected to surpass 1977's turnout of 887,143 aiming for 1.4 million. Larry King insisted attendance was up 67% in 1976 over 1975, with a 50% boost over that in 1977. Other officials said turnout was up 26–31% with receipts up 82%. Evert's Phoenix squad led WTT, drawing 6,752 at home and 6,384 away. L.A. drew 3,000. Indiana and Boston around 2,500. WTT unveiled a new slogan: "Everyone Wins With World Team Tennis." Owners may have disagreed.

The ten-team league proved able to sign every Top 10 woman, but no Top 5 men signed. Still, going into 1978, most franchises seemed solvent and competitive. In the West, the L.A. Strings became the team to beat after signing Chris Evert to join Ilie Năstase and Vijay Amritraj. The San Diego Friars returned a solid lineup with player-coach Rod Laver, Kerry Melville Reid and Mona Guerrant. The Sea-Port Cascades, now the Seattle Cascades, looked poised to make a run with player-coach Tom Gorman, Betty Stöve and rookie Sherwood Stewart. Phoenix replaced Chris Evert with a mix of ranked British star Sue Barker, and welcomed the return of Evert's former best friend Kristien Kemmer Shaw. The Gaters, WTT's best-run operation with no superstars, were back for a fifth straight winning season.

In the East, the back-to-back league champion New York Apples still featured Billie Jean King and added Vitas Gerulaitis. The Boston Lobsters (1977's surprise team, going from 18-25 last-place to 35-9 and first place in one year) starred Martina Navratilova and Aussie men's doubles duo Tony Roche and player-coach Roy Emerson (nine Wimbledon doubles titles between them). The Indiana Loves, after a sub-.500 1977 season with Barker and Gerulaitis, got thrifty with Dianne Fromholtz and player-coach Alan Stone.

Anaheim Oranges, created to replace the failed Soviets experiment, had acquired women's star Rosie Casals. But since their creation came so late, the O.C. squad had to compete in the Eastern Division. Cleveland Nets owner Joe Zingale tried in vain to replace Björn Borg with Guillermo Vilas, so instead he moved the team to New Orleans. Outside of N.O, they'd play as the Sun Belt Nets, barnstorming the South from El Paso and Austin to Baton Rouge and Mobile. The '78 Nets starred tennis' most alluring mixed doubles pair: African-American hoops star John Lucas and transgender Renée Richards.

"I'm thankful to WTT for giving me the opportunity to play professional tennis at the level that I've tried to play—but which has been met with so much frustration that I have been denied the opportunity to do."

—RENÉE RICHARDS, New Orleans Nets, 1978

In a game held May 27, 1978 at Walden Resort in Lake Conroe, TX, the Friars faced the Strings to promote Rod Laver's April Sound resort near Houston. But Friars GM G. Allan Kingston had an ulterior motive. "WTT want a new Houston franchise," he said. "I feel there will be expansion in WTT before next year." He also stated: "This is a financial breakeven year for three or four of the teams. Los Angeles, San Francisco and Phoenix are strong in terms of stability. In terms of having an ability to withstand in-season losses, I think you're looking at every owner this year, as in no other season before."

WTT held what would be its final All-Star event Saturday, July 14 in Las Vegas. East aced West 27-17. Earlier in the month, Navratilova beat Evert for the Wimbledon title, and on this day she erased Evert 6-1. Evert said, "My strength was my aggressiveness and mental toughness, and I don't have it like I used to." The West's only win was Virginia Wade–Kerry Reid over Wendy Turnbull–Jo Anne Russell, 6-4.

Sunday, August 13, aiming to get its franchises into the black, WTT opened its fifth playoffs in four cities. Tuesday, August 22, the four winners moved on to a second round best of three. The intra-divisional semis pitted lopsided series, with the Lobsters playing the Cascades and the Apples facing the Strings. The Eastern best Lobsters and Western winning Strings then met in a best of five finals that began September 13. The series was billed as a battle of the world's top-ranked women, but Navratilova missed the first two games with injury, and L.A. took the title.

"It wasn't only money or the lack of talent that ruined the league. It was the concept of tennis played."

—ALAN TAYLOR, WTT publicist, 1987

October 26, 1978 was a lousy day for WTT. The league hung on by a thread with news of two of its key franchises folding, the Lobsters and the Apples. After weeks of denials, both suspended operations, due to the failure of WTT to sign any stars for 1979, with no men's stars, and Evert and Navratilova departing.

Sol Berg ran New York's team since 1974 at a loss of $1 million per season, but held out hope that his franchise could carry on under new ownership. A WTT source said, "The Apples already sold more season tickets than last year. But Sol feels the league had not kept pace. Sol loves the Apples and he enjoyed the exposure, and tearfully said he'd take care of his staff," who received severance and unemployment.

The only New York office worker was a receptionist saying that everyone left for the day. The Seattle Cascades and New Orleans Nets stopped answering calls,

Vitas Gerulaitis, Pittsburgh Triangles, 1976
First issue of WTT's *Super-Tiebreaker* magazine

confirming they too were going under. There were rumors WTT would operate in 1979 with six teams—L.A., S.F., S.D., Seattle, Phoenix and Indiana.

The colorful sport begun five years prior looked like a goner. November 4, on the heels of the Apples' and Lobsters' demise, Jerry Buss declared the end of his L.A. Strings, after losing $2.75 million in five years, even while winning the 1978 title with a league-leading average turnout of 7,219, and with 1,500 season tickets sold for '79. Buss stated, "The past weeks have convinced me continuing team tennis is not economically sound."

Along with financial issues came fighting between Buss and the other owners. Buss owning, in full or part, four of ten teams became a source of friction. He'd been demanded to dilute his interests. With his back against the wall, he told the other owners to forget it all. Asked about the future of Anaheim (co-owned by Buss and Frank Mariani), Indiana (with Buss associate Larry Noble) and San Diego (Mariani's team funded by Buss), Jerry jibed, "I expect there will be other defections."

He said that while he viewed WTT as a seven-year plan, "internal differences resulting in a interruption of operations in both New York and Boston have led me to believe that we're now four or five years rather than two years away." Buss said he wanted to move on from tennis, and purchase the NBA L.A. Lakers.

The San Diego Friars folded the next morning. Mariani said rebuilding "will involve more expense than I'm willing to undertake." Florida's *Palm Beach Post* wrote that Indiana Loves majority owner Larry Noble would address his team's future within a day.

"Based on current attitudes of other teams and new pressures on top players by major sponsors, we're not confident quality players will be in the league next season. This cannot continue."
—ROBERT KRAFT, Boston Lobsters owner, 1978

Buchholz met in Oakland with other owners at the Golden Gaters offices, and said that WTT would continue in 1979. But all the teams collapsing around him drowned out his words: "We're waiting for the dominoes to fall. We'll wait until all the damage is done, and then restructure. We plan to go ahead with eight to ten teams next year. These withdrawals are regretful but come as no surprise and have been anticipated."

WTT spokesman Bob Steiner in that *Post* piece said owners bled $30 million in five seasons, and that clubs would not show a profit till 1985. When asked why the five-year-old circuit had yet to make money, Buchholz said owners knew their outlays might not pay off for some years, and he believed the team tennis concept was more popular than ever. Loves GM Bill Bereman bashed Butch: "I have no idea of the chances of success. As far as I'm concerned it won't involve me. I am not and will not be involved."

The only surviving teams were the Gaters and Racquets. On November 17, Buchholz said the two-team league just hired a marketing consultant to evaluate new applications, and planned to soon announce new owners. He said, "We intend to have more teams than Phoenix and Golden Gate, but they're the only ones to post letters of credit for next year. The board is confident WTT's concept is viable, and today it pursued play for 1979."

On December 19, WTT announced a new L.A. franchise owned by investment banker Michael Tennenbaum to compete in 1979, along with the Racquets and Gaters, plus new squads assigned to Dallas and San Diego in a ten-team loop with five others TBA. Buchholz said teams would "be awarded on the basis of market size, arena and applicant financial strength."

Buchholz said sports super-agent Marvin Demoff would negotiate all contracts, with salaries to be borne equally by each team after a January 25 draft. Superstars deemed "Class A" players could, on a first-come basis, play for any available team. "Class A" star Navratilova "indicated an interest" in playing for her new hometown of Dallas. Gaters owner David Peterson, after meeting with Navratilova's agent, Sandra Haynie, said, "Now that we have Dallas, Marvin should be able to sign her." Chris Evert planned to skip 1979, but Butch said that Evert's cousin told him: "In my family women change their mind."

On March 8, 1979, new WTT president Joseph Heitzler said from his L.A. office that the league would be suspended for the year, but he was hopeful for a revival in 1980. Earlier in the day, the Gaters and Racquets closed shop.

The issues were overwhelming and obvious. WTT failed due to poor attendance, difficulty in signing and keeping star players, and failure to cultivate an adequate fan base—the idea fans would root-root-root for the "home" team was unfounded. Negativity spread by the media, top players, tennis purists, the country club set, the European summer circuit, and other ruling bodies ensured its demise.

Most importantly, WTT could not affordably sign stars. Everyone knew it was a flimsy financial model when Billie Jean King drew over 50% of the crowds in 1974–75, and Evert accounted for 40% of 1976–78's revenue. The stars were drawing the crowds, not the team tennis concept.

There were other issues like the league's lack of a network TV deal. King blamed "owners who destroyed each other" more than the turnout. Bill Bereman asserted, "The real problem developed when the franchises began to understand what it would take to make this a success. Team tennis is different from any other sport in that the players do something else eight or nine months out of the year. Players don't want to commit to team tennis while they're playing in tournaments, and you cannot sell season tickets and run a franchise without knowing what you're getting."

World Tennis editor Ron Bookman said, "It's like the Central Hockey League: You've got a core of maybe 3,000 people in any city who'll come to the game—but the league had no impact outside the cities games were played. Most players were just collecting paychecks and waiting for the year to end so they could go back to playing tournaments."

"The fact that players let team tennis die is amazing. It's stupid to throw away that much money. And it hurts the women more than the men. Team tennis brought parity to men's and women's tennis."

—JERRY BUSS, L.A. Strings owner, 1978

Chapter 3
Philadelphia Freedoms

Billie Jean King, Philadelphia Freedoms player-coach, 1974

FAST FACTS

Year of Operation: **1974**

Team Colors: **Red, white and blue**

Team Record: **39-5 (1st place, Eastern Division)**

Female MVP: **Billie Jean King (568-328, .634)**

Male MVP: **Fred Stolle (492-428, .535)**

Highlight: **Opening Night win over Pittsburgh (5/6/74)**

Lowlight: **Finals upset loss to Denver**

Home Arena: **The Spectrum (capacity 17,297)**

Quote: **"What more could Billie Jean want? More Philadelphia fans—where the heck are all of you?"** **—Philadelphia Daily News**

"In college, I read this book **How I Found Freedom in an Unfree World,** *which I carried around for years. When I met Billie Jean, and we became very close—she lived at my house, where she later trained for the Riggs match—and her favorite word was also freedom. So the team name wasn't just Philadelphia history. It was about Billie, and I, wanting more freedom in our lives. And if you follow her career, it's always been about freedom."*

—DICK BUTERA, Philadelphia Freedoms owner, 2017

In November 17, 1973's inaugural WTT player draft, Billie Jean King got taken as a #1 "preferential pick" in a prearranged deal to play for the Philadelphia Freedoms, the WTT franchise owned by her friend, Hilton Head developer Dick Butera.

The next week, the Freedoms signed a three-year lease to play at the 17,297-capacity Spectrum. Spectrum president Lou Scheinfeld said the lease's terms were on a "rental percentage basis. So the better they do, the better we do. Philadelphia is a great sports town and a great tennis town. We feel the Freedoms are the new league's greatest team."

On hand for November 26's introductory press conference, King promised a winning team for "The City of Brotherly Love." She exclaimed, "I'm more excited about playing in Philly than ever before. Philadelphians are great to me, and I love it. They spoil me rotten."

Robert Ehlinger, the 45-year-old GM of the Philadelphia Atoms soccer team when it won the NASL championship in its 1973 debut, signed on for three years as Freedoms GM. Dick Butera said at Ehlinger's intro: "Bob did a marvelous job with the Atoms. In five months, he created a big-league operation and spirit which produced attendance records, and the first championship for an expansion team in any professional sport."

Butera said tickets would sell for $5 to $7, and be available at the Spectrum box office or directly from the team, at 251 West DeKalb Pike in King of Prussia, or by calling 215-265-3800. Staffers included Dick's part-owner siblings Ray and Ken, future sportscasting legends Merill Reese and Red Hamer, PR director Barbra Shotel (later Johnny Carson's talent coordinator), trainer Al Domenico, and physician Dr. Joseph Torg.

The Freedoms roster came together quickly. King signed her $100,000 deal as player-coach. January 23, the team introduced their first male star, third-round pick Brian Fairlie, a 25-year-old New Zealand Davis Cupper and two-time 1973 WCT winner. Eight days later, in came brash 18-year-old Buster Mottram, son of British national coach Tony Mottram. Over the next weeks they'd come to terms with Fred Stolle, their second-round pick, a 35-year-old Aussie winner of mixed doubles titles with King, as well as 26-year-old sixth-rounder Julie Anthony, and 30-year-old Tory-Ann Fretz, ranked the world's #4 woman in 1967. 17-year-old Miami native Kathy Kuykendall signed with the team but got traded after a few games because her mother didn't want her young daughter around King and her Sapphic entourage.

> **"It's great to work with someone like Billie Jean. I've learned what it's like to be around a winner. She never lets up and keeps trying on every shot."**
> **—TORY-ANN FRETZ, Philadelphia Freedoms, 1974**

King took her role as the first female coach of a pro team with male athletes seriously. One reason the Freedoms got off to a fast start was King's dedication to physical training, demanding three hours of practice per day, and giving her squad few days off. Her workouts involved long runs, shuffle-drills, two-on-ones, service, individual practice, and sets and sets of tennis. The players rejected the regimen until they lost a total of 50 pounds in the first two weeks. Fred Stolle felt he was in his best shape ever. Julie Anthony said some of the boys found it tough taking instruction from King at first, but that Stolle backed her up, and the others fell in line. King also imposed a fine-system to cover anything from tardiness to wearing the wrong socks and fined everyone, including herself. She confessed, "I guess I'm a slave-driver."

The Freedoms prepared for their season opener at the Spectrum with a May 2 exhibition at Ursinus College, an hour north of Philly between Pottstown and

Billie Jean King and Julie Anthony, Philadelphia Freedoms, 1974
Teacher and student root for their winningest team in the league

Norristown. The night's proceeds went to the Pottstown-based Tennis For Youth, which advocated junior tennis. The event's apex was when King smacked balls into the stands; fans catching specially marked balls were allowed to meet her and receive an autograph.

> ***"I'm all for the yelling. It's good for the game. The public needs to have an emotional involvement with the team. It's a pure form of freedom. Right on!"***
> **—BILLIE JEAN KING, Philadelphia Freedoms, 1974**

Of May 6th's WTT debut, King admitted a burden. Her anxiety was evident, and likely behind her losing her first set to Pittsburgh Triangles star Evonne Goolagong, 6-3. But as the night wore on, her tension eased, leading the Freedoms to victory, 31-25. She said, "I was too keyed-up before the first set. But I quickly came back to my game."

Brian Fairlie started the Freedoms' revival with his strong serves and aggressive net game to wreck Ken Rosewall 6-2. Hecklers cheered, "Attaway Brian baby!" and jeered, "Rosewall, ya old bum!" Going into the final set of mixed doubles, the Freedoms clung to a three-point lead. A convincing 6-3 Anthony-Stolle win over Peggy Michel-Vitas Gerulaitis insured a Philadelphia victory before a Spectrum audience of 10,611.

Triangles player-coach Rosewall postgame lamented his team's loss in the historic match, saying he would've preferred his squad practiced for a few days, as opposed to the Freedoms, who'd worked out as a team for over a week. Some players even passed up tournament money to prepare. King admitted that unity gave her squad an advantage.

The next night, Philly again dented the Triangles, this time at Pittsburgh's Civic Arena, 30-25. On May 8, King blanked Boston's Kerry Melville, 6-0, to lead her Freedoms over the Lobsters, 33-25, before a much smaller Spectrum crowd of 1,396. May 11, the Freedoms whipped the visiting Hawaii Leis, 33-20 to just 2,059 paid. King noted, "We drew great that first night in Philly. But it was lousy the second and third."

Two nights later, the Nets came to Philly and got wrecked 35-20, as King saw her win streak end 6-3 to Nancy Gunter. Cleveland's Laura DuPont was upset by bovine shouts of "Moo" until told that was how Flyers fans greeted NHL goon Andre "Moose" Dupont. A bell tolled each time the Freedoms won a set, which this night came often. King, with bells on her skirt and back, to create noise, smoked Betty Stöve 6-3.

May 22 in Miami, the Freedoms (9-0) fileted the Florida Flamingos, 25-16. King blanked Laurie Fleming 6-0 in the opening set, after which Florida never had a chance. The next night in Buffalo, before a Royals record crowd of 8,329 at Buffalo Memorial Auditorium, King won early and often, as the Freedoms never looked back, 23-20. The next night at Nassau Coliseum, the Freedoms won every event as the New York Sets mailed it in, 30-16.

Philadelphia moved on to Minnesota on June 1 and lost their first match of the year 26-21 before a WTT record 10,658 at the Met Center. The next night in Denver, the Freedoms lost again, 25-24, as the Racquets' Françoise Dürr ousted King, 6-4. After a lost weekend, Philly sat atop the Eastern Division's Atlantic Section, a league-best 12-2.

"Like any new organization, we've had screw-ups. But I have so much faith in what we're doing that it's just a matter of time until we get our concept across to the people."

—JULIE ANTHONY, Philadelphia Freedoms, 1974

The Oakland Arena billboard on June 11 read: "Billie Jean King Here Tonight." No mention of the Freedoms, or the home team Golden Gaters, or WTT. That's how it should've been. No one could deny "the bespectacled libber from Emeryville." (*Daily Review*, 6/12/74).

The biggest crowd to ever see the Golden Gaters, a reported 6,508, came for the lady who put Bobby Riggs in his place. It was no accident the Freedoms played to record crowds in every city. People were not coming to see Buster Mottram or Julie Anthony or even Fred Stolle—who said he never thought he'd see the day a woman would be tennis' top draw.

Julie Anthony quickly improved as King's doubles partner: "Billie has a great eye for tennis and explains things well. She acts more like a baseball manager than a tennis coach when she is not playing. She claps her hands, jumps off the bench, and yells encouraging words to her players." One night, she charged the umpire's chair to protest a call. Another time when a line judge called a service let, she shouted, "That was no let. You're out to lunch!" King explained: "I grew up around team sports," a nod to her brother Randy Moffitt, star pitcher for the San Francisco Giants, Houston Astros, and Toronto Blue Jays.

"I am ticked-off about the support we're not getting, goddamn it. Philadelphia's not supporting us, and it's got a bloody nerve. Everybody's been telling me this is a great sports town. I haven't seen it. I have a terrible temper. I guess it's because I care too much."

—BILLIE JEAN KING, 1974

With all the accolades, you'd think Philly would be turning fans away. But only 2,049 turned out compared to the 10,658 weeks earlier in Minnesota to see the Freedoms lose. What made it worse was King was already perturbed over the last night's 2,415 that saw them bash the New York Sets, 30-20. She said she ignores reports that Philly only backs winners.

The usually reserved King was angry, noting the team had reduced ticket prices (now just 50¢ to $5, with both student and senior discounts), increased PR, and attempted to build a strong squad. "I love Philadelphia. But we'll go someplace they'll support us."

Such threats failed to improve turnout or affect team play. King was thrilled by yet another victory and relished revenge over the Buckskins who'd stopped the Freedoms' early-season winning streak. She also expressed delight with her 31-4 singles mark. But one got the feeling that she would have traded another triumph for a large home turnout.

'It was a tough match,
but we won.'

Billie Jean King and The Freedoms return home to Philadelphia and the Spectrum for
15 tumultuous matches during July and August.
The opening match is 8 P.M. Monday, July 8 against the Baltimore Banners. Jimmy
Connors, who plays for the Banners, is the top ranked American player.
Tickets are $6, $5, $4, $3, and $2. (Also student and group discounts.)
They're available at all Ticketron outlets (Sears, Gimbels, Korvettes) and the Spectrum.
If you haven't seen World Team Tennis, you don't know what you're missing.
If you're a tennis player and haven't seen it, shame on you.

Freedoms

Top: 1974 Freedoms
L-R: Billie Jean King, Buster Mottram, Brian Fairlie,
Fred Stolle, Tory-Ann Fretz, Julie Anthony

Above: Freedoms ad with Fred Stolle, created by Elliott Curson, 1974

The Freedoms drew their second-largest home crowd of 9,746 for a July 25 halftime exhibition between Bill Cosby and Elton John. The event was co-sponsored by Cosby's Urban Coalition, promoting tennis to urban youth. In the game, Philly thrashed the Toronto-Buffalo Royals to win their 13th straight. The turnout was solid, given that same night, 64,000 attended the WFL Philadelphia Bell. Butera threw a post-match party at Cafe Erlanger for Elton, Bill, and Billie. Weeks earlier, North Philly-bred Cosby bought a stake in the team; Elton wore Freedoms warm-ups and hit balls into the crowd at his next Spectrum concert.

> **"The Freedoms are putting an awful lot of money—free balls and free racquets—into the lower economic areas. Even though tennis appears to be an all-white sport, it's not like baseball was or even football. Anybody who makes a move in that particular direction, I'm all for it."**
>
> **—BILL COSBY, 1974**

Legendary *New York Times* writer Dave Anderson opined: "The coach of the year just might be Billie Jean King—not the female coach of the year, but the coach of the year: male, female or neuter. If the Philadelphia Freedoms win WTT, she should be right up there with Don Shula of the Miami Dolphins and Fred Shero of the Philadelphia Flyers."

Carol Viguers, 14, and brother Howard retrieved balls for the Freedoms. An application form hung on a bulletin board at the indoor courts where her mother played, so Carol brought it home for her brothers, who all filled them out on notebook paper. She and Howard became official ball people, down to their blue shirts with "WTT" in bold white lettering. Viguers loved the Freedoms. And one day, she aimed to play like Ms. King. "She is the nicest person," Carol gushed. "Most of the other players won't talk, maybe they're nervous or concentrating. But she always says 'Hi' and asks how you are."

King took her 34th of 38 singles sets with a 6-1 win over future life partner Ilana Kloss and then teamed with Anthony for their 19th straight doubles win, crushing Kloss-Denise Triolo 6-2, as Philly bashed the Golden Gaters on July 26 by a 28-16 score. With their 16th consecutive victory, the Freedoms (28-4) clinched the Atlantic Section.

> **"We're not tennis players. We're hackers. We're just two hockey players trying to get the ball over the net. I sure don't expect to win."**
>
> **—RICK MACLEISH, Philadelphia Flyers, 1974**

The next night, in not quite another Bobby Riggs "battle of the sexes," King faced two stars of the 1974 NHL champion Flyers, center Rick MacLeish and winger Gary Dornhoefer, at halftime of the Freedoms home match against the Denver Racquets.

The exhibition spurred interest; as soon as it got announced, a long line formed at the ticket window. The Flyers, the city's darlings since winning the Stanley Cup, had just drawn 14,500 to Veterans Stadium for a Tuesday night charity softball game. King said of these Broad Street Bullies: "What I'd like to know is if these brutes have their teeth in or out." The match was a best of five with $1,000 going to the Flyers if they won, which they did not. When all was over, WTT's hottest team won 17 matches in a row, 27-24.

August 14, the Freedoms cemented their season-long perfect home record with a 29-19 win over the Houston E-Z Riders before 3,500 or so. Philly was 37-5 going into their final two road matches. They won the next night in New York and then Sunday in Detroit to prep for the playoffs—which they entered a WTT-best 39-5.

Philly had two win streaks that stand up to any sport. They won their first 12, and after Wimbledon another 18. They were the odds-on favorites to take the DuPont Teflon Cup.

In Game One of the playoffs, Nancy Gunter beat King 6-2. So Philly had to take the next four sets to salvage an August 11 road victory in Cleveland, 26-22. The next day, the Freedoms won all three doubles sets to earn a 23-22 home triumph over the Nets in Game Two, advancing to the semi-finals with a cumulative score win, 49-44.

Despite King having injured her thumb, Philadelphia was the odds-on favorite to seize the crown. The team drove to Pittsburgh on August 22 to open a Keystone State showdown against the Triangles (30-14) who'd mangled the Detroit Loves in the quarterfinals. In Game One before 5,362 in Pittsburgh, Philly prevailed 31-21. The next day to 7,112 Spectrum fans, Fred Stolle helped clinch a 24-21 Freedoms victory to advance to the first WTT finals.

On August 25, before a Denver record crowd of 4,405, the Racquets took the opener of the three-game series, 27-21. Philly's elite women fell as Françoise Dürr beat King 6-4 in singles, and then with Kris Kemmer toppled King-Anthony, 6-3. King, visibly upset with line calls, ascribed her team's loss to Denver's two stars. "It helps when you have two good players. Denver has Dürr and Roche," she said. "Plus, the Denver crowd was all over us. We couldn't concentrate." She assured different results in Philadelphia.

> ### "Buster Mottram is a helluva player and could be great—but he won't. He doesn't have the guts or fortitude. We needed him, but then Buster let us down. And he knows it."
>
> **—FRED STOLLE, Philadelphia Freedoms, 1974**

The next night, Andy Pattison's 6-0 shutout of Buster Mottram propelled the underdog Racquets to a 28-24 victory. A rowdy Spectrum crowd of 4,850 saw the shocking 2-0 series sweep—as Denver, who started the season 2-8, became WTT's first champions.

From the losing locker room, a shocked King, Stolle, and Fairlie focused their anger on Mottram for choking under pressure, and for denying them a chance for title glory. Ironically, King had recently taken pride in molding him into a budding star.

After a tumultuous off-season, the Freedoms bowed to King's request to trade her to New York for the rights to Stan Smith and Kerry Melville. Butera knew he was taking a risk. But he said the 31-year-old star that won every major women's title "isn't getting any younger." The trade hurt Philadelphia, but helped New York and the WTT. King felt

British teenager Buster Mottram, Philadelphia Freedoms, 1974

Billie Jean King in her Freedoms uniform, Nassau Coliseum, 1974
Wire photo displaying her power and intensity

The Elton John Band, "Philadelphia Freedom," 1974
Picture sleeves of Elton's hit single inspired by Billie Jean King's team

that playing in America's media hub would boost the WTT brand, though she believed that commuting from Philly to New York to play hurt her game.

Butera said: "It was not easy to let Billie go. I feel like King Faisal, giving away his oil wells." He refused to discuss his real estate business issues, where interest rates soared to 18%, or address his inability to fund a franchise that drew 2,450 to the Spectrum.

WTT owners met March 12, 1975, to discuss the Freedoms' future. John Korff, GM of the folded Lobsters, said a Boston bloc sought approval to buy the Freedoms and move them, to become the Lobsters. So the Freedoms' team shell moved to Massachusetts. In late March, Elton's Billie Jean anthem "Philadelphia Freedom" shot to #1 on the charts.

> *"The end of my story is I sold the team to Robert Kraft, now the owner of the New England Patriots. Elton was going to buy it, and when we did the final accounting, and the team lost $800,000, I called Elton's lawyers in L.A., and they told me he'd changed his mind!"*
>
> **— DICK BUTERA, 2017**

In 1985, the International Tennis Hall of Fame inducted Fred Stolle. Tory Fretz entered the Intercollegiate Tennis Hall of Fame in 1999. Julie Anthony and Dick Butera married for 15 years and lived in Aspen; Anthony became a top sports psychologist. Buster Mottram, of illiberal views, failed at runs for British Parliament. Billie Jean King carries on.

Chapter 4
Houston E-Z Riders

John Newcombe, Houston E-Z Riders, 1974

Year of Operation: **1974**

Team Colors: **Orange and brown**

Team Record: **25-19 (2nd place, Gulf-Plains Section)**

Female MVP: **Karen Krantzcke (338-362, .483)**

Male MVP: **John Newcombe (489-372, .568)**

Highlight: **ABC-TV Monday night victory over L.A.**

Lowlight: **Folding two weeks before the 1975 season**

Home Arena: **Sam Houston Coliseum (capacity 9,217)**

Quote: **"I plan to play, but who knows if the thing will last? I have little confidence in the people behind this."**

—John Newcombe (4/19/75)

"For the first time, pro tennis will benefit from the large audiences and widespread enthusiasm that other Houston pro sports have long enjoyed."

—E.Z. JONES, Houston E-Z Riders owner, 1974

Houston earned its place in tennis history on September 20, 1973, hosting at its famed Astrodome "The Battle of the Sexes" match between top-ranked Billie Jean King and tennis hustler Bobby Riggs, an event that redefined the competitive playing field.

E.Z. Jones played tennis at San Antonio's Trinity College and earned his fortune in Texas oil. He would be one of the first to invest in Chuck Reichblum's National Tennis League (NTL) that transformed into WTT. Jones named his Houston franchise the E-Z Riders, a blend of his name and the popular outlaw film *Easy Rider*. Jones served as team president, while his wife Betty, once president of the Houston Ladies Tennis Association, ran day-to-day operations as VP. Mr. Jones' assistant Ray Bovett, ticket manager Brenda Small, and team trainer Bobby Brown rounded out the front office.

Clarence Mabry, the dean of Texas tennis coaches, who for two decades ran the small-college powerhouse program at Trinity—where he posted a 320-35-9 dual-match record—came aboard as E.Z.'s senior adviser. But when taking money from a pro team created a conflict for the NCAA Tennis Committee chairman, "The Father of Trinity Tennis" resigned from Trinity to become the E-Z Riders' coach-GM.

On February 11, 1974, E.Z. and Mabry introduced their top draft choice—the world's top male player, three-time Wimbledon champion, John Newcombe—signed to a five-year contract for $100,000 per year for the three-month season. Like Billie Jean King's pre-draft deal with Philadelphia, Newcombe was a "preferential choice" of Houston due to his business interest in nearby New Braunfels, the John Newcombe Tennis Ranch (co-owned by Mabry). John was the third Aussie to come to terms, joining third-round pick Karen "Kran" Krantzcke, and fifth-round 1971 French Open finalist Helen "Flo" Gourlay.

Mabry's evaluation skills proved evident by his impressive roster, tabbed as the team to beat in the Western Division. His squad included Newcombe, Krantzcke, Gourlay, Dick Stockton, Mabry's former Trinity student ranked #8 in the world, and two Aussie married couples, Lesley and Bill Bowrey, and Cynthia and Peter Doerner.

Newcombe and Krantzcke were smashing with the press at San Antonio's Northern Hills Country Club on March 13, promoting the E-Z Riders' four matches at S.A.'s HemisFair Arena—June 3rd against L.A., July 8th vs. Hawaii, July 12th with the Golden Gaters, and August 10th against Chicago. Pro Sports Ltd., original owners of the ABA San Antonio Spurs, handled the E-Z Riders' Alamo City gambit. Mabry told reporters if the Houston team proved financially satisfactory, their city could have a WTT entry within a few seasons.

Dressed in bright orange sweatsuits, the E-Z Riders started the 1974 season with three dominant road wins. On May 7, topping the Minnesota Buckskins, 30-28; May 8, slamming the Chicago Aces, 37-15 (billed as a battle between Newcombe and Marty Riessen, but neither played); and May 10, pounding the Denver Racquets, 37-28.

"I'm a rookie. And since they were undefeated without me, I might have trouble making this team."
—JOHN NEWCOMBE, Houston E-Z Riders, 1974

All three Houston wins were accomplished without Newcombe, who was busy beating Björn Borg in the WCT Finals at Moody's Coliseum in Dallas. So the morning after the tournament, he drove to meet his teammates for May 13th's home opener against the Buckskins at Sam Houston Coliseum, but was delayed when the Texas Highway Patrol caught him on radar doing 68 in a 55 zone. Newcombe arrived one hour before game time, and took no warm-ups before routing Aussie friend Owen Davidson 6-1, leading Houston to their fourth straight, 30-23.

That opening night crowd of just 2,167 included various Houston bigwigs. Mayor Fred Hofheinz joined Australian Consul General Phillip Searcy, British Consul member Roy Fox, and envoys of other local pro teams to mark the occasion. Fans realized that the whole thing was on the up-and-up when NFL Houston Oilers wide receiver Eddie Hinton double-faulted. Uncle Freddie, an overweight actor employed by Shakey's Pizza, paraded around as the team mascot in short shorts and a ten-gallon hat. The fans enjoyed music provided by the T.H. Rogers Junior High School Band, raising funds for a European tour.

Few bodies remained in the stands after the grueling four-hour slugfest. The planned "Ride On" war cry, to inspire the Riders, fizzled. A Youth Tennis Association promotion to its members, including half-priced tickets, an autograph, and photo session with Riders players, drew eight people. Veteran umpires Charles Lemaster and Jason Morton looked spent. Mabry moaned, "We have to look at our games. The shortest one we've played is three hours, 14 minutes. We need a new format, and the sooner, the better." Houston served as the case study for WTT, immediately trimming its match lengths.

Newcombe was soaking his tired muscles in the Coliseum whirlpool when E.Z. asked him to attend a post-match party. The last of tennis' "awesome Aussies" said, "I'll stay long enough to have a few." Newcombe was a complicated chap: on the court, so competitive nearly possessed; off it, almost devoid of ambition except to be with his family, provide for his old age, and drink a lot of beer. Dick Stockton called him "a 30-year-old boy." The next day, Newcombe left his team again, this time for Vegas to compete in the Alan King Classic.

Despite opening night's dismal turnout, coach Mabry predicted that WTT had "about a 60-40 chance of survival" and "originally figured the chances were 50-50." May 15's crowd was even smaller, 1,200 or so. The emptiness got to the Riders as the visiting Chicago Aces overcame a final set rally to hand Houston their first loss, 29-28. On May 24, Newcombe led an E-Z Riders win, taking all five sets in New York from the Sets, 32-23. May 31 in Miami, the Florida Flamingos ransacked the Riders, 28-27. June 2, the Gaters got smoked in Houston, 29-22. The next night, WTT debuted in San Antonio before an unreported crowd under 1,000 at the HemisFair Arena (original capacity 10,146), as Houston sliced the L.A. Strings 27-15.

In a June 10 nationally televised Monday night match on ABC with Bill Cosby as a color commentator, the Riders rammed the Strings in Houston 29-21. Due to the poor turnout, lack of excitement, and dismal ratings, Steve Nidetz wrote in *The Chicago Tribune* (7/17/74): "That first World Team Tennis telecast was such a fiasco, there will be no more unless league officials can talk one of the major networks into it."

Hours before the second half of the season begun—with a home loss to the Detroit Loves—Houston signed Texas Tech star Emily Burrer Foster to replace the injured Nancy Gunter. Foster mostly sat the bench during a 3-1 streak: though Houston lost July 17 to the Gaters 26-25 in Oakland before 4,125, they slammed the Aces 28-26 on July 19 before an alleged 3,987 Chicagoans, ripped the Denver Racquets 30-25 on July 22 to nine hundred or so Lone Star onlookers, and broiled the visiting Boston Lobsters 30-19 on July 24. The next night, Gunter returned, and before another sparse crowd at Sam Houston—so small that spectators could hear the gunshot sounds of the police shooting range next door—the Riders looked sharp in trimming the Cleveland Nets, 26-24, led by Newcombe in singles, and Krantzcke-Gourlay in doubles.

> **"I don't expect Newcombe to win every game. I expect the superstars in this league to peak during the playoffs, and play down the to the wire."**
> **—CLARENCE MABRY, Houston E-Z Riders coach, 1974**

WTT made no friends in the South Texas town of Kingsville after a July 27 match between the Riders and Gaters at Texas A&M-Kingsville Health and Physical Education Building. Estimates pegged the crowd at 2,600, which was at least 1,100 over the Riders' average Houston turnout, and far above San Antonio, where a religious convention had kayoed this match. The Corpus Christi Tennis Association sold the Riders on hosting the event, but Memorial Coliseum, the only viable site in Corpus Christi, was already booked. So the game wound up in Kingsville, a hundred-mile round-trip drive.

John Newcombe and Ray Emerson, drawing cards in the ticket sales, failed to show, with Newcombe playing tournaments in Europe, and Emerson just not coming. *Corpus Christi Times* (7/30/74) wrote: "That is Emerson's right. But WTT had better learn that people of today don't cotton to being conned. When someone is advertised as a leading attraction, people shell out good money to see him or her in real life action, and they expect a promise kept. When it isn't, they're going to be hard to sell tickets the next time around."

The end of the Riders' regular season was a blur: July 29, Houston jetted to Baltimore and got ripped by the Banners 28-27. The next night in Miami, the Flamingos flayed them 26-25. August 1, the Lobsters clawed their way to Sam Houston Coliseum but got baked, 29-21. August 3, the Riders beat the visiting Royals, 29-19; August 5, the Riders ripped the Buckskins 26-23 before another woeful three-digit H-town crowd. The next night at Oakland Coliseum, they crumbled to the Gaters 26-22, still unnerved after their flight made an emergency landing at SFO. Mabry sent in ace John Newcombe to play Dick Bohrnstedt, and he was his usual impressive self—leading one onlooker to say, "Is John bad or is he BAD!"

> ## "The hecklers are just small-minded idiots. I'm not a clown for them to have fun. I won't put up with that crap. We're in a pennant race. We're not horsing around. I'll walk out; I'll quit WTT."
> ### —JOHN NEWCOMBE, 1974

Choice seats were available for August 10's San Antonio finale, when the E-Z Riders took on Chicago. Houston had played twice in town, whipping the Strings 27-15 in June, and returning in July to lay it on the Leis 27-21 on "Hawaiian Night." On this night, Newcombe and Helen Gourlay trampled the Riders 28-16 over the Aces before five hundred or so S.A. fans. August 13, the Riders got a paid vacation to Hawaii, winning by forfeit after their game against the Leis in a high school gym got canceled after the gym was too small for tennis. After an August 18 home-finale romp over the Flamingos, Houston (25-19) ended the season second place behind Minnesota in the Gulf-Plains Section, and playoffs-bound.

For Game One of the playoffs, Houston trekked to Minnesota and belted the Buckskins, 28-19. Minnesota faced a large nine-point deficit in Game Two in Houston to advance to the Western Division finals. The next night, in a gauge of local interest in WTT, a paltry 1,504 at Sam Houston saw the Buckskins dominate 29-19, and steal the semifinals based on a total 48-47 combined score—dashing the Riders' championship

Top: Houston E-Z Riders bumpers sticker,1974
Above: pocket schedule for the E-Z Riders' never-played 1975 season

John Newcombe, Houston E-Z Riders, Lake Conroe, Texas, 1975
In a preseason "WTT Spectacular" days before the franchise folded

1974 game program ad for "The Official Hotel of the E-Z Riders"

dreams. From their sad locker room, Newcombe and Krantzcke kvetched about their shocking demise. Newcombe's big year resulted in post-season accolades, awarded "WTT Super Star" status for his top ranking in singles play (.593), and #1 men's doubles duo with Stockton (.583).

In the offseason, things began to look shaky when Betty Jones announced that no signings, trades or roster changes would take place until further notice. On October 18, Union Bank of Houston sued in district court to recover funds loaned team organizers that were to be paid back by E.Z. Jones and local contractor Archie Manes, Jr. Despite a letter to the editor in *Sports Illustrated* by E.Z. and Betty extolling a feature on Newcombe: "Like WTT, John Newcombe is here to stay!" the Aussie star admitted that with the new season approaching, "I plan to play again, but who knows if the thing will last? I have little confidence in the people behind this."

WTT ushered in 1975 with "Spectaculars," exhibitions in which a few squads partook in a two-day orgy of tournament-style play. The poorly received idea led by L.A. owner Jerry Buss proved antithetical to team tennis. At one poorly attended tennis lollapalooza April 26-27 in the Houston resort town of Lake Conroe, Newcombe lost a 5-1 tiebreaker to the Nets' Marty Riessen. That would be the final time the E-Z Riders took the (tennis) court.

Two weeks before the season, with posters and schedules printed, E.Z. and Betty denied reports they were behind in league dues and payroll debts. The league gave them until noon May 2 to post a $50,000 letter of credit, but Betty felt that WTT bylaws would spare Houston due to their pricey deal with Newcombe. In the end, the Joneses posted no funds for operating expenses nor paid off their bills. Betty said, "We protested the action, but the other owners didn't want to take a chance with Houston, so more it looked like total termination." WTT Chairman and Pittsburgh owner Frank Fuhrer fumed about Houston's last-minute demise, "It's something that should've been done six months ago."

Chapter 5

Sue Stap, Chicago Aces press photo, 1974

FAST FACTS

Year of Operation: 1974

Team Colors: Red and white

Team Record: 15-29 (last place, Gulf-Plains Section)

Female MVP: Sue Stap (346-382, .475)

Male MVP: Graham Stilwell (250-318, .440)

Highlight: "Stap v Chicago Aces Tennis Team" win in Illinois Appellate Court (7/21/78)

Lowlight: Methadone Maintenance Institute of Chicago benefit loss to Denver (7/28/74)

Home Arena: Lakeshore Racquet Club (capacity 4,200)

Quote: "For many Chicago citizens, the prospect of another sports team about to begin life is about as exciting as going down to the lakefront pilings and watching the graffiti."
—Chicago Tribune (5/1/74)

"It's nice how people get into these matches. It's like football or baseball, which may or may not be good."

—SUE STAP, Chicago Aces, 1974

Hoity-toity tennis had roots in meat-&-potatoes Chicago from the sport's earliest days. It dated back to the 1800s in Lincoln Park, and FDR's New Deal jobs programs saw 330 asphalt courts built citywide in the 1930s. Tennis peaked in America by the '70s, when the Chicago-based Wilson Sporting Goods company saw its tennis sales exceed even its golf sales.

Indoor tennis exploded in Chicago due to the city's severe weather. In 1972, Walter and Jordon Kaiser opened Lakeshore Racquet Club, a sprawling indoor facility on West Fullerton. Jordon, a former tennis bum and top amateur, promoted local tournaments; his money came from the family's real estate firm, H.S. Kaiser. The Kaisers also owned and operated the WHA Chicago Cougars. Jordon was one of the first team tennis proponents, linked to the original NTL. In 1974, he simultaneously served as WTT president and owner of his Chicago Aces franchise, named not just after the tennis term for an unreturned serve, but also in tribute to the city's gangster/gambler past.

Graham Stilwell, Chicago Aces press photo, 1974

Jordon presided over a July 1973 media event to introduce Aces GM Jock Miller. The Quincy, IL tennis star and teaching-pro-turned-promoter impressed the Kaisers when he brought the 1973 Virginia Slims of Chicago to the Lakeshore. Jordon said Jock "was the guy you searched out to lend credibility to a tennis event." The two announced 1940s local legend Frank Parker as head coach—a move that, like much else with the Aces, never came to fruition.

Miller and the Kaisers oversaw the Aces' ill-fated August 1973 player draft. The team made waves—less for #1 pick Marty Riessen, #2 Julie Heldman, #3 Bob Lutz, #4 Judy Dalton, #7 Billy Martin, or #8 Marie Neumannova, but more for #9 Bobby Riggs, who would've been an immediate Windy City star. In the end, only #5 Ray Ruffels, #6 Janet Young, and #13 Graham Stilwell ever wore Aces uniforms.

Things already began to sour by March 1974, after Miller told the *Chicago Tribune*, "We hope to announce a big name player next week." Newspapers reported 33-year-old Marty Riessen—a four-time Illinois high school champion from Evanston and a Big Ten titlist at Northwestern, ranked Top 10 since 1969—had signed as Aces player-coach.

> ### "The Aces have a contract in their office. I'd love to be their player-coach. All they have to do is sign and agree to terms."
>
> #### —MARTY RIESSEN, 1974

One week before the team's May 8 home opener, Riessen had agreed in principle but had yet to sign a contract. Yet the overzealous Aces heavily promoted his opening-night showdown with the Houston E-Z Riders' John Newcombe. Calling the advertising "an incredibly flagrant misuse of a man's name," Riessen's agent Dennis

Dell demanded more money. Despite the dilemma, team spokesman, retired *Tribune* sportswriter Ralph Leo felt confident that they'd sign "the greatest Chicago-raised player to yet play pro tennis."

With Riessen saying he'd "probably never sign," Jock Miller hurriedly hired as player-coach Earl "Butch" Buchholz, of Lamar Hunt's WCT "Handsome Eight"—the roots of the modern men's tour. So Riessen, with his long sandy hair and flat stomach jokingly referred to as the "Björn Borg of The Prairie State," instead played celebrity exhibitions for Samsonite, like July 15 in Milwaukee against NBA star Oscar Robertson.

The Aces unveiled a roster that would not set WTT afire. Aside from Buchholz, there were Sue Stap and Sue Eastman, both 19-year-olds from the Chicago suburbs; British star Graham Stilwell, a Top 100 player at 5'5"; Barbara Downs, 20, of Alamo, CA; Kim Warwick, a 22-year-old four-time Australian Davis Cup player; Janet Young, of the 1973-1974 Australian Federation Cup teams; and Billie Jean King's mixed doubles partner, yet another Aussie, Ray Ruffels.

Tam O'Shaughnessy of Fullerton, CA, made the opening roster and then retired to work for the Kings' King Enterprises, and live with her life partner, future tragic NASA astronaut Sally Ride. So the Aces brought in for a few games 20-year-old Marcie Louie, oldest of the four Louie sisters (the youngest being top-ranked junior tennis player Maureen "Peanut" Louie).

Aces tickets for single games (from $6 to $10) and season boxes ($880 for four) did not sell briskly. "The only folks lonelier than the Maytag repairman must run the Chicago Aces box office," quipped Second City sports columnist Art Mugalian. Ralph Leo said the Lakeshore, with seating for about 4,200, needed to attract 3,000 per match to break even.

Chicago excelled early in the season. At May 7's opener versus the Racquets in Denver, the Aces prevailed 33-32 before just 1,481, paced by Ray Ruffels 6-4 over Andy Pattison.

The next night, in their long-awaited home opener, the Aces threw a party to celebrate WTT's birth in Chicago, with free liquor for press and VIPs. John Husar of the *Tribune* dubbed them "The Chicago Cases" for all the booze drunk, noting they were the first pro sports team to have its players at a cocktail party *before* the game. Hours later, the Houston E-Z Riders spoiled the festivities, taking every set in a 37-13 rout.

"They didn't seem to be paying attention to us. They were way more interested in the refreshments."
—GRAHAM STILWELL, Chicago Aces, 1974

The Aces played better in their second home match, edging the Toronto-Buffalo Royals 32-31. The May 10 event—in front of just 307 at the Lakeshore—featured WTT's first super-tiebreaker, won by Janet Young-Graham Stilwell 6-3. The next evening, a Saturday night crowd "estimated at 300" saw the Aces defeat the Minnesota Buckskins, 36-30. The squad ended that weekend in Miami Beach, fleecing the Florida Flamingos, 29-21.

To bolster their nonexistent Lakeshore turnout, the first-place Aces slashed ticket prices for the rest of the season—to $4 for general admission and $3 for children—starting with a May 17 rematch with last-place Florida. GM Miller admitted, "It was believed our team wouldn't do well because it lacked a big-name player. We've played our last two home matches before small crowds, so drastic measures had to be taken."

In that Chicago match before a reported 1,442, Florida disposed of the Aces, 34-21. Cigar-chomping *Tribune* columnist David Condon wrote (5/19/74): "Friday's matches opened with Betty Ann Grubb, a divorcee, and Miss Stap, who is 19 and also a major league looker."

May 20 in Minnesota, the Aces folded again, 28-18, in front of "under 1,000 Buckskins fans." May 22, Chicago lost every set to the Cleveland Nets 24-18, before a Lakeshore record crowd of 2,120 (announced as 3,180). Most came for a pre-match exhibition by Bobby Riggs, who got $5,000 plus expenses for 25 minutes of tennis, facing 23 women in one-point games. Riggs said after, "I like soft touches, like the lovely girls of Chicago."

Player-coach Butch Buchholz's decision to stick with Sue Stap proved to be a wise one. The older sister of future tour staple Sandy Stap proved herself the Aces' heart and soul, pacing the Aces' 31-24 over the Buckskins on June 2 before a league-low crowd of 276 in Chicago. Before the match, the Lakeshore announced the opening of The Aces Tennis School.

Then the bottom fell out. June 7, the Aces got slammed by the Denver Racquets 31-24 and would've lost every set were it not for Buchholz's 7-6 win over Andy Pattison. The next night, a tiny audience of 310 saw Chicago crush the Golden Gaters 26-22, led by Buchholz's 6-0 over Roy Emerson. June 11, the Aces let the Lobsters claw a 33-32 win. June 12 in Chicago, the New York Sets won after Buchholz-Warwick lost 6-4 to Manuel Santana-Niki Pilić. June 14, the Detroit Loves came to town and ousted the Aces, 28-19, as Rosie Casals, the #3-ranked American woman, gave Sue Stap a lesson she'd not soon forget: after her 6-1 loss, Stap muttered, "Butch told me just to step up and hit the ball." June 19, the visiting L.A. Strings shuffled the Aces 25-21, before 721 fans, dropping Chicago's mark to 8-15. Then Coach Buchholz left his team for a week to partake in Prince Rainier's celebrity tournament in Monaco with Charlton Heston, Clint Eastwood, and Burt Bacharach.

> ## "It hurts to lose this much. It hurts your confidence. I thought we'd turn things around."
> **—BUTCH BUCHHOLZ, Chicago Aces player-coach, 1974**

The second half of the season offered even fewer highlights. As the ship went down, Chicago turned to benefits and charity events. July 28, the Aces lent a helping racquet to victims of drug abuse in a home match with first-place Denver. The Methadone Maintenance Institute of Chicago got feted in a halftime tribute to the clinic's 70 staffers, who ministered to recovering users. The Aces (12-20) lost all five sets in a 31-18 beat-down to the Racquets, their sixth straight defeat.

August 2's match with the Sets, in cooperation with the Chicago chapter of the March of Dimes, drew just 612 to see the Aces rally 25-20 over an exhausted New York. August 4, the Aces, in their final road win, flew to Miami and edged the Flamingos 29-26. August 18 was the Aces' finale, a home victory over a lifeless, Jimmy Connors-less Baltimore Banners, 25-23.

**Above: Chicago Aces' March of Dimes benefit, Lakeshore Racquet Club, 1974
L-R: Marcie Louie, Graham Stilwell, Butch Buchholz, Sue Stap, Sue Eastman,
Ray Ruffels, Janet Young, Barbara Downs**

Below: Marcie Louie, Chicago Aces press shot, 1974

MARCIE LOUIE

CHICAGO
ACES

World Team Tennis

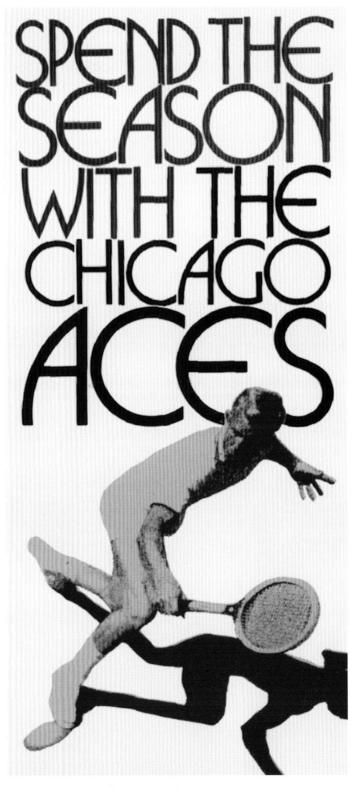

Chicago Aces, pocket schedule, 1974
The lowest-drawing team in WTT history

Chicago finished 1974 with WTT's third-worst record of 15-29, 12 games out of first place, and 9½ out of playoff contention. Aces netters graded rock bottom in every single statistical category. In the 16-team league, Stap ranked #12 in women's singles; Buchholz rated #15 in men's singles, as did Stap-Young in women's doubles. Stilwell-Warwick was #16 in men's doubles, as was Young-Stilwell in mixed doubles.

"The City of the Big Shoulders" with its blue-collar Bears-Cubs fan base never bought into the Aces. Clifford Terry wrote in the *Tribune*, "For many Chicago citizens, the prospect of another sports team about to begin life is about as exciting as going down to the lakefront pilings and watching the graffiti." Lakeshore crowds often numbered more media freeloaders than paying customers. The players lost their swagger due to the lousy turnout, and lost interest when their paychecks began to bounce.

> ### "The Aces told us for blowing the whistle on them we'd be the last to get paid. They said they lost plenty, and that the players got plenty."
> —TONY MENCONI, attorney, 1974

Six weeks after the season, the Kaisers put their bankrupt Aces up for sale. Buchholz sent the Kaisers a promissory note for the $15,400 he was owed and brought in potential buyers in hopes of getting paid. Stap and Warwick each filed a breach of contract lawsuit; their agent Tony Menconi said Stap sought $12,175, and Warwick his $1,875.

The lawsuits began after the team canceled a post-season meeting regarding the owed money. Menconi hired bulldog barrister Arnold Silvestri to sue for the Aces' assets, which caused a PR nightmare for WTT—it looked terrible to have a league executive sued for back pay—so Kaiser stepped down as president.

For November 26's player draft for 1975, Miller picked 13 netters over the 20 rounds, like American star Julie Heldman, Manuel Orantes of Spain, Adriano Panatta of Italy, Australian former E-Z Rider Cynthia Doerner, and Brooklyn playground legend "Fast Eddie" Dibbs.

On January 13, 1975, Larry King expressed confidence in Chicago: "There are several groups interested in having a team in Chicago, and I know Jordon Kaiser is interested." But despite inquiries, owners could not be found. A Kaiser press release said: "potential investors said the absence of an adequate air-conditioned arena was a deal-breaker."

> ### "I think it's best if they couldn't afford the team not to try and do it again."
> —SUE STAP, 1975

In the end, the Aces joined the Banners, Buckskins, Riders, Flamingos, and Freedoms as franchises unable to meet the January 15 deadline of a $50,000 letter of credit and the settling of all unpaid debts. It took until July 21, 1978, for the Illinois Appellate Court to rule on "Stap v Chicago Aces Tennis Team"—judging that Jordan Kaiser was *not* liable for her unpaid salary and bonuses.

That legal decision would be the Aces' biggest win.

Chapter 6
Baltimore Banners

Byron Bertram, Baltimore Banners, 1974

Year of Operation: **1974**

Team Colors: **Blue and white**

Team Record: **16-28 (3rd place, Atlantic Section)**

Female MVP: **Betty Stöve (420-391, .518)**

Male MVP: **Jimmy Connors (106-63, .627)**

Highlight: **Signing Jimmy Connors (1/19/74)**

Lowlight: **Connors' vacation with fiancée Chris Evert "to recover from their Wimbledon titles" (6/8/74)**

Home Arena: **Baltimore Civic Center (capacity 12,000)**

Quote: **"We need World Team Tennis like we need a hole in the head."**
—Baltimore Afro-American (5/11/74)

"Who the hell is Francis Scott Key? I thought we were named after some guy named Banner."
—JIMMY CONNORS, Baltimore Banners, 1974

On August 9, 1973, WTT approved the transfer of Gary Davidson's Phoenix franchise to a Baltimore bloc willing to pay five times the $50,000 fee. The Santa Ana, CA native, claimed that he relinquished control to avoid a conflict in his dual roles as WTT co-founder and WHA president. WTT president Dennis Murphy presented the Maryland group of Joseph A. Rivkin (Baltimore Luggage Company), Howard Fine and Gerald M. Klauber (Fine & Klauber legal firm), and '60s Baltimore-area tennis pro Bob Bradley, Jr.

November 1, Baltimore's newest sports team enjoyed its finest hour, naming a coach, Don Candy, a 44-year-old legend of Australia's Golden Age of Tennis who lived in Baltimore since becoming the teaching pro at the Orchard Indoor Tennis Club in 1967. They also introduced as vice president Walter R. "Bud" Freeman, the mellifluous radio voice of the Bowie Baysox, lured from his post as Baltimore Orioles promotions director. The team declared its name the Banners—as in Francis Scott Key's "Star Spangled Banner."

But the event was marred by media questions over the team's inability to sign any of its 18 draftees. Not Jurgen Fassbinder (Germany), Elly Appel (Holland) or Steve Krulevitz (Israel). Top pick Jimmy Connors, co-ranked #1 in the U.S. with Stan Smith, said he'd only play WTT in Florida or Cleveland. Joseph Rivkin expressed confidence that Connors "would play in the WTT," but declined to say if that meant for Baltimore.

Citing her role in promoting the team locally, Bud Freeman helped sign Towson University's Audrey Morse, the top women's player in Maryland. Days later, Gerald Klauber said the Banners would play at the 12,000-seat Baltimore Civic Center for the 1974 season. His signature appeared on promotional brochures flashing the team motto: "We serve you right."

Jimmy Connors, the 21-year-old from Belleville, Illinois, shocked the world when he signed a December 6 letter of intent with Baltimore. "The offer was too attractive to ignore," said William F. Riordan, Connors' mentor, and agent, a reformed alcoholic who operated out of a dress shop in Salisbury, Maryland. "But there will be a stipulation in the deal that Jim can play in any tournament he wishes." Freeman proved persuasive, trailing Connors to tournaments from Cleveland to Newport Beach—the Banners felt it crucial to their marketing to roll out the home schedule by Christmas with a star attached. Connors signed to the Banners on January 19, the day after WTT won USLTA recognition.

The Banners made local headlines on January 5, when Freeman sprung season tickets on an unsuspecting Baltimore Mayor Schaefer. Then the team hired publicist Pete Porter, a famous local Country & Western radio DJ and TV sportscaster who covered the Orioles and Colts. Porter told his hometown Upstate New York paper the *Hamburg Sun* (12/8/83): "I got to see another side of Jimmy. We used to travel with the Banners by station wagon. Like we'd drive to Philadelphia, and he'd ride with me. We never talked about tennis. Jimmy loved rock & roll, and we had nice discussions about music."

"The Banners were trying to infuse local blood, and they drafted me because I was the No. 1 player in the region. So, I was the face of local promotion. But things did not work out as envisioned."

—AUDREY MORSE, Baltimore Banners, 1991

The Banners unfurled their season ticket drive on April Fool's Day. Persons who bought season passes to all home matches also earned Banners Club membership, with free entry to the clubroom, buffet dinners and cocktails, and private parties with the players. Access to the air-conditioned, 93,000-square-foot Perring Racquet Club in Parkville, MD, was also included free to any season ticket procurer. Complimentary VIP parking went to those that purchased at least two lower concourse season tickets.

Front office turmoil began with April 6's hiring of Fred Neil from WCB-AM. GM Bud Freeman would neither confirm nor deny reports of his imminent departure. But after signing South African doubles star Byron Bertram on April 19, Bud stepped down citing personal reasons. The Banners had already expected his resignation, naming Neil as GM.

Team spokesman Dave Ortiz announced (*Hagerstown Daily Mail*, 4/20/74) a pre-season training camp roster of Connors, Morse, Bertram, and Kristy Pigeon (of the Virginia Slims "Original 9," the roots of the pro women's tour). They also brought in Janet Newberry (the #9-ranked U.S. woman); 33-year-old Aussie carpenter Bob "Nails" Carmichael; and injury-ravaged local star Lenny Schloss, who'd played the most extended doubles match to date, at six hours and ten minutes over two days. Also, in came Scottish pro, Joyce Williams Hume, who told the *Glasgow Herald*: "In Baltimore, we'll play evening matches in air-conditioned arenas, and give tennis clinics."

Days later, the Banners held a press luncheon to announce the signing of #2 pick Betty Stöve, Holland's top female netter, and Ian Crookenden, a left-handed New Zealander turned Roanoke teaching pro, off the professional circuit since 1966. Then Neil made two poor decisions: trading Janet Newberry to Boston for the rights to Paul Gerken, who never joined the team, and sending Kristy Pigeon to Hawaii for the contractual rights to Czech star Jan Kodes, who'd never play WTT. Neil cited Audrey Morse's local popularity, and her development under Candy, as factors allowing the team to trade.

> ### "I admit that I was a little bit scared about entering this new league. I can't say I believe in it, but I hope it does well."
>
> **—BETTY STÖVE, Baltimore Banners, 1974**

Candy put his players through the paces with morning and afternoon workouts until May 8's Civic Center opener vs. the Hawaii Leis. Candy cooed: "I'm looking forward to rounding things into a routine. We will put a top-notch team on the court for Baltimore." A May 6 press release for the opener hyped Jimmy Connors' "bitter feud" with Dennis Ralston, his Davis Cup captain, now Leis player-coach. The press release also said that fans could save 10% by pre-paying for ten or more tickets, which GM Neil called "A Great Net Worth!"

May 8, Baltimore Civic Center rocked with loud cheers, boos, and applause. The Banners had a productive debut, trouncing Hawaii 35-20 before a sparse crowd of 2,722. Connors swept in singles, as did Joyce Williams Hume-Bob Carmichael in mixed doubles. The fans screamed and whistled when Hawaii's Valerie Ziegenfuss served to Betty Stöve. Once when Valerie faulted, a fan yelled, "Can you do it again?" Another had callous advice for Ralston with an elastic bandage on one knee: after failing to reach a sideline shot, roaring, "You can't cover what you used to have Dennis!" At halftime—during the induction of six tennis locals into "The Banners Hall of Fame"—a society matron marched into the team office to bitch about the crowd. "If those people continue to yell like that, I'm not coming back again!" True to her word, she never returned.

May 11's *Baltimore Afro-American* set the record straight with an editorial about WTT. It opened: "While 95% of the players are not native, the league sells the idea its teams are competing for the honor of good old hometown, and the locals are expected to respond." And it closed: "While there's no evidence that a single black person is involved in the operation at any level, we are hopeful that it won't be long before this is rectified. Otherwise, we need World Team Tennis like we need a hole in the head."

The next day, the Banners repelled visiting Toronto-Buffalo 31-28, in front of a Civic Center crowd announced as 1,261, but calculated at 761 by the turnstile. Charm City fans rooted for hefty lefty Betty Stöve with boisterous chants of "Boog"—like how Orioles fans serenaded rotund first baseman, Boog Powell.

May 13 was a wild evening, even by Philly Spectrum standards. Connors rushed the stands during his set with Buster Mottram and had to be restrained by Spectrum security after three drunkards razzed him over fiancée Chris Evert. The incident incited a melee involving Baltimore's Connors and Candy, and Philly's Mottram and Billie Jean King. Umpire Col. Richmond A. Skinner gave Connors five seconds to resume play or forfeit. He settled down to beat Mottram, 6-3, and then courtly bowed to the crowd. Asked later how he planned to attack the goons, Connors, still wielding his racquet, replied, "I'd get one with the forehand, one with the backhand, and the third guy would then beat the shit out of me." When the smoke cleared, despite Jimmy's win, his Banners fell to the Freedoms 34-26.

In front of just 556 at the 17,600-seat Nassau Coliseum on May 20, the Banners edged the Sets, 24-23. A personality clash marked the opening set, as Connors faced volatile Croatian star Niki Pilić for the first time. Pilić failed to handle Connors' double-fisted backhands, and lost 6-3. Connors left the court chuckling; Pilić walked off cursing. In the next event, Morse replaced Hume mid-set, with the women's singles score 2-2. Coach Candy cracked, "We wanted to give Audrey playing time in front of the 'it' folks." The victory elevated Baltimore to a second-place tie with Boston in the Atlantic Section.

After the Sets match, Connors got driven to JFK for a flight to Rome to resolve the flap over his banning by the Italian Open for joining the renegade WTT. The team announced that he would not return until after Wimbledon, and could miss up to 14 matches. On May 21, the Connors-less Banners drove to Boston and rolled the Lobsters, 27-22, before 2,201 onlookers. The next night, John Newcombe and his Houston E-Z Riders came to Baltimore; but the advertised Newcombe-Connors battle was not to be. The high-flying Riders managed a 29-25 victory before an announced Civic Center crowd of 1,089. Three weeks in, the Banners, averaging 1,290 spectators at their home matches, ranked 15th in attendance in the 16-team league.

The Cleveland Nets won 26-17 before just 425 fans at the Civic on May 29. Despite weak turnouts and blasé play without Connors, co-owner Klauber insisted he was not giving up. "People who come here have liked team tennis. But we just can't get people here." He also stated, "We're making all the seats $2, and if that doesn't draw for us, I don't know what will." That Nets loss stung because it was a co-promotion with the NASL Baltimore Comets, with soccer fans admitted free to experience WTT. When asked of his squad's winning prospects, Candy complained, "We're literally out of our sorts without Connors."

> ## "I was a bit optimistic at one stage, but I don't know. Our girls were terrible. They were something like 1-19. They were always putting us behind at the start of a match."
> —BYRON BERTRAM, Baltimore Banners, 1974

On June 12, Baltimore purchased the contract of Kathy Kuykendall from the first-place Freedoms. The 17-year-old Miamian—the youngest player to ever sign a pro deal at the time—had played in only three matches for Philly. Kuykendall immediately stabilized the Banners' women's game with her ravaging baseline work and cross-court forehands.

That night, the blue-clad Banners whipped the visiting yellow-uniformed Detroit

Top: Baltimore Banners bumper sticker, 1974
Bottom: Baltimore Banners, 1974
L-R: Don Candy, Bob "Nails" Carmichael, Byron Bertram, Ian Crookenden,
Audrey Morse, Joyce Williams Hume, Betty Stöve

Loves, 32-17 before a reported 887 fans. However, insiders pegged it closer to 450, as Kuykendall competed strongly in her 6-3 loss to Rosie Casals, while Carmichael, dealing with a pulled Achilles tendon, jostled Phil Dent 6-2. *The New York Times* jabbed: "It will be some time before Howard Fine and his partners recoup their $500,000 investment."

In a last-ditch effort to make the playoffs, Baltimore signed Jaidip "Jay" Mukerjea, the #2 player in India. Candy crowed: "With Connors coming back and Kathy Kuykendall giving us more in women's singles, we should have a chance for one of the wild-card berths."

> ### *"Winning Wimbledon won't change me as a person. I've been successful as whatever I am: Jimmy Connors anti-establishment, Jimmy Connors controversial. I'm not gonna change. See you in Baltimore."*
>
> **—JIMMY CONNORS, 1974**

Connors' triumphant return after winning Wimbledon resulted in a roster jam. So the Banners cut Ian Crookenden, who took a swipe at WTT on his way out: "They're making the players conform to what the fans want instead of the other way." Then Byron Bertram got detained in London over minor visa issues, so the team used that as a pretext to fire him.

Despite Mukerjea's addition and Connors' return, Baltimore opened the second half of the season by losing again to the Philadelphia Freedoms at the Spectrum 28-23. The next day the Banners drove to Pittsburgh for an identical 28-23 loss to the Triangles. In a repeat of his Wimbledon victory, Connors crushed Triangles player-coach Ken Rosewall 6-2. That night, Connors displayed his bratty bad boy best, exploding over line calls against him. From the locker room, Connors clowned, "I must be the most unpopular champion in Wimbledon history!" Candy later told *Sports Illustrated* he dreamed of going postal over some of those line calls: "Kicking over the umpire's chair would be magnificent. All kinds of havoc, with him lying there, all smashed up and me ranting and raving."

GM Neil held a hastily arranged and slightly awkward July 8 press conference with Connors to announce that he and Chris Evert were off to California to recover from the rigors of their Wimbledon titles and would not return until July 17. "I've gotta catch up on my sleep," Connors joked. But by his planned return date, the struggling squad, having snapped a five-game losing skid, disclosed that Connors would miss three additional matches—their next two at home, July 17 against the Florida and July 20 vs. Toronto-Buffalo, and July 22 in Detroit. The team said they expected him to partake in nine of their 19 remaining matches.

> ### *"Barring injury, illness, or an act of God, Jimmy will play in Baltimore. If he doesn't show up because of contractual problems, we'll refund the ticket price, plus parking."*
>
> **—FRED NEIL, Baltimore Banners GM, 1974**

Connors' return resulted in the Banners' winning four of their next five matches. July 31's standings showed Baltimore (14-19) still alive in the playoff hunt, two games behind second-place Boston. That night, the Banners rallied to snag a 27-20 win over the lifeless Strings before a guesstimated home crowd of three hundred. Kuykendall trailed L.A.'s Marita Redondo when Candy substituted in Stöve, who got burned, 6-3. Then Connors-Carmichael rocked in men's doubles, 6-2.

The Banners' tailspin began August 1 at Detroit's Cobo Arena with a loss to the Loves, 28-19. The next night, the Pacific Division-leading Racquets invaded the Baltimore Civic, where Denver routed Baltimore 28-20, as Connors lost twice, to Andrew Pattison in singles, and with Carmichael to Pattison/Tony Roche, in what would be Connors' last match in Baltimore. Afterward, Jimmy flew to Indianapolis to play in the National Clay Courts.

On August 4, with Connors away and Kuykendall hospitalized after an allergic reaction to a fish dinner (with eyes swollen and fingers numb), 2,636 Pittsburghers saw their Triangles ruffle the Banners, 28-26. The three-hour epic, described in the *Post-Gazette* as "An Evening Without Jimmy Connors," featured 19 ties and 15 sudden death points, 12 won by Baltimore. One Pittsburgh fan berated Carmichael, "You're rusty, Nails."

Three nights later, the visiting Lobsters lashed the flagging Banners in a 23-21 match more lopsided than the score indicated. "Howling Harry," a crazy Baltimore sports scene character known for howling from the stands, began doing his thing from the upper deck. Boston's Roger Taylor stopped his singles set to ask, "What does that guy want, and why can't someone help him?" After the details got explained, the British lefty saluted Harry.

On August 9, Philly eliminated Baltimore from the playoffs 29-23, sweeping their season series before a franchise-record 6,160 at the Civic Center. Kuykendall put up a spirited fight against Billie Jean King before yielding 6-4. In hindsight, had Connors played a full season, the Banners were a postseason squad. But without him, they had no shot.

> **"I have been struggling. The girls I face are so strong, and they know exactly what to do. Against some, I can hold my own, but others kill me."**
> **—JOYCE WILLIAMS HUME, Baltimore Banners, 1974**

The next morning, Audrey Morse and Jay Mukerjea taught a free clinic at the Baker Park West Second Street Courts in Frederick, MD. The two Banners proved a smash with their training tips. Morse was a hit, showing the women how to step to the ball and hold their racquets. Mukerjea got a pleasant surprise when Jamno Bhagat, a Fedders engineer from his hometown of Calcutta, greeted him. Frederick citizens who attended an upcoming home match won Banners Courtside Club membership. Thirty percent of all money raised went to Alcoholics Anonymous.

That evening, Baltimore sports media covering the team honored Bob Carmichael—and not Jimmy Connors—as Banners MVP. Candy urged Carmichael's draft selection

Above: Betty Stöve, Bob Carmichael and coach Don Candy argue line call with umpire, 1974

Below: TV camera behind Banners bench of Joyce Williams Hume, Audrey Morse, and Ian Crookenden

despite a lackluster tour record, confident that he was in a slump and would return to form. Nails proved his coach prophetic, offering startling power during Connors' absences, excelling in singles, in men's doubles with Connors or Mukerjea, and mixed doubles with Stöve.

August 17, the Banners ended their home schedule on an up note, shredding the Nets 25-23 before a reported 1,065 onlookers, as Kuykendall-Mukerjea preserved the victory in the final set, 7-6. Their season ended the following day in Chicago after a 25-23 loss to the Aces before a too-small-to-announce crowd at Chicago's Lakeshore, in what would be the last matches for both franchises. Baltimore ended its 44-game slate 16-28 (.364).

Joseph Rivkin denied rumors his franchise was folding or moving, but he conceded that front office expenses forced the dismissal of Fred Neil and all but a skeleton crew at the Civic Center. He would not comment on rumors that by season's end, Gerry Klauber prayed Connors would not show up to collect his $3,000 match fees; Connors' deal called for him to play in 22 of 44 games, but he played 18. Yet when Jimmy partook, he was #1 in WTT singles and unbeaten at home. As for other useless stats, Banners ladies ranked dead last; Kuykendall (.349) and Hume (.286) rated #19 and #20 in the 16-team circuit.

On November 6, the Banners effectively ended when they traded Jimmy's contractual rights to Pittsburgh for Isabel Fernandez, Gerald Battrick, plus cash. Triangles owner turned WTT president Frank Fuhrer addressed the Banners' situation: "When Connors was with Baltimore, it was never known when he'd play, and as a result, attendance suffered. There were many people to blame for the Baltimore situation. But I can say this: there's no way I'd ever be interested in him for one-third of a season."

"I can't say exactly the amount of money we lost. But 'considerable' would be a proper adjective to describe it."

—GERALD KLAUBER, Baltimore Banners co-owner, 1974

There were no mourners, wreaths, or epitaphs, just a brief February 1, 1975 newswire from WTT meetings in Houston: the Banners were no more. The reason for the team's demise—failure to meet a deadline for a letter of credit—also put to rest the Buckskins, Flamingos, Aces, Royals, and Freedoms. Coach Candy cried, "We're literally out of our jobs." In one last attempt, the Banners enlisted Mayor Schaefer to lower their Civic Center rent. But the best offer was $500 per match. "We could never meet our budget," Klauber conceded.

Stöve went on to an all-star career with the Golden Gaters and Seattle Cascades. Kuykendall signed to Hawaii, making her the first to play for three different WTT teams. Candy (later the coach of Pam Shriver) and Carmichael both left the team owed money. In 1976, Klauber got convicted of unrelated racketeering and mail fraud charges. Morse became a State Farm agent in Havre De Grace, MD. Connors never returned to the original WTT.

Chapter 7

Florida Flamingos

Frank Froehling, Florida Flamingos player-coach, 1974

"As soon as I heard [Betty Ann Grubb] was the best-looking girl in tennis, I wanted her on this team. And that's my wife over there."
—TED COHEN, Florida Flamingos owner, 1974

WTT sought synchronicity with South Florida's tennis culture—though there were questions if all these sunny outdoor netters would root for team tennis played indoors. The first traces came on Christmas 1973 with Miami-area newspaper ads for "Team Tennis." One could write to player-coach Frank Froehling at his home in Coconut Grove or call him for a team brochure with ticket plans.

With the season opener less than a hundred days away and an alleged 2,000 season tickets sold for the unnamed Miami club, Froehling still ran the team as a one-person operation. The 31-year-old Ft. Lauderdaler, the #3 American player in his college days, was relying heavily on signing #1 overall draft pick Chris Evert, stating, "I'm certain Chris will play here" after offering her a $1.35 million multi-year deal. But he quickly realized her engagement to Jimmy Connors, playing for Baltimore, "threw everything up in the air." Then in late February, businessman Ted Cohen—part of a St. Louis investor group with Butch Buchholz—outbid three others to purchase the Miami franchise. A naming contest resulted in a tropical, avian moniker: the Florida Flamingos.

"The Froehling Stones" quickly gelled. They signed Cliff Drysdale of South Africa, winner of the 1974 Saga Bay Tournament in Miami, who had once been

ATP president, then Mark Cox, from Leicester, England, living in Vancouver, who earned a then-hefty $60,000 in tennis in 1973. Evert spurned the franchise's offer, so the team signed her childhood friend Laurie Fleming, a women's tour regular with 100-plus trophies. Froehling planned to play mixed doubles with Maria Bueno, the 34-year-old Brazilian star retired five years and coming off surgery; Fleming and Bueno were to star in women's doubles. Betty Ann Hansen Grubb, a former UCLA star, married with a child at 20, divorced and then returned to tennis after three years off, would dominate with bruising baseline play. Detroit drafted Grubb, but traded her to Florida, and she signed her Flamingos contract the day after her divorce settlement. Froehling said that he saw his role as player-coach as "getting our players psyched up for matches."

"The only problem is, I won't be able to miss school every other week. I don't want to drop out of high school, as some people do."
—LYNN EPSTEIN, Florida Flamingos, 1974

Days before the season opener, Florida signed Miami Beach High sophomore Lynn Epstein, the state's top 16-and-under player (unpaid to retain her amateur status). They also introduced 28-year-old Mike Belkin, a Montreal-born University of Miami star and Canadian Davis Cupper, noted for his two-handed backhand and fiery temper. Belkin was bidding to return after shredding his knee in the 1971 U.S. Open—against Drysdale.

Other 1974 lady Flamingos: Bunny Smith (tennis pro at Miami Beach's Fontainebleau Hotel), Donna Fales (another blast from the past), and Donna Ganz (discovered in the crowd). Publicist Mike Kram said: "We waited too long to sign Chris Evert, and when we saw we couldn't get her, we looked around for other talents, and there were none left."

The Flamingos debuted May 8 at Miami Beach Convention Center. Before the 8 p.m. match against the L.A. Strings, Betty Ann Grubb walked on the court, joined by the team's shocking pink mascot, Flora Flamingo. The 11,000-seat arena drew 5,126 to see Florida win a 27-26 cliffhanger. But the match dragged on over four hours; the final set began at 11:45 p.m. to a fraction of the original crowd. Froehling felt that the crowd's stomping and yelling inspired Drysdale's win over Jerry Van Linge in the opener and Cox-Grubb over Karen Susman-Geoff Masters in the finale. Gushed the winning player-coach: "This is the most unbelievable thing I've seen."

On May 11, a reported 1,581 at the Convention Center saw the Flamingos fold to the Aces, 29-21, a game in which they benched Maria Bueno after getting swept in singles and doubles. The *Chicago Tribune*'s David Condon observed that the "suntanned, superbly stemmed" Grubb "heard more whistles than a railroad crossing." Two nights later, 2,014 Miamians saw the Pittsburgh Triangles dominate, 27-19. That kicked off a losing streak that included May 14 in Denver, 26-23 before 1,000-ish "Racquet Rowdies" who politely greeted Mark Cox, winner of the 1973 Denver Open (over Arthur Ashe), in for Froehling playing the Alan King Classic in Las Vegas.

Curiosity tore 5,362 Floridians from their TV sets and crossword puzzles on May 22 to visit the Miami Beach Convention Center for "the Philadelphia Freedoms starring Billie

Florida Flamingos, fan pennant, 1974
Miami Beach's World Team Tennis entry

Jean King." A band playing cool pop tunes and led the sporadic "charge" to urge crowd support, as vendors sold beer, peanuts, and ice cream, making fans feel as if they were at the old ball game. Flamingos pennants dotted the crowd. King blanked Laurie Fleming 6-0 in singles and then won 6-2 with Tory Ann Fretz in doubles. At halftime, scores of fans descended on the Philly bench seeking King's autograph. The 25-16 final score looked less shameful after Froehling-Grubb swept 6-0 in the last set of mixed doubles.

After the loss, Froehling railed: "Betty Ann Grubb has been solid, but we need a number-one woman. It's the women who've hurt us. Laurie Fleming hasn't played well at all. That puts us so far behind we can't give the other team a good match. They've been losing 6-0, 6-2 every time, and that's bush for the fans. We've only played one match worth seeing, and people will stop coming if we don't get better." Fleming told her local *Palm Beach Post*: "There's pressure here different from the tour. I'm playing for a team, and I haven't done that since high school." One month into the season, Fleming, May 1973's *World Tennis* cover girl, got demoted to women's doubles substitute.

> ### *"I haven't been playing well. I've been practicing four hours a day. But I can't get going."*
> **—Laurie Fleming, Florida Flamingos, 1974**

At May 21's Chamber of Commerce breakfast, Miami Dolphins owner Joe Robbie told Ted Cohen and NASL Toros coach Jon Young "I'm confident that pro tennis and pro soccer will make it in Miami with a little hard work and the willingness to look at red ink for a while." Cohen backed that up: "We expect to lose money for the first two, three seasons. But in the end, we will make it."

Florida fans showed zero interest in seeing the Banners without Jimmy Connors. On May 24, just 647 saw the Flamingos win 24-21, as Cliff Drysdale beat Connors' stand-in Byron Bertram, 6-2. The Convention Center marquee read "Baltimore Banners starring Audrey Morse," who also didn't compete. Donna Ganz, a former Miami Beach High standout, attended the Freedoms game and convinced Cohen and team consultant Arthur Mickelson to schedule her a tryout. Ganz got her chance, signing at 4:30 that afternoon and playing in mixed and women's doubles versus Baltimore, with 50 or so friends and family—a sizeable segment of the audience—cheering wildly in the crowd.

The Flamingos won a 28-27 home thriller on May 31 over the Houston E-Z Riders. Froehling said of his Flamingos (3-9), last place in the Gulf Plains Section: "Our record isn't great, but we're starting to play. We have an exciting team with an excellent chance to get into the playoffs. We're only 3½ games out of first and have time to make it up."

Two weeks later, Cohen gave Maria Bueno her walking papers, calling it "one of the hardest things I ever had to do." Bueno's most competitive showing in four women's singles sets for Florida was a 6-3 loss; Cohen said, "I felt bad about it because I was the one who convinced her to leave Brazil and play WTT. But the cold, hard fact was we could not depend on Maria on a match-to-match basis. You're talking about one of the great women ever to play the game sitting on the bench. She was unhappy in that position, and I was unhappy having her in that position. We talked about it for a few weeks, and worked out a settlement."

To end the season's first half, Florida faced Denver in a home match at West Palm Beach Auditorium. The June 16 affair was sponsored by Dennis Burchell of the Palm Beach Tennis Club and promoted by Boca Raton radio exec George Liddy. Froehling told the media: "We named ourselves the Florida Flamingos because we wanted to identify with the entire state, and matches in West Palm Beach is the first step in this direction. We believe Palm Beach is ready for big-time tennis. If we have a reasonably large crowd, we'll come back. If not, we won't. Simple as that." Despite considerable publicity, less than 2,000 spectators came to see the Racquets batter the Flamingos 30-26.

After the Wimbledon break, Laurie Fleming excelled as Florida came from behind on July 13 to belt the Banners in Baltimore, 23-22. With the home team leading 20-17, Fleming-Froehling fried Betty Stöve-Jay Mukerjea 6-2 in the final set. July 18, before 2,510 at Nassau Coliseum, the shorthanded Flamingos fell to the Sets 28-22, after their aged player-coach Manuel Santana zapped perennial benchwarmer Mike Belkin 6-0.

> ## *"This is perfect for me. I'm happy to be here, and I play when the team wants me to. Besides, I'm getting paid for sitting."*
> ### —MIKE BELKIN, Florida Flamingos, 1974

Before ending their road trip in Cleveland, Florida signed Ken Stuart as the third man on the bench. Drysdale was out with a leg strain, and Cox was in Vancouver at a hotel tennis commitment, and WTT rules levied a $5,000 fine on teams not dressing three men and three women. So Stuart, on break from running the John Wayne

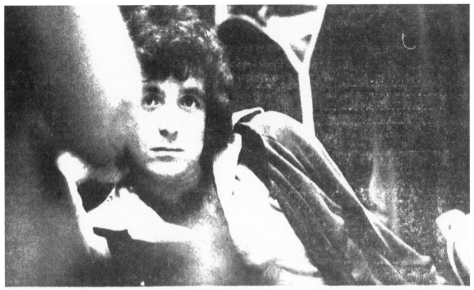

Mike Belkin does his part as Flamingos' designated benchwarmer

Mike Belkin, Florida Flamingos, "designated benchwarmer," 1974

Tennis Club in Newport Beach, made sense, as he was traveling in the team station wagon with his girlfriend, Grubb. Stuart's debut came in front of a July 24 "Nickel Beer Night" of 2,397 inebriated onlookers—most of whom paid little attention to the Flamingos' 29-17 loss to Minnesota.

Stuart on the Flamingos was a "touchy" situation. He and Grubb had been teen crushes before she married another man in 1970. According to Ken, "We engaged the day she got a divorce. Those plans changed, but have re-changed." What he meant was he dumped Grubb after the Flamingos' first road trip to L.A., before things rekindled three weeks later during the break. But in those three weeks, no player and coach ever shared a closer relationship. A Miami reporter described Froehling as "Betty Ann's constant off-court companion." Frank said of Stuart: "I think it's fine they're together. She's happy, and he helps her tennis. He's been cooperative, but it is awkward with a boyfriend on the road."

> *"There have been so many Nickel Beer Nights recently. The people attending the last few matches weren't involved in the tennis. At least they weren't junkies and alcoholics."*
>
> **—BETTY ANN GRUBB, Florida Flamingos, 1974**

Team publicist/consultant Art Mickelson admitted: "The Flamingos policy is we pretty much have to play on a regional basis to be successful." Taking a page from the playbook of the ABA's Floridians (model for Will Ferrell's *Semi-Pro*) who barnstormed the Sunshine State 1970-71, the Flamingos played home matches in West Palm Beach, Jacksonville, and St. Petersburg. Mickelson mused, "All we want to do is leave people happy"—while announcing Nickel Beer Nights for all future Miami home events.

"Phase 1" of the Flamingos' deep Sunshine State infiltration began August 9 at Jacksonville Coliseum, where 1,628 saw Drysdale rally Florida over the Nets, 26-18. Over the loudspeaker from his midcourt chair, umpire Stu Winston urged the crowd to cheer or jeer: "It's your team. Let them know if you like it or don't." The lack of spunk may have been because it wasn't their team. Cohen addressed his squad's J-ville flameout: "I was satisfied with the crowd reaction but not with the crowd size. I expected around 4,000. I hope we can have that type of crowd in St. Petersburg."

Monday, August 5's media event at the St. Pete Hilton introduced the Flamingos before August 10's match at Bayfront Center Arena against last-place New York. Art Mickelson offered: "If this experiment goes well, we may split our schedule next year, playing half our matches in Miami and the other half around the state." The day before the game, team reps still hoped to draw 3,000 for the tennis-perfect 6,400-seat Arena. An alleged 2,234 saw the Sets abuse the Flamingos 28-13. The night's tone was set with an off-key rendition of the national anthem by the geriatric trio Men of Note. By halftime, New York led 18-3, at which point Florida could not mathematically win.

The Flamingos fell out of playoffs contention after falling 24-17 to the Houston E-Z Riders before 3,206 drunkards at Nickel Beer Night. The *Miami News* (8/14/74) quipped: "There have been so many Nickel Beer Nights at the Convention Center that they should rename WTT, 'World Team Beer, this week's attraction, Flamingos Night.'" Mickelson and his wife sold the beer tickets; one vendor offered 2½¢ beers (two 5¢ tix for a nickel).

"My job is not the easiest thing to do. There've been some tough teams. I'd be better off playing instead of coaching. I'm looking forward to next year."
—FRANK FROEHLING, Florida Flamingos player-coach, 1974

Not to imply that the Flamingos were a Mickey Mouse operation, but on August 14, Mickelson said that he'd travel to Orlando to discuss holding future Flamingos matches at Disney World (the idea to erect stands and a tent). For 1975, the team scheduled 13 games in Miami (one per week) and nine in West Palm, Jacksonville, and St. Petersburg.

Flamingos director of operations Bob Shapiro met with the Flagler Kennel Club to use Flagler Amphitheater as the team's new Miami arena. Also considered were Miami Jai-Alai Fronton, Dade Community College, and Miami Beach Auditorium. Mickelson explained: "Obviously you can't use 'successful' to describe the season. The first half was sad, but the second was enthusiastic. It showed we had something."

Miami Herald (9/1/74) reported the Flamingos significantly padded attendance figures. The team claimed before May 8's opener that they'd sold over 1,000 season tickets. But reports to the Convention Center showed 191, with many freebies. Donna

Betty Ann Grubb, Florida Flamingos press photo, 1974

Above: Niki Piliç and Virginia Wade (New York Sets) argue a line call at the Flamingos' only match in St. Petersburg, 1974

Below: Laurie Fleming, Florida Flamingos press photo, 1974

Frank Froehling, Florida Flamingos vs. Hawaii Leis, Honolulu, 1974

Fales said team officials "went to tennis clubs and gave out handfuls of tickets. All the teams did it. On the road, we'd scan the crowd, and teams often announced double what we just counted."

> **"Each team had to reach certain criteria, and Miami didn't. They didn't come up with a $50,000 letter of credit, and they didn't pay their players. We just can't have that as a league."**
>
> **—LARRY KING, 1974**

Bob Shapiro said the Flamingos lost $250,000 in 1974, averaging 1,900 fans where it took 3,300 to break even. Mounting losses meant that players and creditors had difficulty getting paid. Betty Ann Grubb never received $13,000; Cliff Drysdale failed to collect on most of his $60,000. The franchise folded right before 1975 league meetings, unable to secure the letter of credit required to continue play. A *Fort Lauderdale News* (2/2/75) franchise obituary trumpeted, "The Froehling Stones are now just a golden oldie."

"The Flamingos were not well promoted," Laurie Fleming reflected. "But we could never compete with the Dolphins. They were undefeated champions. If we ran away with the league, people might've come seen us play. But most would rather play tennis than watch it."

Chapter 8
Minnesota Buckskins

Owen Davidson, Minnesota Buckskins player-coach, 1974

"Team tennis can be as good if not better than individuals' efforts. Of course, that remains to be seen."

— OWEN DAVIDSON, Minnesota Buckskins player-coach, 1974

Minnesota holds a rich tennis legacy, with a high school history rivaling the state's storied high school hockey programs. From "dynasty" teams like Edina, Rochester, and St. Cloud, to "Cinderella" squads such as St. James, Minneapolis South and Minnehaha Academy, to small-college powers like St. Olaf and Gustavus Adolphus, the state has deep tennis roots. Such popularity played into The Northland's WTT squad dubbed the Buckskins, in tribute to the region's Scandinavian trapper past.

The Buckskins began at May 22, 1973's league meetings in Chicago, where a franchise was approved for Lee Meade, a Litchfield, MN sports journalist and ABA co-founder, joined by St. Paul hockey players Len Vanelli and John Finley, co-owners of the WHA Minnesota Fighting Saints. Weeks later, Burt McGlynn of Twin Cities-based McGlynn Bakeries, long active in amateur tennis, invested in the team and named Meade GM.

At August 3, 1973's player draft, Minnesota made solid choices in top-ranked male Stan Smith, Aussie pro Owen Davidson, and National Clay Courts titlist Linda Tuero. The franchise scheduled an August 27 press event to announce a two-year deal with New Orleans native Tuero. But the next day, Meade said Tuero's lawyer Gene Scott told him his client was warned she'd be barred from the U.S. Open if she signed with WTT. USLTA head Walter Elcott rejected Meade's charges, but Tuero never came to terms. Only four of Minnesota's 19 picks signed.

Meade said of Stan Smith: "I met with Stan for five minutes in Toronto. He gave me his ideas on team tennis. He felt the concept would destroy the men's circuit. But I feel there's room for WTT as a supplement to tournament tennis. He doesn't feel it will happen this way."

Lee Vanelli divulged that the Buckskins had offered Billie Jean King a five-year deal worth $1 million at the draft, with most of the income tied to marketing. "We had heard Billie loved candy, so we approached candy companies and worked out a major ad campaign," Vanelli unveiled. "The deal was for five years with payments spread out over ten." Meade also spoke of choosing a home arena between St. Paul Civic Center, Minneapolis Auditorium, and Bloomington's Met Center. They opted for the latter.

February 5, the Buckskins introduced their first signing, Australian doubles star Owen Davidson as player-coach, and announced the trade of Stan Smith's rights to Pittsburgh for Mona Guerrant-Schallau (one of the Virginia Slims "Original 9"). Meade disclosed, "We had to get a #1 woman. We signed Linda Tuero but we can't force her to play." The Buckskins also coaxed out of retirement 1969 Wimbledon champion Ann Haydon-Jones.

Going into the 1974 season, the Gulf-Plains Section entrants fielded a squad of gifted but blasé netters. Fifth-round pick Bob Hewitt, an acerbic 34-year-old South African, was described by Florida Flamingos player-coach Frank Froehling as "the greatest doubles player in the last ten years and still in the Top 20 in singles." Wendy "Rabbit" Turnbull, a 22-year-old Aussie from Brisbane, won nine Grand Slam titles. British Davis Cup captain David Lloyd from Essex, England, was the older brother of Chris Evert's future husband John Lloyd. Maricaye Christenson of Grand Junction, CO, and Shari Barman, daughter of WTT co-founder Fred Barman, made the opening roster but never played; she opted for a job as team publicist.

Player-personnel decisions and on-court action were never the issues—everything else was. Two weeks before the season, McGlynn and Meade met local media to announce they'd acquired 100% ownership from Vanelli and Finley, and had sold "substantial interest" to Northstar Financial Corporation, the moneymen behind the NHL North Stars.

"We were fiddling and faddling out there. Most of the time we didn't know where the ball was going." —ANN HAYDON-JONES, 1974

In May 7's home opener, the Buckskins lost a grueling four-hour match to the Houston E-Z Riders, 30-28, in front of 2,317 at The Met, to a chorus of cheers, boos and catcalls. When Bob Hewitt surged in his set against Dick Stockton, fans shouted, "We're number one!" and "C'mon Hewitt you can do it." Team officials agreed that their debut match was too long but said they were thrilled with the fan reaction to the new sport. McGlynn muttered. "We must speed up the game. It took too long."

Top: Minnesota Buckskins, 1974
L-R: Owen Davidson, David Lloyd, Bob Hewitt, Wendy Turnbull,
Mona Guerrant, Ann Haydon-Jones

Above: Ann Haydon-Jones, Minnesota Buckskins, 1974

Hewitt howled, "I didn't mind the rowdy crowd. Crowds make no difference as long as they're on your side."

Minnesota won again at home May 10 over the L.A. Strings, 35-22. Owen Davidson whipped John Fort, 6-1, and then with Wendy Turnbull crushed Geoff Masters-Kathy Harter, 6-2. May 15, Minnesota came from behind to bash the visiting Golden Gaters, 32-30, led by Bob Hewitt in singles, and David Lloyd-Ann Haydon-Jones topping Frew McMillan-Denise Triola in doubles, 6-3. May 20, fueled by Ann Haydon-Jones and Hewitt, Minnesota ousted the Chicago Aces 28-18 at The Met for their third straight. May 22, the Buckskins buried the New York Sets at Nassau Coliseum with superior women's play, 25-17. May 26 at Miami Beach Convention Center, the Flamingos fleeced the Buckskins, 26-24. Hewitt-Davidson beat Cliff Drysdale-Frank Froehling 6-4, during which Hewitt went berserk after a double-fault, and slammed a serve at an abusive fan.

The Buckskins' all-time highlight came Saturday June 1. Before a WTT record turnout of 10,658 at the Met, Minnesota beat the undefeated Philadelphia Freedoms. In the final set, David Lloyd-Mona Schallau topped Fred Stolle-Julie Anthony, 6-4. The next night, the 'Skins seized first place in the Gulf Plains Section with a 25-20 win over Baltimore before 2,142 in Bloomington. June 10 at The Met, the Buckskins slayed the Flamingos 28-16. Schallau said of her spent squad to SI: "My volley is blah. I'm a dead elephant on the court. My serve has no sting and I'm confused. Other than that I'm fine."

The Buckskins opened the season's second half on July 14 by edging the Sets at home, 26-25; the turnout was 3,770, although most tickets were given free to the Minneapolis Aquatennis Association. July 24, they knocked back a few after a 29-17 win over the Flamingos on "Nickel Beer Night" in Miami Beach. July 29-30, they went to Honolulu, and split two, falling to the Leis, 26-24, and then winning, 31-24. The next day, with two weeks left in the season, GM Meade said that the team had begun printing playoff tickets. It seemed certain they'd at least qualify for one of two Western Division wild card seeds.

August 7, a Jones-Lloyd mixed doubles win fueled the Buckskins over the surging Denver Racquets, 26-22. On August 14, with Jones and Hewitt out due to illness, Denver exacted revenge, taking four of five sets, 28-20. The next night—in Minnesota's season finale—was a 26-17 home victory over the Leis before 1,294 as the Buckskins (27-17) finished 1974 as Gulf-Plains Section champions.

The playoffs began August 19 with Houston walloping Minnesota in Game One at The Met, 28-19. Since cumulative points in two games would decide the series, the Buckskins had to win handily in Game Two to advance. The next night in Houston, the Buckskins dominated 29-19, fueled by a final set 6-4 Davidson-Schallau mixed doubles victory. The margin gave Minnesota a 48-47 cumulative score, to advance against the Racquets.

In the Division semi-finals on August 22, the Racquets bashed the Buckskins 29-18, as Denver's Françoise Dürr drubbed Ann Haydon-Jones, 6-1. Twenty-four hours later, Denver prevailed in Bloomington 26-25 to take the two-game series with a cumulative score of 54-44. The final match would be the Buckskins' last call of the wild.

Bob Hewitt, Minnesota Buckskins, 1974

"I never would have gotten into this if I thought that anybody would lose a nickel."

—BURT McGLYNN, Minnesota Buckskins owner, 1975

A month earlier, the league took over the financially troubled franchise. Burt McGlynn insisted the situation was temporary "to meet the latest payroll." The Buckskins were one of the premier squads but suffered a capital shortage so WTT had to cover the final two payrolls. Meade said, "We can reclaim the franchise by paying the league back." He felt $250,000 to $350,000 was needed to pay off 1974 and compete in 1975. He also said he'd "found another party from out of state interested. That means the team might move." After McGlynn's admission, a PR firm handling their preseason sued for unpaid services.

The financially strapped Buckskins announced inquiries from ownership contingents in Indianapolis and Washington, D.C. McGlynn said on November 6 that the team would move to one of those cities or it would fold. Meade said there was a "90% chance" that Indiana indoor court operator Bill Bereman's bloc would exercise their option, but they instead bought the Detroit Loves and relocated them to Indy. Meade and McGlynn were on the hook for all debts if no buyers were found—and no buyer materialized.

Before November 26th's player draft for 1975, the Buckskins players got auctioned to other teams, raising $22,500 toward their payroll debt. Owen Davidson went to Hawaii, Ann Haydon-Jones to Cleveland, Mona Schallau to New York, and Wendy Turnbull to Boston, while Bob Hewitt got shipped to L.A. (and re-routed to join Turnbull in Boston). "In retrospect, I never should have gotten in," Burt McGlynn reflected.

Years later, McGlynn returned to Twin Cities sports as part owner of the original NBA Minnesota Timberwolves. Lloyd briefly ran the soccer club Hull City. Hewitt flamed out after a 2011 *Boston Globe* inquiry into abuse of underage girls he coached, and at the time of this writing had recently been paroled on sexual abuse charges in South Africa. Meade went on to work for the World Hockey Association, Canadian Football League, and Major League Volleyball. He told *Sports Illustrated*: "I guess you could call the Minnesota Buckskins a failure."

Chapter 9
Toronto-Buffalo Royals

Tom Okker, Toronto-Buffalo Royals player-coach, 1974

"I don't know what's wrong with this team. I've tried everything. We can't win, and we can't attract an audience. I don't know what to do."
—TOM OKKER, Toronto-Buffalo Royals player-coach, 1974

Toronto, with its ties to British culture, was big into tennis early on. Toronto Lawn Tennis Club in midtown Toronto greatly impacted the evolution of Canadian tennis. In 1881 the club hosted Canada's first International Tennis Championship, won by member Isidore Hellmuth. Over the years, WTT stars like Newcombe, Laver, Borg, Navratilova, Connors, and Evert all made their mark in Toronto-area tennis events and tournaments.

Toronto was undergoing a '70s tennis boom, and there was a belief in the viability of team tennis. In May 1973, businessmen John F. Bassett and John C. Eaton, behind the WHA's Ottawa Nationals, bought one of 16 teams to be called the Toronto Deuces.

Bassett, son of Canadian media mogul John W.H. Bassett, was a 1959 Canadian Davis Club player and former Toronto Maple Leafs Board Chairman. He also owned the WFL's Toronto Northmen, who relocated to become the Memphis Southmen, infamous for poaching NFL Miami Dolphins stars Larry Csonka, Jim Kiick, and Paul Warfield.

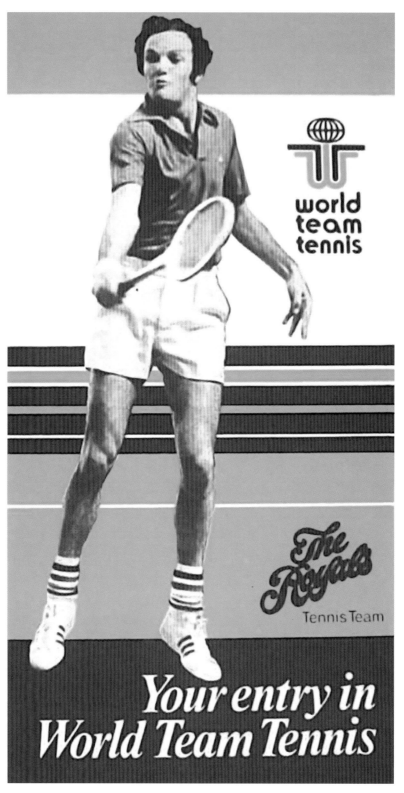

Your entry in World Team Tennis

Toronto-Buffalo Royals sales brochure with Tom Okker,
promoting the only season of WTT in Canada

In November 1973's player draft, Toronto had the 13th pick. They selected Tom Okker of the Netherlands, a star in singles and men's doubles (with Marty Reissen). Noting his high draft position, Okker said, "If they offer me enough money, I'll play."

Canada's only squad then picked American teens Marita Redondo and Laurie Tenney, Germany's Karl Meiler and Helga Masthoff, France's Pierre Barthès, Mexico's Raúl Ramírez, and Australia's Lesley Hunt. Everyone got a good chuckle for the team's final selection, Toronto sportswriter George Gross. None of the names above came to terms.

John Bassett announced on March 13 that he cut a deal for playing dates at Buffalo's Memorial Auditorium ("The Aud"), sports mecca of Western New York. Gus Villanueva, a Philippine star named Toronto GM, told press the team would split 22 home games between The Aud and TO's Canadian National Exhibition (CNE) Coliseum. Bassett created a regal name: the Toronto-Buffalo Royals.

Days later, Tom Okker signed on as Royals player-coach. The diminutive Dutchman would reportedly earn $136,000 per year for the next five years. Boston Lobsters owner Ray Ciccolo fumed: "I'm no expert, but from what I've seen of the owners' mistakes, I see why 80% of them are in trouble. Most made their first mistakes at the draft, before the first set of tennis. They came unprepared or didn't have enough money to do it right. But Okker's signing was the worst thing Toronto-Buffalo could've done to the league."

The Royals built a roster strong on the men's side. Okker with his wicked topspin and backhand; Ian Fletcher, a rangy Aussie ranked #7 on the USTA indoor tour; and Mike Estep, a Waco-bred Rice University legend. The women's side starred Wendy Overton, the #1 women's college player 1965-69 at Florida's Rollins College, 33-year-old Aussie veteran Jan O'Neill, and 27-year-old South African Davis Cupper Laura Rossouw.

> ## "It'd be a lie to say that we didn't put pressure on Tom Okker to play in the home opener. Our argument was he's a professional, and we pay him a lot of money."
> **—GUS VILLANUEVA, Toronto-Buffalo Royals GM, 1974**

May 7, the Cleveland Nets traveled to Toronto's CNE Coliseum for the Royals' home opener. Okker was scheduled to play the next night in Dallas against John Newcombe in the quarterfinals of the WCT $50,000 eight-man championship and had previously said that he couldn't play the WTT opener due to these commitments. But his plans changed after a frank discussion with management. So Okker arrived in Toronto via private jet at 8 a.m. and then left after the match back to Dallas at 2 a.m. WCT officials were livid.

In the end, Okker saved the opening night, as the Royals shredded the Nets 32-21. A reported 4,458 kinda-into-it Ontarians lightly booed the Nets during intros, and occasionally heckled. Okker swept Cliff Richey to give the Royals a lead, and in the final set, Mike Estep-Jan O'Neill razed the Nets' Clark Graebner-Laura DuPont, 6-3.

In the Detroit Loves' May 9 home opener, the Royals lost 28-19 before a Motown crowd of 3,611. The final outcome—highlighted by a singles set in which Detroit's Phil Dent smacked a forehand that cracked Tom Okker's racquet in half—got eclipsed by a 20-minute, first-half dust-up, when Okker fumed over a fault call by umpire Walter Orline on Jan O'Neill. Coaches Okker and Detroit's Jack Shaw feuded with officials, amid taunts and catcalls. Okker waved his team off the court, and only returned after further heated chat. Okker's official protest was the first in the young league's history.

> **"The way we've been playing lately, I could beat most of our own players."**
> —JOHN BASSETT, Toronto-Buffalo Royals owner, 1974

Friday, May 10 in Chicago, the Royals lost in a wild final-set super-tiebreaker, seen by just 307, as they lost to the Aces 32-31. T-B played without Okker, who'd arrived a few hours earlier from Dallas after losing to Stan Smith in the WCTs. Okker went over to the hotel restaurant, got food poisoning, and was ordered bed rest. GM Villanueva filled in as coach, saying, "Tommy was in bad shape. He was still sick the morning after."

May 13's Buffalo premiere (billed locally as the Buffalo Royals) resulted in a big victory over the Hawaii Leis, 30-20, with 3,000 in attendance. Ball girl Debbie DiCarlo recalled the dozens of teens who snuck in by helping load in umpire chairs and other gear from a nearby tennis club.

With Tom Okker away playing in Las Vegas, the understaffed Royals jetted to JFK on May 15 to face the New York Sets. Ian Fletcher's 6-3 win over Charlie Owens, insured Toronto-Buffalo's victory, 33-22. The next night, Boston rousted the Royals in Toronto, 36-22, led by Lobster Kerry Melville's obliteration of Wendy Overton, 6-0.

> **"It's been particularly tough for us because we're a split franchise. Half our games are in Toronto and half in Buffalo. Most of us have apartments in Toronto. So it's like having 11 home games and 33 on the road. Everybody's exhausted."**
> —WENDY OVERTON, Toronto-Buffalo Royals, 1974

Pittsburgh Civic Arena officials on May 19 rolled back its silvery dome to play "under the stars." Figuratively speaking, the roof caved in, as the Royals romped 31-22 in front of 1,857 on "T-Shirt Night." Okker defeated Ken Rosewall, 6-3, then with Estep smacked Rosewall-Gerulaitis, 6-2. May 20, the Royals raged in a 24-21 comeback at Toronto's CNE over the E-Z Riders. In the main event, Okker bested legend John Newcombe 6-4.

Billie Jean King's unbeaten Philadelphia Freedoms traveled to Buffalo on May 23, and before a T-B record crowd of 8,329, rankled the Royals at The Aud, 23-20. King beat Overton 6-2 and then paired with Tory Fretz to zap Overton-O'Neil 6-0. The crowd never got into the game, as the Royals trailed 16-8, and never caught up.

Wendy Overton, Toronto-Buffalo Royals, 1974

Jan O'Neill and Wendy Overton prepare to return volley from
Boston Lobsters Janet Newberry and Kerry Melville, 1974

Tennis pioneers would've done a double-take if they'd seen May 29's Tom Okker-John Alexander game in Buffalo. There was Okker, carping at the linesmen after some close calls, backed by a rowdy crowd of 3,472 in a stinging 24-23 defeat to the L.A. Strings. The usually polite Alexander had to be physically escorted by security out of the arena. The Aussie smirked afterward: "They turned this thing into a shit circus."

Toronto-Buffalo's season quickly unraveled going into the three-week Wimbledon break. Toronto-Buffalo netters made more headlines for their rude comments to the press rather than their quality play. Wendy Overton, in particular, was not amused by Okker's saying "I can't stand women's doubles" or Estep's "The worst male player at Wimbledon can easily beat the women's champion."

The Royals lost their 12th straight match on July 8, to the Florida Flamingos 29-25, this time in Buffalo. In a battle of player-coaches, Okker defeated Frank Froehling, 6-3, fueling a shoving match between Froehling and a linesman. Team officials estimated the turnout at seven hundred.

T-B endured another defeat July 22 to the Golden Gaters at the CNE, 25-24. Okker offed Gater rookie Dick Bohrnstedt 6-4, but then O'Neill-Estep lost 6-4 to Ilana Kloss-Frew McMillan in mixed doubles. July 24 saw yet another loss in Toronto, this time 28-24 to Jimmy Connors' Baltimore Banners. July 30, 6,126 beer-fueled Buffalonians at The Aud saw the Royals' Overton-Estep finally win, over the Triangles 27-25.

"I've never traveled so much in my life. I recall seven matches in eight days, flying from Toronto to Buffalo, Philadelphia, Houston, San Francisco, L.A., and Denver."

—JAN O'NEILL, Toronto-Buffalo Royals, 1974

Okker traveled 15,000 miles in eight days, including a Honolulu-to-Toronto flight. August 12, the defending Canadian Open champ eked by 19-year-old Paul Kronk in the Toronto Open. Then he boarded a private plane to Buffalo to face the Sets' Nikki Pilic in another Royals loss, 25-22. He left the team again to defend his Canadian Open title, losing in the semis to 1974 champion Guillermo Vilas. On August 18 he re-joined the Royals in Cleveland to close out the 44-game slate with a 25-19 loss before 1,834 fans, ending 1974 a woeful 13-31 (.295), 17 games out of first.

In October, John Bassett spoke of his franchise's impending sale to a Hartford, CT bloc, but that deal fell through. Then on April 2, one month before the 1975 season, the Royals folded, with the Gaters picking up Okker's rights in a dispersal draft. The Gaters deal was contingent upon Okker's contract release, which was granted—in return for Bassett agreeing to help the Gaters pay Okker, and WTT releasing Bassett of other legal claims. Bassett, father of '80s tennis star Carling Bassett, returned to ill-fated pro sports leagues as co-owner, with actor Burt Reynolds, of the USFL Tampa Bandits, pulling out of that league shortly before his death in 1986.

Chapter 10
Detroit-Indiana Loves

Rosie Casals, Detroit Loves, 1974

FAST FACTS

Years of Operation: 1974 (Detroit)
1975-1978 (Indiana)

Team Colors: Blue, yellow, and white (Detroit)
Green, maroon, and gold (Indiana)

Team Record: 1974 30-14 (1st place, Central Section)
1975 16-28 (4th place, Eastern Division)
1976 19-25 (4th place, Eastern Division)
1977 21-23 (3rd place, Eastern Division)
1978 13-31 (last place, Eastern Division)

Female MVP: Rosie Casals 1974 (484-350, .580)

Male MVP: Vitas Gerulaitis 1977 (314-359, .496)

Highlight: First-place finish, 1974

Lowlight: Last-place finish, 1978

Home Arenas: Cobo Arena (capacity 12,000)
Indiana Convention Center (17,500)
Market Square Arena (16,530)

Quote: "With WTT's existing problems, it would be
imprudent to continue."
—Bill Bereman, Loves owner/GM (11/9/78)

"Women hate to lose more than men. We're fierce competitors. That's why I joined this league."
—MARY ANN BEATTIE, Detroit Loves, 1974

Detroit Loves owners Seymour "Sy" Brode and Marshall Greenspan made their riches running the International Tennis Corporation—five tennis clubs in Michigan, and one in Toronto. Their uptick in tennis business after the King-Riggs "Battle of the Sexes" convinced them to invest $50,000 in one of the original 16 WTT teams.

The Loves rolled out a "preferred season ticket plan" for their matches at downtown Detroit's Cobo Arena, for which the first five hundred "Marquee Club" members got valet parking with armed security, waiter service, "Court Club" access, plus events like a cocktail party with the players. But unlike $7 "Centre Court Seating," it cost $330 for Marquee Club entry.

Rosemary "Rosie" Casals, one of the world's top-ranked women, was the Loves' #1 pick in August 6, 1973's player draft. The outspoken 25-year-old quickly came to terms with the team and was expected to draw crowds and lead the roster. On March 20, 1974, men's star Phil Dent, a 24-year-old Aussie who sat out most of 1972 due to an auto accident before becoming a 1973 Australian Open finalist, signed a one-year contract.

On April 3, Detroit presented 49-year-old Aussie coach Jack Shaw, who gave interviews at Detroit Sports Broadcasters luncheon, and then held an in-store at Hudson's Franklin Park with tennis films, tennis fashion show, tips from Loves pros, and 25 pairs of Loves tickets.

Along with Dent, Detroit's male roster included Aussie Allan Stone, Columbia U. coach Butch Seewagen, and was completed with the signing of African-American netter Lendward "Lenny" Simpson, tennis pro at Square Lake Racquet Club in Bloomfield Hills, who learned the game with his childhood friend Arthur Ashe. The women's side featured Casals, Kerry Harris, and Mary Ann Eisel Beattie, who'd compete until eight months into her pregnancy.

"We've got a team that can get it done. When people hear of it, attendance will build and build."
—SEYMOUR BRODE, Detroit Loves owner, 1974

Before May 9's opener at Cobo Arena, Sy Brode expressed cautious optimism. "The first year we can break even if we average 4,000 people for our 22 home matches. If we give Detroit a winning team, it will be easy. If we don't, it won't." Brode said the Loves had sold four hundred season tickets, and he expected 5,000 fans at the opener. He felt that Detroit residents would make up the early crowds, but outstaters would attend once interest built. Hours before game-time, only 1,400 tickets sold, around ten percent of seating capacity.

The first protested match in WTT history was the Loves' home opener, eclipsing Rosie Casals' big win over Wendy Overton as she led Detroit 28-19 over the Toronto-Buffalo Royals. Before the game, George Maskin, the voice of the NBA Pistons, introduced players and explained the rules. Midway into the first set, T-B player-coach Tom Okker exploded while Mary Ann Beattie-Allan Stone beat Jan O'Neill-Mike Estep, 6-2. Beattie returned a serve long, but umpire Walter Orline ruled that a line judge missed the call. That incident led to a 15-minute rhubarb, as Okker pulled his squad off the court. The sparse crowd booed as debate raged. Commissioner George MacCall later ruled in Detroit's favor.

Pennants waved in the stands for the yellow, blue-and-white-clad Loves. No one knew what to expect or how to behave. Some fans yelled support, others wisecracks, or taunts. One fan roared a "shut up" to another, rooting for the visitors. Casals tried to support her teammates, smashing a serve at the T-B bench. "I did it on purpose," she later shared. "They were saying nasty things to me, so I wanted them to know I was paying attention."

But Casals was visibly distraught by the turnout: "There's no reason for this small a crowd. I hope by the time we return here, they'll know we have a winning team. When I was here with the Virginia Slims, this place was packed!" At intermission, an inebriated

Detroit Loves, 1974
Above L-R: Jack Shaw, Rosie Casals, Mary Ann Beattie, Kerry Harris, Butch Seewagen, Allan Stone, Phil Dent

Below: Detroit Loves ticket sales brochure graphic depicting Rosie Casals

Detroit Lions fan spewed, "This is one league that'll have no expansion." One item foreign to Detroit's beer-drinking blue-collar sports scene felt evident when a waitress serving the $330 section got overheard asking: "Who's got the vodka and water?"

May 17, the Loves reigned atop the Eastern Division's Central Section, after pounding Pittsburgh 34-25 before just 2,072 onlookers at Cobo. Casals ran her league-leading singles mark to 11-1, deploying her racquet strings with the mastery her legendary uncle Pablo Casals showed on his cello strings. World Team Tennis in fact seemed to be Rosemary's baby.

> ### "It really helps when the crowd yells and screams for me to win. You'd never have that in tournament tennis."
> **—PHIL DENT, Detroit Loves, 1974**

June 10, Detroit won their ninth of ten home matches, prevailing 22-19 over Pittsburgh. But the tennis press was abuzz over Casals calling Evonne Goolagong "overrated," and Goolagong answered decisively by obliterating Casals 6-1. Evonne would become just the third WTT woman, after Cleveland's Nancy Gunter and Boston's Kerry Melville, to defeat Casals all season. June 14, Detroit had a banner night, unfurling the Banners before 500-ish at Baltimore Civic Center, led by Casals' 16-minute rout over teen Kathy Kuykendall 6-3, and Dent's 6-4 romp over Jimmy Connors' stand-in Bob Carmichael.

Everything came up Rosie at Miami Beach Convention Center on July 10 as Casals crushed Betty Ann Grubb 6-1, leading the Loves over Florida, 25-23. Before game-time came distractions, like the two Playboy bunnies that played with two reporters in a mixed doubles exhibition fiasco, a flurry of pink Flamingos banners, and three hundred balloons dropped from the catwalks that fans popped with cigarettes and pins. But most got popped when Casals served, to no effect. She roared: "Fans paid money, so they're entitled to do what they want. That's what WTT is all about. When I win, it's a way to get back at them." WTT's second-best team (after Billie Jean King's Freedoms) went into the Wimbledon break with a 24-9 mark.

> ### "We're very close to the playoffs, and I've played almost every singles match. Everybody's tired. It's hard to maintain your psyche for 44 games."
> **—ROSIE CASALS, Detroit Loves, 1974**

After the break, the winning continued. Jack Shaw thought rest would help Rosie and Phil—and he was correct. The two sat out August 8 in Pittsburgh against Goolagong and Rosewall, replaced by Harris and Stone, as the Loves dented the Triangles, 26-20. Shaw said, "I didn't consider it a gamble as Kerry is world-class, and Stone did a nice job." August 16, in game #43, they poached the Lobsters at Cobo, 31-18, assuring Detroit (30-14) a Central Section title, despite averaging under 2,000 fans at a 12,000-seat arena.

In August 19's quarterfinal Game One against Pittsburgh at Cobo, the Triangles handed the Loves their worst defeat, 31-10. Detroit's ten points were the lowest-ever for a WTT team. Dent reinjured his back against Rosewall and then sat while Butch Seewagen lost 6-1; Casals chose a lousy time to play her worst tennis, whipped by a fired-up Goolagong 6-1. August 20 in Pittsburgh, Detroit limped home after another thrashing, 32-17. The lopsided defeat by a 63-27 combined score ended a sweet Loves season on a sour note.

Sy Brode later conceded: "Yes, we're trying to sell the team." VP Marshall Greenspan divulged, "We've had offers from Indianapolis, D.C., and Buffalo" and were "all very, very interested." As for the odds of remaining in Motown, he said: "The climate is not right in Detroit. The people who could keep the team here aren't coming forward." On November 18, a group led by 34-year-old Indiana tennis promoter William H. Bereman bought the Loves and moved the team to Indianapolis. Brode offered: "The amount was nice in that I'm satisfied with the sale. More importantly, I'm happy to see a second home for the Loves." Detroit GM Bob Love said the team lost $300,000. Brode called Love an ex-GM "because we're not active now," and stated "Bob does not know," while admitting, "we don't have the resources to hang on" and "nobody brought us money to stay in Detroit."

> **"We lacked a superstar. We had more of a positive attitude going into every match: 'Anyone can beat anyone on any night.' Billie Jean can lose, Rod Laver can lose, and Björn Borg can lose."**
> **—TRISH BOSTROM, Indiana Loves, 2019**

Indiana Convention Center in Speedway City was a far cry from Cobo, and the new team colors of green, maroon, and gold were a nice departure from the deep yellow hue of their Motor City uniforms. Bill Bereman preached team play over stars, and after futile negotiations with Casals, built such a squad. Player-coach Allan Stone; Australian Ray Ruffels; late-'60s UCLA star Roy Barth (teaching pro at Kiawah Island, SC); Carrie Meyer, '73 NCAA Women's Singles Champion at nearby Marymount College; Seattle-bred former Lobster Trish Bostrom, and to replace Casals, Toronto-Buffalo Royals alum Wendy Overton. Ownership failed to sign any draftees, not Olga Morozova, Beth Norton, Lele Forood, Barbara Jordan, Barbara Hallqist, Marina Kroschina, or Candy Reynolds. The owner held a press conference at the Indianapolis Hilton announcing five televised home matches on WTTV Channel 4, starting May 1 opening night.

The Loves' 1975 season got off to a rocky start. They finally won their first match on May 9 over Margaret Court, John Newcombe, and the Hawaii Leis at San Diego Sports Arena, 28-22, after which Bereman said, "I emphatically believe team depth can beat individual brilliance." On July 4, the Loves played an exhibition in nearby Carmel, joined by the Buffalo Brothers Wild West Show and 60-unit horse and buggy parade at Carmel Junior High School. July 15, the Loves fell behind 18-1 to the Triangles and lost 27-22 before 5,199 drunken Pittsburghers there for $2 tickets. July 15, Indiana lost again in Pittsburgh, 27-22. July 18, they outlasted the visiting Friars, 25-21.

BE A LOVES-LOVER IN 1977

SUE BARKER   VITAS GERULAITIS

Top Left: Indiana Loves program, 1975

Top Right: Indiana Loves pocket schedule, 1977

Bottom: Indiana Loves, 1975
L-R: Carrie Meyer, Allan Stone, Trish Bostrom,
Roy Barth, Wendy Overton, Ray Ruffels

The Loves kept their vow to improve by midseason, taking four of five sets on July 23 to crush the visiting Racquets 30-18, in Indiana's first-ever victory over Phoenix. It was Indiana's sixth win in their last ten matches over 12 days, raising them to a third-place tie in the Eastern Division with Cleveland. The Loves lost all five sets on August 1, fried at home by the Lobsters, 31-12; Boston took the final event in a 6-0 forfeit over an illegal substitution. Indiana ended 1975 at 18-26, fourth place, and out of the playoff picture.

In an offseason trade to benefit both teams for 1976, the Loves traded Phil Dent to New York for Billie Jean King's women's doubles partner Mona Anne Guerrant-Schallau. The 25-year-old Guerrant became an All-Star in Indiana, while Dent proved crucial to the Sets' title run. The 1976 Loves roster starred Stone, Ball, Ruffels, Bostrom, Meyer, and '74 Lei/'75 Gater Ann Kiyomura, reuniting the Guerrant-Kiyomura Wimbledon doubles title duo.

Before the season, the Loves hired their "Loves Court" of seven young ladies, ages 18 to 25, to escort sponsors and celebrities to promotional events and matches, and to model Lazarus tennis fashions at all home games. May 13 in Indianapolis, the Loves fried the Friars 32-24, led by Allan Stone's thrilling tiebreaker win over Rod Laver. May 20, the Loves shredded the visiting Nets 28-18. May 25, a season-best crowd of 3,240 saw Racquets new addition Chris Evert crush Guerrant as Phoenix reigned 30-25. "There's no question the league will make it," Bereman proclaimed. June 3, before the Wimbledon break, a scant crowd of 1,704 at Hartford Civic Center saw the Loves lose four of five events, and fall again to the Lobsters, 30-26.

August 10, the Loves lashed Cleveland 30-22, as Guerrant-Kiyomura beat Navratilova-Overton, 6-2. The teams played before 1,799 at the 17,500-capacity Indiana Convention Center—many there for "Band Night" with 12 local rock bands. When the Loves faced the Triangles in Pittsburgh on August 11, there was one Indiana figure at the press table, Bill Bereman: owner, GM, and announcer of Loves games on WART-FM. If Indiana lost this match, they'd miss the playoffs, and they did, by a final score of 29-21. Indiana ended 1976 slightly better than 1975 at 19-25, but again fourth place in the East.

In September, Bereman sold 80% of his Loves stake to Florida mogul Larry Noble, a business partner of L.A. owner Jerry Buss and San Diego owner Frank Mariani. Noble's entry signaled a shift from Bereman's low-budget style. In February, Indiana signed 20-year-old British blonde Sue Barker, voted "Sexiest Player In Women's Tennis," while ex-Triangle Vitas Gerulaitis came to terms on a pricy deal that included a Rolls-Royce Silver Shadow. In the 1977 draft, they took, and nearly signed, Argentine icon Guillermo Vilas.

Ruffels, Guerrant, and Bostrom got traded, and Meyer left WTT, so 1977's opening roster featured player-coach Stone, Ball, Kiyomura, Barker, Gerulaitis, his 21-year-old sister Ruta, and three-time Indiana Closed Tennis Championship winner Mike Smart. "We will be 100 percent stronger," Bereman insisted. Ruta would miss most of the season with mono.

"People think that tennis is a glamorous, romantic life, even with the Loves. They think we've got it made. I've lost lots of friends because they've been jealous of what they believe is my fantastic life. Ha!"

—RUTA GERULAITIS, Indiana Loves, 1977

The Loves kicked off 1977 on April 26 against the Soviets, the first Eurasian team to compete in an American league. Before the match, the Loves wheeled out a birthday cake for USSR star Teimuraz Kakulia, but they left no gifts, winning for 2,938 onlookers at the Convention Center, 28-19. Funniest was Vitas' antics—blowing at balls headed out of bounds or throwing his racquet at balls out of reach.

On April 29, reigning Wimbledon champion Björn Borg made his WTT debut in Indianapolis, edging Gerulaitis 7-6. But Indiana won in a final set super-tiebreaker to best the Cleveland-Pittsburgh Nets, 25-24. May 4's Nets rematch drew flies in Pittsburgh. The game drew 908 (a headcount said 731) as the Loves prevailed 27-21. "This match should have been played in a two-car garage," cracked one attendee. "Excedrin should've sponsored this match," joked another. The night sorely missed organist Vince Lachaud, hired by the NHL Penguins and ABA Condors, but not by the Nets in a cost-saving move.

Gerulaitis and the Apples' Sandy Mayer were best friends, but one wouldn't have known by the way Mayer throttled Gerulaitis 6-1, as New York thrashed Indiana on July 15 at the Felt Forum 31-20. Loves fans were confused by Vitas' mediocrity (ranked #8 in WTT). The

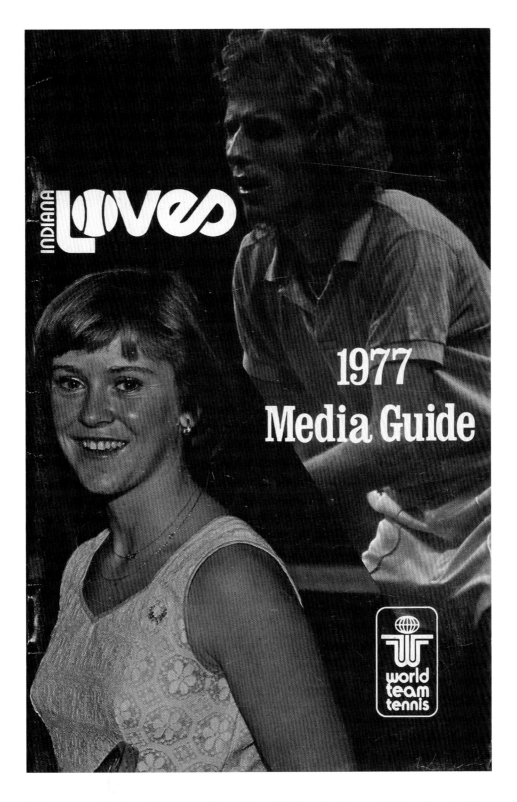

Above: 1977 Indiana Loves media guide with Sue Barker and Vitas Gerulaitis

Opposite: Vitas' sister Ruta Gerulaitis, Indiana Loves press photo, 1974

Dianne Fromholtz, Indiana Loves, 1977

GM said, "People don't get how he can win the Italian Open or play as he did at Wimbledon against Borg, and then lose in World Team Tennis. They don't feel like he takes it seriously."

August 3's Borg-Gerulaitis rematch never materialized due to Vitas' thumb tendinitis. The Swede blanked Stone 6-0, yet Indiana clipped the Nets before 5,715 in Indy, 25-22. August 10, the Lobsters lashed the Loves 32-20, as Indiana had to endure the ignominy of Boston celebrating their clinching the Eastern Division. Indiana finished 1977 at 21-23, securing third place in the East, and a playoff spot versus second-place New York.

August 16, the Loves lost to the Apples at the Felt Forum in Game One of the best-of-three 33-21. August 17 in Indianapolis, the home team forced a Game Three, 27-25. The next night in NYC, the Loves lost in a laugher of 31-15, as Billie Jean King and Virginia Wade convulsed with hilarity on the bench, watching Sandy Mayer and Ray Ruffels eliminate Indiana.

> ### "Vitas was not happy in Indianapolis. It was not his kind of place. I was as happy to be rid of him in Indianapolis as he was to leave Indianapolis."
> —BILL BEREMAN, Indiana Loves GM, 1983

Days before April 22's 1978 opener at their new home, Market Square Arena, versus the rebranded New Orleans Nets, Bereman admitted that his team had no stars after trading Barker to Phoenix and Gerulaitis to New York. But he expressed confidence in the combo of lithe import Dianne Fromholtz, joined by Geoff Masters, "This team can play as well as or better than when we had Sue Barker and Vitas Gerulaitis, on paper two of the top players on the circuit. We can finish as high as second in the Eastern Division."

The Loves finished 1978 a WTT-worst 13-31.

> ### "To cut a long story short, Jerry Buss refused to pay us unless our agent gave back money as well. So, it left a sour taste in my mouth because I played for 12 weeks, and I didn't earn a penny. I spent $6,000."
> —GEOFF MASTERS, Indiana Loves, 2019

After the season on November 9, the Loves, not broke but losing $1,500 a day, followed four other Buss-Mariani-affiliated franchises and folded. Indiana was never on a solid financial footing, but they survived with low expenses. The GM told a gathering at Loves HQ: "After two days of negotiations with owner Dr. Larry Noble in Santa Monica, he decided to disband based on economic considerations."

Bereman said the team tennis concept was good, but there were too many issues with promotion. "We were on the brink of failure so many times; the feeling developed that no matter what happened, we'd make it. We thought we were making progress in terms of profit and loss, but with WTT's existing problems, it would be imprudent to continue."

Chapter 11
Denver-Phoenix Racquets

denver RACQUETS

phoenix RACQUETS

Chris Evert, Phoenix Racquets, 1977

"These fans get me mad. And when I get mad, I play better."

—FRANÇOISE DÜRR, Denver Racquets, 1974

Denver, with a 1970s population exceeding one million, became the sports capital of the Rockies, a trajectory begun in 1960 by the American Football League Denver Broncos. Frank Goldberg and Bud Fischer bought a franchise to connect with their ABA Denver Rockets and called it the Denver Racquets. They issued a press release "presenting residents with the chance to be part of the formation of a new major league, not just a single franchise."

Françoise Dürr, who grumbled about Denver's 5,280-foot altitude making balls travel faster and farther, was the first Racquets player signed. "I haven't played well here on the Virginia Slims," admitted the 31-year-old Paris-raised Algerian. "But with time, I can get used to it." Dürr, the #1 French women's netter, who finished fifth on the Slims tour in 1973 despite a bout with hepatitis, would become a fixture in Denver social circles.

Bud Fischer declared that negotiations were underway with Denver's other draft picks and he expected all players to sign. He said that 28-year-old Aussie first-rounder Tony Roche—who a year earlier thought his career was over due to an arm injury, but through friends' urging visited a faith healer in the Philippines and returned to form—would be ready for the season. To prepare, he wanted to play Davis Cup matches in Pakistan, so his contract stipulated a $500,000 insurance policy against illness. Fischer noted: "It's an interesting situation after him having not played much the past years because of his arm for me to show my hand too soon."

Fourth-round pick Kristien Kemmer, a 21-year-old San Diegan voted the most improved player on the 1973 Slims tour, came to terms. So did husband and wife Andrew and Daphne Pattison, Andrew a fifth-rounder, and Daphne, a free agent, both 25 years old from Bulawayo, Rhodesia. Andrew, who signed to back up Tony Roche, was a hot commodity, having knocked off Ilie Năstase in Monte Carlo for the WCT title. The Pattisons partook in a March 13 preseason match, but Daphne didn't make the team.

Pam Austin, 24, and Jeff Austin, 22, of Rolling Hills, CA—the oldest of four tennis siblings (the youngest being phenom Tracy Austin)—sat the bench, Jeff behind Pattison and Roche, Pam behind Dürr and Kemmer. The siblings would hate not playing.

Eight-rounder Stephanie Johnson, 28, one of the first players on the Slims circuit under her maiden name Stephanie DeFina, came out of retirement as a tournament director in Hollywood, FL. Thirteenth-rounder Cliff Buchholz, 30 (brother of Chicago Aces player-coach Butch Buchholz), a 1965 All-American at Trinity College turned St. Louis lawyer, signed days before the season. Cindy Ursich, a 19th-rounder from San Diego, made the squad but never played. Bud said, "We've got to be considered contenders in the West."

The Racquets debuted May 7 at Denver Arena against the Chicago Aces. Dürr's Airedale terrier, team mascot Topspin, carried her racquets to the court, while yellow-shirted "Racquet Rowdies" in the balcony beat rubber chickens. Racquets publicist Bob King got sensational press coverage for the squad's unisex showers. In the match, the Aces in red and white ousted the blue-and-gold Racquets 33-22 after Pattison lost 6-4 to Ray Ruffels. A WTT-low opening night crowd of 1,481 in the 6,841-seater took in the tennis action.

> ## "A lot of us are depressed because we're not playing—and it wouldn't bother me if this team was winning. But we're not."
>
> **—PAM AUSTIN, Denver Racquets, 1974**

The next day, the Racquets jetted to Oakland to take on the San Francisco Golden Gaters before a crowd of 4,012, only to blow a second-half lead, 35-26. Then came May 10's 29-21 home loss to a John Newcombe-less Houston E-Z Riders. May 14 in Denver, the Racquets won their first, 26-23 over the Flamingos before 1,000 or less. Two nights later, to a similar-sized crowd, the Racquets beat the visiting Hawaii Leis, 28-24. Then came more losses: May 18 at Cleveland's Public Hall, May 19 at Detroit's Cobo Hall, May 24 at Oakland Coliseum, and May 25 at L.A. Sports Arena, and May 27 to Detroit at Denver Arena.

Denver started the season 2-8. Player-coach Tony Roche needed to act decisively—so he took his players out drinking. "We did not get off to a good beginning," Roche explained.

Françoise Dürr and Andy Pattison with umpire, Denver Racquets, wire photo, 1974

"There was lots of tension, so we all went to a bar and blew off steam, which really brought the team close together" (*Greeley Daily Tribune*, 8/28/74). May 29, the Racquets silenced the Sets 28-18 before 1,132 in Denver. June 2, the Racquets stunned the surging Philly Freedoms 25-24; June 4, they wrecked the Royals at Toronto's CNE 28-22. The Racquets went into the midseason break on an upswing after flummoxing the Flamingos on Nickel Beer Night at Miami Beach Convention Hall, 29-21. Pam Austin decided against the expense of Wimbledon, instead opting to work as a Denver cocktail waitress.

The season's second half began with home wins on July 6 over the Gaters and July 7 over the Triangles. By late summer, a brigade of "Racquet Rowdies" celebrated with confetti, drums, and bugles in front of a banner declaring Denver Western Division's Pacific Section champs, clinched after an August 13 win over Hawaii. Tony Roche said the ruckus thrilled his players. Corks popped and champagne flowed in the locker room as Roche toasted his players, fans, and reporters.

The Pacific Section crown gave the Racquets (30-14) top seed in the playoffs. Denver drubbed the fourth-place Gaters, rolling to a 29-17 Game One home victory to 2,404 on August 20, and 32-24 in Game Two the next night in Oakland. Denver then made short work of Minnesota in the semifinals, winning 29-18 at home to 3,126 fans on August 22 and losing the next night at the Buckskins 26-25 in Bloomington. The Racquets advanced with a cumulative score of 54-44, to play in the first WTT finals, against the heavily favored Philadelphia Freedoms.

"Beating Billie Jean King is like sticking a pin in a balloon for Philadelphia. Our players never saw how big this title would be. We all felt the pressure."
—TONY ROCHE, Denver Racquets player-coach, 1974

In a David vs. Goliath scenario, the Racquets won Game One on August 25 at Denver Arena, 27-21. As pop star Elton John sat on the Philly bench in a Freedoms warmup suit, Pattison turned in a superstar performance, with a 6-0 destruction of Buster Mottram. The next night, Denver took Game Two 28-24 at the Philly Spectrum. Roche's Racquets celebrated on the Philly court, hoisting the first DuPont Teflon Cup.

Roche pointed to Dürr's dominance over King, holding her iconic opponent to just seven points in two matches: "Françoise isn't Billie Jean. But she knows she can beat her or stay close, and that's a big lift to our team." Roche, still dealing with the arm issues that ravaged his career, edged King out for the title of WTT Coach of the Year. Pattison earned the Smirnoff Silver Cup as playoff MVP, and each Racquets player received a set of Wear-Ever cookware.

Roche praised Denver's fans, saying that he was sad they had not won the title at home. "We got great support during the last few playoff games. We'll just have to start again in February." King extolled the champions' balance and all-around team play: "Give Denver credit. They're a solid team and deserved to win. We got beat by the better team. The year was good for us. But tonight it ended, and what we did before getting washed away. But there will be another time. Denver does not have to wait. Their time is now."

The first-year champion franchise's demise was a toxic blend of mismanagement and disinterest. The Racquets claimed 2,134 fans at their 25 home games, including playoffs. But so poorly attended were some matches, one could hear the hot-dog vendors in the stands. The team got put up for sale on December 9, with ownership seeking local investors. Bud Fischer explained: "We've found it impossible to devote the time needed to both basketball and tennis to be successful. We've pledged to continue to build the best pro basketball team. The decision was more than financial." Weeks later, a Phoenix bloc, led by Oakland A's slugger Reggie Jackson and majority owner Jimmy Walker, bought and relocated the Racquets.

> **"I am the first black owner in tennis. I play baseball with world champions, so I don't want to be associated with a loser that can ruin my image. There's no hesitation on my part that we'll be a success. It's going to work."**
> **—REGGIE JACKSON, Phoenix Racquets co-owner, 1975**

The 1975 Racquets fielded a similar roster to 1974. They also signed New Zealand's Brian Fairlie, Britain's Roger Taylor, American Stephanie Tolleson, and USC doubles champion Ken "Butch" Walts Jr. Phoenix's strange schedule included three "home" series: in San Diego May 9-11; Philadelphia May 22-24; and L.A. June 6-8.

The franchise felt welcome in the Valley of the Sun. The Phoenix Jewish Community Center Racquet Club bought ads wishing the Racquets "The Best Season Ever." The team, in turn, held free clinics at the Camelback resort in Paradise Valley. Governor Raul Castro proclaimed May 2 "Phoenix Racquets Day." But the team lost opening night to Billie Jean Kings's new team, the New York Sets, 30-21 before a crowd of

5,534 at the 12,000-seat Veterans Memorial Coliseum Arena. Home attendance took a downward curve.

On June 25, the Racquets paid $15,000 in rent to the Arizona State Fair Board after they pushed to evict the team from the Arena. The Board said it was considering ending the lease because they were already $20,000 behind in rent, and that would start by canceling the next home match July 9 with the Hawaii Leis. Team officials told comptroller Mike Conforti that it was all a mix-up involving accounting procedures, and had nothing to do with solvency—and that all back rent would get paid in its June billing.

The Racquets finished the year 22-22, second place in the West. They clipped the third-place L.A. Strings 22-8 in a one-game playoff August 17 before 1,214 at the Coliseum, and then advanced to face the Golden Gaters in a best-of-three semifinal. But the Racquets lost by a 25-24 score in front of 1,308 in Phoenix fans on August 18, and again the next night 26-20 to 1,819 in Oakland. In all, the Phoenix franchise lost over $1 million in 1975. Weeks after the season, Walker bought out Jackson, who wished to cut his losses.

> ## "I've achieved about everything there is in tennis. I'd like to try everything before I retire. And I wouldn't have signed if the financial figures weren't pleasing."
> **—CHRIS EVERT, Phoenix Racquets, 1975**

October 28, the Racquets traded Françoise Dürr to the Gaters for the rights to Chris Evert. Gaters owner Dave Peterson said that after two months of talks with the world's top female player, she preferred to start her WTT career in Phoenix: "If it were just a matter of money, we would've signed. But money wasn't a major factor." He felt she wanted the Racquets to be with her best friends, Kristien Shaw (the former Miss Kemmer became Mrs. Shaw in November 1974) and PR director Brenda Bricklin. Evert gushed, "We're like sisters, I could never get mad at Kristien."

The next day, Walker held a press conference to announce: "We've made the best offer of any player active in WTT." Sources said the team offered Evert a 1976 salary as much as Billie Jean Kings's $150,000. The golden girl eventually signed a two-year deal worth $160,000 per season, ahead of Evonne Goolagong's $140,000, and Martina Navratilova's $100,000. Walker said Evert's signing "would do for WTT what Joe Namath did for the AFL."

She addressed what was to come: "I'm sure I'll notice the noise. I won't mind the home crowds that favor me, but away crowds will take some adjustment. Focus is the strength of my game, so I'll be put to the test. Players on the bench rooting for me will mean a lot."

Evert was the last significant woman star sought by the league, with King, Goolagong, Wade, Casals, and Navratilova all under contract. Evert had recently said, "I've played the European and American circuits for years, and it's not any more interesting. I'd like to try everything before I retire. I'm supposed to win; otherwise it's a tragedy."

Photo by Paul Markow, court

Phoenix Racquets pocket schedule, with insert artwork of the roster, 1976

Tournament organizers were irate. Clay Court chairman Steve DeVoe vented that the entire women's summer circuit teetered on uncertainty: "If the top women play WTT next summer, we'll have to look at the tournaments we will have. If Chrissie goes, it'll put women at a serious disadvantage to men in terms of the top purses."

At May 5's 1976 season opener at the neutral court of Salt Lake City's Special Events Center, Evert led her Racquets over the Loves, 28-21. Evert, who aced Indiana's Carrie Meyer 6-0, admitted her pre-match jitters. The star stated, "I can't describe it because it's a feeling I've never had before." She called WTT's multicolored surface "weird" and offered, "I don't mind loud colors, but the surface was too fast."

In their home debut—before a raucous May 9 crowd of 8,143—the Racquets laid it on the Leis 27-26, as Evert crushed Marcie Louie 6-1, setting the tone for Phoenix starting the 1976 season with a perfect 7-0 record.

In the final match of the year, the Nets gnashed the first-place Racquets (30-14) in Cleveland, 31-14. The August 15 win left Nets owner Joe Zingale fuming because neither Evert, Roche, Shaw, nor Pattison made the trip. Zingale said that many other owners were as mad as he, and reiterated that Phoenix should pay a fine. In the end, Jimmy Walker paid the league $10,000 plus damages to rest his players for the playoff run.

Title talk abounded as the first-place Racquets took on the second-place Gaters in the playoffs, but on August 16, a fired-up home crowd of 5,848 left disappointed after a 32-16 rout. The next night, 6,025 Oakland fans rooted on the Gaters as they advanced to the finals, blasting the Racquets, 24-18.

Evert's two-fisted backhand and faultless backcourt game led to her Rookie of the Year and WTT Super Star honors, and she was singled out in December 1976's *Sports Illustrated* as "Sportswoman of the Year." After the team's first-place finish and an 85% uptick in attendance (148,544), Walker was named Executive of the Year.

> **"The first half of the team tennis season was the best I've ever played. Before that, I didn't know what real training was. After training three hours a day with men, I was strong and eager."**
> **—CHRIS EVERT, 1976**

Phoenix went into 1977 as the team to beat. For April 29's opener in Atlanta, the Lobsters lashed the Racquets 27-18, as Greer "Cat" Stevens whipped Evert 6-2. May 12, Evert won twice, in singles and with Kristien Shaw, to jerk the Strings 26-20. May 14, the Racquets stuffed the visiting Nets, as Evert drubbed Wendy Turnbull 6-3. May 19, back in SLC, Evert had a rough night, yet her Racquets soared to first place over the Cascades 27-21.

WTT's most massive turnout of the first four seasons was June 6, as Evert and Walts helped Phoenix polish off the Apples 27-24 in OT before 13,675 at Madison Square Garden. The previous high mark was 13,492, also set by the Racquets the previous summer in Pittsburgh.

Phoenix (28-16) finished 1977 atop the Western Division. In the playoffs, they faced third-place San Diego (21-23). August 21, Phoenix lost on the road, 29-26, but the next

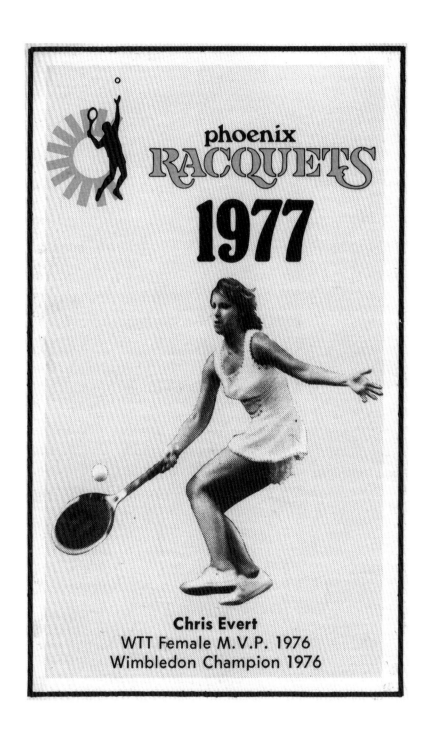

Chris Evert
WTT Female M.V.P. 1976
Wimbledon Champion 1976

Chris Evert, Phoenix Racquets pocket schedule, 1977

Kristien Kemmer-Shaw and Chris Evert, Phoenix Racquets, best friends and teammates, 1977

night at the Coliseum squared it up, 27-20. August 23, a home crowd of 8,025 saw Evert carry PHX over S.D. in OT, 30-22, to face defending champion New York for the crown.

For August 26's Game One, the Apples diced the Racquets at MSG's Felt Forum 27-22. Two nights later, at the Coliseum, the Apples wrecked the Racquets 28-17. Phoenix won just one set in that two-hour rout, and Evert cringed as WTT's first back-to-back champions celebrated on her home court.

> ### *"After last season, I realized I had to develop a more positive outlook and be more aggressive. I used to get depressed when I lost. Now I just get mad."*
> #### —KRISTIEN KEMMER-SHAW, Phoenix Racquets, 1976

December 14, Jimmy Walker admitted Evert's Racquets days were over, and that he'd lose his drawing card to the Strings: "I spoke for 11 hours with Jerry Buss, and we are continuing talks to determine compensation. Jimmy Connors has a house in Beverly Hills, and he may also play WTT next year for the Strings." Walker claimed any deal would have to include much cash plus Indiana's Sue Barker, which L.A. could sort out. Strings GM Bart Christensen said, "It's a done deal. I don't see snags."

The biggest issue involving Evert's departure was Kristien Shaw. Married to a Manhattan banker and living nouveau riche on Riverside Drive, Shaw helped make Evert chic with upscale fashion, shopping, and pampering: dinners at Nicola's or The Palm, shopping at Bergdorf and Saks, hair and nails by Jean Pierre. But the sisterhood ended bitterly over Shaw's mild dishing to *Sports Illustrated*'s Curry Kirkpatrick about Evert's previous fashion faux pas, and her "sobbing, moaning tantrum" upon learning of Jimmy Connors' new girlfriend.

February 8, 1978, Sue Barker signed a two-year deal. Walker told a press gathering at the Racquets' 1130 E. Missouri offices that Barker would replace Evert in singles and team with Shaw in doubles. The Barker signing surprised some, as she had recently got into a nasty spat with Billie Jean King after saying her season with the Loves wore her out. March 21, the team signed Dean Martin, Jr., son of boozy crooner Dean Martin.

But playing a mix of Martin, Barker, her fiancée, new player-coach Syd Ball, and Village Tennis Club pro Brian Cheney, was no answer at all. Evert had been the heart of the Racquets. Her move to L.A. made the Strings 1978's team to beat, but left Phoenix in disarray. Opening night April 29, a Racquets win came when Strings player-coach Ilie Năstase got docked three penalty points after obscene tirades, and Phoenix left with a 28-26 triumph. But mostly, 1978 was about nights like May 1, when an injury-riddled Racquets—with Barker or Walts both hurt days earlier by slipping on a faultily-laid court surface—got crushed at home by the Lobsters 28-21, as Martin fell 6-2 to Roy Emerson. The next night in Anaheim, the expansion Oranges won every event.

May 30, the Racquets, struggling to avoid the Western Division cellar, shocked their players when Walker sold the team to Jerry Simmons of Simmons Professional Sports, and Buel Wetmore replaced Walker as president. Wetmore named Brian Cheney to replace Ball as player-coach. Syd stayed on as #2 men's player with Cheney the #3.

> ### "I'd be unhappy if I hadn't given either football or tennis a try. I've been very fortunate, but I want to go as far as I can in tennis with no favors."
> —DEAN MARTIN JR., Phoenix Racquets, 1978

Dean Martin Jr., with his strong forehand and powerful serve, played 14 competitive matches before leaving WTT for the movies—as the Racquets and Hollywood producers announced his departure to make his acting debut. Billed as Dean-Paul Martin, he starred in Robert Evans' *Players* (opposite Evans' ex-wife Ali MacGraw), a story of a 23-year-old tennis hustler's affair with a 30-something kept woman. Martin and MacGraw won their starring roles over Vince Van Patten and Farrah Fawcett.

The oldest of Dean Martin's three children with his second of five wives—getting his blond, blue-eyed, strong-chinned look from his mother Jeanne Biegger—Martin played for UCLA's famed 1971 tennis squad with Jimmy Connors. But he dropped out of college at age 19 to marry actress Olivia Hussey (*Death on the Nile; Romeo and Juliet*). Jr. also played wide receiver for the semipro Las Vegas Casinos and got drafted by the Southern California Sun of the World Football League before resuming college at USC.

At age 13, coached by Pancho Segura, Martin quit the juniors' circuit to form the '60s pop group Dino, Desi & Billy with Desi Arnaz, Jr. and future Beach Boy Billy Hinsche, but he later regretted missing two years of tennis. He took the *Players* role only if he could play early 1978 for Phoenix, stating, "I'm not thrilled with movies, but I can make more in a year acting than Connors or Borg playing." A puzzled Evans replied, "Dean would rather be Borg than Redford, but I think he'll be Redford. Women love him the second he's on screen. In this film, he plays himself: a player good enough to play Wimbledon."

Dean Martin Jr. and Ali MacGraw in *Players,*
Paramount Pictures press photo, 1979

Sue Barker, Phoenix Racquets press photo, 1978

Phoenix Racquets sew-on patch, 1977

Not his father's son, Martin played tennis six hours daily. He didn't drink, and stopped smoking grass: "It thuds me out, and tennis means more to me than getting high." Jr. also rued: "I don't know my dad well. We've never had a heart-to-heart conversation."

Players, released in November 1979 with cameos by Pancho Gonzalez, Ilie Năstase, and Guillermo Vilas, got panned and flopped. Dean contracted hepatitis during filming in Mexico, derailing his movie career. Martin later married America's sweetheart Olympic skater Dorothy Hamill for 21 months (1982-1984). In 1987, as a California National Guard pilot, he died at 35 when his F-4 Phantom crashed in the San Bernardino Mountains.

The Racquets improved a bit as the season wore on, but on August 9, in one of the last games of the season, only 350 fans in the 80,000-seat Superdome watched the Racquets lose to the New Orleans Nets 28-19. One year before, Phoenix had first place sewn up and was preparing for a deep playoff run. In 1978, the Racquets (14-30) resided in the last place of the Western Division and missed the playoffs for the first time in team history.

Weeks later, WTT folded.

> **"There were no major earthshaking disagreements. But we had four solid months of absolutely nothing going on."**
>
> **—BUEL WETMORE, Phoenix Racquets GM, 1978**

Chapter 12
Pittsburgh Triangles

Vitas Gerulaitis playing to empty seats, Pittsburgh Triangles, 1976

FAST FACTS

Years of Operation: **1974-1976**

Team Colors: **Green and yellow**

Team Record: **1974: 30-14 (1st place tie, Central Section)**
1975: 36-8 (1st place, Eastern Division)
1976: 24-20 (3rd place, Eastern Division)

Female MVP: **Evonne Goolagong 1975 (449-290, .608)**

Male MVP: **Vitas Gerulaitis 1974 (218-216, .502)**

Highlight: **1975 WTT Championship over**
Golden Gaters (8/24/75)

Lowlight: **Coach-GM Dan McGibbeny dies of cancer**
at age 27 (9/6/77)

Home Arenas: **Pittsburgh Civic Arena (capacity 16,400)**

Quote: **"I don't want to put up with crap and lose**
money at the same time. I've paid my price in
blood to keep this team going."
—Frank Fuhrer, Triangles owner (12/14/76)

"We're taking love out of the game. But we're putting excitement in!"
—JACK HILLMAN, Pittsburgh Triangles co-owner, 1973

The Pittsburgh Triangles—named for the city's confluence of three rivers—began with three National Tennis League founders: businessman Chuck Reichblum, lawyer Bill Sutton, and industrialist John Hillman III, joined by insurance tycoon Frank Fuhrer. As per a July 1973 stock issued in 1,000-share increments, the Triangles Board of Governors consisted of Reichblum, Sutton, Hillman, Fuhrer, and Gary Brown.

The Triangles roster featured player-coach Ken Rosewall, 39, famed for his backhand and shot placement, and Evonne Goolagong, 23, 1971 Wimbledon champ, and one of the world's top players. Both Aussies got introduced at the William Penn Hotel's Allegheny Room after signing "generous" multiyear pacts (Goolagong's included an annuity providing 20 years of income). The franchise also came to terms with NYC-bred, second-year professional Vitas Gerulaitis; U.K. Davis Cup star Gerald Battrick; Cali girl Isabel Fernandez, the top-ranked Colombian since 1966; Peggy Michel, two-time NCAA doubles titlist at Arizona State; and Carole Graebner, estranged wife of Cleveland player-coach Clark Graebner.

To ensure Goolagong's signing, Pittsburgh hired her coach and guardian Vic Edwards as player personnel director. Vic discovered the young aborigine at ten years old, and since age 14, she lived and trained with Edwards, his wife Sara, and five daughters, with the blessings of her sheepherder father from Barellan, New South Wales (population 936). Vic's hiring led to acquiring Michel, her doubles partner, and his coaching client.

A week before the season, Reichblum insisted Steel City's rough-hewn sports fans would not find WTT too sissy: "The average Pittsburgh fan will appreciate big-time tennis as a fast-moving action-driven sport." He said the team sold 1,000 season tickets and needed 5,000 a night to break even, "so about we're 20% there." Brochures stated, "When the Triangles Tennis Team launches its first championship season, you'll want to be there."

May 6, WTT's inaugural season began at Philadelphia's Spectrum, with the Triangles facing Billie Jean King's Freedoms, who won easily 31-25. In the next night's rematch before 5,000 at the first tennis game in the 16,400-seat Pittsburgh Civic Arena, Philly won again, 30-24. Pittsburgh fans banged on triangles called "Goola-gongs," and Kenny Rogers sat courtside by trainer Henry Kush as the Triangles dazzled in green and yellow uniforms. Of the nasty catcalls and slurs, Rosewall grumbled, "A lot of good that did for tennis!"

May 12, as Pittsburgh took on the Hawaii Leis before a modest Mother's Day crowd of 2,104, Goolagong was miles away from the Civic Arena in Italy representing Australia in Federation Cup. But that's not why Pittsburgh lost 33-25. Rosewall admitted: "We have problems. Everyone was picking us to win it all before the season. That was premature."

Their next home match, May 18, for "T-Shirt Night" at Civic Arena, Pittsburgh lost their fourth in a row without Goolagong, to the lowly Toronto-Buffalo Royals 31-22. The match was the Triangles' first "under the stars" with the venue's retractable roof open. Rosewall offered: "The lighting was worse than when the roof was closed, but the atmosphere was quite pleasant." Pittsburgh ended their losing streak May 21, slashing the L.A. Strings in their largest victory margin of the season, 28-16. A home crowd of 1,911 sat beneath the open dome for two hours and ten minutes and welcomed Goolagong back from Italy.

"I feel that our signing of Evonne Goolagong will mean as much as the signing of Bobby Hull did to the World Hockey Association."

—CHUCK REICHBLUM, Pittsburgh Triangles founder, 1973

Running the team proved too much for Chuck Reichblum, so he sold a majority interest to partner Frank Fuhrer, an ornery George Steinbrenner-like character to the core that never drank, smoked, or took a pill. At Allegheny College, he played every sport but tennis, earning 13 letters before becoming an über capitalist and self-made millionaire. Gerulaitis called Fuhrer "fair, generous and competent—and the most obnoxious owner in sports."

Above Left: Pittsburgh Triangles pocket schedule, 1974
Above Right: Pittsburgh Triangles roster, from New York Sets program, 1975

Below: Pittsburgh Triangles promotional poster, 1975

A month into the season, the team fired Carole Graebner, who was attempting a comeback after years of semi-retirement. On a recent night when Carole found it was all she could do to meet the ball with her racquet, Fuhrer sitting at a front-row seat threw his head back, shut his eyes, and flapped his hands in derision at every point she blew. Gerald Battrick charged Fuhrer at intermission, "How could you do that to the poor girl?" Fuhrer roared back, "I'll do what I damn well please!" as Graebner slumped on the bench. Days later, during a Fuhrer postgame chew-out, the Triangles' three other women picked up their gear, with tears streaming down their cheeks, and left the locker room. He then resumed his tirade about the value of winning, after which all of his male stars also walked out.

Rosie Casals' big mouth provided drama fodder when she called Goolagong "overrated" in a June 13 newspaper. "The quote came out wrong," Rosie roared after 4,187 watched her Detroit Loves annihilated, 31-12, in the biggest victory-margin in league history. Goolagong crushed Casals 6-3, and then Pittsburgh won 16 of the next 18 points to clinch the match by intermission, up 18-4. Then, teacher defeated student, as Detroit's Butch Seewagen, Gerulaitis' coach at Columbia the one year that he attended college, won 6-2.

To open the season's second half, the Triangles faced the New York Sets on July 21 and won in a mixed doubles super-tiebreaker 28-27. Michel-Battrick led the comeback, after which Gerald jumped into his street clothes. Out for a few weeks after a freak accident, cutting his right hand on Venetian blinds, Battrick was fighting mad at the fans screaming "Put Vitas in," as well as by the playing surface he called "a joke." A kid in the second row was holding a sign that irked the Sets' Virginia Wade: "The New York Sets are the worst team in WTT." The Sets were unavailable for post-game comments because their PR man was so busy asking where to party in Pittsburgh that his players had left for their hotel.

Pittsburgh ended the year 30-14, tied with Detroit for first place in the Central Section. On August 20, for Game One of the quarterfinals, the Triangles drove to Detroit, where they mugged the Loves 31-10. The next night in Pittsburgh, the Triangles mangled the Loves 32-17 and won the series by a cumulative 63-27. Fuhrer roared, "I've never seen this team so determined. The Triangles want to prove that they're the best in the league."

August 22, in the opening game of the Eastern Division finals, 5,369 at the Civic Arena watched Philadelphia bash Pittsburgh, 31-21. August 23, the Triangles bounced back before 7,122 at the Spectrum, 24-21, but lost the series by a combined score of 52-45. Pittsburgh did reasonably well in their first season, second in overall attendance despite small crowds. In some ways, the Triangles caught on, with newspaper headlines above the MLB Pirates and ABA Condors. Plus, they had rising superstars in Gerulaitis and Goolagong.

After the season, Fuhrer presided over an October 23 press luncheon at Pittsburgh's Duquesne Club for new Triangles coach Vic Edwards. The move assured the return of Goolagong and Michel for next season. The gentlemanly Rosewall, who always seemed uneasy as player-coach, said that he was unaware Edwards had replaced him, or that the team had acquired Mark Cox, Britain's top male player, from the Florida Flamingos. Edwards admitted, "I was deeply opposed to World Team Tennis at the start. I called the players the clowns, the owners monkeys, and the whole thing a circus." But he expressed confidence in Pittsburgh winning it all in 1975: "I think this thing is going to skyrocket."

On November 6, Fuhrer made two moves that he hoped would benefit the team, and balance the league: acquiring from Baltimore the rights to Jimmy Connors for Isabel Fernandez and Gerald Battrick, and then trading their rights to Stan Smith to the Sets for a #1 pick, plus cash. Fuhrer, recently elected to serve as WTT president, said that he understood the value of a premier New York team: "Plus I hear Smith plans to marry a Long Island girl, so he'll be happy to play in New York." Fuhrer expressed the belief that he would sign Connors after negotiations with Bill Riordan, stating, "Connors is the best player in the world. If I didn't think I could sign him, I wouldn't have made the deal."

The Triangles offered Jimmy Connors a deal "in the category of" the $3 million Jim "Catfish" Hunter had recently received from the New York Yankees. But before bait got snapped, talks broke off over full-season commitment to WTT. Bill Riordan raged, "We talked in generalities in October, so if negotiations broke off, it's news to me, and I'm honestly confused." The team said it would look to another world-class pro like Tony Roche if Connors' talks fell through. Riordan said Connors was excited to join his friend Vitas in Pittsburgh but retorted: "Jimmy's one of the great sports personalities today. And as a millionaire, it's not like he doesn't know where his next meal's coming from."

The night before Christmas, Vic Edwards gave his new boss a lump of coal, stating that Evonne Goolagong's Triangles' future was in doubt. As her manager, Edwards refused to let her re-sign until he was satisfied with the contract. The two parties quickly came to terms.

Bill Sutton finally announced Connors would not join the team, stating: "We got three votes out of four: his mother, his attorney, and manager all said yes, but Jimmy said no. Connors wanted to play only part of the season, and we couldn't agree to that." Fuhrer said that he understood: "I can't blame Connors. I'd go for the big bundle, too."

February 20, 1975, Pittsburgh signed Rayni Fox as their #3 female behind Goolagong and Michel. The U.S. Juniors champ from North Miami Beach via Rollins College was 107 pounds of power packed into a 5'4" frame. The Triangles also re-signed Gerulaitis to a "substantial pay increase," and traded for Kim "Ace" Warwick, a rising Aussie male coached by Edwards, from the E-Z Riders, for "not much" in return.

"I was never sure what Evonne was all about. You just couldn't get inside her head."
—VITAS GERULAITIS, Pittsburgh Triangles, 1975

Love was in the air for the Triangles. Peggy Michel stayed in Pittsburgh not just to continue her doubles pairing with Goolagong, but because the California girl from Pacific Palisades found true love in the Steel City, marrying NHL Penguins marketing director Terry Chambers. Then, from Triangles HQ at the Monroeville Racquet Club, Goolagong and Roger Cawley met the Pittsburgh press to announce their impending nuptials, and that bridesmaids Michel and Fox, along with Coach Edwards, would give away the bride.

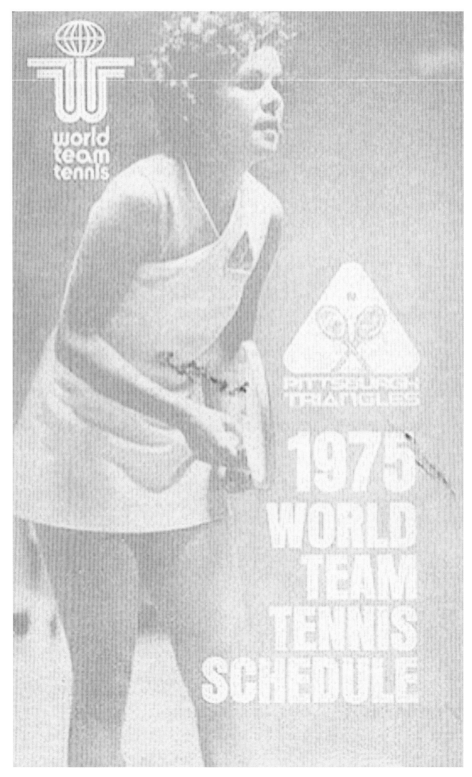

Evonne Goolagong, Pittsburgh Triangles, 1975
Pocket schedule for their championship season

Cawley had another reason to attend—to debunk reports from his native England that he'd become Goolagong's business manager. "That's rubbish," Roger roared. "That began when someone put words in my parents' mouth." Goolagong glanced fondly at Cawley, holding hands with her fiancée as she gushed about a "church wedding in Sydney," where they planned to live—although he had never actually been there.

Pittsburgh opened the 1975 season on May 1 in Indianapolis against the Loves, with Mark Cox absent for tournament play, and Edwards and Goolagong preparing to represent Australia in the Federation Cup. Goolagong blasted Wendy Overton 6-0 in a 13-minute "love match" to lead the Triangles 23-22. At Pittsburgh's May 3 home opener, in front of 4,300 fans, Gerulaitis sparked a 25-24 win over the Lobsters. With his colorful style, stinging serves, and grueling ground game, Gerulaitis' 6-4 win over Bob Hewitt was a stroke of genius.

For May 5 at home against L.A. and May 9 against Cleveland, coach Edwards left specific orders with his stand-in, team trainer Paul Denny, as to whom to play and when. Fuhrer said, "We were lucky to win our first two matches by the skin of our teeth. You can't play like that in this league and expect to win." In a pregame exhibition, Fox and Warwick blasted radio deejays, Don Cox and Bob McClain. In the main event, Pittsburgh marked their first loss of the season 25-24. After the mixed doubles set, as L.A.'s Casals and Geoff Masters flummoxed Fox-Warwick 6-4, Fox expressed, "I could have used Mr. Edwards tonight. He helped me so much in just one week." Gerulaitis blanked Bob Lutz 6-0, and then spewed about the light crowd of 1,437: "I like the team concept, but this turnout is a real letdown." Fuhrer seethed: "The attendance has been a bitter disappointment," adding: "I have two questions: am I doing the right thing, and is team tennis promotable? I don't know the answer. But I do know that if people don't show up, we're in trouble."

The Triangles savored a 29-20 victory on May 29 over the league-worst Friars before 4,676 fans—after offering 12,000 seats for $2 each. Goolagong flogged the Friars in singles and women's doubles, inspired by festivities earlier that day when she got awarded keys to the city by Mayor Pete Flaherty as part of Pittsburgh Triangles Day. Mayor Pete told her, "You don't really need this; the doors are always open to you." Cox missed the match after flying to BWI at 4 p.m. and getting a flat tire in the Fort Pitt Tunnel.

May 31, the Triangles returned home, after two straight beat-downs in Honolulu by the Leis, to face the last-place bottom-feeding Lobsters. It was Pittsburgh's third win against Boston, 26-20, before 2,158 at the Civic Arena, who saw Gerulaitis prevail 6-4 over Bob Hewitt—after which the 36-year-old South African drilled a ball into the crowd, and lit into referee Tom Huzella.

June 7, Pittsburgh swept all five sets over the visiting Golden Gaters 32-18—avenging a 31-17 humiliation earlier in the year. In a cultural low point, Vitas' fan club, Gerulaitis' Guys (GG), reduced to tears Gaters star Lesley Hunt, with leather-lunged drunkards yelling "lesbian," "dyke," and "queer" because she'd worn shorts instead of a dress.

June 10, a crowd of 5,199 at the Civic cheered from the start and stayed until the end, enticed by more $2 tickets. Triangles fans were known to only rise for the national anthem, to use the restroom, and to leave. In this game, Pittsburgh made short work of visiting Indiana 32-13. The match was over in 53 minutes; Goolagong routed Wendy Overton 6-0 in 16 minutes. Edwards said: "That might be the best tennis I've seen Evonne play." After intermission, Davey, the ball-boy, yawned at the press table. When told that two events remained, the young man frowned.

"I love showmanship in tennis. That way, even if I play lousy, people will enjoy it."
—VITAS GERULAITIS, 1975

July 26 saw records smashed at the Civic. Pittsburgh bashed Billie Jean King's Sets 26-19 in front of 10,236, the largest turnout to ever see a tennis match in Greater Pittsburgh. The Triangles excelled with 6-4 wins—Goolagong over King, and Gerulaitis' 21st birthday bashing of his buddy Sandy Mayer. Gerulaitis made PA announcer Jack Henry (popular with Penguins fans for his "sudden death" alerts during tie games) invite the crowd to his post-game pajama party at a nearby hotel. Explained new GM Dan McGibbeny: "Vitas took the top floor of a hotel. They came all night, in waves. I've seen heavy damage at parties before, but this was the first one they literally broke a bathtub."

July 29, the first-place Triangles won their 12th straight match, gnashing the last-place Nets in the season's third and final $2 Fan Appreciation Night. After a disastrous May that saw crowds under 1,500, Fuhrer initiated $2 nights—that on this night drew 4,446. Pittsburgh had not lost to a Division foe all year. With Cleveland player-coach Marty Riessen on crutches, leading B-listers like Clark Graebner, Sue Stap, Valerie Ziegenfuss, and Bob Giltinan, the Triangles were not facing the finest netters to drive the Ohio Turnpike.

July 31, the Triangles faced the Western Division-leading Gaters on Wristband Night at the Civic. The Oakland squad had lost three of four times to Pittsburgh in 1975 (winning 31-17, and losing 32-18, 29-17, and 32-21). Edwards warned his team not to overlook the visitors: "Unless we play on top of our game, we will have trouble." The Triangles promised wristbands to the first 2,000 fans, and if they gave away 2,059, every attendee would've had one. Weak at the gate but strong on the court, they gored the Gaters 29-20.

On July 31, arena organist Vince Lascheid angered Golden Gaters' player-coach Frew McMillan with his keyboard cleverness. Frew bristled: "Do you want to see tennis? Or do you want to hear a guy play the organ?" Considering the weak play, Lascheid might've been the first choice, but the Gater had a point. Fans also deserved criticism, especially those yelling "out" or "fault." "The crowd was uncouth," said uppity Mark Cox. "It reduced tennis to a barroom brawl."

In an August 16 first-place battle, New York returned to Pittsburgh. The feature bout was Goolagong vs. King. Vic Edwards implied that Sets player-coach Fred Stolle was employing psychology by not announcing his starters: "Tell them I'm unsure who I'm also starting." Fuhrer put it bluntly: "Saturday night, all the marbles will be on the table." Iron City Beer, not NYC champagne, was the post-game quaff, as 7,105 saw the home team prevail, 26-22.

Pittsburgh (36-8) expected to fly to JFK for the WTT semifinals. But on August 17, the sub-.500 Lobsters took out the Sets in a one-match qualifying round tiebreaker, 25-24. "Boston winning threw us for a loop," admitted Fuhrer. "But I think maybe we took the heart out of them and were flat against Boston."

August 19, the Eastern Division champion Triangles breezed into the WTT finals with a 2-0 sweep of the third-place Lobsters. They took Game One 23-14 before just 912, who saw the game called off in the fourth set after Pittsburgh took an insurmountable lead. The Triangles were favorites in the finals over the Gaters, opening at San Francisco's Cow Palace. Repeating a question thrown his way after the win, Edwards said, "Do we have the momentum to keep going? Sure, the players are ready and psyched to win the title."

On August 21, the Gaters stunned the Triangles in the best-of-three opener 26-25. Pittsburgh led 24-20 before Frew McMillan-Betty Stöve pasted Michel-Warwick 6-1 in the final set. Both squads moaned about the multicolored "Sporteze" playing surface—rolled up after the All-Star Match, it buckled when applied to the arena floor, causing irregular bounces. For the next game, Larry King told the Triangles if another court did not arrive in time, they'd have to paint the court red, blue, orange, and brown. Fuhrer raged, "There's no way I'll paint our court. I'd rather play on concrete."

August 23, Coach Edwards regrouped his squad before a nationally televised Game Two for NBC's "Super Season." Fuhrer felt elated as a sports person but deflated as a capitalist. "I didn't make enough money, but this positions us well to bring another title to Pittsburgh," he said after the Triangles won 28-25 to tie the series. The 2 p.m. crowd of 2,182 got bunched together so that the TV cameras wouldn't have to pan the sparsely populated areas. "The telecast wasn't blacked-out locally, and that certainly hurt us," Fuhrer grumbled. NBC expressed happiness with its WTT broadcasts like July's All-Star Match, but NBC Sports publicity director Chuck Adams said that he knew of no impending TV deal for WTT.

August 24 at the Civic before 6,882 euphoric fans, Gerulaitis got voted Playoff MVP after he broke Tom Okker's service three times in a 6-1 win, carrying Pittsburgh to the 1975 WTT championship over the Gaters 21-14. Before the match, the Triangles' most famous fan Kenny Rogers fired up the crowd singing "Ruby, Don't Take Your Love to Town," while Gerulaitis blew taps during Gaters player intros. The Triangles played so well that the match got halted when they did not have to play the final mixed doubles event.

"This is my career highlight," voiced Gerulaitis, jubilant after being carried off the court on the shoulders of Mark Cox and Kim Warwick. His rowdy "G-Men" fan club turned out in force, cheering wildly for their Adonis and heckling opponents. Fuhrer, in Triangles cap and G-Men shirt, clutching the Bancroft Cup, joked, "I'll have my green Triangle blazer and championship ring to show for the million I lost." Fuhrer, who'd lavish jewelry on stars, bought his squad gold rings when WTT offered nothing. Reminded of his pricey roster, he roared, "You don't win the Kentucky Derby with a mule, right?"

> ## *"This is the highlight of my career. There is no other feeling like sharing this championship with seven others."*
>
> **—EVONNE GOOLAGONG, Pittsburgh Triangles, 1975**

Less than 48 hours after winning the title, Fuhrer traded one-third of his championship roster, sending Rayni Fox and Kim Warwick plus their rights to Jimmy Connors and Wendy Overton to the Nets, for 20-year-old rising star Sue Stap, who excelled in 1974 with Chicago and 1975 with Cleveland.

Fuhrer shocked again at a September 9 luncheon at the Duquesne Club, announcing that he was looking to replace Vic Edwards, whom Frank fired two weeks after winning the title. Goolagong's husband/de facto manager Roger Cawley made it clear the Aboriginal racketeer wanted to drop her guardian/mentor, under whose tutelage she rose to stardom.

Fuhrer said the dismissal had nothing to do with Edwards' abilities: "It was my decision, and I made it based on events during the season. I just decided that we couldn't bring Edwards back without a conflict. Let's just say he won't be back because I don't want him back." Edwards admitted he expected his firing since the two had "certain difficulties" negotiating a new contract, "But I'm wondering why I'd get fired after having won the championship." Years later, Fuhrer confessed: "Cawley told me, 'Evonne doesn't want to play next year if he coaches.' That stuck me in a box. My gut instinct was to say, 'The coach stays; you must go.' But the reality was, we needed her."

"I was like her father for years, and I don't believe a father should speak out against his own, so I make no comment," Edwards offered about Goolagong. One of the world's top tennis instructors, he later split his time as the tennis pro at Pittsburgh's The Mews on Town North, running Australia's Victor A. Edwards Tennis School, and serving as New Zealand's National Tennis Coach. Edwards said of his WTT encounter: "It was a hell of an experience. Tennis is staid—team tennis was different. At Wimbledon or Forest Hills, you never saw anyone pick up a beer can and toss it down the court."

"I've reached a point where I'm not putting any more money into this franchise. Sure, I'm eating every day, but I want to continue eating."
—FRANK FUHRER, Pittsburgh Triangles owner, 1975

Fuhrer found himself confronting an issue he never counted on when he said the team would remain in Pittsburgh. Scheduling conflicts between the Triangles and the Civic Arena sparked talk of the franchise's demise. Fuhrer said he'd move his squad unless the Arena cooperated with decent 1976 playing dates. Frank directed his ire at arena manager Charles Strong for booking events for the NHL Penguins, the Shrine Circus, and an ethnic folk festival, without allowing for the Triangles. "Charlie gives us garbled garbage," seethed Fuhrer. "The dates he's offering are unacceptable, but his answers are even more unacceptable." Strong, in turn, said that the Triangles, Arena tenants of two seasons, deserved equal treatment but that the venue was booked far ahead with few available dates. "We're hopeful we can find more dates. But Mr. Fuhrer doesn't realize the building is not dealing with an empty page. Frank went berserk when "Charlie suggested we play in Johnstown, Steubenville, Wheeling, and Erie. We're a Pittsburgh team, and we'll play in Pittsburgh. I'm damned mad. Phooey!" He continued,

Isabel Fernandez and player-coach Ken Rosewall with autograph seekers, 1974

"You can't be gutless or spineless. We've shown we should be entitled to some good dates without this Mickey Mousing around!"

But no preferential treatment was coming for a franchise that drew under 70,000 fans for 25 dates, including a championship. Fuhrer faced an October 1 deadline for submitting his 1976 home schedule. September 29, the two parties signed a deal brokered by the mayor. Fuhrer said, "We're pleased with the dates, and I'd like to thank Mayor Flaherty. I'm sure WTT and the Triangles will succeed, and as long as I own the team, we'll attempt to be a credit to this city in every way. As long as I'm owner, the Triangles will stay here."

Fuhrer hoped to break even in 1976 and sell 2,500 season tickets. The East Brady, PA, native also detailed re-signing Gerulaitis after a bitter stalemate. While no terms got disclosed, Gerulaitis was driving a new yellow Rolls-Royce Corniche. "We had a tough time because he was a valuable asset. But I would not pay more than he was worth," Frank said. The Triangles also signed Bernie Mitton of South Africa and JoAnne Russell of Seattle. Now they needed a coach.

> ## "I'm so excited to get named player-coach of the defending champions. But because we won it all last year, there is nowhere to go but down."
> —MARK COX, Pittsburgh Triangles player-coach, 1976

March 15, the Triangles introduced veteran Mark Cox as player-coach, to replace fired Vic Edwards. During negotiations, Cox wanted a clause that read, "you must agree not to interfere," to which Fuhrer replied, "I'll interfere any time I damn well please!" Frank said, "While I've never been a fan of player-coaches, I have great confidence in Mark."

Recently acquired Sue Stap—voted WTT most improved female player of 1975—got shipped to Hawaii before the season for former Houston E-Z Rider Nancy Gunter. Fuhrer was irate that Stap refused to make any personal appearances. He ranted: "I did not like her attitude. Besides, we decided that everybody would be much happier with just three girls on the team. That way, everybody will get playing time." Peggy Michel concurred: "We will see a lot more court time than with four girls. That would've caused conflict."

May 1, the champion Triangles made their 1976 home debut, drawing 5,108—more than twice 1975's premiere—as they poached the Lobsters 31-14 in a flawless display by Goolagong in singles and women's doubles. Goolagong was on a roll, having become the world's #1 woman after beating Chris Evert in the Virginia Slims. GM Dan McGibbeny, at age 25, the youngest pro sports executive, pushed for the blaring ads between events.

Pittsburgh edged the L.A. Strings on May 7, in front of 3,458 at Civic Arena. Goolagong won her opening set with Peggy Michel, 6-3, and then roasted Rosie Casals 6-2, as the Triangles triumphed 22-19. Goolagong got diagnosed post-game with heel tendinitis.

Without Goolagong, the Triangles tanked. On May 23, Pittsburgh lost their fifth straight, 29-17 to the Gaters before 2,809 at the Civic. Goolagong warmed up before the match but left before the action. Gerulaitis was en route to Rome to compete in the Italian Open. Cox confessed, "I know my play was poor, and when the coach fares poorly, that filters down. Not having Evonne and Vitas hurt, but that's no excuse." Fuhrer stewed: "We can't wait for things to happen. I won't get into it, but believe me, things are going to happen."

Before Pittsburgh's June 2 win over the surging Sets, 31-14, Billie Jean King got hospitalized with severe stomach cramps later diagnosed as spastic colon (colitis). Organist Vince Lascheid played "I'll Take Manhattan" and "Happy Days Are Here Again" for the 3,877 in attendance. After the game, Fuhrer and Cox feuded over the squad's 5-10 start. Two days later, the GM declared: "In a meeting yesterday morning, Frank and Mark looked at each other, broke into wide smiles, and got down to fixing the Triangles."

The Triangles then relegated Peggy Michel to the disabled list for sketchy reasons. The idea conveyed by Fuhrer's wording "hampered with an injury since last year" was that her shoulder wasn't hurt so much as her feelings. Fuhrer inspired the *Post-Gazette* (6/8/76) to write, "Are the Triangles giving Peggy the cold shoulder?" and an angry fan-made banner read, "Fuhrer's Brain Should Be On The Disabled List." Before June 9's game with Cleveland, Fuhrer angered his team for discussing fining players for losses. Ranted Goolagong: "So Frank says he'll fine us if we lose. Well, I went through the hassle of calling my lawyer to say that I'll sue." Cox required shots for a rash caused by his frayed nerves. Gerulaitis voiced, "Mark will have gray hair by the end of the season. He's not the same person."

"Loyalty goes two ways, and I've given my players total commitment. I've gotten damn little in return. I'm fed up."

—FRANK FUHRER, 1976

Fuhrer fought tooth and nail with his top female Goolagong, top male Gerulaitis, player-coach Cox, and Goolagong's doubles partner Michel. "I'm upset Evonne won't do promotions. With her salary, she owes us." Goolagong and husband Roger Cawley again threatened to quit. Worse to Fuhrer were Gerulaitis' views: "Vitas lied to the media. He was unhappy with himself, so he blamed me." Goolagong and Gerulaitis stayed, but Fuhrer fired Mark Cox as coach, keeping him as a player.

On July 8, Chris Evert's Phoenix Racquets drew a record Triangles turnout of 13,492, as Pittsburgh conquered, 24-23, led by Goolagong's 6-4 win over Evert. Seeking yet another five-figure crowd, on July 10, Fuhrer drew 11,742, though most tickets were freebies. His squad had lost handily to Cleveland, 30-21. Arms folded and blood boiling, Fuhrer said, "This is the worst match since I owned the team." Afterward, Gerulaitis slumped in the dressing room, a smashed racquet at his side, revealing that he'd expended the last of his energy by slamming it against a cement wall. "The wall already was cracked," the star netter shrugged.

Dan McGibbeny, son of the *Post-Gazette*'s sports editor, was named coach of the 9-16 defending champions, though he didn't want the job and had never played tennis. The ousted Cox said he wanted to devote more time to his play. McGibbeny joked at his June 15 introduction, "I certainly don't plan to tell Evonne how to hit a backhand." Fuhrer hired McGibbeny out of Point Park College in 1974 as PR agent and then in 1975 appointed him publicity manager, before starting him as GM/PR director in 1976. The flack-turned-coach said, "I'll do anything to help this team. If Frank wants me to fix the court before a match, I'll do that. I can't play the game or teach it, but I can take off some pressure and get us winning."

McGibbeny's first victory came July 17 "under the stars" against Rod Laver's Friars 27-18 before 5,369 at the Civic. Gerulaitis, off a two-game benching, returned for a doubles win with Bernie Mitton, 6-3. The Triangles then had a 6-2 road mark that started with a July 19 win in Honolulu and ended with a July 26 loss in Cleveland. Going into the final stretch, Pittsburgh had eight home games in 16 days. McGibbeny said glibly, "I told the team that we're in the best position to make the playoffs since the rest of the league wrote us off. With our momentum, we can repeat as champions."

"I feel awkward being interviewed. I'm used to rounding up the person to be interviewed. I'm not comfortable, but I'll give it my best shot."
—DAN McGIBBENY, Pittsburgh Triangles GM/coach, 1976

"I am exhausted," growled Gerulaitis. "We haven't had a day off in a month. Even now, we have to come back to practice on a Monday. I'd just like to have a few days to rest. I am just not into the game." Coach McGibbeny insisted he was totally behind Gerulaitis despite his on-court nosedive. "Vitas is a big-play man. He's always tough when you need him."

In mid-July, Pittsburgh could've been the Bermuda Triangles because every time they took the court, they looked lost at sea. Then they won nine of 12, with their best wins of the year. "A reluctant McGibbeny is holding the torch, but he doesn't know which end holds the flame," wrote the *Pittsburgh Press* (7/28/76). Much change was due to Cox not carrying the weight of the world on his slender shoulders. McGibbeny noted, "Mark drove himself that much harder because we were losing, and it began to inhibit his game. His whole personality returned when he dropped the title of coach."

Under McGibbeny, rookie JoAnne Russell solidified her play. She noticed a whole new team spirit: "The entire attitude of the team changed. I noticed it in Phoenix during warm-ups with a Frisbee football game. Imagine the tense team of the first half doing that." McGibbeny's motto was "sacrifice," a belief they could play together like last year's champions: "The team practices together, and stays on the same floor when away, offer each other encouragement and constructive criticism at the match, and cheer on each other. My job is to keep spirits high and to keep everything organized." His Triangles also did all they could to sell tickets and build awareness, appearing at schools and Kiwanis Clubs.

A July 30 game at the Civic was another "Must Win" night, where if Pittsburgh lost, every fan got invited to the next game free; luckily for Fuhrer, they won 30-22. July 31, the Triangles lassoed the Loves 28-22 on "Jacket Night," but the promotion got nixed when the manufacturer failed to deliver the product. An August 6 home match against L.A. featured a halftime show by comic Marty Allen. Before their next game against Boston, Victor The Wrestling Bear took on all comers, including the Lobsters' bear-like player-coach Ion Țiriac.

At a shocking August 4 press conference, the Triangles announced that team physician Dr. Lowell Lubic would coach the team for ten days as McGibbeny convalesced at Montefiore Hospital from the treatment of a blood clot in his upper thigh. McGibbeny stated: "It's a real shame because I was just getting a feel for what I was doing. But I'll be the first to admit that it hasn't been anything that I've done. Actually, I'm kind of embarrassed by the whole thing."

"It's like a Walter Mitty story for me. I've jazzed up the medical community—and the medical community is falling against the wall!"
—DR. LOWELL LUBIC, Pittsburgh Triangles interim coach, 1976

Lubic, an enthusiastic, intelligent man respected by the players, whom McGibbeny referred to as his "wily mentor," and whom bad boy Ilie Năstase called "The Germ," felt the Triangles would respond well. Insiders felt trainer Paul Denny would get the nod, but Fuhrer's instincts proved spot-on. Lubic would take the reins August 4 against Hawaii, in a playoff drive that carried Pittsburgh within a game of second-place Cleveland. McGibbeny joked: "I can see the new coach in the locker room now, telling them to win one for the Gibber."

August 4, in Honolulu, the Leis sought to convey an idyllic tone by giving away 2,100 orchids. Ilie Năstase was his nasty self, but it didn't do him any good in a shouting match with Mark Cox. Cox kept his composure as the Triangles won 30-22. With Pittsburgh ahead going into the final event, Năstase began firing balls at Cox, who scowled and furrowed his brow as he walked to the net. Harsh words got exchanged, but no blows struck.

The Triangles ended their season with a 24-23 victory over the playoff-bound Racquets. After edging Phoenix, returning McGibbeny got named the night's MVP. "I thought it was a fix," he joked. Asked if other coaches respected his "coaching," he said, "Some could be rightfully upset, and I wouldn't blame them. But everybody gets the situation."

August 13, in a one-game playoff to reach the Eastern Division finals, Pittsburgh edged the visiting Cleveland Nets on the last point of a super-tiebreaker 25-24 before 3,158. Tony Tato, a cigar-chomping 50-something Triangles quasi-employee, abused his press-table privilege, yelling at Martina Navratilova, "If you weren't a woman, I'd punch you in the face." From the locker room, she moaned, "I'm sick, and he's a Triangles employee." Classless Pittsburgh fans threatening the Nets angered their player-coach Marty Riessen: "It was like bows and arrows against bazookas."

"There have been disquieting trends in the last few matches. Maybe we should all put on crash helmets and go to town."
—MARK COX, 1976

For Game One of their best-of-three playoff series with New York, Pittsburgh seemed to be firing on all cylinders. Of the August 16 home turnout of 3,385, Fuhrer grumbled: "Very poor crowd, there's no excuse for this"—as his Triangles edged the Sets, 26-25. Said

Photo: Clint Burton

**Dan McGibbeny, second from left, with trainer
Paul Denny, Bernie Mitton, Mark Cox, 1976**

Billie Jean King, who lost in women's and mixed doubles: "This place is a tough place to play. The lights are vicious, and the balls just fly. It's the league's only tennis court on top of a basketball floor."

Game Two took place 48 hours later in front of just 3,227 at Nassau Coliseum, where the Sets tied the series 29-21. McGibbeny was bothered by Gerulaitis' erratic play (3-7 in his past ten games) but stayed loyal: "Vitas is a money player. He rises to the occasion." Such trust would be the Triangles' ultimate undoing. For Game Three, the Sets won at home before 2,608 on August 19, to end the Triangles' season. *News-Dispatch* (8/17/76) mused: "How long can Moneybags Fuhrer continue losing cash with his athletic toy?"

With Goolagong expecting her first child, Fuhrer saw the writing on the wall. The owner said on October 13, "I'm not confident that we're going to be playing here another year," and "[Her motherhood] will hurt the sale of the team in the trade market." He also said he spoke with prospective buyers from Atlanta, Minneapolis-St. Paul and New Orleans, and that "a bona fide offer will get weighed against taking a total loss on my part."

December 14, Fuhrer announced he'd dissolve the team for at least a year because he didn't have the stomach to handle all the controversies. He opened his press conference at the Carlton House third-floor Drawing Room with, "We're here not to honor Caesar but to bury him," and joked, "We're going out the way we came, in style," referring to the free roast beef and Bloody Marys. The rich man who lost $1.4 million over three years on his "toy" said: "Tennis players in this age of freedom are made to feel like kings and queens, and it's very difficult to get them to play on a team. I don't need the aggravation. I'd rather play golf." He cited issues with Goolagong and Gerulaitis, McGibbeny's illness, and the fans ("always looking for something for nothing"). But Fuhrer admitted, "Not one of those reasons stopped me, but it made it impossible to continue."

Fuhrer boasted of the Triangles' league-best 90-42 record over three seasons. He said if he could swing a $10 million insurance deal, he might seek another Pittsburgh franchise for 1978 if he could retain Goolagong's rights. Cleveland owner Joe Zingale joined Fuhrer at the podium to announce that his team would play half their 1977 home games in Pittsburgh to carry on interest. While thanking his staff, Fuhrer's voice quivered as he turned away from the lectern, wiped a tear, and confessed, "It hurts to leave a loser."

"If I get out of this hospital bed, nothing will keep me from the Arena."
—DAN McGIBBENY, 1976

Joe Zingale's rebranded Cleveland-Pittsburgh Nets named McGibbeny GM, but he quit after four months to work for Fuhrer's insurance firm. The 26-year-old McGibbeny died September 6, 1977, after 17 days in the I.C.U. at Pittsburgh's Presbyterian Hospital, of histolytic lymphoma discovered during his blood clot. Weeks later, the city declared "Danny McGibbeny Day," and named a baseball field in the Brookline neighborhood in his honor. In 1978, he received a posthumous tribute, with WTT honoring him with the Daniel Patrick McGibbeny Award.

Chapter 13
Cleveland/New Orleans Nets

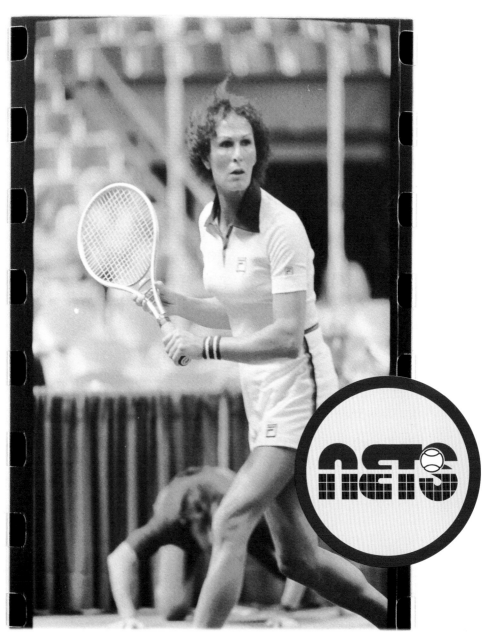

Renée Richards, New Orleans Nets, 1978
WTT welcomed pro sports' first transgender star

FAST FACTS

Years of Operation: 1974-1976 (Cleveland)
1977 (Cleveland-Pittsburgh)
1978 (New Orleans)

Team Colors: Red, white, and blue

Team Record: 1974: 21-23 (4th place, Central Section)
1975: 16-28 (5th place, Eastern Division)
1976: 20-24 (3rd place, Eastern Division)
1977: 16-28 (3rd place, Eastern Division)
1978: 20-24 (4th place, Eastern Division)

Female MVP: Martina Navratilova 1976 (453-388, .539)

Male MVP: Marty Riessen 1975 (398-350, .532)

Highlight: Signing Björn Borg and fiancée
Mariana Simeonescu (2/1/77)

Lowlight: Nancy Gunter mugged in Cleveland Public
Hall parking lot (7/25/74)

Home Arenas: Cleveland Public Hall (capacity 5,000)
Richfield Coliseum (20,000)
New Orleans Superdome (80,000)

Quote: "The Nets have as much chance of signing Björn
Borg as he has swimming the nearest fjord."
—*Pittsburgh Post-Gazette* (1/31/77)

"Either this town isn't ready for us, or we're not ready for this town. Where were all the people?"

—RAYNI FOX, Cleveland Nets, 1975

Cleveland tennis dates back to the 1880s. The city's first tournament was in 1881, run by George Worthington at the East End Tennis Club. Elizabeth Dean Sprague won the Women's City Championship three straight years 1899-1901; local Mary K. Brown, the U.S. women's champion 1912-14, won the women's doubles title in 1921 and 1925 (with Helen Wills). Cleveland tournaments varied from junior, public-park, and amateur to pro, to semi-pro city tourneys called "The Munis." In 1960, Davis Cup games came to the city.

Joe Zingale, a '50s-'60s Cleveland rock & roll disc jockey known as "Mr. Rhythm," bought Cleveland's WTT franchise. The 41-year-old 1260 WIXY-AM executive dressed with '70s style: balding, bearded, and lots of denim. The brash cousin of

Cleveland sports czar Nick Mileti owned shares of baseball's Indians and basketball's Cavaliers, and in late 1973, Zingale paid Mileti $60,000 for his $50,000 Nets stake. (In 1979, Joe bought out his cousin's Cavaliers stake, and in 1983 sold out to controversial Ted Stepien, acknowledged as the worst owner in NBA history.)

For November 1973's draft, fourth-round selection Cleveland native Clark Graebner, chosen as the team's player-coach, insisted that his wife, the former Carole Caldwell—once one of the top U.S. women players, now raising two children—be drafted by the team, too. So by special dispensation, WTT declared pick #4A a "family selection." But love quickly soured when coach Graebner filed for divorce. He pled his case to owner Joe, and in a "play me or trade my wife" scenario, the Nets sent 31-year-old Carole to the Triangles for 21-year-old Laura DuPont. Carole insisted the feeling was mutual, so she returned to her native Pittsburgh. Zingale zinged, "Clark's a helluva lot more important to me than Carole." Clark joked that he'd love DuPont madly if she didn't choke on the court with him in mixed doubles. His numerous inappropriate remarks included blaming a road loss to Denver on menstrual issues.

The Nets, in red, white, and blue, played in 1974 at the old 5,000-seat Public Hall. Their opening roster featured Graebner, DuPont, Texas siblings Cliff Richey and Nancy Richey Gunter, Australia's Bill Lloyd, aging South African Ray Moore, and Jane "Peaches" Bartkowicz, one of the Virginia Slims "Original 9." Player-coach Graebner embraced WTT team spirit: "I get nervous worrying about my game and that of six others, and I love it."

> ### *"The team can't be in a position where a player can, at his or her whim, decide they can breach a contract in the middle of the season. I like her personally, but Peaches Bartkowicz has some serious personal issues."*
> —JOE ZINGALE, Cleveland Nets owner, 1974

Cleveland got off to a fast start in 1974. May 30, the Nets went to Boston and won their fifth game in a row 29-25 at Walter Brown Arena, led by Gunter-Bartkowicz in women's doubles, and Graebner-Bartkowicz in mixed doubles. June 5, the Nets jetted to L.A. and rained on the parade of just 855 fans at the Sports Arena, tweaking the Strings 29-25. But after a 10-5 start, things quickly went south, beginning July 15, when the Nets asked Peaches to turn in her uniform after her sixth contract renegotiation. The two sides parted ways when Bartkowicz told Zingale that she still wanted more money.

"I hear from her agent every day, but it's all over," Zingale uttered, referring to lawyer Pete Huthwaited, trying to trade Peaches to another squad. The owner went on: "I signed her when she was seven months pregnant and hadn't played in three years. I renegotiated her deal five times, and then she gave me this ultimatum that she wouldn't play if she didn't get more money." Zingale upped her money with the proviso she'd play the whole season. Then, one week later, she failed to show up for a press conference to announce she'd remain with the Nets. So the team signed Winnie Shaw Woolridge, ranked #3 in the UK.

Peaches Bartkowicz, Cleveland Nets, 1974
Fired after her sixth contract renegotiation

On July 25, the Nets lost to the Triangles in Pittsburgh, 26-22, after forfeiting 6-0 in women's doubles. Nancy Gunter got sidelined before the match after aggravating an injury to her right foot in the afternoon practice. Her absence left the Nets with one female in DuPont, who lost in singles to Evonne Goolagong, 6-3.

Gunter was not having a great week. Days earlier, after her 6-0 obliteration of Florida Flamingos star Laurie Fleming, she and her 73-year-old great uncle got mugged on the exit ramp into Public Hall's parking lot by two thugs wielding tire irons, who assaulted the old man and made off with cash, traveler's checks, and paychecks.

With the season in the home stretch, Cliff Richey was furious over his benching in an August 4 loss to Detroit, 25-17. Richey blamed Zingale, but Clark Graebner said he decided to play aging Ray Moore, who upset Loves' star Phil Dent in singles 6-1, as the Nets got swept in every other event.

Cleveland finished the season 21-23 (.477), fourth place in the Eastern Division's Central Section, and qualified for the final playoff seed. Billie Jean King's heavily favored Freedoms swept the Nets in the best-of-three. For Game One on August 19 at Public Hall, Cleveland lost 26-22 before 2,148. The next night 2,173 in Philly saw the Nets fall again 23-22. The Nets led before Gunter-Graebner lost to Fred Stolle-Julie Anthony, 6-3, to end Cleveland's first year on a downswing. Zingale hailed his heroic "street fighters."

"WTT taught me that I play much better when I'm mad. I really need to get fired up."
—WENDY OVERTON, Cleveland Nets, 1975

A month before the 1975 season, the Nets partook in a three-way trade, shipping Nancy Gunter to the Houston E-Z Riders and Kim Warwick to Pittsburgh, and welcoming former Toronto-Buffalo Royal Wendy Overton. Gunter wanted out after she and her brother feuded with Graebner and Zingale over their lack of playing time.

Gunter griped about the Nets, "I don't care for the owner. He's difficult and has double standards. Peaches was the reason we were winning, and she was earning nothing. Cliff and I urged her to demand more money and not to budge. But he took a stand that no one player is too important. Here's a guy who knows nothing about the game, yet refuses the advice of people with 20 years in the business. Anyhow, she left at the halfway point, and we'd won 12 or 14 with her and lost 15 of the last 20 without her. For a bit more money, we could've been good. If you confronted him, he pled ignorance. Yet he set the policy."

Cleveland then signed 33-year-old Marty Riessen, the nation's #3 ranked men's player, to a three-year deal, $250,000 contract—to serve as player-coach, and to team with Clark Graebner, reuniting the three-time National Clay Courts men's doubles titlists. Riessen, who nixed the 1974 Chicago Aces, would play a vital role with the Nets moving forward.

Before opening night, the Nets signed WTT's first African-American woman, Margot Tiff, 22, of Shaker Heights, OH. The Cal State L.A. graduate was also the first AA woman on the Virginia Slims circuit. Zingale said he "followed Margot and watched her improve for the past year," stressing he signed the local pro "not as a black tennis player but as a good tennis player." Tiff said of WTT: "I like the people yelling and screaming. It makes you feel like the fans care, and it makes the game exciting." With Riessen, Graebner, and Tiff, the Nets' 1975 roster included assistant coach/radio analyst Bob Giltinan, Ann Haydon Jones (ex-Buckskins), Sue Stap (Aces), and Valerie Ziegenfuss (Lobsters).

Cleveland opened its 1975 season 0-3 after a May 9 defeat to fewer than 1,000 fans in Pittsburgh, 27-26. The other 12,000 needed to fill the arena missed an action-packed night, as Graebner-Stap lost to Rayni Fox-Kim Warwick in a super-tiebreaker. On June 7, player-coach Riessen fined himself $100 for smacking a ball at a heckler in a home loss to the Triangles, 26-23. Then he imposed the same fine on Graebner for foul language. Riessen reasoned: "I fined myself for smacking a ball too close to a fan, and did the same to Clark for his talk. I could've hurt an innocent person."

The Nets finished the year 16-28, fifth place in the Eastern Division, and missed the playoffs. After moving home games from downtown Public Hall to suburban Richfield Coliseum, they drew just 1,000-plus per match at the 20,000-capacity arena. Zingale caustically praised his audiences as "the politest in the league." Riessen ranked #1 in men's singles (.570), and got voted 1975 WTT Rookie of the Year. Riessen-Graebner was top-ranked in men's doubles. Tiff struggled to find playing time behind DuPont, Stap, and Jones, losing 6-1 in just one set of mixed doubles.

> **"They put us in an arena for 25,000 people, and only an average of 1,500 showed up. By the time the applause got to you on the court, you'd already played the next point."**
> **—MARTINA NAVRATILOVA, Cleveland Nets, 1977**

In the offseason, the Nets shocked the tennis world when Zingale signed the 20-year-old Czech defector Martina Navratilova to a multi-year deal worth $150,000 per season. The owner sealed the deal by giving Navratilova a "#1" diamond necklace. Three weeks before the opener, they cornered the market on famous Pakistani netters by signing doubles star Haroon Rahim. So Cleveland's 1976 roster would consist of Riessen, Rahim, Overton, Giltinan, Navratilova, and 19-year-old college star Rayni Fox, acquired from Pittsburgh. Hot Chilean netter Hans Gildemeister filled in admirably during the season's second half.

On August 15, Cleveland ended 1976 on the tennis court and prepared to take it to the legal courts. Zingale fumed after his Nets wrecked the Racquets, 31-14, because Phoenix's top four—Chris Evert, Tony Roche, Andy Pattison, and Kris Kemmer Shaw—did not play, killing hopes of drawing 10,000 for the season's finale. Instead, Richfield Coliseum announced a crowd of 4,615 but a WTT insider estimated 1,800 fans. Zingale said that if the four had played that week in the playoff's opening round, he'd file a suit. Dr. Lowell Lubic found each to have different injuries and prescribed rest. After the fiasco, Lubic said: "I did not certify them as disabled. I said the injuries were bona fide."

Cleveland finished 1976 at 20-24 (.455), third place in the East. They finished the first half of the season strong, but lost four of their five final matches, and got edged out of the playoffs by their rival Triangles. The Nets' improved attendance, from 1974's 48,887 to 1975's 55,924 to 1976's 73,108 (2,323 per match)—but Zingale kept all options open.

Pittsburgh owner Frank Fuhrer announced on December 14 the demise of his Triangles, after admitting that he'd lost boatloads on WTT. Zingale joined Fuhrer on the podium to announce his Nets would play 1977 as the Cleveland-Pittsburgh Nets, with 11 matches in Richfield, and 11 at Pittsburgh Civic Arena.

January 31, at league meetings at the New York Hilton, Zingale introduced GM Dan McGibbeny, the 26-year-old, coach, GM and PR director of the 1976 fallen Triangles. Zingale also presented former Triangles director of operations John Felman to run the rebranded "Tri Nets" Cleveland-Pittsburgh "regional franchise." He also said in a move to improve the revenue that they'd play "home" matches from Nashville to New Orleans. Soon after, McGibbeny left to work for Fuhrer's insurance firm, before succumbing to cancer.

Zingale liked his 1977 roster: player-coach Riessen, Navratilova, Rahim, Overton, Fox, Gildemeister, and Giltinan. Laughs broke out when Joe said of Swedish star Björn Borg, "I've chased him for three years now and I may catch him." *Pittsburgh Post-Gazette* wrote, "He has as much chance of signing Björn as he has swimming the nearest fjord."

"I've been thinking about playing Team Tennis. I like to try new things. Another reason I signed was to see my fiancée Mariana very often."
—BJÖRN BORG, Cleveland-Pittsburgh Nets, 1977

On February 1, the Nets introduced Borg and his 19-year-old Romanian fiancée, Mariana Simionescu, in a "love conquers all" deal. The highest-ranked men's netter got $40,000 weekly, in a pact financed by the Nets and WTT. The "sweetheart deal" also included $20,000 annually for Simionescu, the 1973 Wimbledon Juniors titlist. Mariana denied seeking political asylum: "I have many rights from my country that I didn't think I'd get. My government lets me do what I want and go where I wish." Joe rejoiced: "It's a fantastic breakthrough for WTT to sign tennis' most famous player, a dominant force in tennis."

The fiery owner leased a jet to pick up Borg in Little Rock, where he played the previous night, and fly him to New York. Borg then departed for more press in Cleveland and Pittsburgh, then back to Little Rock for more tournament play. From the dais, Borg lobbed: "Europe holds no challenge for me. I've done everything there. I thought, why not try team tennis? I think we can win the league. I know I'll try my best." Zingale operated "Cleveland's Entry In World Team Tennis" without a Xerox Telecopier for intraleague messages or a full-time publicist. But his team was the only franchise with Borg. Posters hung around Cleveland and Pittsburgh proclaimed: "A Nets Star Is Björn."

After the Borg-Simionescu signing, Cleveland cut Wendy Overton and Haroon Rahim. Then they brought in Peggy Michel—Evonne Goolagong's Triangles doubles partner, out most of 1976 with shoulder injuries—to pair with Navratilova. But between Riessen, Borg, and Navratilova, the Nets took on a glut of pricy stars, so something had to give. As the 1977 season began, the Nets traded Navratilova to Boston for Virginia

Björn Borg, Cleveland-Pittsburgh Nets press photo, 1977

Slims Rookie of the Year Wendy Turnbull plus cash. Navratilova said she'd quit WTT if she had to play another game for Zingale. She told reporters she hated Cleveland's "too much pollution." Joe said, "She didn't like Cleveland, but there wasn't much I could do... Three years ago, I had trouble with Cliff Richey and his sister, and I vowed never to have an unhappy team again."

"I wanted to be traded. I didn't care where I was going to play unless it wasn't Cleveland or Indiana."
—MARTINA NAVRATILOVA, 1977

Navratilova, no longer the star after the Borg signing, forced the trade. But the heart of the issue was that the owner and the Soviet Bloc defector "couldn't stand each other's catgut" (*Pittsburgh Post-Gazette*, 4/30/77). Player-coach Riessen called Martina a royal pain: "She did what she wanted, and it was hard to control her. But the contracts are too weak to control anyone. It puts you in a begging position."

Slumped in his dressing room cubicle after April 26's season-opening 28-21 defeat to the defending champion New York Apples, Riessen raged, "We don't have the talent to compete." He noted Martina's trade to the Lobsters left the Nets a shell of what they required. In the loss, Borg bested 1976 WTT MVP Sandy Mayer 6-4.

May 4 at the Civic Arena, a crowd of 908—the press table tally was 731—saw Borg's second game in Pittsburgh. Zingale raged, "I'm sure there aren't even that many. That must have included no-shows." May 13, the winless Nets (0-4), greeted by empty seats and gaping yawns, lost four of five sets, and the match, to Indiana, 27-21. The only Nets win was Borg crushing Vitas Gerulaitis 6-1. Cleveland-Pittsburgh ranked last in the ten-team league, a failure conceptually, competitively and financially. Zingale saw that even a star like Borg couldn't overcome the fact Pittsburghers did not relate to World Team Tennis.

Pittsburgh hosted Boston on May 23, and before a headcount of three hundred crushed the Nets, 27-11. In a reversal of roles, Borg lost 6-1 to Tony Roche while his fiancée Mariana Simionescu figured in the only Nets win, with Riessen over Greer Stevens-Mike Estep 6-3. Autograph seekers by the locker room chased Mariana and ignored Borg. Riessen said the empty orange seats made him see red: "It was like a morgue. I have no idea how they promote. Pittsburgh thinks they're a major-league sports town. It's an insult to the players and an affront to pro sports that 200 or 300 people came." Riessen should've registered his complaints with the owner, who treated Pittsburgh like a spy agency, with little public information and no listed phone number.

Just 1,100 Pittsburgh fans came June 2 to see Chris Evert and her Racquets prevail over the Nets, 30-22. Zingale was coy when asked if this would be his franchise's final visit to Western PA, saying, "I'm gonna look at what's happening. I'm no idiot." When pressed if the city deserved another shot, he snapped, "Listen, I gave Pittsburgh two Wimbledon champions tonight with Borg and Evert. What else can I do?" The game would be the last of six home games in Pittsburgh. Joe said he'd provide refunds to the three hundred season ticket holders, and that any Pittsburgh ticket holder who'd drive to Cleveland would receive up to six free tickets. June 4's game with the Gaters, moved at the last moment to Cleveland, had no issue with refunds since Ticketron punched only one ticket sold. Vince Leonard in the *Post-Gazette* wrote "Requiem for a Lightweight" about the end of Cleveland-Pittsburgh tennis, "The services smack of Siamese twins: stab one, and the other one feels it in Cleveland." Zingale said, "I'm pulling out of Pittsburgh, and I don't intend to return."

Then the Nets stunned the sports world by signing 42-year-old Renée Richards to a two-year deal. The former Dr. Richard Raskind, an ophthalmological surgeon famous for treating cross-eyed children, played semi-pro baseball with Yankees great Whitey Ford at age 16, then married, had a son, and was a ranked American netter. Raskind then gave it all up to become Renée, the towering maverick that underwent three years of painful gender reassignment surgeries, and got signed by the Nets as a female.

Zingale claimed that he made the move, not due to curiosity value, but because "she's popular and a helluva good player," and "a tremendous drawing card." He conceded the Nets were in dire need of female talent, after failing to replace Martina adequately. Joe pointed out that he and Richards came to a quick agreement, and that while he hadn't "polled" other owners, he admitted to a mixed reaction. Richards told the press, "All I want to do is prove myself as a woman. This is a great opportunity. I can help the team."

The owner said that Richards would play for the Nets Saturday night in Cleveland against the Golden Gaters. But new commissioner Butch Buchholz, in his first political hot potato, cited "league policy" in subjecting Richards to the karyotype chromosome test created by the International Olympic Committee, to determine if her chromosomes were male (XY) or female (XX). Butch later revealed, "I was afraid whatever action I took would be misinterpreted. If we refused to accept her, we could be accused of bias. If we took her in, people might say we're promoting WTT through burlesque. So I told Joe that if Renée passed the IOC test, I'd okay it. If she can play Wimbledon, she should be able to play WTT."

Buchholz feared a rumored walkout of women in the league. For example, the L.A. Strings' Diane Fromholtz called Richards "a freak," and when asked what she would've done had she lost to the transgender star, replied, "drowned myself." Days later, Richards failed the test and got barred from WTT. A distraught Richards, who planned to quit tennis and resume her medical practice, was unavailable for comment.

A July 6 Nets game against Boston planned for Pittsburgh got moved to Columbus, and then to Hartford. During the midseason break, Borg basked in his Wimbledon title but said that he had no trouble, mentally or physically, getting up for his WTT re-entry with his fourth-place Nets. A Lobsters record crowd of 6,118 saw the re-rebranded Cleveland Nets triumphant 26-23, as Borg blasted Boston in singles and doubles competition.

Zingale offered to lease Borg a Corvette if he won Wimbledon. So when he did win, the owner presented him the keys to the white sports car in front of a July 9 announced crowd of 8,312, the largest to see the Cleveland team. But a press table regular heard the attendance report and exclaimed, "If you believe that number, you believe in the Easter Bunny." Borg also got feted for his #2 rank in men's singles play (.667). The Nets set another home attendance mark July 18, this time in New Orleans, as 9,952 saw Borg spark his Nets, 25-23 over the Sea-Port Cascades. Zingale raved about fan support.

The Nets ended the 1977 season a mediocre 16-28 (.364) yet backed into the playoffs to face the first-place Lobsters (36-9). August 16, the Nets got trimmed at B.U. 30-26, as Borg fell to Tony Roche 7-6. August 18 in Cleveland, the Nets tied the series, 21-20; the Nets competed short-handed, between Turnbull's shoulder tendinitis, and Borg's ear infection. August 19 in Boston, the Nets' season ended by a score of 28-21. At WTT post-season awards in L.A., Borg—the top men's singles star and #3 with Riessen in doubles—got named Rookie of the Year. Renée Richards, finally cleared to play after being declared a female by the New York State Superior Court, never got on the court.

December 29, Borg announced that he would not return to the Nets in 1978. The svelte Swede spoke of the mental and physical fatigue he suffered, and of his inability to focus on the big tournaments. Borg complained that his season-long shoulder discomfort, for which the Swede retired from the 1977 U.S. Open, was due to his WTT overuse. Zingale said Borg's deal had a clause letting him leave at year's end, and that Borg felt pressured to play for Sweden's Davis Cup, and in Italy, where he had lucrative endorsements.

February 14, Zingale announced the Nets' relocation to New Orleans. He said the team would play nine home games in the 80,000-seat Superdome, plus 13 in other Southern cities like Baton Rouge, Shreveport, and Thibodaux, Louisiana; Huntsville, Birmingham, and Mobile, Alabama; Biloxi and Jackson, Mississippi; and Lakeland, Florida. The squad would also return three times to Cleveland's Richfield Coliseum: a May 28 exhibition with the Gaters, plus August 2 versus Indiana, and August 12 against Anaheim.

"I am pleased that the press is beginning to refer to me as 'Renée Richards the tennis player' instead of 'Renée Richards, the transsexual.'"
—RENÉE RICHARDS, New Orleans Nets, 1978

Zingale, seeking local funding, said that with neither Borg nor Simionescu returning, all he'd signed for 1978 were Richards, Wendy Turnbull, and Peggy Michel. No men had come to terms, but he hoped to import Argentina's Guillermo Vilas, Romania's Ion Țiriac, or Florida's Brian Gottfried. The Nets players loved the move; N.O. was paradise compared to Cleveland. A week later, the owner said the team would be called the Sun Belt Nets: "Sun Belt got chosen because it's a term for the growing South." When not playing in secondary markets, they were the New Orleans Nets.

After re-signing player-coach Marty Riessen on March 8, the oldest team in WTT, with an average age over 30, now featured Richards, Turnbull, Trish Bostrom, Helen Gourlay, Andy Pattison, and NBA star John Lucas. The hoops icon obtained in a trade with Phoenix to play behind Riessen and Pattison came to terms with a paltry $15,000 salary.

What does an owner do when his team draws just 704 fans to an event? He fires the promotion director. That's what Zingale did after his franchise brought 704 to see the Nets beat the Cascades 27-22 at the Superdome—looking like a postage stamp in the middle of the arena. Zingale said that Barry Mendelson, former EVP of the NBA New Orleans Jazz, was told he'd no longer work for the Nets. Zingale said, "I think we've done

Marty Riessen, Cleveland Nets player-coach, 1976

John Lucas, New Orleans Nets, 1978
#1 overall NBA Draft pick, #2 African-American netter after Arthur Ashe

a bad job of getting the word out. Barry's been too busy with other things," going on to say he'd handle all promotions: "I'm the owner, I'm the guy responsible."

May 20, in a Sun Belt apex, Richards upset Billie Jean King 6-2 as the Nets gnarled the Apples 28-26, at a home match in El Paso (1,100 miles from New Orleans). May 24, the Nets stomped the Apples at Madison Square Garden, as New Yorkers gave Richards an ovation. Lucas, last time at MSG leading his Houston Rockets to 17 points and nine assists, sat on the bench for all but two of the Nets' first 11 matches. Then Riessen rolled out a new mixed doubles duo—Lucas-Richards, who went on to earn WTT's second-best record.

Richards and Lucas became known as The Odd Couple. They'd pal around like kids, psych up each other on the court, and root wildly for each other when not together. Richards said, "When I first heard of John, I guessed he couldn't play tennis. But I saw him hit one ball, and I knew he could." In doubles, the two lefties comprised the most unique duo in tennis history. Lucas said, "We have a Tasmanian [Gourlay], an Australian [Turnbull], a Rhodesian [Pattison], another basketball-tennis player [Riessen], a Black, and Renée."

> ## "It's not often you see a black basketball player and a transsexual playing tennis. But when you're black, everything else pales by comparison."
> —JOHN LUCAS, New Orleans Nets, 1978

Zingale spoke of the incident after a Nets-Gaters match in Lakeland—halfway between Orlando and Tampa, among the orange groves and cattle ranchers—when the pair went to a rural roadhouse for beers. "Someone said, 'Lookee here…' Richards walked up and settled the matter." Lucas gushed, "I love Renée. She's one of my favorite people, along with JFK, Martin Luther King, and my parents. Five minutes with Renée, I forgot what she used to be." For her stubborn determination, the Nets dubbed her "No Way Renée," which became the title of her second autobiography.

After the Wimbledon break July 15, the Nets wrecked the Racquets in Phoenix 26-20, as Richards-Turnbull and Riessen-Pattison led the way. July 28, before four hundred fans at the Superdome, the Nets crushed the Lobsters 23-20. On July 31, before a WTT record-low 126 at LSU Center in Baton Rouge, the Nets beat Seattle 26-23; August 9, just 350 at the Superdome saw the Nets again overtake the cellar-dwelling Racquets 28-19.

New Orleans came on strong late-season to go 20-24, decent enough for the eighth and final playoff spot. Richards was sidelined for the last ten games with Achilles pain, but planned to make their playoff opener against Boston. But August 15's Game One was too easy for the Lobsters, winning the first four sets, and sending a Boston crowd of 2,120 into delirium, as they battered the beat-down Nets, 31-24. For August 19's Game Two in N.O., the Nets made their last stand but lost to the Lobsters 25-23 to end their season.

Two weeks later, the team's phone calls went unanswered. Big-talking Joe Zingale never even announced his franchise's demise. In the end, the Nets team never finished above .500 or higher than third place despite some real high-profile stars.

Chapter 14
Golden Gaters

Frew McMillan, Golden Gaters player-coach, 1976

FAST FACTS

Year(s) of Operation: 1974-1978

Team Colors: Maroon and gold

Team Record: 1974: 23-21 (2nd place, Pacific Section)
1975: 29-15 (1st place, Western Division)
1976: 28-16 (2nd place, Western Division)
1977: 25-19 (2nd place, Western Division)
1978: 21-23 (3rd place, Western Division)

Female MVP: Betty Stöve 1975 (340-307, .526)

Male MVP: Tom Okker (429-348, .551)

Highlight: Tom Okker WTT Male MVP;
Frew McMillan Coach Of The Year (11/5/75)

Lowlight: Losing the WTT finals to Pittsburgh
(8/25/75) and New York (8/27/76)

Home Arena: Oakland Coliseum Arena (capacity 12,000)

Quote: "Some people go to the spas of Europe for
relaxation. I coach the Gaters."
—Frew McMillan, Gaters player-coach (8/15/76)

> *"It was all over so quickly. The only way we'd come out on top was if the San Andreas Fault opened up and swallowed them all."*
>
> —TOM OKKER, Golden Gaters, 1976

WTT's blend of team spirit, progressive politics, and gender equality played well into the Bay Area's post-hippie mindset. The San Francisco-Oakland team, with the regional moniker of the Golden Gaters, proved to be the league's most stable franchise, never signing stars; instead, they focused the roster on players that fit the team tennis concept.

October 25, 1973, co-owner Cathie Anderson confirmed that the Golden Gaters signed a long-term deal with #1 draft pick Margaret Court, the 31-year-old Aussie star winner of 22 titles in tennis' "Big Four" events. That news made her WTT's 13th player in the fold. Court's signing was a $100,000 offer, but a franchise press release put asterisks next to her name with "Court is pregnant and will not play WTT until 1975." Unsigned Gaters draftees included Pancho Segura, Jürgen Fassbender, and Jim Delaney. Anderson also announced that the Gaters would play their 22 home games at the 12,000-capacity Oakland Coliseum Arena, joining as tenants the NBA Golden State Warriors and NHL California Golden Seals. She emphasized, "We felt it important the Bay Area entry start on the right foot by providing our fans great viewing and comfort." The squad promised two home games with L.A., Hawaii, Denver, Houston, Miami, and Chicago, and one with Toronto, Pittsburgh, New York, Philadelphia, Baltimore, Boston, Detroit, and Cleveland.

One month before training camp, the only two Golden Gaters signed were foreigners: Roy Emerson 35, from Blackbutt, Australia, and the era's top doubles star, Frew "The Mad Hatter" McMillan of Springs, South Africa. Two women were about to sign— again, not American: Perth, Australia's Lesley Hunt, and Johannesburg, South Africa's Ilana Kloss. That made the squad's chasing of local pro, San Mateo's Ann Kiyomura, extra special. Team negotiator Dick Wright said that the Gaters were keen on the 1973 Wimbledon junior champion (who beat Martina Navratilova in the semifinals) "because of her doubles prowess. She has great potential and a proven record." The 19-year-old daughter of tennis coach Harry and former #2 Japanese netter Hisayo offered: "I'd be lucky to play near home. And I like the team concept. It gives me an incentive. WTT will be interesting, and it'll work out." But she signed for 1974 to the Hawaii Leis.

Court quit WTT on March 13, after which the Gaters signed 24-year-old Denise Triolo from Los Altos, and came to terms with Whitney Reed, 43, the #1 ranked American in 1962 who drank and drugged his way into oblivion. Their final preseason signing was Redlands, CA-raised 23-year-old USC star Dick Bohrnstedt. So 1974's maroon-and-gold opening roster consisted of Emerson, McMillan, Hunt, Kloss, Triolo, Reed, Bohrnstedt, and co-owner Cathie Anderson.

"I put up a stink with WTT as I was concerned about the financial situation. It's hard to concentrate when you've got other things on your mind."
—LESLEY HUNT, Golden Gaters, 1975

One could've bet their last tennis ball that the Gaters ownership of Cathy Anderson, Jerry Diamond, and Larry King didn't sleep well before May 8's home opener against Denver. Player-coach Roy Emerson said he'd wait to choose between Lesley Hunt and Ilana Kloss in women's singles. Diamond had the right mindset: "We expect to go two years before making money. But who knows? We may be surprised." They hoped to outdraw baseball's Oakland A's, playing across the parking lot that night—the Gaters won before 4,012, while Reggie Jackson and the A's lost in front of just 2,980.

Two days later, Boston came to town, and things got loud. A Gaters fan yelled at Lobsterette Kerry Melville, "Break her serve!" Another screamed, "Break her leg!" May 15, the Gaters jetted to Minnesota and got pelted by the Buckskins, 32-30. June 5, the night after losing at home to John Newcombe's Houston E-Z Riders 31-22, the Gaters battered the Florida Flamingos, in their only Bay Area appearance. Coach Emerson then missed the next two matches, attending the opening of Murrieta Hot Springs, where he'd later work as a tennis pro. But Emerson missed much of the season due to other tennis camp commitments. The team tried to fill the void by signing mid-level pros such as

Jeff Borowiak, veteran of the champion UCLA Bruins team with Jimmy Connors and Haroon Rahim.

In their final home match before midseason, the Gaters took on Billie Jean King's Freedoms and lost before 6,500, the season's largest home crowd, 25-18. King detractors said her show-biz style was better suited for a circus tent than a tennis court. She made faces and argued line calls, egged on her players, and sulked. It was her show.

Ilana Kloss started the season playing doubles before Emerson shifted her into singles. Said Kloss: "When I grew up, tennis was a very personal thing. It was against everybody else. It's not that way anymore. If I lose, I lose for the team, and letting the rest of the team down is not a responsibility I want on my shoulders. The team feeling makes you want to win a bit more because it means more." Emerson elucidated: "Ilana is young, and I expect she'll make some mental mistakes. With more experience, she won't."

July 16, the Gaters lost by 26-25 to the Pacific Section-leading Racquets in Denver. August 5, the second-place Gaters coasted over Tom Okker's visiting Toronto-Buffalo Royals; the 21-15 win put them 2½ games ahead of Florida for the final playoff birth with seven games remaining. After a 28-21 home victory August 6 over the E-Z Riders, the Buckskins came to town on August 9 and dismantled the Gaters 31-15. August 16, the Gaters bested the Leis in Oakland 29-20—to qualify for the 1974 playoffs. The night's low point was Lesley Hunt getting smacked in the eye by a ball deflected off her racquet.

The Gaters ended the 1974 season 23-21 (.523), qualifying for the playoffs, which opened against the top-ranked Denver. August 19, the best-of-three series began with the Racquets thumping the Gaters 29-17 in front of 2,404 on a Monday night in Denver. August 20, the Racquets slapped the Gaters out of the playoffs 32-24 before an estimated crowd of 1,600 at Oakland Arena; Lesley Hunt rebounded from an accidentally self-inflicted eye injury (got smacked in the eye by a ball deflected off her racquet in a match against the Hawaii Leis), only to blink in defeat to Denver's Françoise Dürr, 6-3. Just like that, the Gaters' first year was over.

Post-season contract talks broke down with Margaret Court, around whom new owner David Peterson hoped to build his franchise. The club offered Court a two-year deal, but she wanted just one. GM Jerry Diamond offered her a pact larger than Billie Jean King's, yet she demanded more. "You get into that, and you either have to say no, or you raise your ticket prices, and we were lowering ours." Diamond also said they had spoken with three other stars, but nothing had resulted. He abruptly traded Court's rights (in exchange for the rights to Chris Evert) to Hawaii, a franchise more likely to indulge her demands.

Peterson bought co-owner Cathie Anderson's shares in the team for pennies on the dollar. The 1961 Stanford grad, who once owned a well known Bay Area restaurant chain, got into tennis after attending the King-Riggs "Battle of the Sexes," and applied shrewd low-cost methods to selling a new sports concept to the local populace. He explained: "If I can sign a superstar and it makes economic sense, I'd do it. But remember that having a superstar doesn't bring out more people. Our attendance is due to my staff marketing."

Peterson wouldn't re-sign Emerson, who couldn't commit to a full season, so he and Larry King named Frew McMillan player-coach. They also signed two Dutch stars from folded franchises: Betty Stöve (Baltimore) and Tom Okker (Toronto-Buffalo). They got Ann Kiyomura from Hawaii to join Kloss, Hunt, Bohrnstedt, and Reed (1974's feel-good story, who went AWOL after one game in 1975). Among the team's unsigned draftees included Raúl Ramírez, Bob Lutz, Sue Mehmedbasich, and Joaquín Loyo-Mayo.

The release of 1975's schedule meant that Bay Area tennis buffs would see more of Billie Jean King, but less of the Gaters. The team would host King and her new team the New York Sets twice in their second year, including May 13's home opener. King made it to Oakland once in 1974 with the Freedoms, and the Gaters drew their most massive home crowd. Instead of 22 home and away matches, the Gaters agreed to help spread the WTT brand by playing 18 home dates with 26 on the road, but 11 were on neutral courts.

"It's unbelievable, isn't it? We're both 19, on the same team, won Junior Wimbledon titles, and both our surnames start with the letter K."

—ILANA KLOSS, Golden Gaters, 1975

1975 started strongly for the Gaters. On May 16, against Pittsburgh, Frew McMillan gambled in women's doubles by pairing pint-sized "K-Kids" Kiyomura and Kloss. The hunch paid off in spades, with the 19-year-olds standing 5'2" and 5'5" crushing the Triangles' Peggy Michel-Evonne Goolagong Wimbledon title duo, 6-1, then May 18 in Indianapolis over the Loves' Trish Bostrom-Wendy Overton 6-2, and again May 19 in Honolulu over the Leis' Margaret Court-Brigitte Cuypers, 6-3. A media release hailed the Kloss-Kiyomura "Teenie Corps"—WTT's #1 ranked women's tandem.

From May 30 through June 7, the Gaters endured a grueling five-game losing streak. They returned to form with June 8's home win over the San Diego Friars 24-21, and June 10's wallop of the visiting Boston Lobsters, 28-18. June 11, the Gaters increased their Division lead to two games over the Phoenix, trouncing the Racquets 33-23, and winning every set, to quiet a boisterous Phoenix crowd of 4,021. The night's apex was Okker's win over Brian Fairlie when there was a disputed call that had McMillan hopping mad. When the contest reached the final set, the Gaters margin had proven impossible.

In the Western Division playoffs, the Gaters (29-15) made short work of the Racquets, sweeping a series that began August 18 with a 25-24 win before 1,308 in Phoenix, and the next night 26-20 to 1,809 home fans, to advance to the finals. The Gaters' home court in Oakland had already booked a circus, so their playoff games got moved to S.F.'s Cow Palace. (The previous year, the Golden State Warriors won the NBA title after they had to vacate Oakland Arena for an ice show, so the Gaters hoped for similar results.)

The Triangles won four of five matches over the Gaters in 1975, 6-1 in the two-year-old league. Both squads flashed impressive stats: Pittsburgh's Goolagong ranked #2 in women's singles, while Stöve was ranked #5. In men's, Pittsburgh's Mark Cox rated #2, directly followed by Okker at #3. Both squads handily swept their best-of-three semis.

"I was hot tonight. That's why they call me hot Stöve."
—BETTY STÖVE, Golden Gaters, 1975

In the title opener August 21 at the Cow Palace, the Gaters only won two of five sets, yet they beat the favored Triangles, 26-25. For August 23's nationally televised afternoon match in Pittsburgh, the Gaters lost four, 28-25. Arena organist Vince Lascheid annoyed the Gaters players; McMillan fumed: "I don't mind the organ playing during the breaks, but not when he interrupts play." In the decisive Game Three, the Gaters overcame Vitas Gerulaitis' 6-1 opening set annihilation of Okker. Play got suspended when a Triangles win was assured 21-14, as the Gaters season went down in flames. In the post-season, Okker got voted WTT Male MVP while McMillan was named Coach of the Year.

After acquiring Chris Evert's rights, Dave Peterson confirmed that the Gaters traded her rights to the Racquets, admitting he'd spent two months futilely negotiating with the Ft. Lauderdale phenom. "Chris indicated her preference for starting her WTT career in Phoenix," Peterson said. Evert received from Phoenix more money than the Gaters' entire 1976 player budget. In return, the franchise received 1975 All-Star Françoise Dürr.

Having failed to sign Court and then Evert, the Gaters found themselves in a bind with Dürr. Peterson said Kloss would not return for 1976, and that Kiyomura was a maybe. At the crux was that the players' agents found Peterson challenging to negotiate with. Having taken hard lines with Court and Evert only to wind up trading the stars to other franchises in a pro league with few big stars, Peterson was firm that he'd sign Dürr or she would not play. Jerry Diamond offered her more than she could've earned if she made the finals in every summer tournament. Dürr's powerhouse agent Marvin Demoff said his agency was not out to make a rep by asking so much for her services. March 8, Dürr signed a two-year pact of undisclosed terms, reuniting her top-ranked 1975 tour doubles duo with Betty Stöve. The Gaters opened 1976 with McMillan, Okker, Stöve, and Dürr, joined by Kiyomura and Borowiak, plus Argentine professional Raquel Giscafré.

The Gaters lost their May 1 season opener to the L.A. Strings 28-24 at Oakland Arena, as Borowiak excelled in doubles, and Dürr lost her set, and the match. Borowiak filled in admirably for Okker—who arrived an hour before the game, sat the bench, and wasn't missed. After Borowiak-McMillan's 6-2 quick start, the Gaters quickly blew the lead after Dürr lost her singles event 6-3. Dürr spoke of her difficulty seeing the ball, and getting a feel for the gaudy multicolored courts: "I rely so much on my ground-strokes that I need to feel the ball. But it'll get better. Even on the Slims tour, it takes me a few days to get in gear."

May 5 at Fresno's Selland Arena, the "hometown" Gaters humbled the Friars 31-15, taking all five events, as Borowiak-McMillan excelled in men's doubles over Rod Laver-Ross Case, 6-1. May 10 in Oakland, Okker-McMillan defeated Dennis Ralston-Charlie Pasarell 6-3 in the final event to pace the Gaters over L.A. 24-21; June 4, the Gaters outlasted the visiting Leis, 31-15, after which Dave Peterson rushed to sue AWOL star Ilie Năstase for breach of contract. June 12, versus the Indiana Loves in Oakland, the Gaters won 27-22, in a match with some ticket proceeds going to Institute of Noetic Sciences, a nonprofit co-founded by astronaut Edgar Mitchell, researching mind power.

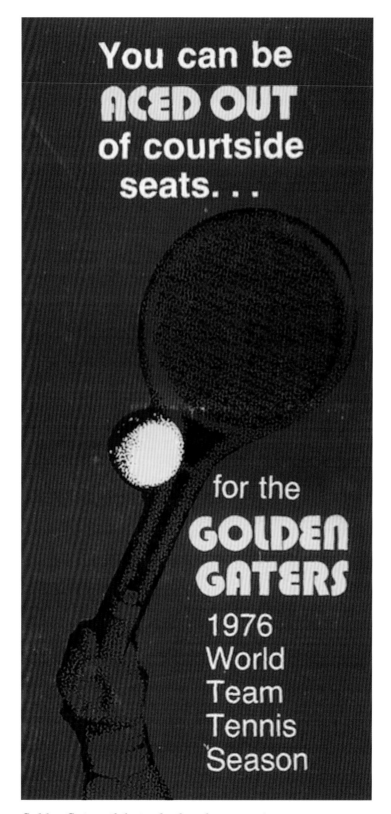

You can be **ACED OUT** of courtside seats. . .

for the **GOLDEN GATERS** 1976 World Team Tennis Season

Golden Gaters ticket sales brochure, 1976

"I'm quite excited about playing World Team Tennis. I have all the strokes, but my court strategy is very poor. But through tennis, my anticipation and footwork have made me a much better basketball player."

—JOHN LUCAS, Golden Gaters, 1976

John Lucas, #1 pick in the NBA draft who signed an $850,000 five-year deal with the Houston Rockets, made news on June 11 when also signed with the Gaters, resolute to play two pro sports. The contract gave the 21-year-old, 6'4" left-hander what amounted to a three-year commitment, with a team option to move on after each season. In addition to being a consensus All-American basketball guard, Lucas was one of the nation's top college netters, on a junior national team with Gerulaitis and Connors, winner of two ACC singles titles and one doubles crown, and went 20-1 in a Maryland tennis season before losing in the third round of the NCAAs. Lucas' agent Donald Dell declared him "the nation's second-best black tennis player [after Arthur Ashe]." Diamond said, "We're not worried about the overlap of basketball, but we did not want a one-year deal." Peterson joked, "The Gaters won't be his primary income for the next few years."

The team was gambling that the athletically gifted Lucas could mature into a star under Frew McMillan's stewardship. McMillan, with his team in second place and on a seven-game winning tear, pledged to help but expressed doubts of the squad's latest addition. "I don't know a thing about him. I've never seen him play tennis or basketball. I reckon if he's a star in one sport, he ought to stop, right? I think it's a tough assignment. One has to be so into your chosen sport that it doesn't allow enough time for a second sport." Lucas would spend most of his short season with the Gaters riding the bench.

The Gaters finished the 1976 season with a 28-16 record good enough for second place in the Western Division and making their third straight playoff appearance. A reporter asked the boyish McMillan if being the coach had aged him in any way. "Some people go to the spas of Europe for relaxation," McMillan mused. "I coach the Gaters."

For August 16's playoff opener, the Gaters felt confident about their chances. Game One of the semifinals, they smashed the Racquets 32-16 before 5,848 in Phoenix. The next night in Oakland, 6,025 saw the Gaters dominate 24-18, to face the New York Sets in the best-of-five finals. While not available on TV, all Gaters playoff matches were listenable on KFFG-FM 97.7 in Los Altos and KRE-AM 1400 in Berkeley.

An August 21, a crowd of 3,075 at Oakland Arena saw Billie Jean King and Virginia Wade pace the Sets 31-23. Sandy Mayer, the Sets' cocky NCAA champion from Stanford, trounced Okker 6-2 to seal the deal. The Gaters' play so irked Frew that he said to expect drastic lineup changes for the next match. But the following night in Oakland, the squads endured similar results: Sets 29, Gaters 21. Interesting was the pre-game parking lot interaction between the sharp-dressed tennis crowd and maniacal Oakland Raiders fans. No violence occurred, but incidents of sexual epithets and bullying were reported to Arena security by unnerved tennis fans.

August 27, the Gaters seemingly played dead at Nassau Coliseum, swept in the finals, 31-13—the only time all year that the Gaters lost all five sets in a match. With the loss, the Gaters joined the Buffalo Bills and Minnesota Vikings in that sad pantheon of sports bridesmaids with many title games but no crowns. For the third time in three seasons, the Gaters made the playoffs; but for the second straight season, they ended second-best.

"I think we've had a good deal of luck. But I hope we've created some of our own fortunes."
—DAVE PETERSON, Golden Gaters owner, 1977

One week after the Gaters' season-ending humiliation, Diamond and Peterson said that the Gaters would re-evaluate their structure. The two did not rule out a switch on the men's side, where Okker flopped in the second straight finals. But the Dutchman re-signed for one more year when they decided his low salary price was right. Diamond declared: "We might not want to give him up, and we'll pick up a good third male to sit Jeff Borowiak"—who "was unhappy with his playing time" and "did not fit in emotionally with WTT." The musically minded Borowiak, best friend on the pro tour with Danish star Torben Ulrich, later bankrolled Lars Rocket, Ulrich's son Lars' band, which went on to change its name to "Metallica." And finally, before the 1977 season, Diamond left to run Women's Tennis Association.

The Gaters began 1977 with the league's best record (3-0) and the largest crowd (6,113 against Chris Evert's Racquets). Opening night April 28 in Oakland, Rod Laver's Friars got shamed 29-25; St. Petersburg, FL's Betsy Nagelsen, signed days earlier to replace an injured Betty Stöve, teamed with Francoise Dürr over Mona Guerrant-Julie Anthony 6-1.

The New York City Blackout struck Wednesday July 13, at 9:34 p.m. The Gaters, at Madison Square Garden's Felt Forum, trailed the Apples 21-15, with Okker and Mayer tied 5-5. The MSG staff activated emergency lights for the 3,345 in attendance, but it wasn't enough to resume competition. Okker joked, "We stunk, we blew up the place."

Most failed franchises fold due to poor management. The Gaters were WTT's most durable because of Dave Peterson, who, in three years, turned the team into a showcase. Had he sold his team in 1976-77, it could've fetched $1 million. Although the Gaters had no stars, they increased turnout every season and made the playoffs every year under his stewardship. Apples owner Sol Berg offered, "Dave's team typifies the concept if WTT is going to make it. He's gone to the community, and built a team from the grass-roots."

August 9, a record crowd of 11,277 at Oakland Arena rose to its feet after Okker's dramatic 7-6 win over Björn Borg led the Gaters over the visiting Cleveland-Pittsburgh Nets, 30-26. August 10, the Gaters flew to Portland and prevailed 30-26 over the Sea-Port Cascades, led by a men's doubles duel won by Okker-McMillan over Tom Gorman-Steve Docherty 6-4. It was the last of the six away Gaters matches aired on KTVU Channel 2. The next night in Oakland, the squad repelled the invading Soviets, 28-17.

The Gaters held WTT's most extensive radio network, selling out all their commercial time. On the 50,000-watt KNBR, Bob Mansbach and Jerry Lee announced all 44 Gaters games plus playoffs. One match, after an official threw Okker off the court, he went up to the booth and sailed paper airplanes down at the ref while delivering salty analysis.

August 16, the Gaters (25-19) began their 1977 playoffs in Oakland against the Friars, ceding a five-point lead in Game One, 24-22. The next night in San Diego, the Gaters' flew home after a 30-21 defeat, after Rod Laver mauled Okker in singles and doubles.

"I knew it was over quick. But I didn't know it was over that quick."
—FREW McMILLAN, Golden Gaters, 1976

"Gaters Fever '78" became the slogan on the team's posters and pocket schedules. Printed matter featured 1978's netters in maroon and gold: player-coach McMillan, Wade, Kloss, Marise Kruger, Sandy Mayer, Michael Wayman, assistant coach Henry Schneiderman, trainer Charley Black, and GM Bob Horowitz.

The Gaters lost April 23's 1978 season opener at Oakland Arena to the Cascades, 27-24. A Gaters bright spot came in the third set as their new "K-Kids"—the returning Kloss and Marise Kruger—burned former Gater Betty Stöve and Brigitte Cuypers, 6-3. After April 26's loss to the expansion Oranges in Anaheim, 28-24, the Gaters rebounded the next night at home to defeat Anaheim, 27-23. June 12 in Boston, Mayer-McMillan beat Tony Roche and ex-Gater Roy Emerson in a 24-23 super-tiebreaker over the Lobsters.

The Gaters signed Ken Rosewall on August 9 to replace Sandy Mayer, sidelined by a foot injury. Dave Peterson said the 44-year-old Aussie great was unsure he could remain with the team for the playoffs due to commitments. Rosewall left the club after just two matches. One day before the playoff opener against L.A., they landed Tom Leonard, the world's 36th-ranked male netter, and then threw him into the fire to face Ilie Năstase in singles, and paired him in doubles with Frew McMillan.

August 15, the soon-to-be-titlist Strings won the opening playoff game 29-17, then two nights later shut the Gaters down. That night in Oakland, McMillan and Leonard fell in a 7-5 super-tiebreaker to lose a close night 30-29. A Bay Area crowd of 6,721 loved seeing Leonard bash Năstase 6-1, but it'd be the final Gaters match.

November 7, Dave Peterson vowed he'd press on following the demise of eight of the league's ten teams. He stated, "We have a strong franchise without a league in which to play," and that while there would be no WTT in 1979, stressed that they were not folding. Dave felt the league, with only the Gaters and Phoenix left, could've played a six-week schedule, but "the pressure of time and the adverse effects of teams pulling out made the 1979 season impossible." He also vowed refunds for the 2,000 season ticket holders.

Peterson said the Gaters would maintain its office and focus on promoting tournaments and tennis packages, along with finding new owners to restart WTT for 1980. "The key thing is, we're not folding." Then Phoenix owner Jerry Simmons suspended operations despite the Racquets' four seasons averaging a league-high 6,000 per match.

The league's lone remaining team cited an inability to find long-term owners for other franchises to make the circuit healthy for years to come. Peterson vowed to press on but admitted, "I recognize we must have someone to play against." Golden Gaters Productions (GGP) remained active in promoting women's tournaments through the '80s.

Chapter 15
New York Sets/Apples

Billie Jean King, New York Apples press photo, 1977

Years of Operation: 1974-1976 (Sets)
                  1977-1978 (Apples)

Team Colors: Blue and white (Sets)
            Red and green (Apples)

Team Record: 1974: 15-29 (last place, Atlantic Section)
            1975: 35-9 (2nd place, Eastern Division)
            1976: 33-10 (1st place, Eastern Division)
            1977: 33-11 (2nd place, Eastern Division)
            1978: 22-22 (2nd place, Eastern Division)

Female MVP: Billie Jean King 1975 (568-328, 634)

Male MVP: Sandy Mayer 1976 (467-366, .561)

Highlight: Winning the first 16 games of the
          1975 season

Lowlight: Losing a *one-game* playoff to Boston to
          end the 1975 season (8/17/75)

Home Arenas: Nassau Coliseum (capacity 18,600)
             Felt Forum (capacity 4,500)
             Madison Square Garden (capacity 19,693)

Quote: "If I did as well on-court as I did off the court,
        I'd be #1 by now."
           —Vitas Gerulaitis, New York Apples (2/19/78)

"We need a drawing card. It's the only possible way to sustain the New York franchise."
—JERRY SAPERSTEIN, New York Sets owner, 1973

New York failed spectacularly in November 1973's first WTT draft, selecting with no advisors or game plan, like a rotisserie draft. There were okay picks between Aussie Roy Emerson in Round One, Pam Teeguarden of L.A. Round Two, Sandy Mayer of Wayne, NJ third, and Cliff Richey of San Angelo, TX fourth, and Manuel Santana of Spain ninth. But there was no excuse for taking Kazuko Sawamatsu, Wanaro N'Godrella, or Herb Fitzgibbon. Only Santana and Mayer came to terms. WTT's New York's franchise took the tennis-themed name Sets, to rhyme with the NFL Jets and ABA Nets.

Bill Riordan, agent to Ilie Năstase, sent a 27-page letter to notify WTT the fiery Romanian would play only for New York in 1974, if at all. Drafted by San Diego #62 overall, Năstase avowed, "I do not want to play with San Diego. I hope to play in

New York." A source close to the Sets reported Ilie was anxious to sign. Up to this point, the Sets had only one player under contract in player-coach Santana. Two weeks later, Commissioner George MacCall said he cleared the final hurdle for Năstase to play in New York. The Sets offered $125,000 per year, but San Diego refused to cede their rights.

Three weeks before the first ball got served, the Sets were a source of concern to league officials. New York's time-consuming chase of Năstase proved fruitless. MacCall increased the Sets' salary cap to $400,000 and looked into signing top-ranked pros to satisfy New York's sports appetite, as the Pam Teeguarden-Manuel Santana mixed doubles duo wasn't going to cut it. Sets owner Jerry Saperstein, son of Harlem Globetrotters founder Abe Saperstein, at league meetings in Chicago, presented "facts" about his team's issues in a new sports league that could ill afford to fail in the largest cities.

Apparently still swooning over irritable Eastern Europeans, the Sets traded British netter Roger Taylor to the Boston Lobsters for volatile 34-year-old Slav Nikolai "Niki" Pilić. Also from the Lobsters came Tuscaloosa's Charlie Owens, #8 on the Indoor Circuit behind Connors and Gerulaitis. For $25,000 to Detroit, they acquired 28-year-old Virginia Wade, who showed no interest in WTT but then signed with the Sets for the second half of the year.

The Sets 1974 roster consisted of non-stars Santana, Teeguarden, Owens, Argentina's Beatriz Araujo, Peru's Fiorella Bonicelli, S.F.'s Ceci Martinez, and New Jersey's Sandy Mayer. Saperstein desperately sought investors and met Sol Berg, a tennis-crazed cocoa futures broker that bought the franchise—and then hired Saperstein as GM.

WTT debuted in New York on May 7. Paid turnstile count at Long Island's Nassau Coliseum was said to be 4,999. Sandy Mayer called the audience "typical New York—crude and obscene." The visiting Hawaii Leis, by a score of 29-25, slammed the blue-and-white Sets, beginning a losing trend that surely did not endear the team to NYC sports fans accustomed to star players and championship teams—the Nets won only one of their first 13 games.

> ### "There will be noise in New York, and I will probably enjoy it. It would be nice if there were nobody in the arena, but you don't make money that way."
> #### —NIKI PILIĆ, New York Sets, 1974

Pilić, absent from WTT to play for Yugoslavia in the Davis Cup, returned to face a new war of nerves on May 17, with the Sets losing to rival Lobsters. "I've heard some ideas about team tennis," he said, referring to the shouting and informality urged at WTT events. Yugoslavia's Davis Cup success vs. Egypt assured that he'd miss more matches in July, when his nation would face the USSR.

May 20, before the echoing screams of just 556 fans at Nassau Coliseum, the visiting Baltimore Banners edged the Sets 24-23; May 22, the smallest crowd for any event at the Coliseum of 457 saw the Minnesota Buckskins bash the Sets 25-17. After Pilić beat Bob Hewitt, 6-2, Hewitt slammed a serve into the balcony.

Sol Berg, tired of weak returns on his investment—tiny turnouts at Nassau Coliseum, and the Atlantic Section's worst record—began a roster overhaul. After May 24's home loss to John Newcombe's E-Z Riders, seen by 1,076, they cut Beatriz Araujo and signed the Bay Area's Sharon Walsh. New York then signed Carol Graebner, of which GM Bob Kain said: "We're sure Carol will bolster our lineup and add value with her following."

June 3, the Sets shocked the Central Section-leading Detroit Loves 27-26, for just their second victory, and their first home win. June 5, Tony Roche's surging Denver Racquets thumped the Sets 24-15, observed by a purported home crowd of 1,469. July 12, Walsh-Pilić beat Janet Young-Graham Stilwell 6-3 in the final event to lead the Sets over the Chicago Aces at Nassau, 26-23. After the game, Sets player-coach Santana left to oversee Spain's Davis Cup squad, replaced by Pilić, who'd coached Yugoslavian, Italian, and East German Davis Cup. Pilić's coaching debut was spoiled July 7 in a 25-21 setback to the Lobsters. July 15, Santana temporarily rejoined to fill in for Pilić, busy with his own Davis Cup duties. July 22, Pilić returned to lead his Sets over the Gaters, 26-23, in front of a more robust home audience of 5,204.

There was no love between NY's Virginia Wade and Philadelphia's Billie Jean King. In the past, they exchanged strident words and volleys, and their squads adopted the stars' animosity. New York and Philadelphia played July 26 in front of 7,535, the Sets' biggest turnout at Nassau, as the Freedoms reigned supreme 28-20. Two days later, New York endured a 30-10 disgrace at the Spectrum, swept in all five events. August 16, the Sets ended their home schedule on a downswing, surrendering a lead to lose to Philly 25-24, before 7,187 at Nassau. The Sets finished 1974 at 15-29, for fourth place in the four-team Atlantic Section, averaging 2,869 at the 18,600-seat Coliseum.

"My outside interests will not interfere with my playing for the Sets. I will be available anytime."
—BILLIE JEAN KING, New York Sets, 1975

Neil Amdur posited in *The New York Times* (2/5/75): "Is Billie Jean King headed for the New York Sets in a desperate lob to save World Team Tennis?" Later that day, the Freedoms traded "Mother Freedom" to the Sets, for the rights to Stan Smith and Kerry Melville plus cash. At the Essex House by Central Park, Sol Berg promised to win a title in New York—and said he'd just begun that process by signing King to a four-year deal.

Reports persisted that the 1975 Sets wanted Jimmy Connors as male star and Pancho Gonzales as head coach. "Last year at this time, we had Fiorella Bonicelli and Beatriz Araujo," Berg snarled. King said she'd focus on WTT, spend most of her other time in NY as a TV commentator, and oversee her women's sports magazine. King requested relief from coaching duties, so the Sets named her Freedoms mate Fred Stolle as player-coach. The former Aussie Davis Cup captain joked, "Billie made decisions last year. This year, it'll be up to me." He also disregarded any ill will between new teammates King and Wade: "When both are on the same team and want to win, I foresee no problems." To make room, the Sets jettisoned Teeguarden and Pilić. They also endured another lousy draft, between Helga Masthoff, Nathalie Fuchs, Jas Singh, and Marjory Gengler Smith.

The Sets stabilized their roster by adding King and Stolle, returning Wade, Mayer, and Owens, and signing Mona Schallau and Betsy Nagelsen—the latter hired to replace Wade as she played for England in Federation Cup. That lineup won "The Walden Goblet" for winning an eight-team preseason "Spectacular" near Houston in Lake Conroe, Texas.

The Sets flew home following May 2's 1975 opening night 27-24 win over the WTT champion Racquets in their new home of Phoenix. The Sets won their home opener against the Cleveland Nets 26-21 before an announced 4,010 attendees, but only two hundred watched the first few sets before new star King played. For 1975, the Sets reworked their Coliseum seating; so, instead of matches in the center to thousands dressed as empty seats, the court got moved to one corner seating 8,800 fans, and bringing fans close to the action as the Sets began the season undefeated with a WTT-best 16-0 record.

Sol Berg threw a July 15 party to celebrate the recent Wimbledon titles of his two top players, King and Sandy Mayer. King took the women's singles title, while Mayer and Vitas Gerulaitis took the men's doubles crown; King thanked Sandy for helping her win with tough daily training with her Sets. August 1, a record home audience of 6,055 saw New York's first-ever win over the Pittsburgh Triangles, 31-19, in a five-set sweep, to sit atop the Eastern Division. With King missing her third straight match with a stomach virus, Wade led the way, thrashing Goolagong, and in doubles with Mona Schallau outlasting Goolagong-Peggy Michel, both 6-3.

The Sets would end 1975 with a 35-9 record, second place in the East, behind the Triangles. All that stood between the Sets and an epic New York-Pittsburgh playoff battle was a one-game wild card against the lowly Lobsters. On August 17, a stone-silent Coliseum crowd of 1,025 saw Boston edge New York, 25-24, as the league's second-lowest paid squad defeated King's superstar squad, ending the Sets' season.

"We don't want too many superstars on our team. Parity is the key to WTT's success."
—BOB KAIN, New York Sets GM, 1975

After the season, GM Bob Kain made an under-the-radar move to upgrade the 1976 Sets, sending Mona Schallau to Indiana for Loves men's star Phil Dent. January 14, 1976, Kain made his last move as GM: re-signing player-coach Fred Stolle as per King's desires. Kain left to join Mark McCormack's new IMG sports management firm, and later became Björn Borg's agent and IMG's president. Soon after, Sol Berg hired his latest GM Billy Goldstein, former football/baseball coach at St. Agnes in Rockville Centre, LI.

The Sets' 1976 roster retained King, Wade, Stolle, and Mayer, and added Dent, Linda Siegelman of Roslyn, LI, and 26-year-old Brit Lindsey Beaven, who lost to Chris Evert in the 1975 Wimbledon quarterfinals. Sets salaries ranked as followed: King $130,000; Wade $90,000; Mayer $55,000; Stolle $55,000 and Dent $50,000, with Lindsey Beaven and Linda Siegelman $8,500 apiece. Charlie Owens, cut at the end of the 1975 season, said of his two-year Sets daze: "I liked it when I got to play, but not when I sat the bench. I was tired from all the traveling and not playing. WTT was the worst thing for my game."

June 10, led by Mayer's 6-3 routing of Vitas Gerulaitis, the Sets dented the Triangles 26-22 before 3,393 in Pittsburgh. Mayer, a thoughtful 24-year-old, when asked about his

Sandy Mayer and Phil Dent, New York Sets 1976

Above: 1976 New York Sets
L-R: Phil Dent, Virginia Wade, Lindsey Beaven, Fred Stolle, Linda Siegelman, Billie Jean King, Sandy Mayer

Below: 1976 Sets championship banner
L-R: Stolle, Dent, King, Mayer, Siegelman, Beaven, Wade, GM Billy Goldstein

improved 1976 play, replied in a manner worthy of his Stanford diploma. "I've reached a level of consciousness as to what the difference is. I had an attacking style, but you've got to live within yourself." About losing, Gerulaitis said, "There's so much shit going on."

"Last year, I felt I had to win every point. Now, I hang in there and let others lose."
—SANDY MAYER, New York Sets, 1976

New York only played 43 matches in 1976, due to Hurricane Belle forcing a cancellation that was never made up. Home attendance improved to a reported 3,264 per. Sol Berg quelled rumors that King might sign with the L.A. Strings. His squad dominated end-of-season stats: a 33-10 team record, with King #3 (.615) and Wade #4 (.531) in women's singles, #1-ranked "WTT Super Star" Mayer (.595) in men's singles, Mayer-Dent #8 in men's doubles (.548), King-Wade (.560) #3 in women's doubles, and King-Dent (.594) #10 in mixed doubles. King made good on her vow to crush the Lobsters, bashing them in all five in-season matches, and then eliminating them from playoff contention.

At Game One of the Eastern Division playoffs, an August 17 audience of 3,385 in Pittsburgh saw the defending champion Triangles win the opening match of a best-of-three series, 26-25. Stolle's tactic to open with women's doubles fizzled when King-Wade lost to Evonne Goolagong-JoAnne Russell, 7-5. August 18, with their season on the line, 3,227 at Nassau watched the Sets bash the Triangles 29-21 to even the series. Fans saw vintage King darting, slashing, and fighting in 6-4 wins over Goolagong and in mixed doubles with Mayer over Goolagong-Gerulaitis. Wade said, "We didn't wanna lose to them again. Particularly not at home." At Game Three, the Sets beat the Triangles 28-26, seen by a Nassau crowd of 2,608—to advance to the WTT finals against the Golden Gaters. Wiping champagne off her face in the locker room, King bellowed, "I've waited three years for this one. We won the division title when I played for Philadelphia, but we lost the big one. Now I have a second chance for that title, and it's crucial to me."

August 21, led by a fired-up King, the Sets invaded Oakland Arena, and trounced the Gaters 31-23, to take Game One. Sandy Mayer mocked from the locker room: "So they can't believe we beat them? Well, let me tell you that they better!" King offered, "We made an effort to get off the dime right away." August 23—blasting off to a 12-1 lead after King blanked Betty Stöve 6-0 in 14 minutes—the Sets routed the Gaters again 29-21. Gaters player-coach Frew McMillan lamented of Mayer's 6-1 trouncing of Tom Okker, "He was just taking Okker's serves and knocking it down his throat."

August 27, in a scene devoid of all the elements of a title series—fans, banners, and competition—New York swept the Gaters, thoroughly dominating Game Three 31-13 in front of the Sets' third largest-ever crowd of 5,730, to win their first WTT title. Before the match began, the Gaters faced the possibility of playing without Betty Stöve, who was stuck in traffic on the N.J. Turnpike, but she arrived 30 minutes before game time. Mayer enthused, "We were on top of them from the start. We never let them breathe." Even with no trophy to raise, MVP Billie Jean King felt content. A WTT crown was the only title that eluded her. She told *The New York Times* (8/28/76): "This has been of paramount importance to me."

> ## *"Pressure, pressure, pressure—I love it. It's been no secret that I wanted the WTT title badly."*
> ### —BILLIE JEAN KING, 1976

Furious with the turnout for his champions, Sol Berg hired Billie Jean's spouse Larry King as team president. WTT officials knew the importance of a powerhouse New York franchise, and could not afford to let the titlists fold. Larry rebranded the team, with a re-naming contest. All things considered, the winning "Apples" was better than some others submitted: The Whips, The Noodniks, The Muggers, The Whiz, The Bagels. Of the 5,000-plus entries, 43 suggested the Apples or Big Apples. GM Billy Goldstein admitted, "Poking fun at the nickname is inevitable." The team also said that the 1977 Apples, wearing green and red, would play two games at Nassau for the old fans, eight times at Madison Square Garden, and the rest in MSG's smaller room, the Felt Forum. With King, Wade, and Meyer—the first star developed within the WTT system—and a front office run by King and Goldstein, the Apples seemed to be building a dynasty.

The Apples won their 1977 opener on April 28 at the Felt Forum over the Sea-Port Cascades 24-23, as the former Hawaii Leis proved greener than their uniforms. June 3, Wade rallied the Apples over the Soviets at Nassau 26-23. June 6, Chris Evert led her Racquets to a 27-24 win before 13,675 at MSG, the fourth-largest crowd in WTT history.

On July 13, the Apples, before 3,345 at the Felt Forum, were leading the Gaters 21-15 with the men's singles set between Sandy Mayer and Tom Okker tied 5-5 at 7:34 p.m., when the 1977 New York Blackout struck. Staff activated emergency electrical gear, but there was not enough light to resume play. July 17, the Apples became WTT's first team to win twice in one night, scorching the Gaters 29-18, to finish that Blackout match, and then routing the Loves 24-14 in the scheduled event, seen by 3,170 at the Felt. July 23, after getting shelled by the Lobsters 24-21, the rather proper Virginia Wade went berserk over a penalty call by referee Jon Glazer. She called him an "imbecile," and stated, "I can't even call him a man. If I had my way, I would've rapped him with my racquet."

> ## *"There was a tremendous amount of pressure on us to win. But I deserved to win. I conquered the balance of tension."*
> ### —VIRGINIA WADE, New York Apples, 1977

The Apples relied on King to stay in first place. Back from the flu, King won both sets July 21 against the Nets, solo and with Wade. With King's substitute Linda Siegelman at the Maccabiah Games in Tel Aviv, they signed Siegelman's teenaged practice partner Anne Fritz. The Apples (33-11) ended the 1977 season two games behind Martina Navratilova's Lobsters.

New York began its playoff drive for another title. August 16 at the Felt Forum, the Apples lashed the Loves in Game One, 33-21, as Mayer fended off Gerulaitis 7-6, and Wade routed Sue Barker, 6-2. The next night in Indy, the Loves eked out a 28-25 victory, in which King raged at the abusive audience, exiting the court with an angry fist-on-bicep-pump "Italian salute." Game Three, on August 19, back in New York, the Apples

Sandy Mayer, New York Apples, 1977
Billie Jean King called Mayer "WTT's first homegrown star"

swept all five sets to advance 31-15. Stolle extolled: "We got back to our system tonight."

August 20 and August 22, a pair of tense super-tiebreaker wins involving Sandy Mayer returned the Apples to the finals, as they fried the Lobsters, 28-24, 29-26 for the Eastern Division title. New York's victory was considered an upset because Boston (35-9) had WTT's best regular-season record. With teammates screaming on the sidelines, Mayer edged Tony Roche 7-6 and then paired with Ray Ruffels to top Roche-Mike Estep, 7-6. Afterward, the Apples chilled, as the Racquets and Friars beat on each other in the West.

For Game One of the best-of-three WTT Finals, New York blasted visiting Phoenix 27-22. Two nights later, on August 27, the Apples retained their crown before for the 11,294 fans in Phoenix who saw the Apples' 28-17 Game Two rout of the Racquets. Virginia Wade's 6-0 "golden bagel" over Chris Evert in the second set was both the crucial element and the hot topic of conversation. The Apples became the first New York team to win consecutive titles since the Yankees won the World Series in 1961 and 1962.

Sol Berg beamed in post-match photos with the Apples of his eyes: King, Wade, Stolle, Mayer, Ruffels, Beaven, and Siegelman. Stolle hailed Wade for her obliteration of Evert, saying, "Maybe Chris wasn't at the top of her game, but Ginny was terrific." At a victory party serving champagne and spaghetti, sportsmanship was served by the appearance of Evert and Ross Case to propose toasts and offer salutations. And no one loved it more than Berg, after all the money he'd spent. Sol responded with a salute involving honesty: "We're glad to be in our position rather than yours. But we are sorry you had to lose."

"I'm excited to be playing for the Apples. New York is my kind of town."

—VITAS GERULAITIS, New York Apples, 1977

1978's big preseason trade involved New York-bred best friends and doubles partners when the Apples' 25-year-old star Sandy Mayer and 23-year-old Vitas Gerulaitis swapped cities in a straight deal with the Gaters. In "a deal of convenience," Mayer, two-time male MVP and a proven team tennis dynamo who'd just built a house in the Bay Area, was traded for the box-office potential of the Brooklyn-bred "Lithuanian Lion" (462-461 in four WTT seasons). At the press conference, new team publicist Marty Appel (Yankees historian of 18 books) stood on the podium next to Sol and new GM Ella Musolino to announce Vitas' one-year $200,000 contract with the two-time champions.

Vitas was a rock star by the time he joined the Apples, and Berg acknowledged that they traded for his New York roots and Big Apple flair, hoping the deal would translate into ticket sales, with his team now team playing all 22 home matches at the Garden. MSG president Mike Burke said the free-swinging Gerulaitis had the "chemistry of stardom." Sol swooned: "Vitas is a product of New York. Joe Namath was transplanted, so are Tom Seaver and Reggie Jackson. His flamboyant lifestyle and personality earned him the undisputed title of New York's first homegrown Broadway Joe."

Gerulaitis grew up idolizing such sports heroes but said, "I don't think anyone is gonna replace Namath or [Knicks star Walt] Frazier. I'm my own person with my own style of living." He also joked, "I told the Apples to reserve number 54 for me," referring to his off-court reputation at Studio 54, Le Club, and Regine's. Asked of winning a WTT title, Gerulaitis joked: "I'd trade one of my cars in for it" (at his LI mansion with a racquet-shaped pool sat two Rolls-Royces, a Mercedes, a Porsche, a Cadillac, and a Lamborghini). He also quipped: "If I did as well on-court as I did off the court, I'd be #1 by now."

Unlike most of his peers, Vitas learned the game on lower-middle-class concrete playgrounds. He announced plans to host a fundraiser at Studio 54, and to run clinics promoting the sport to urban youth as national director of Pepsi's Mobile Tennis drive. He said: "I know what tennis has given me and I want to give that back. I'm trying to stimulate any interest I can get for city kids." Gerulaitis laughed about his *People* feature titled "Vitas Gerulaitis Is Known As a Hustling Tennis Player—But Is it on the Court or at Studio 54?" Gerulaitis also responded to John Newcombe's *Sports Illustrated* piece referencing his recreational drug use: "There were a few misquotes in the article."

> ## "If you don't have team spirit, you don't win in this league. We have enough talent to win the whole thing."
>
> **—FRED STOLLE, New York Apples, 1978**

One month before the 1978 season opener, the Apples re-signed Fred Stolle—after his second straight year as WTT's outstanding coach. They also signed Mary Carillo, a 21-year-old local star who won the 1977 French Open mixed doubles championship with her Douglaston, Queens neighbor John McEnroe.

The club sent some of their seasoned samples to the Bay Area with Mayer and Wade traded to the Gaters. For 1978, the Apples were ripe for the picking with critical injuries and roster changes. For the two-time champions to three-peat, they'd have to face heavy competition.

Former Sea-Port Cascade JoAnne Russell's lethal serves led the Apples in their 1978 opener on April 21 over the expansion Anaheim Oranges 28-25; New York won the first two sets, but then eased up. Home-baked banners hung from MSG's balcony with slogans like "Vitas To Lead Us" or "Sock It To 'Em, Solly" denoted an artificial enthusiasm.

A crucial factor in the Apples' drive for a third title was whether Vitas Gerulaitis was serious about WTT, or if it was just a cozy payday? The question surfaced April 25, after the Nets' 25-18 romp over the Apples at MSG. With NY up 14-13, Rhodesian Andy Pattison blasted Gerulaitis 6-3. The Apples had shredded the Nets in 18 of 21 previous matches.

April 27, at halftime of the New York-Indiana match, the Apples rewarded 12 ticket holders by giving them a racquet, and a chance to return serves by an array of Apples, of which only one fan succeeded. The Apples won all five sets, 31-19. The team also declared Mary Carillo out for the season with knee surgery. Sol Berg slammed: "When all was said and done, that money got wasted."

Just seven games into the season, the Apples played the Loves four times and won all four. On May 5, New York won 31-25 in OT, in their fifth straight over Indiana. The Loves prevailed in men's singles when Gerulaitis got assessed two penalty points for arguing line calls, handing a 7-6 victory to his ex-Loves teammate Allan Stone. The Apples won a

Billie Jean King, New York Apples, wire photo, 1978
The Apples failed to three-peat as WTT champions after her heel injury

wild 25-24 game on July 31 over the Lobsters at Cape Cod Coliseum in South Yarmouth, MA. Next came home losses to Seattle August 1, Boston August 3, and San Diego August 5.

"The injuries and absences have been ridiculous. When we eventually get a team together, then we can win."

—RAY RUFFELS, New York Apples, 1978

King was trying to regain form after a heel injury. JoAnne Russell was doing crossword puzzles. Gerulaitis was griping about the fans. Ray Ruffels lost his cool. And New York kept losing. August 8, after a series of home losses, the Apples lost their fifth in a row, falling to the Cascades in Seattle, 24-23. At the end of the game, Ruffels throttled the hometown official scorer by the neck. Stolle said: "That was dumb for a Cascade employee to trash-talk us while the teams were playing." Seeking a four-letter answer to her crossword clue, "Wimbledon champion, 1977," Russell—blanked 6-0 by 110-pound Marita Redondo, and last seen storming off the court—correctly wrote "Borg," the Swede who bowed out of WTT after one year.

The Apples profited August 9 from L.A. Strings player-coach Ilie Năstase's war with WTT officials over his obscene gestures. Năstase got penalized one point for his extended middle digit toward the head umpire and then refused to continue against Gerulaitis, who got awarded a 6-3 win in the Apples' 26-23 victory. After losing their final two games of 1978, August 11 in Oakland and August 12 in Phoenix, New York finished the season 22-22, mediocre enough to secure a playoff birth against third-place Anaheim.

August 15, the Apples obliterated the Oranges 29-16 in the opening game of their first-round playoff series at Felt Forum. Gerulaitis played brilliantly, pasting Mark Cox, and then with Ruffels subdued Cox and Anaheim player-coach Cliff Drysdale, both by 6-1. Two nights later, New York swept the series with a 27-24 win at Anaheim Convention Center. August 22, the defending champions began an inter-division semifinal against the L.A. Strings, losing 28-20. Game One, seen by 3,483 fans at the Felt Forum, was marred by Năstase's ejection for foul language and obscene gestures, losing again to Gerulaitis, 6-3. August at the L.A. Forum, the Apples got dethroned 26-22, as the New York operation ended abruptly.

On October 26, Sol Berg told his staff he was suspending operations after losing nearly $1 million per year since 1974. The last straw was learning that no major stars had signed to WTT for 1979. Sol loved his Apples and all the exposure, but he felt the league had not kept up. He assured that he'd make good on his debts, and his staff received full severance pay.

All that remained of the Apples was a receptionist. The owner told his workers that the league would announce the team's demise—but commissioner Butch Buchholz insisted that New York had not dropped out and "we have received no notification in this matter." A rumor floated that the Apples' departure was to prompt the rest of the league to intensify efforts to sign name netters, but WTT officials rejected that claim. "Sol would not fire his front office staff to light a fire under anybody," said one unnamed source. But all indications showed that 1978 stars Evert, Navratilova, Gerulaitis, Wade, and King planned to forgo WTT participation.

Chapter 16

Boston Lobsters

Martina Navratilova, Boston Lobsters press photo, 1977

"I think the fans enjoy WTT because it's like a prizefight. If there's a knockout in the first round or one fighter is crippled, and you know the outcome, it's not as good."
—JANET NEWBERRY, Boston Lobsters, 1974

The Boston Lobsters began in 1973 with well-known local Volvo dealer Ray Ciccolo. He chose the tasty crustacean name from scores of contest entries. Then he scheduled 22 home games at Boston U.'s Walter Brown Arena, a 3,806-seat skating pavilion home to B.U.'s vaunted ice hockey program.

At a December 17, 1973 press conference, the team introduced top draft choice Kerry "Pixie" Melville of Australia, one of "The Original 9" that launched the Virginia Slims women's tour. Days earlier, the team had picked among their 20 choices Yugoslavian Wimbledon semifinalist Nikola "Niki" Pilić, Americans Sharon Walsh, Chris Evert's kid sister Jeanne Evert, Paul Gerken, and Pat Bostrom, and Romanian Ion Ţiriac. Ciccolo announced that Arnie Brown, teaching professional at Tennis Now in Watertown, MA, would become the team's head coach, but a deal never panned out.

For four months, the Lobsters lived on paper. Draft lists. Dotted-line contracts. Airline tickets. Hotel reservations. Plus reams and reams of red-and-black stationery. On April 23, Boston traded cantankerous Pilić to the New York Sets for Brit star Roger Taylor. Ciccolo stated: "Strong players forming a cohesive and cooperative team is an obvious hurdle—which is where the Pilić trade comes in."

The move left the team with dashing left-hander Taylor, voted man with the best legs on the WCT tour, Janet "Strawberry" Newberry, a 5'7" blonde Slims star schooled on California's hardcourts, and Grover "Raz" Reid, king of the Spartanburg (SC) Invitational. They were joined by Pat "Trish" Bostrom, a Phi Beta Kappa star at the University of Washington, and National Indoor Amateur titlist Andrea Voikos of Pawtucket, RI.

Player-coach Ion "The Count" Țiriac—a 6'2" 220-pound former Romanian Olympic hockey star drafted in 1965 by the NHL Philadelphia Flyers turned national tennis legend that mentored Ilie Năstase (and later Boris Becker)—led the Lobsters. During Țiriac's job interview, GM John Korff bet him $100 that he couldn't eat a wine glass; Țiriac chewed twice and got the position.

> **"Ion Țiriac was 'The Wild Hungarian.' He'd say to me, 'Trish, the first shot you hit, hit right at the woman. I don't care if we win the point.' It was to intimidate them. So, the first return I'd hit as hard as I could at them. And sure enough, she'd be a step behind after that. He was a forceful coach."**
> **—TRISH BOSTROM, Boston Lobsters, 2012**

Ray Ciccolo spoke of WTT reclaiming Tinseltown glitter glory. "It's like putting together a Broadway show," he offered. Since their inception, the Lobsters sold a reported 1,000 season tickets and signed a TV deal with Boston's Channel 38 ("The Lobster Station") to air 20 home matches. Ciccolo chimed: "We're a colorful team, and should attract a strong following because we have altered the game to serve the fan."

May 8, the Lobsters debuted in Philadelphia, in front of just 1,396 fans at the 18,000-seat Spectrum, losing 33-25. Billie Jean King's Freedoms won four of the night's five events—of note gangly 19-year-old Buster Mottram blanked his heavily favored countryman Roger Taylor, 6-0.

The Lobsters played their first home match May 9 before 3,574 fans at Walter Brown Arena, where they laid it on the Hawaii Leis, 33-25. A Dixieland band jammed between sets, but not between points. The Lobsters' mascot, a six-foot dude in a red cloth lobster suit with a racquet in one claw and pink pantyhose under the tail, flapped his claws after points. A halftime contest allowed fans to serve balls with a 38" racquet to hit a "Lobster Trap" (built by John Foley of North Shore Tennis Club). One hit won Lobsters tickets; two won tickets plus lobster dinners; three, all of the above plus two racquets; four, a weekend at Boston's Sonesta Hotel, while five won a Honolulu trip for a Leis rematch.

May 17, before a scant Nassau Coliseum crowd of 1,181, the Lobsters roasted the Sets 31-28. The match was also the NY debut of Niki Pilić, who returned from Davis Cup to pound his ex-team, and his replacement Roger Taylor, 6-2. May 22, Boston won every set as the Chicago Aces folded in a 25-16 laugher on Family Night at Brown Arena.

On May 29, Ţiriac led his Lobsters off the court after a disputed call by referee Kurt Wallach and forfeited their match in Miami to the Florida Flamingos, 23-20. With the score tied 20-all, neither the linesman nor Wallach saw Ţiriac's serve. So the referee ruled the point replayed. Ţiriac protested in vain, zipped up his racquet cover, and stormed off. Boston didn't return within five minutes, resulting in WTT's first forfeit.

GM John Korff filed a protest with commissioner George MacCall and chief umpire Scotty Deeds. The penalty for forfeit could've been as much as $5,000. Ţiriac said: "Due to my play in World Team Tennis, I've been banned from European tournaments, banned from playing Davis Cup, and banned by my own Romanian Tennis Foundation. I break my back for my team, we all fight together, and this is what we get—this is not tennis."

> ## "Tennis players are not team-oriented. There are jealousy and egos involved. As for the fans, some nights I don't hear the shouting. Other nights, all the noise is irritating—particularly at away games when the crowds are hostile."
> —ROGER TAYLOR, Boston Lobsters, 1974

Though aggravated, Ţiriac remained a colorful character—he assailed a Boston sports reporter: "Hey midget, why are you writing trash about me? I'm gonna bite off one of your fingers, chew it up into pieces, and spit it into the Charles River." Days later, he stunned his squad during a pre-match pep talk, grabbing a live lobster out of an aquarium tank and munching on it.

Boston markedly improved after Wimbledon. June 12, in front of 2,328 fans at Brown Arena, they won their fifth straight, garroting the Gaters 30-18. July 10, the Lobsters won all but one set, trampling the Buckskins in Minnesota 28-16. July 14, Ţiriac set the lineups for their home match with the Royals before leaving for Logan Airport to fulfill Davis Cup duties after Romanian officials decided to ignore his ban for playing WTT. But Roger Taylor, Ţiriac's player-coach stand-in, had difficulty with the dual tasks, losing to fellow player-coach Tom Okker, 6-3, as Toronto-Buffalo beaned Boston, 27-24.

Amid a late July swoon—connected to Janet Newberry's stress fractures in both legs—the Lobsters boiled in turmoil, having trouble coexisting and playing tennis. July 20, in their only win, they still lost four out of five sets in a 24-20 victory before just 930 fans at L.A. Sports Arena. The Lobsters became crabs: snapping among themselves. Ţiriac vowed: "I'm finding out what's wrong. I must suck out all I can from my Lobsters."

Ownership grew so desperate that GM John Korff hired college students to bring three busloads of institutionalized mental patients to a July 24 Lobsters-Leis match. Earlier that day, Ciccolo met with Hartford business people interested in hosting games in 1975. Ray said, "While we're open to the possibilities, under all circumstances, the franchise identifies with the city of Boston." He also said to expect a verdict on the team's future.

The Lobsters finished 1974 a mediocre 19-25 (.432). They missed the playoffs by one game, so that Miami forfeit stung. In advance of the 1975 draft, Boston dropped Andrea Voikos from their roster and Jeanne Evert from its protected list. John Korff pointed to Voikos' lack of court time and said Evert didn't fit Boston's plans.

During February 1, 1975's owners' meetings, Boston and four other franchises got voted out for not securing $50,000 letters of credit. Ciccolo got granted a seven-day stay to find capital from four investment blocs; one included Boston Bruins legend Phil Esposito. Ciccolo explained: "I've met with all four, and they've all been very interested. It's time for them to fish or cut bait. Their only concern was whether WTT was solvent."

Korff expressed optimism about cutting a deal to save the Lobsters, which lost well over a half-million dollars in 1974, despite averaging 2,200 fans, and having a decent TV deal. Korff said the way it would work was, once funding got secured, he would contact Larry King, who'd fly to Boston to assess the investors, so any statement of a Lobsters rebirth would come within a week. But they had to beat the clock.

February 12, in a convoluted move, Ciccolo stepped aside, as one of the four interested ownerships, consisting of eight Boston business people, met with the folding Philadelphia Freedoms to buy the shell of the franchise which traded Billie Jean, and make that a reconstituted Boston Lobsters. Philadelphia owner Dick Butera, who lost $800,000 on one season of WTT, said of his team's likely move to Boston: "Time is running out."

The group, pared to five partners, pitched a proposal to the other owners at March 12 league meetings in Pittsburgh. *The Boston Globe* mused: "In past weeks, the Lobsters have died more times than the Cambodian army. So often has WTT been pronounced out of breath, cash, and franchise that I hesitate to throw another briquette on the funeral pyre—or raise the hopes of you screaming team tennis fans."

The sale got approved March 18, but for a short time after that, they couldn't be called the "Lobsters," so temporarily they were "the Lobs." Newton, MA realtor Paul Slater was named chairman, and Somerville meatpacker Bob Mades became team president. Mades, who bought 1974 Lobsters season tickets, and then bought the team through his "tennis nut" wife Marilyn's urging, understood that his main job was to avert repeating Ray Ciccolo's losses. He said: "At this point, we've got more questions than answers: I'm talking about the roster, sites, dates, ticket prices, and advertising schedules." The franchise's other owners were Newton meatpacker Harold Bayne, Brookline jeans distributor Herbert Hoffman, and Brookline product packager Robert Kraft.

Korff later said Butera "planned to sell the club to them on February 12. But Elton John came out that month with 'Philadelphia Freedom' dedicated to Billie—so that upped the ante. More than that, he didn't want to sell due to the pleasure he derived from owning it." Butera finally sold his Freedoms—recouping some losses, and reviving the drowning Lobsters.

> **"With a married couple on the team, we save on expenses. They room together, and we furnish one car."**
>
> **—JON KORFF, Boston Lobsters GM, 1975**

Kerry Melville, Boston Lobsters, 1974

Boston Lobsters mascot, with pincers and tennis racquet, takes the court, 1974

On April 8, Bob Mades announced the 1975 return of 36-year-old player-coach Țiriac, and he re-introduced Kerry Melville, shipped to Philly in the Billie Jean King trade. Days later, Boston reunited Kerry with her fiancé, purchasing Raz Reid's contract from Indiana.

Melville and Reid got married on April 27 in Greenville, SC, becoming the first pro sports teammates to tie the knot. The unlikely pair never met until sharing adjoining Lobsters lockers and found bliss in each other's claws. *Sports Illustrated* (8/5/74) covered the Lobsters' first season and wrote of Melville snuggled in Reid's lap the entire flight to Honolulu. Melville sewed her wedding dress. The couple later held a ceremony with Lobsters teammates on the home court at halftime—days after a ring service in Robert Kraft's family living room.

Other Lobsters came and left: Taylor to Hawaii, Newberry to Phoenix, and Bostrom to Indiana. In came South African former Buckskin Bob Hewitt, Aussie Wendy Turnbull of the Nets, Californian Val Ziegenfuss of the Leis, and teen Boer, Greer "Cat" Stevens. The players resided at Windsor Village in Waltham—the place Melville and Reid fell in love.

The Lobsters started the season slowly in 1975. Boston bashed the Leis 29-27 on May 27 in Honolulu, posting their second victory in 13 matches. The Lobsters played without Bob Hewitt or Kerry Melville-Reid; Hewitt needed a rest after losing his first six games. Then, with Wendy Turnbull injured, Boston activated 18-year-old Quincy native Sally Rickson (later Sally Goodman), daughter of local 1950s netter Dr. Ken Rickson.

A strange altercation occurred during a June 13 road loss to the Triangles, 27-21—anger arose after Hewitt-Țiriac lost to Mark Cox-Kim Warwick 7-6. Hewitt charged at the Pittsburgh bench and went after coach Vic Edwards, warning him that if Warwick didn't settle down, "he's gonna get himself killed." Warwick said he had no idea what Hewitt meant, and neither did Edwards. Whatever it meant, it didn't affect the outcome.

> ## "The way Raz Reid is playing, I think he should adopt his wife's name and become Raz Melville. Something might rub off."
> **—ION ȚIRIAC, Boston Lobsters player-coach, 1975**

Bill Drake of West Concord, MA—the #1 player in New England and a 1974 Lobsters fan—joined toward the end of the 1975 season, and impressed despite limited action. July 20, he and Greer Stevens combined for a 6-2 gem over Brigitte Cuypers-Ashok Amritraj, but the Lobsters lost to San Diego, 26-21 before just 1,029 fans at Walter Brown Arena. August 3, in their home finale in front of 2,042, Boston exacted a form of revenge, frying the Friars 29-19, led by Turnbull-Drake. The Lobsters (20-24) finished 1975 in third place, 17 games behind first-place New York, and yet they backed into the last playoff spot.

The high-flying New York Sets (35-9) crushed the Lobsters seven times during the regular season, so when they were to meet in a one-game playoff on August 17 at Nassau Coliseum, the outcome seemed inevitable. But this time, the Lobsters edged the Sets 25-24, as seen by a reported 1,025 Long Islanders in stunned disbelief. A bitter Billie Jean King avowed afterward: "The Boston Lobsters will not beat us once in 1976."

But the Lobsters' season ended swiftly, swept in a best-of-three semifinal by the to-be-champion Triangles: 25-16 on August 18 in front of 912 home fans, and August 19, 23-14 before 2,803 in Pittsburgh. After the season, Țiriac-Hewitt ranked #2 in WTT men's doubles, and Greer Stevens was awarded 1975 Female Rookie of the Year.

For 1976, GM John Korff left for a Harvard Business School MBA program but stayed on as a consultant. Țiriac and Kerry Reid returned, joined by Waco-bred Mike Estep of the 1974 Royals, Pam Teeguarden of the 1974 Sets, and #1 pick John Alexander—the 24-year-old Aussie ranked 11th in the world—who played half of 1974 with the Strings. The Lobsters also signed a deal with West Coast surfwear kings Hang Ten to produce uniforms and warm-ups, in one of the first merchandise deals of its kind.

The 1976 Lobsters got off on the wrong foot (claw?) but improved over time. May 6, Ion Țiriac was irate—about losing at home to the Strings, 25-23, and over Kraft screaming at him about his lineups and on-court decisions. May 8, Alexander and Țiriac led the Lobsters over the Loves in Indiana's home opener 26-24. May 17, the Lobsters bashed the defending champion Triangles 31-26, in Pittsburgh's first of two local visits.

1976 would be Boston's worst-ever season at 18-25, last place in the East, behind lowly Cleveland and Indiana. But ownership took solace in the fact that attendance purportedly doubled that of 1975, to 2,690 per match. The Lobsters made late-season headlines with rumors of their impending signing of 19-year-old Czech defector Martina Navratilova for the rest of the season—but the deal imploded when Nets owner Joe Zingale offered her three years. After the season, the team parted ways with Alexander, Țiriac, and the Reids.

> ## *"We have a big winner and a real star in Martina. If we can't draw under these conditions, then it will tell me I'm not in the right business, or that we should move to another city."*
> **—ROBERT KRAFT, Boston Lobsters owner, 1977**

November 15, the Lobsters introduced Roy Emerson as 1977 player-coach. The young oldster at 39—a titleholder in every "Big Four" singles and doubles crown at least once—Emerson said he planned to retain the Stevens-Estep mixed doubles duo and revamp the rest of the roster. Robert Kraft admitted, "We can't hold him to his promise to put the Lobsters into the playoffs unless we give him a free hand." Emerson got introduced by new GM J.W. Wilson, a promoter at the Hazel Wightman Tennis Center in Weston, hired after Robert Gilbertson left to run Portland, Maine's WGAN-TV. Weeks earlier, Kraft bought out three others to become the majority owner with one partner, Robert Morse.

April 28, 1977, Kraft announced "the most important thing that's ever happened to the Lobsters." His WTT entry had finally acquired the world's #2 ranked woman, Martina Navratilova, in a trade involving Wendy Turnbull, $50,000, and breaking Navratilova's contract with the Nets. "She didn't like Cleveland; there wasn't a heckuva lot I could do about it," her team owner Joe Zingale admitted. "She refused to play here. I could've made her play, but it would've been disruptive and not good for the franchise."

Above: Ion "The Count" Țiriac, Boston Lobsters player-coach from Transylvania, 1974
Below: Boston Lobsters season schedule, 1977

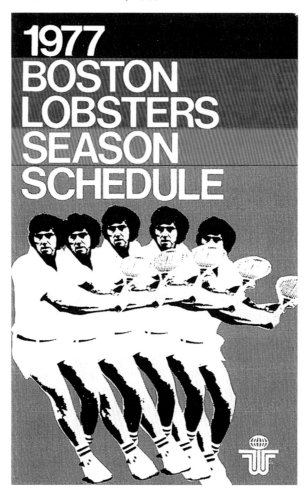

May 5, the Lobsters won their 1977 home opener at Brown Arena over the Sea-Port Cascades (formerly the Hawaii Leis) 27-23. Boston presented an upgraded roster, with player-coach Emerson, Mike Estep, Greer Stevens, Aussie southpaw Tony Roche, Romanian diva Virginia Ruzici, joined by the Czech Navratilova. The next night, in a bona fide blowout before 2,022 fans at B.U., the Lobsters crushed the Strings, 30-12.

Navratilova had much to prove on May 25 against her nemesis Joe Zingale's rebranded Cleveland-Pittsburgh Nets. Just three hundred people at Pittsburgh's Civic Arena saw Navratilova annihilate in singles 6-1, and then in women's doubles with Greer Stevens 6-2, as the Eastern-leading Lobsters won 27-11. "I guess you can't say there was much atmosphere here tonight," said Roche. Navratilova leaned against her locker, cradling her racquet, and said: "Tonight's crowd was the smallest we've seen, and the smallest I've played to by far."

June 7, in their final match before midseason, Navratilova-Stevens bested Betty Stöve-Trish Bostrom 6-3, as the Lobsters scaled the Cascades 30-14, before eight hundred onlookers in Portland. June 11 at Oakland Arena, Boston edged the Gaters 25-24 in a seesaw battle that went down to the last service, as the Lobsters improved at midseason to 18-4.

Navratilova credited her start to weight loss. The Czech gained 20 pounds in her two years in America. She said: "I cut down portions. But I still adore the American hamburger." Or as her previous team's owner Zingale bluntly put it, "Martina's handicap was her weight—the 20-pound brick she was carrying around with her."

When WTT action resumed July 5, the Lobsters rejected the Loves 29-16. Navratilova-Stevens won their 21st straight set, equaling a league mark set by the 1974 Freedoms duo of Billie Jean King-Julie Anthony. Before the match, the Lobsters cut high-strung Virginia Ruzici, who could not get along with fellow Eastern Bloc diva Navratilova. Kraft insisted that the split with Ruzici was on "the best of terms." In her place as a benchwarmer for WTT's top team, they signed Sweden's Marie "Mimmi" Wikstedt, ranked #7 in the world.

July 19, the red-hot Lobsters crushed the visiting Cascades 27-20. Mike Estep celebrated his 28th birthday with a set-point ace over Cascades player-coach Tom Gorman. Halftime offered an exhibition pitting Navratilova and Massachusetts Governor Mike Dukakis against Betty Stöve and Commerce Secretary John Marino. July 26 in Hartford —in front of 8,924, the largest home crowd for a Lobsters game— Boston overcame Phoenix 28-20, as Navratilova beat Chris Evert 6-4, and then teamed with Stevens to paste Evert-Stephanie Tolleson 6-2. July 31, the Lobsters shredded the Nets 27-15 in Cleveland to remain in a first-place lead ahead of New York in the Eastern Division, as Stevens-Estep blasted Björn Borg and fiancée Mariana Simionescu 6-4.

The Lobsters finished 1977 a league best 35-9 and opened their playoff drive August 16 against Borg's Nets. The Lobsters won the opener 30-26 at Brown Arena before the Nets kept the series alive the next night in Cleveland, 21-20. Game Three began on August 19 with Navratilova-Stevens blanking Simionescu-Peggy Michel 6-0, as the Lobsters celebrated on their home court to advance to the WTT semifinals, 28-21.

The Lobsters went to City Hall to honor their playoff push, and Boston Mayor Kevin H. White issued a proclamation affirming "our next great team" in front of owner Robert

Kraft. But perhaps the Lobsters counted their chickens before they hatched—they lost two straight nights to the Apples, and ending a soaring season with a thud. The scene was what one came to expect of 100-plus years of urban rivalry: the hollering from Manhattan's Felt Forum gallery, the knot of Boston fans tucked away in a corner, live mice sailing down, and a home-court playoff seed at stake.

"I think we've got one of the best teams in the league, and I mean T-E-A-M. We're tough."
—ROY EMERSON, Boston Lobsters player-coach, 1978

For 1978, the Lobsters promised improved tasty competition. GM J.W. Wilson and player-coach Roy Emerson prepared a squad that practiced at Northmeadow Tennis Club in Tewksbury and resided at the Howard Johnson's Motor Lodge in Cambridge. PR director Betsey Hickey provided the press with statistics and telecopiers at home games.

April 23, Boston opened defense of their Eastern Division title in Sacramento, beating Rosie Casals' Anaheim Oranges 30-24. May 24, the Lobsters blasted the Gaters 31-18 at Brown Arena. On June 8, in WTT's only Worcester game, they lashed the Loves, 30-16.

The best-laid plans of mice, men, and coaches went astray on June 17 when Fred Stolle, New York player-coach, made some poor personnel decisions that allowed the Lobsters to nip the Apples 28-26. July 12, the Lobsters acquired 19-year-old Trinity College star, Anne Smith; that night, her new team wrecked the Racquets 28-26. Emerson, Roche, and Navratilova played at the weekend's All-Star Match.

Recent Wimbledon champion Navratilova, traveling to Anaheim on July 18 with her toy poodle Racquet, blasted teen prodigy Tracy Austin 6-3, but the Oranges ultimately squeezed the Lobsters in a 26-25 super-tiebreaker. July 23, Boston beat Rod Laver's Friars, 32-36, in front of 3,005 San Diegans expecting a different result. Navratilova was home in Dallas with shoulder tendinitis (complicated by calcium deposits), so Anne Smith, in her first WTT singles match, defeated ex-Lobster Kerry Melville Reid 6-4. In Smith, the franchise knew they'd found a diamond in the rough. The next night, WTT's version of The Lou Gehrig Story unfolded a second chapter, as the Lobsters won with Terry Holladay doing what Navratilova did before her Wimbledon Shoulder. In front of 3,015 summering fans at Cape Cod Coliseum, Holladay's icy demeanor and violent shot-making helped the Lobsters roll 30-20.

Dale "The Animal" Collings was a burly 22-year-old Australian who lived and died by his lethal 130 mph serve. He made a huge impression in his short late-season stint with the Lobsters but then got sidelined by throat surgery. A young Lesley Visser wrote in *The Boston Globe* (8/3/78): "He has the body of a linebacker and looks like a rock star." Other late 1978 Lobsters included Ferdi Taygan, a 5'8" right-handed Turk from Worcester, Una Keyes, New England's #1 woman from Brookline, and Barbara Hunter-Estep, an NBC sportscaster married to Mike Estep, who did not get to play.

The Lobsters (33-11) finished 1978 favored to win it all. Boston dominated WTT with an 1187-999 (.543) overall winning percentage. Navratilova ranked #1 in women's singles (.644), as did her duo with Terry Holladay (.608). The hen play of Holladay (.544),

Martina Navratilova, Boston Lobsters press photo, 1978
Due to injuries, her anticipated finals battle vs. Chris Evert never materialized

Stevens (.566), and Smith (.507) outpaced cock Lobsters Roche (.527), Emerson (.526), and Estep (.508).

August 15, Boston began the 1978 playoffs against third-place New Orleans at Brown Arena, winning 28-23. The Nets had it all—black NBA star John Lucas, white South African Andrew Pattison, and transgender sports pioneer Renée Richards. But the Lobsters swept the series with another win August 19 in New Orleans 25-23. In the interdivisional semifinals, Boston faced Seattle, and swept the series, winning on August 22 by 30-27 at home, and August 24 by 27-22 on the road.

"I was dying just sitting there on the bench, watching this team lose. I had to play this series."
—MARTINA NAVRATILOVA, Boston Lobsters, 1978

Fans expected a WTT Finals world-class matchup between Navratilova (.644) vs. Evert (.614). But Navratilova remained injured the first two games, as Boston lost at home to L.A. 24-21 on September 13, and again 27-23 on September 16. On September 19, in the opening set of Game Three, Navratilova overcame Evert 7-5. Then in the third set, Roy Emerson paired Anne Smith with veteran Tony Roche, and tweaked the Strings' bickering Ann Kiyomura-Ilie Năstase, to lead the Lobsters to victory in a shocking super-tiebreaker, 27-26. The win kept the Lobsters' slim championship hopes alive. "It was the smartest thing he did all night," Smith joked of Emerson pulling her off the bench.

Had Navratilova not been hurt, Boston should've dominated the series. But the next night, L.A. won it all. Jibed *Boston Globe* writer Gil Peters: "If the Lobsters make a 1978 highlight film, they should entitle it, 'Injured Pride.'"

Robert Kraft held an October 23 press conference to deny reports that his team had disbanded. He declared, "Rumors circulating to the effect that the Boston franchise has ceased day-to-day operations are unfounded." But he conceded that operations could be "altered in 24 hours or the near future." Owners of the ten WTT teams met in Boston October 12-13, and Kraft said he left with questions about the league's viability.

Four days later, the Eastern Division champion Lobsters—with WTT's best record over the past two seasons—suspended all business activity. Kraft stated, "Based on the current attitude of other teams, and new pressures being put on top players by major tournament sponsors, we are not confident the quality level of player will be in the league next year."

Kraft's late wife Myra Kraft recalled when the Lobsters treated everyone like a family, when Țiriac and Navratilova were more than employees, and when the media felt part of the process. Reporters even got invited to parties at the Krafts' home in Chestnut Hill. Myra played an integral role with the team, although she didn't deal with trades and contracts. For instance, at one point, it became clear that male media couldn't have equal access to female players, and vice versa. Robert Kraft spoke to his wife, who ordered the players to come out to a room for all to interview.

Sixteen years later, Kraft applied his Lobsters knowledge to his next pro sports foray, the NFL New England Patriots.

Chapter 17

Los Angeles Strings

Ilie Năstase, Los Angeles Strings player-coach, 1978

Years of Operation: 1974-1978

Team Colors: Orange and yellow

Team Record: 1974: 16-28 (3rd place, Pacific Section)
1975: 20-24 (3rd place, Western Division)
1976: 22-22 (3rd place, Western Division)
1977: 11-33 (last place, Western Division)
1978: 27-17 (2nd place, Western Division)

Female MVP: Chris Evert 1978 (449-310, .590)

Male MVP: Ilie Năstase 1978 (408-320, .538)

Highlight: Owner Jerry Buss celebrates 1978 WTT championship (9/21/78)

Lowlight: Comedian Johnny Carson sells ownership stake (11/27/74)

Home Arenas: L.A. Sports Arena (capacity 14,795)
L.A. Forum (capacity 17,500)

Quote: "If you love tennis, the ultimate is to own a team."
—Jerry Buss, Strings owner (5/5/75)

"After reviewing all the alternatives, we are convinced that this is the best way to allow Southern California fans an opportunity to see world-class tennis."

—JERRY BUSS, Los Angeles Strings owner, 1975

When WTT launched in May 1973, it awarded one of the original franchises to the ownership group of WTT cofounders Dennis Murphy and Fred Barman, lawyer Jerry Fine, and realtor Dr. Jerry Buss. Due to the "ins" of Murphy and Barman, they also got a break on the $50,000 entry fee. To capitalize on L.A.'s star power, they brought in TV star/tennis buff Johnny Carson, who purchased Barman's minority partnership share in the L.A. Strings.

October 9th, the Strings signed top draft pick John Alexander of Australia. Marita Redondo, an 18-year-old from the San Diego suburb of National City, signed next, in a rags-to-riches tale for a Filipino-American girl from a family of nine children. Thanks to the Strings, she had a condo in Marina Del Rey with saunas, pools, underground parking, tennis courts, a new car, and an expense account.

April 15, Jerry Fine said that the Strings had acquired negotiation rights to Australian legend Rod Laver, in exchange for fellow Aussie Geoff Masters and Seal Beach, CA's Kathy Harter—a trade rescinded when Laver failed to come to terms. Laver laughed it all off: "They made me an offer I could afford to refuse." Fine also presented 1974's co-head coaches, Jon Douglas and Bob Harman. The unique set-up, intended to impart generational wisdom to the players, instead resulted in contradictory messaging and poorly delineated authority.

One day before May 8's season opener, the Strings signed 25-year-old juniors star John Fort to replace John Alexander, who missed the first three matches due to Davis Cup duties. So L.A.'s opening roster featured Fort, Masters, Redondo, Harter, former Wimbledon champ Karen Hantze Susman, and Santa Monica College's Jerry Van Linge. Midseason acquisitions included Frenchman Jean-Baptiste Chanfreau and South African Pat Cramer.

The Strings launched their WTT campaign on the home court of the Florida Flamingos in Miami Beach. Experts felt that sans Alexander, L.A. would get their strings snapped, which they did in a 27-26 loss. On May 10, Los Angeles, dazzling in yellow and orange, went cold on the road against the Minnesota Buckskins 35-22, as Owen Davidson tore apart John Fort, 6-1. The next night in Oakland, the Strings won their first-ever match by bashing the Golden Gaters, 33-27, fueled by Marita Redondo's 6-3 win over Lesley Hunt.

In a rematch of the past week's debut, WTT finally held its Opening Night in L.A. on May 15—and the reaction was uninhibited ambivalence. Of the 4,666 at Sports Arena to see the Strings bash Florida 34-33, 1,500 must've been dressed as empty seats. A team official admitted to many complimentary tickets, "but it wasn't a complete papering job." In true L.A. style, the women players sported midriff, and the linespeople sat in director's chairs. Before play, Johnny Carson did a monologue imploring fan support, and there was music by the USC marching band. Mike Waldon, in a blue batik suit and red leather shoes, introduced the rosters with the zeal of a boxing emcee. Dan Rowan (Rowan & Martin) was a season ticket holder, and advertised to play in a halftime exhibition, but never showed up.

> ## "If people are happy with the format of team tennis, they'll keep coming back. If not, we'll have to make changes or move on."
> —JOHN ALEXANDER, Los Angeles Strings, 1974

As the Strings reached the Wimbledon break, they made one last try to sign Rod Laver for the season's second half, before talks broke off. Of the Strings, only Alexander, Fort, and Masters qualified for Wimbledon. Susman spent the break relaxing with her husband, while Harter and Van Linge chilled at home. Redondo was on the path to stardom until a torrid midseason affair with married teammate J.B. Chanfreau resulted in her pregnancy.

The Strings finished 1974 at 16-28 (.364), third place in the four-team Pacific Section. They drew 1,750 per match and lost over $500,000. The stats reflected such on-court dysfunction: Marita Redondo ranked 13th (.491) in the 16 team loop; Harter-Susman #13 (.498); John Alexander rated #7 (.534) in singles, and #4 (.544) with Masters in doubles.

It was newsworthy that the Strings would extend their marketing radius with home four matches at Anaheim Convention Center, but GM Bart Christensen really made waves when he announced that Florida-bred Chris Evert was interested in joining the Strings. But when her talks with Jerry Buss reached an impasse, L.A. signed California girl Rosie Casals. The 1975 Strings roster featured Harter and Masters, plus Casals (ex-Loves), Betty Ann Grubb-Stuart (Flamingos), Ross Case (Leis), Mike Machette (Friars), and UCLA star Bob Lutz. African-American netter Delroy Reid made the team, but he never played. The Strings failed to sign any of their draftees: Jeff Borowiak, Madeleine Pegel, Mal Anderson, Dean Martin, Jr., or joke pick Johnny Carson—who sold his ownership share to Buss after losing 80% of his principal.

L.A. upped their game in 1975. June 12, Casals won 6-2, and with Stuart won 6-3 in a road victory over Cleveland, 26-22. July 11, Casals led her squad over visiting Hawaii, 28-17, in front of 3,122, as she roasted Margaret Court 6-2. August 12, Casals-Lutz crushed in a dramatic 7-6 final-set super-tiebreaker, to pull the Strings over S.D. 22-21.

The Strings finished the 1975 season 19-24 (.455) and qualified for a one-game playoff against the Racquets. On August 17, L.A. got lashed on the road, 20-8, to end their season. Statistically, Rosie Casals impressed as WTT's #3 woman behind Billie Jean King and Evonne Goolagong. But their men's game bombed: In a ten-team 1975 league, Geoff Masters ranked #19 in singles and Case-Bob Lutz #13 in doubles.

"We are never home for more than a day or so. Some of the players haven't had a chance to move into their apartments in L.A. It's a bit disappointing."
—ROSIE CASALS, Los Angeles Strings, 1975

January 21, 1976, the Strings, having failed in their pursuit of Rod Laver, acquired the rights to another Aussie star, John Newcombe, who spent the 1974 season with Houston, and 1975 with Hawaii. Buss felt "confident Newcombe would sign for the 1976 season" and would "100% recover" from a knee injury. But Newcombe never recovered or joined L.A.

February 10, the Strings signed player-coach Dennis Ralston, one of the top American players of the '60s. The 33-year-old Bakersfield-bred USC star, a Wimbledon doubles champion at 17 and Davis Cup captain, slowed by injuries, served as player-coach of the 1974 Leis and 1975 Friars. Strings publicist, former *Los Angeles Times* reporter Pete Donovan, expressed confidence that the team, now playing at the 11,250-capacity L.A. Forum in Inglewood, would break out of the red and into the black, stating: "We sold only 250 season tickets last season. We feel this year we have a chance of selling 2,000."

On March 19, Christensen announced that Rosie Casals and Bob Lutz re-signed for 1976, joining #1 pick 20-year-old Aussie southpaw Dianne Fromholtz, and India's Vijay Amritraj, acquired from the Friars for Ross Case. The Strings had amassed legitimate talent—unlike the dark days of 1974, with Jean-Baptiste Chantreau and Jerry Van Linge.

At May 1's opener, L.A. toppled the Gaters 22-19, as Fromholtz led the way, belting Françoise Dürr 6-2. May 23, Rosie and Vijay clinched the match with a 6-4 win, as the Strings edged the Friars 25-23, before 3,207 at the Forum. The next night's rematch, Dianne beat Terry Holladay, 6-2, as the ascending Strings won their fourth straight game.

To start the season's second half, the Strings signed Charles Pasarell, who'd just made waves at Wimbledon by pasting Adriano Panatta to reach the quarterfinals. Pasarell, a 32-year-old native of Puerto Rico—a 1966 NCAA champion at UCLA, and a four-time U.S. Davis Cupper—was the #5 men's player in the nation. On July 20 in Boston, Charlie dropped in his Strings debut, with Bob Lutz losing 6-4 in a 25-24 defeat to the Lobsters. Fromholtz and Lutz left after the match to represent the West in the 1976 All-Star Match.

July 28 at the L.A. Forum, 6,237 fans saw the Strings upset Billie Jean King's Sets 28-23, fueled by Casals-Fromholtz in women's doubles, Lutz-Ralston in men's, and Casals-Ralston in mixed. July 30, Lutz led L.A. to a lathering over Ilie Năstase's Hawaii Leis, 32-22. "I tried to make him commit errors," Lutz said of his 6-2 razing of the Romanian. Fromholtz topped Aussie mate Nancy Gunter 6-4, and then in mixed doubles, Casals-Ralston outdueled Margaret Court-Owen Davidson 6-3.

The Strings' 1976 season ended on an up note. An August 13 Forum crowd of 7,425 saw Lutz again overpower Năstase, as L.A. clipped the Leis, 29-23. The Strings missed the playoffs, finishing third with 22-22. But turnout soared, with 4,624 per match.

"You don't have a great team without a superstar. I'm dedicated to getting one because I'm tired of losing."

—JERRY BUSS, 1976

For 1977, the Strings tried to woo Jimmy Connors with a $200,000 per year offer. Jerry Buss affirmed, "We want Jimmy Connors and want him badly, and we'll take him under almost any circumstances. I can't say that he has a blank check because I could ruin WTT with that. But I'm willing to pay him 50-100 percent more than any player in the league." It wasn't the first time Buss pursued Connors. Once, in Palm Springs, the two were chatting. Jerry pulled the keys to his Maserati and said, "You like it, Jimmy? Just sign." Another time, Buss offered five years, $1 million, but received no response.

The Strings went into the season with great optimism. Buss said his team lost $750,000 in its first two years, but in 1976 he claimed to have nearly broken even by surpassing the 100,000-fan mark for the year. No WTT franchise was more lavishly run: Christensen had 12 full-time front-office employees. Veteran Lakers color man Lynn Shackelford became 1977's radio voice of the Strings for 35 games on KGIL-AM. Team trainer Bill "Duck" Norris brought to work a duckling named "William" or "Little Bill" that became the team mascot. Buss' 14-year-old daughter Jeanie sat in during board meetings.

Jerry Buss grew up in the Depression-era coal-mining town of Kemmerer, Wyoming, and by age 24, finished his doctorate in chemistry at USC. By age 30, he became a real estate tycoon with Frank Mariani after one of their first L.A. properties struck oil. Buss

Vijay Amritraj, Los Angeles Strings, 1977

1977 Los Angeles Strings, press photo before signing Ilie Năstase
Back L-R: Bill Norris (trainer), Charlie Pasarell, Ilie Năstase, Dennis Ralston
Front L-R: Rosie Casals, Julie Anthony, Valerie Ziegenfuss

claimed his '77 Strings were on target for 5,000 season tickets, and calculated a $946,000 gross over 22 home dates for a $200,000 profit—thus valuing his franchise at $4 million.

"Ilie Năstase's wife wanted to be in a metropolitan city because she likes to shop. I'm glad they didn't hit us up for a house in Malibu."
—BART CHRISTIANSEN, Los Angeles Strings GM, 1977

After rekindled Connors talks broke down for good, Buss turned his attention to Ilie Năstase. The fiery 30-year-old Bucharest native jumped at the offer of $1.5 million over six years, which included a house in Brentwood, and twin silver Corvettes for him and his wife, Dominique. Tennis' first European star to earn $1 million, "Nasty" joined a Ralston-coached squad featuring Casals, Fromholtz, Pasarell, and Texas star John Andrews. Năstase offered, "I like everything about L.A., especially the weather and the tennis crowds. It's a good place to play—everyone roots for the home team." But one question remained: was Hollywood ready for an award-winning performer the likes of Năstase?

The Strings signed Năstase knowing that he would miss the first two months of his first season in L.A., due to previous tournament commitments. In the Strings' April 28, 1977 opener at the San Diego Sports Arena, the Friars won four of five events, 31-24. May 12, L.A. lost their L.A. Forum opener to Indiana 29-27; Mark Cox, filling in for Năstase, made just $30,000 for his 44 Strings matches, but insisted he got overpaid to play his passion.

With both their seasons imploding, Buss of L.A. (1-12) and Mariani of S.D. (3-8) discussed a swap of rosters that would've left just Năstase with the Strings and Rod Laver with the Friars. There were also talks involving Pasarell and Ralston to Cleveland-Pittsburgh. Buss floated another trade: Casals for Gaters' star Françoise Dürr. But L.A. needed an instant upgrade, so as not to scare off Năstase and cause him to flee in exile.

On May 25, the Strings stumbled to their 11th straight defeat, bowing to the Gaters 30-21, before a Forum crowd of 3,175. May 27, the Friars humbled the Strings 27-20, as Laver rallied to rip Pasarell 7-5. June 2, the Strings lost their 14th in a row, 29-22, to the Loves in Anaheim—tying their 1974 WTT record of futility for consecutive losses.

"I eat the right food, train very hard, and I don't drink alcohol. If you knew me, you'd know how ambitious I am."
—DIANNE FROMHOLTZ, Los Angeles Strings, 1976

On June 3, the Strings traded 1976 All-Star Dianne Fromholtz to the Friars for Julie Anthony. Buss pressed for the trade to improve the team's woeful women's play, despite—or possibly due to—Fromholtz becoming his son Johnny's fiancée. Buss also said that both he and Ralston would attend Wimbledon to seek new talent.

The Strings took solace as they resumed play after the Wimbledon break, knowing they could only get better—and hoping that Năstase would be a plus, not a minus. Năstase, #4 in the world, would play singles and mixed doubles with Julie Anthony. July 4th's newspaper standings listed the Strings soundly out of tune with a WTT-worst 4-17 mark.

In a PR move, the Strings signed, for one game, pigtailed 13-year-old Orange County phenom Tracy Austin. In Austin's July 8 Forum debut, substituting for Casals, the Friars' Kerry Reid dominated 6-3, as the Strings fell 30-24. Rosie insisted she'd told trainer Bill Norris that morning she'd be okay to play after sitting out hurt the past night's match in Portland. She called the startling switch "an insult" to the team's regular women's roster.

July 17, the Strings repelled the Soviets for their fourth-straight win 31-30, as Casals-Anthony seized the final set of women's doubles, 7-6. July 20, that streak ended against Phoenix at the Forum, 28-23 after Chris Evert crushed Casals 6-1. Without Năstase—still playing Romanian Davis Cup and partying in Paris—L.A. (7-24) lost all playoff hopes.

Monday July 25, Năstase returned to the fold. He arrived at 6 p.m. and entered Fresno's Selland Arena by 6:45. Local promoter Al Geller, who enjoyed the biggest turnout by far of the four Gaters home matches there, said: "I'm just grateful he got here and I think the fans got their money's worth." That was debatable since in the men's singles set between Năstase and Tom Okker, Năstase protested an out call on the fourth serve of the first game (Okker later agreed it was a bad call). From that point on Năstase berated linesman Warren Worthimer. With Okker up 3-0, L.A. player-coach Dennis Ralston took off his warmups and replaced the Romanian. Among the catcalls was one Fresno fan screaming, "Go home, Năstase, you creep!" The Gaters won the match, 31-25.

The Strings ended their fourth season August 14 by obliterating the Sea-Port Cascades, 29-13, before 4,706 at the Forum, finishing 1977 a league-worst 11-33. The subpar on-court action resulted in a sizeable attendance drop of over 1,000 spectators per match.

> ### "Năstase was a mix of Mozart and Beethoven. He had extraordinary abilities. Eighty percent of the time, he was funny, and twenty percent he was gross. But as an entertainer, he was unique."
> #### —VIJAY AMRITRAJ, Los Angeles Strings, 1978

For 1978, Mr. Buss promised changes. He spent the off-season in search of a female star, pursuing a post-pregnancy Evonne Goolagong, before reeling in the big catch: Chris Evert of the Phoenix Racquets. Buss beamed at February 2's media event, as Evert called the signing "the best decision for my career," adding, "it was time to move to a bigger city, and L.A.'s a great sports town." Buss said he and her agent Bud Stanner hammered out a $1 million deal nearly identical to that of Năstase. Evert blushed in denial of rumors of her nuptials to Jimmy Connors. "Our situation is simple; we met when I was 17, and I'm 23 now. We've dated six years and never kept out of touch. We see each other and we see other people. I'm not selfish."

February 21, Bart Christensen announced that Vijay Amritraj, star of the 1976 Strings, would return for 1978. The GM said, "With Chris Evert and Ilie Năstase playing singles, and Amritraj teaming with Năstase in doubles, the Strings will be tough to beat." The team also signed Vijay's 20-year-old brother Ashok. The Amritrajes, with older brother Anand, played on India's 1974 Davis Cup squad that boycotted apartheid South Africa.

Two weeks before the April 24 opener, the GM stunned the tennis world by introducing Năstase as Strings player-coach. Naming Năstase coach was like letting an inmate run the asylum. "It really was his idea," Christiansen explained. Impressed by a roster with Chris Evert, Ann Kiyomura, Stephanie Tolleson, and the Amritrajes, Năstase said: "It's important the players play for the team and not just for themselves. I'm like a father and mother to the team." The Strings also announced they'd play 20 home games in the Forum with two in St. Louis. The move was part of a WTT charm offensive to engage teamless regions.

May 12, the Strings faced the Racquets in their third match of the year, and finally won 27-17. But the big news was WTT alums Jimmy Connors and Björn Borg, in town for a tournament, coming to see Năstase blast Butch Walts 6-4 in singles and then with Ann Kiyomura 6-1 over Dean Martin Jr.-Kris Kemmer Shaw. Evert defeated her old team, and her nemesis/former friend Shaw in singles, 6-2. The next night, Evert led her shiny new Strings over the expansion Anaheim Oranges at Anaheim Convention Center 32-28. By midseason, the Strings found themselves in a first-place battle with the Friars and Gaters.

Evert, in her first match since she lost in the Wimbledon final to Martina Navratilova, led a coach-less Strings to a July 12 comeback 28-26 win over the Nets in St. Louis. L.A. played sans Năstase, fined $15,000 for missing the match in violation of his deal, to play in a $300,000 invitational at Forest Hills. The G.M. attempted to clarify that the one game that Năstase missed "was technically allowed in his contract." Năstase said, "the press made a mistake," and his $15,000 fine was what he would've earned with the Strings—and that previously he'd worked it out to play for L.A. between Forest Hills round-robin games. Vijay Amritraj, in for Năstase, ousted Marty Riessen, 6-4. Năstase retorted, "I wish we could play the set here in New York and call in the score, and save us all a lot of time."

Năstase handed a win to Cascades player-coach Tom Gorman when the testy Romanian got tossed from his August 6 match for making obscene gestures toward an official, giving Gorman a 7-6 win and Seattle the 28-26 victory. Năstase got penalized one point after his first middle finger toward umpire Bill Ruhle. When he repeated the motion, another penalty point got assessed, and Năstase got ejected. The loss ended an eight-game win streak. August 11, Năstase, benefitting from unforced errors, beat Rod Laver, 6-1, as the Strings flayed the Friars 27-20, before a sellout crowd of 8,354 at San Diego Sports Arena. The next night, the Strings nipped the Gaters in OT, 26-23. Los Angeles (27-17) finished best in the West. Statistically, Evert (.614) ranked second behind Navratilova in singles; Năstase (.538) ranked Top 10 in singles, mixed and men's doubles.

"I don't cry much. But here I had to. It was one of my happiest moments."

—ANN KIYOMURA, Los Angeles Strings, 1978

Chris Evert, Los Angeles Strings, 1978

August 15, the Strings blasted the visiting Gaters in Game One of the opening round of the playoffs, 29-17. Two nights later in Oakland, Năstase won 7-5 in a super-tiebreaker to take the game, set, match, and series, 30-29. Despite the victory, Evert proved unable to end her Virginia Wade "jinx." "She just seems to get psyched up to play me," she said.

Evert played nearly perfectly in leading the Strings to a 28-20 win August 22 over the Apples, for a 1-0 lead in a best-of-three inter-division semifinal. The match, in front of 3,483 at Madison Square Garden, was marred by Năstase's ejection for foul language and obscene gestures. Năstase, who mildly protested some early calls, boiled over after losing to Vitas Gerulaitis 6-3. Umpire Ken Farrar warned Năstase twice before ejection. August 24 in L.A., the champion Apples got dethroned 26-22, as the Strings advanced to the finals.

Before the Strings took on the WTT-best Lobsters on September 13 in their best-of-five finals, it was evident that the focus would be an Evert-Navratilova showdown. But Navratilova reinjured her left shoulder and had to watch from the sidelines as Evert's Strings won two straight in Boston, before returning to L.A. with a chance to sweep.

Martina got cortisone shots and had calcium deposits removed before September 19's Game Three, won by the Lobsters in a gritty come-from-behind super-tiebreaker win at the Forum, 27-26, before a record turnout of 10,366. The Strings' squabbling Năstase-Kiyomura lost to underdogs Anne Smith-Tony Roche in the final set, 6-4. September 21's Game Four saw Evert's singles and doubles wins to pace the Strings 28-25 over the Lobsters, giving Jerry Buss' Strings the title over Robert Kraft's Lobsters, 3-1. The emotion that surged through the Forum crowd of 7,154—with the din of fans stomping and shouting—inspired Evert's 7-6 win over Navratilova, and Evert-Kiyomura over Smith-Navratilova 6-1.

> **"If you win a major tournament, your parents and your family can share the joy. But in team tennis you've got the team and the whole city — it makes a lot of people happy. And this brings me enjoyment."**
> **—CHRIS EVERT, Los Angeles Strings, 1978**

Jerry Buss shuttered his WTT champions despite an announced average crowd of 7,219 at the Forum and selling over 1,500 season tickets for 1979, after losing a reported $2.75 million over five seasons. "Events of the past weeks convince me that continuation in World Team Tennis is economically unsound." The announcement was significant because Buss and his business partners also owned the Loves, Friars, and a slice of the Oranges.

Jerry later said the millions he lost on the Strings educated him for pro sports with the NBA's L.A. Lakers. Asked if it was worth it, he said, "There are less expensive ways to get the same education. On the other hand, I know what it takes to run a franchise, and you don't get that inexpensively. Not sure what the appropriate tuition should've been."

Chapter 18

San Diego Friars

Rod Laver, San Diego Friars, 1976

Years of Operation: 1975-1978

Team Colors: Gold and brown

Team Record: 1975: 14-30 (last place, Western Division)
1976: 13-31 (4th place, Western Division)
1977: 21-23 (3rd place, Western Division)
1978: 30-14 (1st place, Western Division)

Female MVP: Mona Guerrant 1978 (301-202, .598)

Male MVP: Rod Laver 1976 (388-351, .524)

Highlight: Signing Aussie legend Rod Laver (1/15/76)

Lowlight: Losing 16 of their first 18 matches (1975)

Home Arena: San Diego Sports Arena (capacity 9,500)

Quote: "I don't mind somebody saying I'm over the hill, just as long as the hill's not too steep."
—Rod Laver (4/18/76)

"The Friars are a new team in a new and exciting league. The plan is to develop tennis enthusiasm in San Diego for the team, its players, and WTT as a whole."

—G. ALLAN KINGSTON, San Diego Friars GM, 1975

The first evidence of team tennis in San Diego came May 30, 1973, when orthodontist Dr. Leonard Bloom—the owner of the ABA's San Diego Conquistadors with player-coach Wilt Chamberlain—presented his WTT San Diego Swingers. Bloom saw his $50,000 franchise fee as "earnest money" and expected expenses far above that amount.

Dr. Bloom felt confident about his picks on August 3's first player draft. When a local reporter chastised him with an "are you serious?" Bloom yelled, "Of course I'm serious, why else would I be here?" But he could not sign Ilie Năstase, Linky Boshoff, Nancy Richey, Janice Metcalf, Charlie Pasarell, Kazuko Sawamatsu, Glynis Coles, Jaime Fillol, Jane Stratton, Peter Fleming, Balázs Taróczy, Sue Mappin or Pancho Segura. Six months before the 1974 season, Bloom sold his franchise to a Honolulu bloc for a tidy $300,000. That team became the Hawaii Leis.

As a payback to S.D.—but also in case the Philly Freedoms folded—WTT announced for 1975 the expansion San Diego Fliers, named for the "Birthplace of Naval Aviation." Soon after, they became the San Diego Friars, akin to baseball's

Padres, named for the city's founding missionaries. The ruin of 1974 left the 1975 season to begin as an uneven 11-team loop. So when Houston folded days before the opener, the decision looked solid.

Frank Mariani, Jerry Buss' real estate partner, who'd whetted his WTT appetite as an L.A. Strings minority owner, bought the Friars right before the season. It made sense, as he owned property in San Diego. Former Leis president G. Allan Kingston joined as GM.

Kingston brought with him ex-Leis player-coach Dennis Ralston to serve as tactician, psychologist, humorist, confidant, arbitrator, trainer, mind reader, counselor, and drill sergeant. His roster consisted of Indian brothers Ashok and Vijay Amritraj and 1974 Lei Mike Machette in men's play, and women Lesley Hunt (ex-Golden Gaters), Janet Young (Chicago Aces), Helen Gourlay (E-Z Riders) and Brigitte Cuypers (Leis). In their McDonald's-like gold and brown, the Friars provided weak ammo for WTT's big guns.

The Friars opened 1975 reeling with a 2-18 record as they flew to Pittsburgh on June 12, where they stunned the Triangles 26-23. An ugly incident occurred when "The G-Men," Vitas Gerulaitis' rooting section, taunted Lesley Hunt with hurtful lesbian slurs. In disgust, she whacked a ball into an empty press box. Later, the Perth native fired back: "They weren't very nice, were they?" Vijay Amritraj had different issues related to Friars' home matches in L.A. and Anaheim, both far from San Diego Sports Arena: "We don't have a home. We play 38 times on the road. We don't even go back to San Diego this season!"

On July 27, the last-place Friars wrecked the Racquets at Anaheim Convention Center, 24-20, led by Hunt 6-3 over Phoenix's Françoise Dürr. Other highlights of their lost first season included victories over the Strings, August 6 at L.A. Sports Arena 31-26, and on August 13 by a 26-25 decision in Anaheim.

The Friars finished 1975 a Western Division-worst 14-30 (.318) and drew just 22,274 for their 22 home matches. At times, it felt like linespeople, ball persons, and players outnumbered fans. Vijay Amritraj was the only Friar selected to the All-Star Match. Hunt carried her share, but no Friar rated Top 15 in any WTT category. Sixteen netters, six men and ten women, played for S.D. in '75—Bill Schoen, John Andrews, Sashi Menon, Marita Redondo, Jeff Cohen, Ken Stuart, and Francis Troil each scored under 50 points.

"I don't mind somebody saying I'm over the hill, just as long as the hill's not too steep."
—ROD LAVER, San Diego Friars, 1976

The Friars held a January 15, 1976 media event after signing Rod "Rocket" Laver to be "the highest-paid player in WTT history." The 5'8" 37-year-old left-handed Aussie, a four-time Wimbledon titlist and two-time grand slam winner, was one of pro sports' first millionaires. About his three-year, $200,000 per year pact, Kingston said, "Laver insures the Friars will be competitive, but he gives the entire league added status and appeal."

Laver joined Chris Evert, Martina Navratilova, and Ilie Năstase as the fourth major star to sign for WTT's third season. The 14-year pro, who admitted being out of shape and unfamiliar with WTT rules, told the gathering: "I played some of my best tennis last year.

I feel like a long way from being put in a coffin." Laver said he planned to sell his home in Corona Del Mar south of L.A. to live in Rancho Santa Fe, just north of San Diego. He also said he'd play all 44 games, starting May 4 at home versus the champion Triangles.

Two weeks later, the Friars signed Terry Holladay to power their women's game. S.D. women needed shoring up, with only Janet Young and Betty Ann Grubb Stuart (ex-Flamingos) in the lineup. Akin to 1975's draft letdown, the team failed to sign any of 1976's 12 picks. Before the opener, they traded the Amritraj brothers to L.A. for Ross Case (Leis) and Ann Haydon Jones (Buckskins); the latter traded back to the Strings two days later for Grubb Stuart. The 1976 roster also featured WTT veteran player-coach Cliff Drysdale.

> ### "I didn't think they'd build me up as a star the way they did. It was sort of a dream for the owner and the president of the team, I guess. I slowly lost my confidence."
> —TERRY HOLLADAY, San Diego Friars, 1976

May 13, the Loves humbled the Friars in Indianapolis for the second time in one week, 33-24. Rod Laver lost to Allan Stone, and then Laver-Case rocked Stone and Ray Ruffels, in 7-6 tiebreakers. Stuart-Holladay lost in the opening set to 1975 Wimbledon doubles champions Mona Guerrant-Ann Kiyomura 6-2, and Indiana never looked back. June 5, the Friars bashed the defending WTT champion Triangles before 3,968 at Pittsburgh Civic Arena, 28-26. Laver's handiwork reigned, stifling Vitas 6-2, and then with Case outlasting Gerulaitis-Bernie Mitton 7-5. Laver told the press afterward that the previous night in Phoenix an official's call "robbed" them: "It may not seem right saying this to you, but it's nice to win this one," implying his Friars were owed one.

Rod Laver pulled himself out of a July 6 match with the Nets, and it was not the first time. Laver excused himself on May 29, also citing personal reasons, when his Friars lost to the Gaters 32-28. This time the Friars fell to Cleveland 31-26 to drop to a midseason mark of 9-15. Cliff Drysdale dished gallows' humor: "Of course it matters to the team. But there is a positive side. It lets me get out there and see if I can still hit the ball."

In the second half of the season, 1976, Drysdale's team went a dismal 4-16. So despite Laver's Rookie of the Year honors (the oldest Rookie of the Year in pro sports history), these Friars finished one game out the cellar at 13-31 (above the 12-32 Hawaii Leis). While S.D.'s court play fell short of expectations, attendance allegedly tripled, to a reported 3,392 spectators per match. Terry Holladay ranked #10 in woman's singles.

The 1977 Friars featured a mature roster between 36-year-old Drysdale, 37-year-old Laver, married couple Kerry and Raz Reid (Lobsters), and the recently acquired Mona Guerrant (Loves) and Julie Anthony (Freedoms). The team believed that Reid and Anthony would upgrade their women's game. The Friars also tried in vain to sign Renée Richards to compete as a woman. *The Boston Globe*'s "WTT '77" preview called San Diego, "the most improved team in the league." The Friars would play 18 home games at San Diego's Sports Arena and four at Anaheim Convention Center, with season tickets ranging from $90 loge to $270 box.

The Friars started slowly, but still expected to challenge Chris Evert's Division-leading Racquets. May 17, the champion Apples took three hours and eight minutes, two super-tiebreakers and 11 match points to oust San Diego at New York's Felt Forum, 29-28. May 27, before 3,424, the Friars bashed visiting L.A. 27-20. The Strings (1-14) seemed ready to snap a brutal losing streak until Kerry Reid silenced mouthy Rosie Casals, 6-1.

> ## "We've discovered through surveys that 52 percent of our crowd is female. So we've instructed our sales force to talk to the ladies as much as possible. They should go to their husbands, and demand equal time for tennis."
> —SHELLY HALL, San Diego Friars assistant GM, 1977

The Friars' play significantly improved after July 9's sold-out All-Star Match at San Diego Sports Arena. The squad finished the 1977 season 21-23 (.477), good enough for a playoff spot with a third-place finish. August 16, San Diego opened a best-of-three in Oakland with a gritty 24-22 victory over the Gaters. The Friars lost to the Gaters four of six times during the season. Kerry Reid fueled the victory with a 6-1 win over former Friar Terry Holladay. The next night, the series moved to S.D., where the Friars took four of five events 30-21, to advance against Phoenix in the Western Division finals.

For Game One on August 22, the Friars slammed the Racquets, 29-26, to move within one game of the WTT championship. The next night, Phoenix squared the series with a 27-20 home victory, led by 6-0 singles sweeps by Chris Evert and Butch Walts. August 25, again in Phoenix, the Friars' title dreams crashed and burned 30-22.

WTT stability seemed a reality in San Diego, with 1,743 season ticket holders going into 1978. GM Kingston announced that the 1,800th and 1,900th fans to buy a season ticket plan would win a gift package of two Friars T-shirts and two Friars racquet covers. He went on to say the 10,000th fan to enter the Sports Arena would win an autographed jersey. G. Allan added: "We feel this proves our strength as a legitimate franchise and puts to rest rumors that the Friars are just another team to live and die in San Diego."

March 8, 1978, the Friars announced that Rod Laver would succeed Cliff Drysdale as player-coach. Laver, in his third season with the franchise, "thought about the coaching job all last year, and the more I thought about it, the more I wanted to do it."

The 1978 Friars returned as a largely intact lineup, with Laver, Kerry and Raz Reid, Mona Guerrant, Janet Young, and Ross Case. Kerry Reid won more games than she lost in 1977, playing nightly against King, Evert, Wade, Navratilova, et al. Her doubles partner Guerrant—from that tennis hotbed of Marengo, Iowa—fit the Friars plans if they were to again advance to the divisional playoffs. San Diego also announced a radio deal with KSON (1240 AM) to broadcast 32 of their 44 matches.

May 13, the Friars throttled the ailing Racquets 27-15 at the Sports Arena, to take their sixth straight. Kerry beat Sue Barker 6-3 and then teamed with Mona for a 6-2 win over Barker and Kristien Kemmer. The win elevated San Diego to first place in the Division.

Tennis insiders seemed shocked by Kerry Reid's early successes, as though she were a

1976 San Diego Friars
Back L-R: Larry Williams, Rod Laver, Ross Case, Cliff Drysdale
Front L-R: Connie Spooner, Betty Ann Grubb Stuart, Terry Holladay, Janet Young

youngster showing flashes of potential. She was easy to overlook because she lacked the charisma of Billie Jean King or the shot-making of Chris Evert. The former Kerry Melville had been one of the world's top players for years. Coach Laver did not belabor the point of building her confidence but said she needed to excel due to the intense competition.

"This year, I concluded that I should hit everything as hard as I could. I could play conservatively or just go for it."

—MONA GUERRANT, San Diego Friars, 1978

The week of May 20, Mona Guerrant and Ross Case got named WTT co-players of the week, dependable in all three of San Diego's matches: May 22's 31-24 win in Phoenix; May 26's 26-24 loss to the Lobsters at St. Louis' Checkerdome; and a May 27 win over L.A. near Houston in Lake Conroe, TX to promote Laver's local April Sound resort. But Kingston had an ulterior motive for that match: to find owners for a Houston team for 1979.

The season's hottest night may have been June 3 before a San Diego Sports Arena crowd of 6,074. The Friars, led by Laver, overcame the defending champion New York Apples, 30-25. Bad blood boiled when Vitas Gerulaitis lost his cool over the San Diego Chicken mascot's unruly conduct, slamming an overhand shot to the poultry's gut after a lost point. The win gave the Friars a two-game divisional lead over the Gaters.

June 14, the New Orleans Nets debuted at the San Diego Sports Arena. Renée Richards and her mixed doubles partner, NBA Houston Rockets guard John Lucas, endured their first loss, 6-4 to Guerrant-Case, as the Friars prevailed 32-25. San Diego spent June 15 crushing the Cascades in Seattle 31-21, and June 16 in L.A. succumbing to the Strings

Terry Holladay and Betty Ann Grubb Stuart, San Diego Friars, 1976

30-18 before Wimbledon break. Two Friars women returned with Wimbledon trophies: Kerry Reid, who teamed in doubles with the Nets' Wendy Turnbull, and Mona Guerrant in consolation singles.

"Home court is worth one set," explained Laver, just before San Diego played five straight nights on the road. July 25, in their most painful game of 1978, the Friars, after giving up a seven-point lead in the last two sets, were shamed by the Apples in OT, 26-25. After a tough week, San Diego socked Seattle with a July 31 home victory at the Sports Arena, 28-25. Kerry Reid scored a 6-2 win over Betty Stöve, who quit halfway through the set after she bonked herself in the head with her racquet.

The Friars ended 1978 winning 12 straight—whipping the Apples, their rival Strings, and the stubborn Oranges—to finish atop the West with their best-ever record of 30-14. Laver, celebrating his 40th birthday, said, "It's quite an accomplishment that we're in the playoffs" and called a WTT title his "final career goal." At his new home, the player-coach honored the milestone, crediting his vitality to "all this beer drinking and clean living I have."

August 15, the Friars got cooking in the playoffs. For Game One against the sub-.500 Seattle Cascades (20-24), San Diego won decisively at home, 30-22, paced by singles wins by Rod Laver (6-2 over Tom Gordon) and Kerry Reid (7-6 over Stöve). But the favored Friars shockingly lost May 17 in Seattle, 28-20, and then again May 18 at home, 31-20—and a potential championship season ended.

> **"The dissolution of New York and Los Angeles, combined with a general lack of commitment by the top players, will force us to present an inferior product, which is not the direction I want to go. Our chances of making progress from an income standpoint are now severely hindered."**
> —**FRANK MARIANI, San Diego Friars owner, 1978**

After the 1978 season, San Diego became the fourth WTT team to cease operations. On November 8, owner Frank Mariani, in front of a "1978 Western Division Champions" banner, stated that retooling the franchise "will involve far more of an expense than I'm willing to undertake." The avowal came one day after the champion L.A. Strings folded, due to what Jerry Buss called his "$2.7 million loss over the last five years."

Buss and Mariani had become WTT's most significant enablers. By 1978, they owned or held stakes in four of the ten teams: Anaheim, Indiana, L.A., and San Diego. So their move to pull out effectively sunk the league, which already lost clubs in Boston and New York.

Mariani moved aside to let G. Alan Kingston try to find new owners to keep team tennis alive in San Diego. Kingston, balancing stark financial realities with 1979 season ticket promotional efforts, said, "We feel that by reorganizing, the league will be better and stronger. But at the moment, we want the league to say where it's coming from and where it stands." November 14, Kingston declared refunds for all 1,100 buyers of 1979 season tickets.

Chapter 19
Hawaii Leis

Valerie Ziegenfuss, Hawaii Leis, 1974
The Honolulu-based squad wore lei garlands

FAST FACTS

Years of Operation: 1974-1976

Team Record: 1974: 14-29 (last place, Western Division)
1975: 14-30 (4th place, Western Division)
1976: 12-32 (last place, Western Division)

Female MVP: Margaret Court 1975 (283-298, .497)

Male MVP: Ilie Năstase 1976 (369-358, .508)

Highlight: Opening night streakers hired by owner Bill Schoen (5/20/74)

Lowlight: Năstase goes AWOL (5/26/76)

Home Arena: Honolulu International Center/ Blaisdell Arena (capacity 7,529) McKinley High School gym (2,400)

Quote: "Năstase is Romania's most precious export since petroleum, and just as temperamental a product."
—*Honolulu Star-Bulletin* (5/9/76)

"We have to use all the hoopla we can. We want to do a serve-stroke-and-volley contest for the kids like the punt-pass-and-kick contests. And we will have to go in for a T-shirt night, headband night, and bracelet night too. Our survival is at stake."
—**BILL SCHOEN, Hawaii Leis owner, 1974**

Tennis in the 50th State dates back to 1895, with the first island championship run by the Hawaiian Lawn Tennis Association, in which W.F. Dillingham won in singles and then teamed with Dr. H. Howards to take the doubles title. Pro tennis exploded after the first tournament in April 1920, coinciding with the 100th anniversary of the landing of American missionaries. The incredible weather made Hawaii a tennis destination.

By the 1960s, Hawaii became culturally hip. That led to a push for pro sports in Honolulu. Football thrived with the successful NFL Pro Bowl and the college Hula Bowl, then in 1973, the renegade World Football League introduced The Hawaiians, a.k.a. Honolulu Hawaiians, a.k.a. Hawaii Hawaiians (starring future New York Giants coach Jim Fassel), who lost in the final World Bowl to the Birmingham Americans, 22-19.

Dr. Leonard Bloom, the owner of the 1974 WTT San Diego franchise, sold his $50,000 team to a Honolulu group led by Virginia Slims lawyer Bill Schoen (backed by WFL Hawaiians owner Sam Battistone's Invest West Sports) for $250,000 including the rights to Romanian star Ilie Năstase. A naming contest yielded six hundred entries like the Alohas, Breakers, Sunsets, and Monarchs. A January 14 press event at the Hilton Hawaiian Village unveiled the Hawaii Leis, with their logo of a lei garland wrapped around a racquet.

Schoen's Leis failed to sign any of 20 draft picks. On April 29, they acquired pig-tailed #16th-ranked American Ann Kiyomura of San Mateo, CA, from the San Francisco Golden Gaters in exchange for the rights to Soviet star Alex Metreveli. Dennis Ralston, the former U.S. Davis Cup captain known for his lethal right-handed forehand, would serve as player-coach. They signed San Diego's Valerie Ziegenfuss, versatile in singles and doubles, and Cape Town, South Africa's Brigitte Cuypers, at 18 her nation's #9 woman netter. Mike Machette, a striking 6'2" USC star who reached 1973's Wimbledon men's doubles quarterfinals with Raúl Ramírez, Ross Case, a 23-year-old WCT star from Toowoomba, Australia, and Kristy Pigeon, a 5'8" blonde lefty from San Mateo, one of Virginia Slims' "Original 9" (playing while completing her Ph.D. in wildlife biology) rounded out the roster. Ralston would set lineups and play men's doubles with Case and mixed doubles with Ziegenfuss and Kiyomura.

Owner/GM Bill Schoen—1965 University of Redlands NCAA Division II men's doubles titlist—doubled as KORL-AM color analysis (with Larry Jones doing play-by-play), while Leis VP Dennis Murphy, served as a consultant. Mimi Beams handled publicity. Treasurer Dianne Plotts and ticket manager Pat Monroe had difficult jobs. The team split 22 games between Honolulu International Center (HIC—home of Elvis Presley's famed 1973 "Aloha from Hawaii" concert) and McKinley High School gym.

The Leis faced complicated logistics, with long road trips and extended home stands. They opened 1974 with eight straight road games before returning to Hawaii. Then after five home matches, they left on a grueling 12-game mainland trek. The upside of all the travel was a month in Honolulu to end the year.

Hawaii opened the season by crushing the New York Sets 29-25 at Nassau Coliseum on May 7 before a reported 4,999. Ross Case led the Leis, lashing aging Spanish star Manuel Santana, 6-2. Then the squad flew to Pittsburgh, and before a thin Mother's Day crowd of 2,104, exploited the absence of Triangles star Evonne Goolagong, 33-25.

The Leis' first-ever home match on May 20 was a severe 26-19 loss to the Golden Gaters before 2,689 at the 7,529-capacity HIC in the arena's first tennis event. Fans got given free megaphones, and the crowd laughed over streakers, allegedly hired by Schoen. But it was the Leis that got stripped on the court. The night also debuted a unique fan club, the Oahu Refuse Collectors Booster Club: 193 rowdy Honolulu sanitation workers in Leis T-shirts imprinted with garbage trucks, with a bugler blowing taps when the visitors served.

Hawaii drew a record home crowd of 5,924 on June 12 in a 26-17 loss to Billie Jean King's Philadelphia Freedoms; it was the Leis' 15th straight defeat, dropping to a league-worst record of 2-18. The next day, Hawaii dumped Kristy Pigeon on the Gaters for a fourth-round pick. Hawaii's three men and three women by year's end totaled 11 netters, such as native Charlie Panui, Bay Area vet Barry McKay, and UCLA star Charlie Pasarell.

Hawaii Leis owner Bill Schoen with player-coach Dennis Ralston, 1974

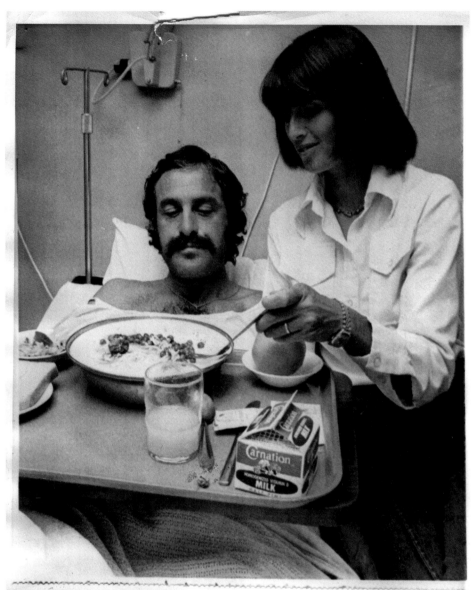

(SA1) SAN ANTONIO, Tex., Aug. 19--TENNIS ANYONE?--
Australian tennis star John Newcombe recuperates at
Bexar County Hospital in San Antonio after damaged
cartilage was removed from his right knee. Newcombe
says he **expects** to regain his form with little
difficulty. His wife, Angie, assisted during Newcombe's
first meal after the operation Tuesday night. (AP
WIREPHOTO) sme 193075

John Newcombe, Hawaii Leis, 1975
The Aussie legend never fully recovered from his WTT knee injury

The Leis markedly improved by season's end. July 29 in Minnesota, the Leis sheared the Buckskins 26-24. On August 3, at least 1,565 Honoluluans watched the Florida Flamingos flame out 24-22. The next week, league officials informed the Leis of a loss by forfeit for August 12's match with the Houston E-Z Riders at Kauai High School after the gym was deemed too small. The Leis finished 1974 in the cellar of the Western Division's Pacific Section with a dismal 14-29 record, drawing an alleged 32,191 in 22 games (1,463 per).

"I haven't played well, but what can you expect? It's the psychological aspect—I'm nervous, and I don't want to let my team down."
—MIKE MACHETTE, Hawaii Leis, 1975

For 1975, Hawaii traded player-coach Dennis Ralston to San Diego and replaced him with the Chicago Aces' Butch Buchholz. The roster returned Brigitte Cuypers, Barry McKay and Charlie Panui, and added Owen Davidson, of the defunct Minnesota Buckskins. Days before the opener, with the E-Z Riders' demise, John Newcombe signed to be the Leis #1 men's singles player and to team in doubles with fellow mustachioed Aussie Davidson. Hawaii then signed 32-year-old legend Margaret Court and Newcombe's E-Z Riders partner, Tasmanian Helen Gourlay. Others to play for the 1975 Leis would include Mary-Ann Beattie (ex-Loves), Freedom/Banner Kathy Kuykendall, Tom Edlefsen, Joyce Champaigne, and taxi squad-ers Peter Burwash, Jim Osborne, and Heather Dahlgren.

Due to logistical issues after the E-Z Riders' folding, John Newcombe couldn't join the Leis for their season opener in Phoenix, but he arrived in time to play two matches that weekend in San Diego. Then he missed the next week's first three Hawaii home games, busy in Las Vegas at the Tournament of Champions. Upon his May 21 return to the HIC, the Leis won four of five sets to mangle the Pittsburgh Triangles before a reported crowd of 5,000. In that game, Newcombe tore knee cartilage against Vitas Gerulaitis. Days later, he saw an NYC specialist who concluded surgery was unnecessary and prescribed three weeks rest, which meant missing Wimbledon. His career would never fully recover.

After the Wimbledon break, Hawaii played without Newcombe or Court, and lost to Billie Jean King's New York Sets, 27-17, in front of 4,870 at Nassau Coliseum. In an August 4 grudge match, the Sets rallied to trim the Leis 22-20 in front of 5,554 Long Islanders. The following night in Cleveland, player-coach Buchholz endured WTT ignominy, aced nine times in one set, losing 6-1 to the Nets' Bob Giltinan in a 30-21 drubbing.

Improved player statistics and an unsubstantiated attendance surge of 72% (based on a 22-game announced audience count of 56,470) failed to reverse Hawaii's losing ways. The Leis (14-30) finished 1975 fourth place in the Western Division. So something had to give. One month after the season, Bill Schoen sold controlling interest to Don Kelleher of Kelleher Lumber Sales—a company that grew from a Quonset hut in San Rafael into one of the world's largest wood molding distributors—and stayed on as GM.

At December 11's league meetings at New York's Essex House before the 1976 draft, the Sets sold their rights to Ilie Năstase back to Hawaii, after which the Leis signed the fiery 29-year-old Romanian to a pricey two-year deal. Năstase said that he, his wife, and daughter would be available for all 44 matches, other than his native Davis Cup duties.

If everyone signed for 1976, the Leis would have fielded an all-star squad with Court, Năstase, Newcombe, Gourlay, and top draft pick Stan Smith. But Smith spurned WTT, and gimpy Newcombe got sent to L.A. before retiring, while Court took extended maternity leave with her third child. So, the Leis opening roster featured Năstase, Gourlay, Buchholz, Ken Rosewall, Dick Stockton, Sue Stap, Marcie Louie, and Nancy Gunter. Before the season started, their home court, the HIC, got renamed Blaisdell Arena.

"Ilie Năstase is a difficult man to like. But he's just too good."

—MARGARET COURT, Hawaii Leis, 1976

Năstase proved to be an instant headache. Opening night May 12, he said he'd pass up his Davis Cup duties and French Open plans to honor his Leis deal. After a testy chat with Don Kelleher, "Nasty" played the season's first six-city road journey—and the Leis began the season 0-6. In that May 12 opener, a 31-20 loss to Pittsburgh, Năstase ran around the court, refusing to let them put leis around his neck, and then lost to Gerulaitis 6-4.

On May 17, the Gaters rushed to court to sue Năstase for skipping the previous night's Hawaii-Gaters match at Oakland Arena. Năstase had signed to play in two different places at the same time—also with the Avis Challenge Cup, in Hawaii—an outside deal in direct violation of his WTT contract. Then he skirted two Leis games to "rest" a pulled groin before his May 23, $100,000 winner-take-all match with Arthur Ashe—infamous for him taunting Ashe with the N-word (in line with his 1973 game in Baltimore where he told the player's locker room, "It was like playing to 20,000 Jews out there"). Reporters had just seen the AWOL Năstase watching the French Open in Paris.

After May 26's Leis repeat loss to the Gaters, Năstase hastily departed Blaisdell Arena for Honolulu International Airport in his Leis uniform, accompanied by his manager-adviser Mitch Oprea, and a lady friend. He told the team Romanian officials issued an immediate order for his return, and then he hopped on a red-eye to JFK via SFO. Schoen said: "We don't feel this is the full reason, but we have no details." Reached in Bucharest, Romanian Tennis Federation secretary Alexander Lazarescu said he knew of no recall. Năstase offered no excuse other than his passport expired and needed renewal. Schoen said the Leis had no idea if or when he'd return and had no option but to consider contract revocation. Kelleher, in turn, spoke of his plans to sue Năstase, asking $4 million in damages for breach of contract, in response to him complaining, "I don't want to play for the Leis anymore, and my federation asked me to break my contract."

The next day, Schoen reported that Năstase told Kelleher via phone from London that he'd return for the season's second half, starting with July 5's home match against L.A., in exchange for the dropping of all lawsuits. Larry King saw Năstase at Wimbledon and coerced his high-priced part-timer to return, as wife Billie Jean tried to pick a fistfight, but got held back. Năstase also surrendered 20% of his salary in the form of a fine. Two weeks later, the Leis, with a suddenly genteel Năstase, and Court back from maternity, played an exhibition with Strings and Friars at the South Coast Plaza Hotel in Costa Mesa.

Valerie Ziegenfuss and Dennis Ralston, Hawaii Leis, 1974

Năstase celebrated his birthday July 18 before 8,150 at Phoenix's Memorial Coliseum as his Leis lost to Chris Evert's Racquets, 27-23. Năstase sauntered about the court, razzing ball boys and umpires, and showing disinterest, as he rattled Rhodesian Andrew Pattison, and then joined Court, in a pair of prim and improper, to top Kristien Kemmer-Butch Walts.

The Leis' 1976 matches at Blaisdell Arena drew between 2,500 and 3,066 per game. On July 2, the franchise announced they might move to Portland or Seattle, or have a joint franchise in those cities in 1977. As a test run, they slated three games in each city, at Portland Memorial Coliseum in late July and Seattle Coliseum in early August. Don said, "The Northwest interests us due to scheduling problems in Hawaii."

At July 27's first audition, the Leis thrashed the Western-leading Racquets 31-18 before 7,344 in Portland, with Evert home in Arizona due to illness. The Leis started the year 2-16 and ended 12-32 (.272). For all of his drama, Năstase ranked as WTT's #6 men's star.

On September 23, Kelleher told a media assemblage the Leis would leave Honolulu for the Pacific Northwest, where they drew best and would split 22 home matches between Seattle and Portland. Kelleher and new GM Marty Loughman said to soon expect a new player-coach and a naming contest. The franchise played 1977 as the Sea-Port Cascades.

In the end, the Leis could never compete with Hawaii's surf and sun. The homestands burned out the fans, as did the feeble play. There was also the transportation factor and an upsurge of top tournaments throughout the Islands. The lack of talent traced back to anemic drafts that found the team unable to sign picks, be it Rod Laver, Jan Kodes, Chris Evert, NBA-er John Lucas or comedian Bill Cosby. Hawaii has not hosted a major pro sports team since.

Chapter 20
Sea-Port/Seattle Cascades

Betty Stöve, Sea-Port Cascades, 1977

Years of Operation: 1977-1978

Team Colors: Green and white

Team Record: 1977: 16-28 (4th place, Western Division)
1978: 20-24 (4th place, Western Division)

Female MVP: Betty Stöve, 1977 (368-400, .479)

Male MVP: Tom Gorman, 1978 (441-353, .555)

Highlight: 7,208 at Seattle Center Arena see Sea-Port lose to Phoenix (7/12/77)

Lowlight: 126 at LSU Center in Baton Rouge see Seattle lose to New Orleans (7/31/78)

Home Arenas: Seattle Center Arena (capacity 4,700)
Portland Memorial Coliseum (12,888)
Mercer Arena (6,500)

Quote: "Joining the franchise was one of my worst mistakes."
—John DeVries, Cascades executive director (11/5/78)

"Tom Gorman and I were the two big local names for tennis. They were looking to us to draw fans. It wasn't a great plan."
—TRISH BOSTROM, Sea-Port Cascades, 2012

Pacific Northwest tennis dates back to 1890 when 39 of Seattle's elites founded the Olympic Tennis Club, later known as the Seattle Tennis Club, with two clay courts at the NW corner of Madison and Minor on First Hill. Pro tournaments and exhibitions came to the area by 1950—although the region's pro "Open Era" did not begin until 1968, when just 5,000 attended the two-day Bobby Riggs' World Championship Tour of Tennis.

WTT came to the Northwest when Hawaii Leis owner Don Kelleher announced that his team with Ilie Năstase and Margaret Court would play three 1976 matches at the Seattle Coliseum plus three at Portland's Memorial Coliseum. Breaking even was something he did not do in Honolulu, where the Leis drew 2,800 per game. The owner stated, "If we move, Seattle's strong, but Portland is under consideration." Kelleher felt that a joint venture between Seattle and Portland was feasible. The Leis' six Northwest matches drew a total of 31,429 (July 28's Leis-Racquets drew 8,450 fans to Seattle Coliseum), and Kelleher felt his franchise could prove profitable drawing 5,000.

After months of rumors, the Leis, with 1976 attendance at an all-time low, headed to the Northwest, to divide 22 home matches between Seattle and Portland, and renamed their squad the Sea-Port Cascades, in tribute to the region's rugged mountain chain. New GM Marty Loughman explained, "It became evident Hawaii cannot financially support a WTT franchise." New league commissioner Butch Buchholz offered, "No franchise has profited, but the losses are going way down."

In Seattle, Kelleher presented his new team. Asked why he picked two cities, requiring two offices, two staffs, two arenas, and different tax laws, the owner said, "I just didn't want to make anybody mad." Năstase was the Leis' star, and Kelleher's choice to coach Sea-Port despite his pricey salary. But Năstase nixed the Northwest, and Kelleher sold his rights to Jerry Buss' L.A. Strings. The Cascades retained no Hawaii Leis after 1976's last-place finish.

The owner also said that he spoke to the agent of Seattle native Tom Gorman—a star at Seattle Prep and in the NCAA semifinals for Seattle University—and felt he might be ready for WTT. In November, Gorman told Puget Sound writers, "Team tennis doesn't let you perform. You're out there 20 minutes at a time, and in 20 minutes, I wouldn't even get my three sweaters off." GM Loughman said, "Tom's our top choice, not only because of his tennis knowledge and playing ability but also since he is the type of person that will represent and promote tennis in the Northwest in a way our fans will be proud."

The Cascades came together quickly. Loughman hired publicist George Hill, office manager Molly Cheshier, and salesperson Dianne Shorett. They had some smart ideas, like promoting the squad through running clinics and setting up youth leagues based on WTT's format. On January 27, the team signed their first player, JoAnne Russell, a 22-year-old from Naples, FL. February 17, they came to terms with fifth-rounder Steve Docherty, a 6'5" Aussie-bred Washington State star ranked #1 in the Northwest, and Trish Bostrom, Seattle's first woman pro, who starred at UW and played WTT for the 1974 Lobsters and 1975-76 Loves. Tom Gorman, signing a $60,000 salary for 13 weeks of work, stated: "All my life I've fantasized about representing Seattle in a team sport."

> ## "At first, I wasn't sure if WTT would be successful. I didn't want to give up tour play for something that didn't look like it would make it—like the World Football League."
> **—ERIK VAN DILLEN, Sea-Port Cascades, 1977**

On March 16, Gorman, in his first press event as player-coach, grumbled, "We need solid women players. That is the pivotal position in WTT." On April 12, Dutch star Betty Stöve, one of the top women doubles players, came to terms. Loughman called Stöve "the best unsigned player available." The team also brought in Erik van Dillen, 26, of San Mateo, CA, for his doubles excellence. The GM said that he'd explore trade options for female firepower, and if that failed, he'd troll the Virginia Slims Tour's lower levels.

Even before the season, the franchise showed warning signs of not connecting with the marketplace. Kelleher refused to invest in advertising, and Loughman signed no stars. After a one-week training camp in Houston, the Cascades began 1977 with seven straight road games, including four in five nights in Knoxville, Pittsburgh, Indianapolis, and New York. Kelleher's promotional idea was to sweep all seven matches, return as conquering heroes, and attract tens of thousands of turned-on sports fans to their home opener.

After a 5-2 start, the Cascades played their Seattle Center home opener May 17 in front of a disappointing crowd of 2,675 fans, who watched the local player-coach return home to repel the Loves 28-22. Robert Julien, the singing bartender at Jake O'Shaughnessy's, belted out the national anthem. Of his slow start in a 7-5 win over Indiana player-coach Allan Stone, Gorman gushed: "I was nervous and had trouble, but the crowd picked me up. You don't get that in tournaments." Stone stewed over his inadequate performance, "I missed shots my mother could've hit."

May 22 in Seattle, Gorman had 3,985 locals cheering, stomping and shouting at every point of the final two sets, as he rallied the Cascades over the defending champion New York Apples 23-20. Gorman, "too psyched" to answer questions, later stated: "There's no feeling of hopelessness on the bench when we're behind." Billie Jean King credited Gorman's "brilliant tennis," and said, "The Cascades have a good shot to be first in the Western Division. Two or three teams could win the league, and Sea-Port has a chance." May 27, the Apples blasted the Cascades 25-21, before 3,440 at Portland Memorial Coliseum.

The rest of the season's first half was a mess; the Cascades lost nine of eleven. After June 2's road win over Rod Laver's Friars, 31-28, the Cascades dropped five in a row: June 3 in L.A., 26-22; June 4, in the second game of a home-and-home to the Strings in Portland, 31-19; June 5 in Seattle to Boston, 28-25; June 7 in Portland to less than 1,000 fans, shelled again by the Lobsters 30-14; and June 9 in Seattle before 1,213 spectators in a defeat to the Golden Gaters, 29-25. On June 10, Sea-Port entered the three-week Wimbledon break on a high note, breaking their losing streak by beating the Friars, 23-22 in front of 2,013 Seattleites. Following the come-from-behind victory, the Cascades ranked third in the West.

"They didn't realize the money needed to promote a team in two cities. You can't bring a new team into a city, not spend, and expect to do well."
—GEORGE HILL, Sea-Port Cascades publicist, 1977

Days into the break, the Cascades underwent a seismic shakeup. In an attempt to boost attendance—averaging 2,471 in Seattle and 2,225 in Portland—Kelleher canned George Hill. The publicist said: "I hear my job is no longer." Dianne Shorett and Molly Cheshier quit over the incident. On her way out, Shorett sued in King County Superior Court, over $3,360.03 in unpaid salary and commissions. Kelleher said, "we are not in danger in Seattle," and, "I think we'll operate in Seattle and Portland next year."

July 6, in Sea-Port's first game after the break, Chris Evert led her Racquets 29-27 with wins in singles over Stöve, 6-3, and doubles with Kris Kemmer over Wimbledon titlists Stöve-Russell, 7-5. The next night, again in Portland, the Cascades blasted the last-place Strings, 27-19. Critical of the weak turnout for the Phoenix game, Stöve praised the L.A. match crowd of 5,181: "They seem to be getting team tennis, and that means a lot."

July 12, a large Seattle crowd of 6,452 (or 7,208) saw the Cascades lose again to the Racquets, 30-23. July 15, they repelled the invading Soviets 31-23, taking four of the five sets in front of 2,143 in Portland. The thrifty Kelleher would not cover the squad's hotel rooms for 11 games in Portland. As all players lived in Seattle, they all ran to catch the last Braniff flight after the match, unshowered in their warm-ups.

As part of a late July swoon, the Cascades fell 24-21 on August 5 against Björn Borg's Nets in Portland. Docherty played the game of his life, with blazing serves and backhands to bash the superstar 6-4; the upset made front-page news in Stockholm. In an August 6 rematch, Borg attracted a season-high Seattle crowd of 7,642, as his Nets romped 27-23. August 14 at the L.A. Forum, the WTT-worst Strings routed the Cascades, 29-13—yet sub-.500 Sea-Port (18-26) backed into the playoffs.

For Game One of the opening round, Phoenix won all five events on August 17, to stifle the visiting Cascades 30-14, in front of an announced crowd of 5,540. Game Two took place the next night in Portland, before 700-ish at Lewis & Clark College's Pamplin Sports Center. "This is ridiculous," said Kelleher. "We can't even fill a building with 2,200. That many alone should want to see Chris Evert." Evert herself noted that the crowd was her "smallest since junior high school."

Loughman was so bothered by advance ticket sales that he drove around downtown Portland with a loudspeaker advertising the Evert game. The GM downplayed that his team had alienated their fan base by requiring fans to buy pricey playoff tickets for the Phoenix match as well as all possible future matches. But the Cascades' season ended after a crushing Game Two defeat, 27-26.

"What should I say about this playoff loss? It was your basic train wreck."
—BETTY STÖVE, Sea-Port Cascades, 1977

After the season, Kelleher discussed the poor attendance and scarcity of playing dates at Portland Memorial Coliseum: "We got turned down cold turkey by the Coliseum for April dates, meaning we'd have to play the first month on the road. But I can't blame the Coliseum as they make more money off the [NBA champion] Trail Blazers than they do off of us." He then stated, "After long deliberation, the Cascades will operate in Seattle next year" as the Seattle Cascades, playing home matches at the 4,700-capacity Seattle Center Arena and 6,500-seat Mercer Arena. He added, "With Tom Gorman, Betty Stöve, and JoAnne Russell, this season should be exciting," without mentioning Docherty, van Dillen or Bostrom. Attendance in Portland and Seattle ran equally weak, at about 2,700 fans.

The Cascades dealt with internal and external issues stemming from Kelleher running the team from his Quonset hut in San Rafael, CA. Marty Loughman, the Leis/ Cascades' fourth GM in three years, quit, leaving only one Seattle office employee. Loughman cited George Hill's messy firing as an indictment of Kelleher's management style. Marty said the Bay Area lumber baron "ran the franchise like a lemonade stand. He felt you could open the doors and people would walk in." Portland-based assistant GM Judy Daigle scoffed, "I have doubts Portland can support these games, and to be

Above: Sea-Port Cascades banner, 1977

Below: Hawaii Leis ad for matches in Seattle that resulted in the franchise's relocation

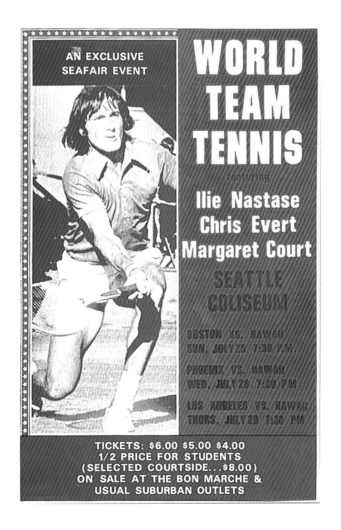

honest, I have doubts about Seattle." The Cascades had a long road to travel before they'd become a Northwest fixture.

New Cascades executive director John DeVries discussed his plans to build a great franchise. But three months after signing, DeVries got ousted in another front-office shakeup, after a dozen sales reps walked out. "Joining the franchise was one of my worst mistakes," DeVries said. "They're like Jesse James trying to get into everyone's pocket."

> ### *"I was always saying, 'Seattle is so beautiful' and 'It's so lovely.' And it was always raining and cold. I thought, 'This stinks.' I always thought 'Cascades' was a detergent."*
> **—JOANNE RUSSELL, Sea-Port Cascades, 1978**

On February 1, 1978, Kelleher announced that a Seattle bloc led by Howard Leendertsen, Mike Nealy, and Dave Ederer bought a 50% stake in the franchise. He welcomed the partners "to ensure Seattle fans the highest value for its entertainment dollar." The team would play 19 home matches in Seattle, plus one in Boise, Corvallis, and Portland.

In a preseason three-way trade, Seattle acquired 22-year-old, five-year WTT vet Marita Redondo, with JoAnne Russell going to New York, and Virginia Wade to the Gaters. The team also added two rookies: Texan doubles star Sherwood Stewart, and 22-year-old Australian Chris Kachel. Brigitte Cuypers (ex-Leis) replaced Bostrom. Gorman trained offseason at Mission Hills Country Club in Palm Springs to improve on '77's mediocrity.

The Cascades began 1978 by losing six in a row, starting with April 21's opener, in which 2,300 saw the 1977 Western Division champion Racquets prevail 30-29. They ended that losing streak May 10 in New Orleans, shredding the Nets in front of just 704 at the 80,000-seat Superdome, powered by Redondo 6-2 over Renée Richards. On June 14, the Cascades lost in L.A. to the Strings 28-16 on a bizarre technicality, as under WTT rules, a team could only make two substitutions per match. Gorman had replaced Kachel after falling behind to Ilie Năstase with Sherwood Stewart, who got hurt, and both he and Kachel had already played in the maximum two events. The next night in Seattle, they finished the season's first half with a 27-24 home victory over San Diego, before 1,536.

On July 31, the Cascades partook in WTT's lowest-attended match, just 126 spectators at the 13,215-capacity LSU Center in Baton Rouge, falling to the Nets, 26-23. The defeat dropped Seattle ten games under .500 with eight matches remaining.

> ### *"We came back strong this season. Now it's going right down to the wire."*
> **—TOM GORMAN, Seattle Cascades player-coach, 1978**

The team ran no ads to promote August 1's match, in which 2,049 at Seattle Center saw the Cascades crush the Apples 24-21. In one of WTT's kookier moments, Billie Jean King and Ray Ruffels passed in front of the scorer's table as the two sides traded courts, when Seattle scoreboard operator Bruce Below blurted, "You guys are in trouble now." At that point, King and Ruffels glared, and King screamed, "Do you work for the team?" When Bruce said he did, King yelled, "Well, then shut up! You shouldn't be saying anything." The Cascades won two of the next three events to take the match, after which Ruffels raced toward Below, grabbed him by the throat and shook him like a rag doll before umpire Brian Howell could restrain him. King then verbally blistered Howell, before shoving him. Then she slammed her racquet on the table.

The next night, the Cascades hosted the Loves at Seattle's Mercer Arena. The 846 onlookers saw the most excellent example of WTT multitasking, as Bruce Below drew double-duty as Mr. Peanut.

On August 4, the fourth-place Cascades flew to Indianapolis and won four out of five sets over the Loves in a 29-16 victory, clinching the final playoff spot with five matches to go. August 7, they nipped the Apples in Seattle, 24-23. Redondo's 6-0 blanking of ex-Cascade JoAnne Russell set the tone with Seattle's first set sweep of the season. The Cascades (20-24)—finishing the franchise's fifth straight losing year dating back to the 1974 Leis—went into the opening round big underdogs to the Division champion Friars.

For August 17's Game One in San Diego, the Friars won 30-28. The next night, the Cascades evened the best-of-three series in Seattle. For the decisive Game Three, the Cascades returned to S.D., and dominated 31-20, earning them a match-up with the Eastern Division champion Lobsters in an intra-divisional semifinal beginning August 22 in Boston. But at Boston U.'s Walter Brown Arena, Seattle got slew, 30-27. Then on August 24 in Seattle, the Lobsters creamed the Cascades, 27-22, in Seattle's final on-court experience.

After the season, Sherwood Stewart won WTT accolades as 1978's most valuable rookie, edging out the Nets' Renée Richards for an award won by Björn Borg in 1977, Rod Laver and Chris Evert in 1976, and Marty Riessen and Greer Stevens in 1975.

"Our priority was to keep the team in Seattle. We looked for other Seattle investors, but there was no money on the surface."
—DON KELLEHER, Seattle Cascades owner, 1978

Kelleher, peeved by weak turnout over two seasons, said he and Howard Leendertsen met September 20 in San Rafael to consider a sale to Houston. Pat Dawson, Cascades 1978 operations manager, said he'd spoken to Tom Gorman about the team's future: "He was very understanding. Tom would likely move with the franchise if that were the case."

A week later, Kelleher said that "it was not economically feasible" to have a team in Seattle for 1979. His team averaged 2,700 per match in 1977 as Sea-Port, but in 1978 as Seattle drew just 1,695 despite another playoff run. The owner also said there was more interest shown in his now-homeless team than only Houston. "It's funny," he said. "We've had three or four cities come out of the woodwork with offers." Kelleher failed to produce a letter of credit for the 1979 season, but that proved moot when WTT folded.

Chapter 21
The Soviets

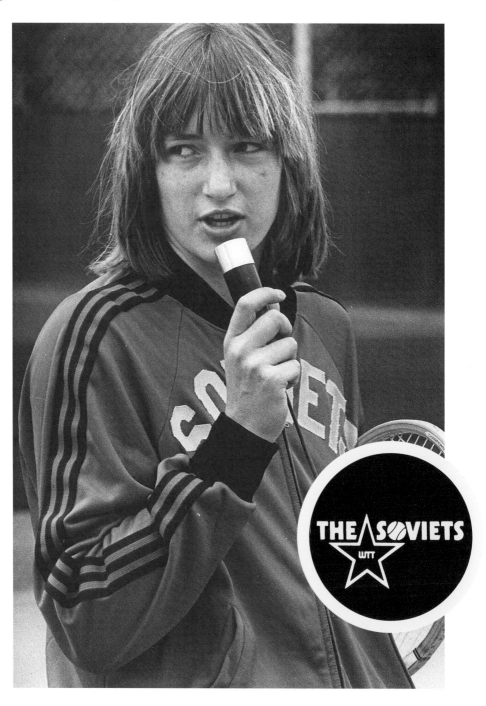

Natasha Chmyreva, The Soviets, 1977

"The Soviets team has an advantage in that they can talk strategy in a language that no else can understand!"

—JOHN KORFF, The Soviets VP, 1974

WTT's connection to the Soviet Union came out of a trailblazing series of U.S./USSR tennis exhibitions. Russian tennis, still in its infancy, went through an explosion, ranking in popularity only behind weight lifting, figure skating, rowing, and chess.

By 1975, the USSR had 60,000 registered tennis players. But the state-controlled system's lack of coaches, racquets, balls, and courts—especially indoor courts—held the game back. While attending Wimbledon in 1975, Larry King broached with Soviet Tennis Federation secretary Vladimir Golenko the idea of a goodwill tennis challenge series—a sports version of détente—between WTT and Russian stars.

After months of negotiations begun in Moscow, King and Indiana Loves owner Bill Bereman announced a deal for team tennis matches in two continents over eight days starting March 8-9, 1976 at Moscow's 13,000-capacity Palace of Sports, in Lenin Stadium Park by the Kremlin. King decreed: "This series between Team America All-Stars and Team Russia All-Stars will do a lot for tennis in both countries, as well as for WTT. The Soviet Union has never won the Davis Cup or Federation Cup. But people will be amazed at how well the Soviets will be in this type of team event. The intense focus and training drilled into most Russian players make them a natural for our scoring tennis."

The 26,000 tickets for the two Moscow matches sold out in hours. The impact of these events foretold Russian tennis glory. Before each game, the squads stood for the national anthems plus "The March of the Tennis Players," the host nation's musical tribute to the event. Then both teams flew to the United States for three more matches, of far less pomp and impact—March 13 before 4,200 fans at the Philadelphia Spectrum; March 14 to 4,100 at Cleveland Coliseum, and March 15 for 3,200 at Indianapolis Convention Center.

The U.S. won four of the five matches—billed as the WTT-USSR Challenge Cup or the Weisman-Toyota Cup—by a total score of 136-95. The $100,000 purse (put up by WTT and Soviet Tennis) split $60,000 to WTT, and $40,000 to the USSR.

The use of WTT's carpet-like surface favored Team America, familiar with the erratic bounces and garish hues. Plus, the Soviet side, for all its international tennis experience, seemed awestruck by larger-than-life young Americans like Billie Jean King, Rosie Casals, Mona Schallau, Vitas Gerulaitis, Sandy Mayer and player-coach Butch Buchholz.

"I'm just glad we won," the admittedly out-of-shape King told the media, "The Russians are much better than they showed, they just weren't familiar with the format." She said the worst aspect was "the lack of American crowds" after the robust Moscow sellouts. A satisfied Golenko stated from the Ministry of Sports: "We are pleased about the matches. It was a meeting of the superpowers held in a friendly atmosphere."

> ## *"This is a legitimate cultural exchange program being done for the good of tennis, and to promote the concept of team tennis. No politics in this series."*
> **—LARRY KING, 1976**

The Soviets' WTT story began in Philadelphia at a December 15, 1976 press event in which Jim Jorgensen, the CEO of King Enterprises, the Kings' Bay Area-based tennis promotions empire, announced that with the decline of the Pittsburgh Triangles and Philadelphia Freedoms, the formation of a new team called the Pennsylvania Keystones to split 22 home games between Pittsburgh's Civic Center and Philadelphia's Spectrum.

Jorgensen, the new franchise's president/co-owner, stated: "We want to reassure WTT fans in Pittsburgh that they will have a local team to back as they have since 1974. And Philadelphia tennis fans to know the WTT is coming back better than ever." He also said he'd travel to both cities to hire staff and arrange capitalization, which needed completion before the January 6 ownership meeting, when WTT would reveal rosters.

Charles Strong, the Pittsburgh's Civic Arena director, confirmed he was ready to sign a lease with Jorgensen's group. That bloc involved Jerry Buss (L.A. Strings), Sol Berg (New York Sets), and GM John Korff (a VP for the Freedoms and Lobsters). Strong said, "It looks like a solid program. We want it to work; a Pittsburgh-Philadelphia relationship makes sense."

The Keystones declaration created a massive rift with Nets owner Joe Zingale, who planned to play at least ten home games in Pittsburgh but had not yet received WTT sanction. Zingale had recently stood side-by-side with former Triangles owner Frank Fuhrer, as Fuhrer said that he'd seek another Pittsburgh franchise for 1978.

League executive director John Schwarz, siding with the Nets, said, "There are no territorial prerogatives, the home city for the Keystones will be Philadelphia." He suggested the owners of Cleveland and Pennsylvania talk it over, "so they don't end up killing each other trying to get into Pittsburgh." Having prevailed, Zingale zinged on a conference call from his Cleveland office: "It's my first victory." That team would sign Swedish star Björn Borg and play 1977 as the Cleveland-Pittsburgh Nets.

After their failed Three Rivers bid, the Keystones made waves with their first pick in the 1977 draft: 42-year-old Renée Richards, the former Dr. Richard Raskind, and a pioneering transgender figure in pro sports. Caught off-guard, Richards said, "I'm a pro tennis player, and I welcome the chance to play other women." The next day, however, Larry King announced the USSR national team would replace the Keystones' in the ten-team league. Richards sat out '77 and joined Zingale's Nets in '78.

> ### "Never before has a Soviet team competed in league play where the results counted in the standings. This is sports history in the making—and another important step in building a spirit of cooperation with the Soviet Union."
> **—JIM JORGENSEN, The Soviets GM, 1977**

With every team drawing 3,000 at 20,000-seat arenas, WTT needed a shake-up. So bringing communist tennistas to the heart of capitalism was a PR no-brainer. Jokes raged over what to name these Cold War netters, ranging from The Nyets to The Really Big Red Machine. Larry King crowed: "This is a huge step in de-Americanizing tennis."

The success of the past summer's series swayed Soviet officials to field a franchise for WTT's 1977 season. The USSR allowed its players to partake for three reasons: firstly, the USSR got paid $200,000 (the team shared no receipts but paid no expenses, and each person received an $18 per diem). Secondly, party leaders felt it was a chance for their players to face top competition. Thirdly, they believed their athletes could win the title.

It served USSR interests to assemble a Westernized roster that spoke fluent English with slang, had long hair, wore blue jeans, and listened to Elton John and The Bee Gees. Olga Morozova—a 28-year-old gym teacher from Moscow, a married mother of two, and a 1974 Wimbledon finalist—had been on WTT's radar since a January 1974 dialogue between the National Soviet Team coach Belitz Hyman and WTT Commissioner George McCall. Moscow native Natasha Chmyreva was a 5'9" freshman at Donetsk University, destined for stardom after winning the junior's titles at Wimbledon and Forest Hills.

Alex Metreveli, 32, an eight-time USSR champ from Tbilisi, ranked #9 in the world in 1975; Teimuraz Kakulia, a burly 30-year-old Tblisian with a devastating forehand, was his nation's #2 male. Konstantin Pugayev, the 6'7" giant with a lethal serve, and a three-time Soviet finalist sat the bench with National Team-mate Jania Biryukova. Early in the season, 23-year-old Marina Kroschina and Vadim Borisov, 22, both ranked #9 in the USSR, replaced Biryukova and Pugayev. The Soviets' staff included coach Shamil Tarpischev, Metreveli's son, a medic, an interpreter, two wives, and six players.

Marina Kroshina, The Soviets, tour credentials

A February 3 press conference presented members of the Russian squad to be called The Soviets. Alex Metreveli said: "Soviet athletes and teams have come to the United States. But this will be the first time a Soviet team will compete in a regular season with statistics kept." In their debut as Western capitalists Metreveli, Morozova, and Chmyreva posed on the corner of Manhattan's Madison Avenue and 55th Street in their red CCCP sweat jackets with a 12" star across the back, bouncing balls for photographers with racquets in hand. When asked by the media, "Why not a hammer and sickle?" John Korff blurted, "We're avoiding political symbols. This is a sports enterprise, a star suffices."

Jorgensen said the Philadelphia-based franchise would play just four times at The Spectrum and twice in nearby Atlantic City, plus "in as many American cities as possible." Over 36 cities offered to host games, including Miami, Baltimore, Washington, Cincinnati, Harrisburg, Norfolk, Nashville, Raleigh, Dallas, Fresno, Butte, and Sioux Falls. The next day at Philadelphia City Hall, Mayor Frank Rizzo's office awarded Soviet Tennis Federation executive Semyon Belits-Geiman an inscribed Liberty Bell replica.

> ## *"Women's lib is not a problem back home. Women are already liberated. That's the way it should be. But they shouldn't forget to be feminine, too."*
> —NATASHA CHMYREVA, The Soviets, 1977

The Soviets kicked off the '77 season April 26 against the Indiana Loves, as the first non-Canadian foreign team to compete in an American sports league. That morning, Chmyreva came to the lobby for her Hilton buffet breakfast wearing a Virginia Slims T-shirt emblazoned "You've come a long way, baby." Indeed, she had come over 10,000 miles.

Kakulia turned 30 that day, so before the game, the Loves wheeled out a birthday cake. In the end, 2,938 at the 17,500-seat Indiana Convention Center watched the Loves subdue the Soviets. Gerulaitis entertained the crowd with his antics, blowing at a ball headed out-of-bounds and hurling his racquet at balls out of reach. The Big G stated, "I didn't expect to win so easily." Morozova mused: "I think they decided they wouldn't make us feel bad by cheering too much for Indiana."

April 28's match against the Boston Lobsters in Champaign, Illinois, got postponed. So the next day, they resumed against Billie Jean King's defending champion New York Apples at the Birmingham Civic Center. The USSR netters diced the Apples in OT, 27-24, paced by a Morozova-Biryukova upset over King-Wade, for their first WTT win. King spewed, "My issue is keeping my head straight and my mouth shut." The Soviets' only loss in Birmingham was their laundry, sent out for service earlier that day by their hotel. The next morning, the Soviets flew to Atlanta and then drove two hours to the Plains, GA hometown of President Jimmy Carter.

On April 30, traffic slowed on Route 280 into Plains, with folks flocking to the rural town (pop. 680) for "The First Annual Peanut Tennis Classic" featuring the Soviets against Phoenix Racquets, led by America's darling Chris Evert. A sellout crowd of 4,250 paid from $10 general admission to $100 per head for the 500 VIP box seats to attend the new courts located across the street from the Carter family home, a gift built by the USSR.

> ***"I would like to hit some tennis balls with Chris Evert. But I honestly don't know one end of a tennis racquet from the other."***
>
> **—BILLY CARTER, 1977**

The gala—hosted by President Carter's mother Lillian and his trailer-park-star brother Billy—began with opening ceremonies at noon, 90 minutes before match time. It included the sounds of a Dixieland band and Instamatics clicking like locusts. An amusing moment came when everyone learned that the three USSR men players came from Soviet Georgia. Metreveli joked, "There's not a single peanut in all of our Georgia."

Many locals hated The Soviets in town. Plains officials flew the Soviet flag next to but lower than Old Glory. The crowd stood dutifully for the Soviet national anthem. One townie, Ed Hollis, told Barry McDermott of *Sports Illustrated*, "I ain't going. Not unless they're invading." Evert and Ross Case enforced U.S. hegemony, as Phoenix won 30-23.

The day's loudest cheers came during a day's-end exhibition. Billy Carter and Chris Evert, with a little help from the scorer making line calls in their favor, defeated Bobby Riggs, the granddaddy of tennis hustlers, and Tandy Rice, legendary manager of, among others, Dolly Parton—and Billy Carter. WTT spokesman Bob Steiner stressed Riggs had no ties to the league but that "Bobby will show up anywhere the product gets national exposure."

Before the match, Billy said, "I've never held a tennis racquet in my hand. But I ain't got enough sense to say no." Evert tried to teach Carter a two-handed backhand, to which he replied: "How am I gonna hold my beer?" When asked about his training, Billy blurted, "Pabst." After it ended, those "in the know" headed over to the barbecue at Miz Lillian's.

> ***"We didn't properly prepare ourselves to compete in WTT. Traveling is a headache. We played last night, tonight, and again tomorrow. All we see is airports and hotels. We need time to work on our game. And I need to sleep."***
>
> **—OLGA MOROZOVA, The Soviets, 1977**

After Plains, The Soviets drove back to Atlanta for two flights to Binghamton, NY. The Russians ended their woeful weekend May 1 with a "May Day" lashing at the claws of the Lobsters 31-17, losing all three doubles events. Doubles would be the Soviets' WTT Achilles heel. It was their eighth match in seven states since the season began.

Two days later, in Greensboro, the Soviets toured a Wrangler jeans factory and went to a Neil Diamond concert. The Wrangler visit was a particular highlight, as the blue jeans they procured were an expensive black market commodity for Soviet Bloc citizens. The next night they edged the Strings, 26-25, led by a Morozova-Metreveli mixed doubles thriller. After that win, Team USSR flew from North Carolina to New York, where the Apples won 28-24 before 2,340 at the Felt Forum. A few motivated protesters tried to disrupt the match on behalf of the plight of Soviet Jewry. The Soviets, with their backs to the crowd, looked stunned and called it all "a big noise."

Alex Metreveli and Olga Morozova, The Soviets, 1977

The exhausted players, barnstorming America five nights a week, flew to Boston on May 26, and the Lobsters stuffed 'em 31-17 before 2,327 chowderheads. The last-place Soviets lost all five events. Czech exile Martina Navratilova took great joy in purging her Iron Curtain oppressors. To honor both cultures, a local McDonald's served lobster and vodka. The Soviets had lost 15 of 18 matches; only the L.A. Strings had a worse overall record.

"Of course, I'm proud to represent my country. But I more like the people who are interested in tennis and my game."

—JANIA BIRYUKOVA, The Soviets, 1977

Over 7,100 Milwaukeeans tried to make The Soviets feel at home as the "home" team. Team USSR reacted with a 33-29 win in a Racquets rematch. Chmyreva crushed Evert, and then in doubles with Morozova, flogged Evert and Kristien Shaw. *Milwaukee Sentinel* (6/4/77): "The Soviets took three out of five sets because everything Evert hit turned to borscht."

The corporate-sponsored affair included ball boys in a local bank's T-shirts and large banners draped on both ends of the court. Crowds paid $5.50 to $8 to make the scene: men wore ties, women flashed pantsuits and summer tans. The two national anthems and player intros ate up the first 20 minutes. Exciting tennis filled the night. Afterward, the Soviets hit buckets of balls into the crowd—with the right ball, you won a case of soda.

WTT was supposed to be the USSR's baptism into American sports—instead, it was their drowning. "I don't know what the problem is," Morozova moaned. "We're tired of losing all the time. We've got to change things, but I have no idea what to do. We may be doing something wrong, but we have no time to correct it." She also said that no Soviets would participate in Wimbledon or Forest Hills due to extreme team tennis burnout.

In their first match after the Wimbledon break, The Soviets flew to Fort Wayne on July 6 to face the Loves. The Russians lost all five events in a 31-20 licking. VP Korff confided: "We haven't been able to find a man who can play better than .500 tennis. However, we have the best Russian men available, so there's no place else to go."

At July 9's 1977 WTT All-Star Match at San Diego Sports Arena, 14,452 fans watched, joined by an NBC-TV national audience. Morozova got named to the Eastern Division side. But she never got off the bench due to her star teammates Virginia Wade and Billie Jean King in the East's 23-18 comeback victory. Morozova left after the game for Spokane to join her teammates for their match against the Sea-Port Cascades.

July 10's "Spokane experiment" tried to decide how many locals had $7.50 to $10 worth of curiosity to experience the best tennis ever played in that city. The last-place Soviets (6-19), 13½ games out of first, arrived that Friday, minus Morozova.

Three days in Spokane would be The Soviets' most extended break. They practiced Friday afternoon, and that night got feted at Playfair Race Course. Saturday, they gave free clinics at the city's Mission Park, sponsored by the Parks Department, Coca-Cola, and KREM-AM, from 10:30 to noon, and then from 1:30 to 3, with more advanced players. They practiced Saturday night and again the next morning. Preceding the Sunday 7:30 event capping off "Spokane Tennis Week" at Spokane Auditorium was a 7:15 doubles exhibition between Chmyreva and Mayor David Rodgers against the Cascades' Betty Stöve and a KREM sportscaster. A scant 1,243 spectators—less than half the 3,000 predicted by promoter Jerry Daugherty—saw "visiting" Sea-Port crush the Soviets, 32-20.

> ## *"Our players feel somewhere between unconscious and dead. Sometimes we only have time to eat, not sleep. Plus, our players have no team experience. So I tell them if they lose, lose very close."*
> **—ALEX METREVELI, The Soviets, 1977**

Cascades player-coach Tom Gorman supported Metreveli: "It's a real disadvantage for The Soviets to play all their matches on the road. They're not playing up to the rest of the teams' standards because they get no time to practice and are always on the road. We're in sort of a similar position splitting games between Seattle and Portland. It's not ideal."

July 11, the Soviets went to Kansas City and blew a lead to lose to the WTT-leading Lobsters, 26-24. Kemper Arena officials expelled anti-USSR protestors and removed a sign hung facing the Soviets from the upper deck that read "Stop Soviet Oppression." Eight members of Friends of Soviet Jewry, singing English and Hebrew freedom songs, unfurled the banner. A group official, while offering and collecting refunds to the match, said: "It's very interesting how the Soviets control free speech in our country and theirs."

July 18, the Philly-based Soviets found a friendly crowd in the least likely of places: North Little Rock, where they fried the San Diego Friars, 26-22. Associated Press wrote of Arkansas' first WTT match: "Call 'Em The Arky Soviets." Afterward, the two teams, invited by Arkansas Tennis Hall of Famer Darrel Snively, partook of ribs and beer.

The Soviets woke up and flew to the Bay Area and got gutted by the Gaters at Oakland Coliseum, 28-17. Then they flew to Seattle to endure another uphill climb and crumbled to the Cascades, 27-23. Asked if their nation coerced them to improve, Morozova mused, "When we win, we're in the papers at home. When we lose, we don't." The next nights were a blur: Thursday, Anaheim; Friday, Portland; Saturday, Phoenix; Sunday, L.A.

> ## *"Anybody can drive a flashy car. Not everyone can be a Master of Sports."*
> **—NATASHA CHMYREVA, 1977**

The Soviets invaded Louisville on July 24 and tore down the Nets before 3,100 at Louisville Gardens. 21-19. Cleveland-Pittsburgh's $1.5 million star Björn Borg railed against the lighting but conceded it did not dim enthusiasm. "The crowd was exciting; I liked it," he said. "But the lighting was bad. The players missed easy volleys." Kakulia agreed, calling the Gardens "the worst lighted place he'd ever played." He also griped about their scheduling: "It's hard for us to win since we do so much traveling. Last night we were in California. We went to sleep late, and had to get up very early to fly here."

Three months into the season, the Soviets played their first Philadelphia home match. Before a July 25 Spectrum crowd of 3,278, they thrashed the Nets for the second time in

Alex Metreveli and Olga Morozova, The Soviets, 1977
The Soviets' season in America helped thaw the Cold War

four days, in the Soviets' best WTT court display, 21-19. The feeling from the team's Philly offices was that the Russian stars got their groove back going into the stretch.

Morozova again lamented the lack of fan support: "The spectators don't want us to win. They want to see the Americans win." Metreveli added: "The people are against us, of course, but they are very friendly everywhere." GM Jorgensen deadpanned: "No doubt, in some locations, people turn out just to see them lose."

The Soviets were in Evanston, Illinois, on July 27 to face the Loves at Northwestern University's McGaw Hall. Earlier that day, Cook County Circuit Court Judge Richard J. Curry ruled against the city seeking to bar the event. The school's Athletic Director John Pont warned the team to expect protests. But the only hassle came when they couldn't find anyone to let their red hotel courtesy bus through the college gates. The Soviets lost 27-25 after Morozova lost to Brit Sue Barker, 6-3. The Soviets then spent the next week traveling to Vancouver, Omaha, and L.A. When asked of their mental state, Chmyreva snapped: "I knew exactly what I was getting into when I started in World Team Tennis."

> ## "We were surprised when the Soviet Federation agreed to this in the first place. So I don't think the Russians will make us or break us. We believe the concept of team tennis will work beyond the point of survival."
> **—BUTCH BUCHHOLZ, WTT Commissioner, 1977**

The Soviets went out with a whimper. They were the only team in WTT history ever to turn a profit, but only because their expenses were so low. The grace and agility of Morozova and Metreveli presented a human face to the cold USSR—and American jingoism got served because the Soviets usually lost.

The Soviets filled their luggage with the keys to cities and other trinkets of Americana. But curiosity only took things so far. In a sport where patience and poise are vital, they lived a suitcase-and-airplane, jet-set lifestyle. The players wilted under the strain of 44 matches in 33 cities in 65 days. And their last-place finish, with no Soviets ranked Top 10 in any category, shamed party leaders.

The Soviets (12-32) left for home after a 31-27 loss to the Apples and pulled out of WTT with no fanfare, eulogies, or press releases. The season's close coincided with an International Tennis Federation edict requiring all Russian players to be declared pro or amateur. The USSR, instead of making such a big decision—its star athletes, registered amateurs subsidized by the state—used that issue as a pretext to sever its WTT deal.

USSR officials, concerned that the hippie-ish Chmyreva might defect to the West, sent her home two weeks before the end of the season. She was later removed from the national team and denied permission to visit or play outside of the Soviet Union.

For the 1978 season, the Keystones/Soviets franchise was allocated to Orange County, California, and mutated into the Anaheim Oranges—starring Rosie Casals, Cliff Drysdale, Mark Cox, Tracy Austin, and no Russians at all.

Chapter 22
Anaheim Oranges

Rosie Casals, Anaheim Oranges, 1978

"We have plenty of talent and experience. With a little luck, we can contend."
—CLIFF DRYSDALE, Anaheim Oranges player-coach, 1978

Orange County was America's tennis hotbed, and WTT spent much of its five seasons trying to tap into the region's upper-middle-class suburbs. There were also a few years of chatter regarding the NFL L.A. Rams joining the MLB California Angels in Anaheim, and WTT saw its role within this new pantheon.

WTT officials promoted a July 25-27, 1975 "Spectacular" at the 7,200-seat Anaheim Convention Center, with five teams over three days. Such "Spectaculars" were eventually abandoned, but they drew well in O.C., so for 1976, A.C.C. hosted "home" matches by the Los Angeles Strings, San Diego Friars, Detroit/Indiana Loves, and Hawaii Leis. In 1977, WTT rolled out weekly Anaheim events, with ten teams playing ten matches over ten weeks. These Convention Center nights aired Saturdays on Channel 11 at 11 p.m. There were also two "home" games for The Soviets (listed in Bank of Newport brochures as "Team Russia"): July 14 against L.A., and July 21 vs. San Diego.

On December 1, 1978, WTT rolled out the Anaheim Oranges, an expansion franchise to replace the departed Soviets as the league's tenth team. WTT officials cut a deal with A.C.C. manager Tom Liegler, who could accommodate 16 of the team's 22 home games. The Strings' Jerry Buss and Friars' Frank Mariani agreed to waive their Southern California territorial rights—because Mariani-Buss Associates owned the franchise.

Since the Oranges came together so late—and after a St. Louis franchise fell through—Anaheim had to awkwardly compete in the Eastern Division, with New York, Indiana, Boston, and New Orleans. Because of their situation with the Convention Center, they also had to host six "home" matches in neutral courts from Pennsylvania to Utah.

GM Dennis Hall said, "We chose this area as our prime expansion position because it boasts the nation's ninth-largest population, with the finest tennis facilities. Support and civic interest have been incredible." To ensure viability, Hall said he'd trade for proven stars and sign draft picks, like Lea Antonopolis and John Evert, younger brother of Chris.

The Oranges quickly announced their first star, purchasing the contract of Rosie Casals, L.A.'s star female the past three seasons. That meant Jerry Buss, who just acquired Chris Evert for his Strings, sold Casals to himself. Hall said the Oranges would also help WTT test other cities seeking 1979 franchises, like Mexico City, Detroit, and Las Vegas. The GM emoted: "The fans will have great fun, but I'll be a nervous wreck every night."

"It's great to contribute to this team. It makes me want to live in the U.S. India's old-fashioned. You can get so many things here—fast food, television, excitement."

—ANAND AMRITRAJ, Anaheim Oranges, 1978

Three weeks before the season, Hall announced the Oranges' 1978 six-member roster—all Mariani-Buss-associated players, versatile and experienced at WTT. For 36-year-old South African player-coach Cliff Drysdale, the new franchise traded a #1 pick to the Friars. UK star Mark Cox, an all-star for the 1975 champion Pittsburgh Triangles, spent 1977 with the Strings. Indian star Anand Amritraj was the older brother of Vijay and Ashok Amritraj (of the '78 Strings). Seal Beach's Kathy Harter, one of the top netters ever from O.C. but slowed by injuries, played doubles with Casals two years in L.A.

For their final spot, the Oranges considered Terry Holladay and Pam Teeguarden before signing Françoise Dürr. The two-time WTT all-star won a 1974 title with the Denver Racquets and a 1975 MVP. An Oranges newsletter said regarding France's #1 player: "Dürr, born in Algiers on Christmas Day in 1942, has a limp-wrist backhand and a patty-cake serve, but she has won 13 major titles including one at Wimbledon and two at the U.S. Open."

The Oranges' season got off to a sour start April 21 at Madison Square Garden. JoAnne Russell (ex-Cascades/Triangles) and her powerful serves carried the night in her debut for the defending champion New York Apples, preventing a fruitful Anaheim WTT premiere, 28-25.

Then the team flew west. April 23, the jet-lagged Oranges lost to the Boston Lobsters in Sacramento, 28-23. The next night, they debuted in Anaheim, losing again to Boston, 29-22. The night after that, against the visiting Golden Gaters, Anaheim withstood the onslaught of Virginia Wade, Tom Okker, Frew McMillan, and Sandy Mayer to win a match, 29-24. May 1 in Oakland, the home team exacted revenge, bruising the Oranges, 27-23.

Mark Cox, Anaheim Oranges, 1978

In the first of four "Tab Discount Nights" sponsored by "The Official Soft Drink of World Team Tennis," last-place Anaheim won their second match May 2 before a dressy A.C.C. crowd of 3,859, pasting the injury-ravaged Phoenix Racquets 31-13. The Oranges refused to look this gift horse in the mouth, as Drysdale blanked Dean Martin, Jr. 6-0, as did Harter-Dürr over Kristien Shaw-Rayni Fox. The Oranges' low point came May 11, allowing visiting Indiana to rally from a three-game deficit, 24-22, before 1,535 fans. Drysdale described his WTT-worst 4-11 squad's spirits as "awfully good, despite a slow start."

> ## "This hasn't been very satisfying in that we have the talent, and we're not putting it together. We can play better. We haven't gotten killed, and when we win, it's by a large margin."
> **—ROSIE CASALS, Anaheim Oranges, 1978**

League experts seemed clueless for predicting that the Oranges would be a .500 team. With one-third of the season down, the Oranges' prospects looked dim—with 21 of their final 28 games on the road, where they had struggled, just 1-5 away from the Convention Center. The good news was all of Anaheim's losses came in close games, their average loss by two points. The bad news was when Elegant Travel of Laguna Beach—"Official Travel Agency of the Anaheim Oranges"—announced that only four people had signed up for special "fan trips" to selected away games.

Then Drysdale and Cox fueled Anaheim on May 22 to a 27-26 comeback over Seattle in a match aired on KCOP-TV. Drysdale said, "Cox and I went out there, hitting all out. We knew we had nothing to lose." He also said Anaheim's sweetest surprise was the play of Anand Amritraj. Two nights later, at the A.C.C., the surging Oranges (7-12) bruised the Billie Jean King-less Apples, 26-21. Vitas Gerulaitis' presence was nearly enough to offset her absence due to bronchitis, but Anaheim outhustled the defending champs. Casals ruled the first set, while Dürr-Amritraj shone, as Anand upped his mark to 15-4. June 3 in New Orleans, fewer than 1,000 fans at the 80,000-capacity Superdome saw Rosie damage her right knee ligaments, getting hurt landing after leaving her feet for a shot.

Dennis Hall predicted Anaheim would average 4,000-4,500 fans. The Oranges did an excellent job with season tickets (1,579), but most home crowds drew in the 1,900-2,800 range—whereas those 1976-77 events at the Convention Center attracted over 4,000 without a home team.

The next matches were a blur. On June 6, what player-coach Drysdale called a "hazy decision" turned into a "stroke" of genius, as his Oranges squeezed the Lobsters, 29-26. He allowed his #3 woman Kathy Harter off the bench, who responded with dominating efforts in singles and mixed doubles. The next night Cox and Drysdale excelled as they edged the Sun Belt Nets in 28-27 in Mobile. June 8 in St. Louis, the Oranges lashed the Loves, 32-19. Casals, hobbled by her injury, sucked it up in a spirited women's doubles pairing with "Frenchy" Dürr, 6-3.

On June 9, the squad played a "home" match nearly 3,000 miles from Anaheim—in Reading, PA, for "The McDonald's Tennis Classic," a benefit for the American Heart

Association of Bucks County. The Oranges fell to the Apples 29-24 in what got dubbed "The Fruit Bowl" before a vocal crowd of 2,300 at Albright College's Bollman Center.

Anaheim came to Reading spent, having trekked 12 hours from St. Louis. Billie Jean King played in mixed doubles but then got held out of singles by team trainers due to a nagging heel injury, while Casals sat on the bench with knee issues. Deprived of singles matches featuring those star players, many fans felt cheated.

Nearly 15,000 fans had gathered earlier in the day at Reading Airport to greet tennis star Billy Talbert and his WPIX-TV team broadcasting the match. An impressed Talbert, doing color commentary, shouted, "Wow, what a reception for World Team Tennis!" The television broadcast created several delays. During one break, Gerulaitis sat on a startled woman's lap and flirted. A nurse sitting courtside by the ambulance crew took a smash to her face off an errant Cox serve. Both squads mingled at a post-match party, boogieing in the hotel's club till 2 a.m. Tennis designer Teddy Tingling held court from his VIP table.

The next night in Indianapolis, the Oranges outclassed the Loves 32-19, led by Kathy Harter's upset over Dianne Fromholtz, and the injured Casals gritting it out with Dürr for a 6-4 doubles win. June 14, in their final match before midseason, Anaheim went to Boston and got routed, 29-15. The Oranges, who started the season poorly—going 1-6 and 4-11—had won eight of their next 13 matches going into the Wimbledon midseason breather.

During the break, Casals underwent season-ending knee surgery in Manhattan. "Rosie is not expected to return to competitive tennis for the rest of WTT or the fall circuit," said her manager Shari Barman, daughter of WTT co-founder Fred Barman. Anaheim officials insisted their team was profitable, and that Casals would return next season.

> **"Things will improve. This is too good an area and too good a product. I have every confidence in Orange County. We'll just have to roll up our shirtsleeves and work harder."**
> **—DENNIS HALL, Anaheim Oranges GM, 1978**

The Oranges on June 29 announced signing 15-year-old tennis whiz Tracy Austin, from Los Angeles County's Rolling Hills Estates, to step in for Rosie. GM Hall said that Austin's deal was for three matches, and to maintain her amateur status, she would not get paid. Austin had World Team Tennis in her blood, with her older siblings Jeff and Pam Austin members of the 1974 champion Denver Racquets.

Austin debuted July 11 at A.C.C., as the Nets lashed the Oranges, 30-28. The squads went into the night tied for third place in the Eastern Division behind Boston and New York. The match's pivotal moment came in women's doubles when New Orleans' Renée Richards and Pat Bostrom edged Austin-Dürr, 7-6. The next night, the wunderkind made her Bay Area premiere, wowing in singles (6-3 over Virginia Wade), and doubles with Dürr (6-1 over Ilana Kloss-Marise Kruger), to raze the Golden Gaters in Oakland, 29-

Françoise Dürr, Anaheim Oranges, 1978

19. July 18 in Anaheim, Austin crushed the Wimbledon champion Martina Navratilova, 6-3, but her team ceded a lead in a 26-25 flameout to the Lobsters. Then the Oranges left town without Austin and got pulverized by the Apples at Madison Square Garden, 24-17.

The Oranges returned home for a run of A.C.C. matches. July 25, Anaheim overcame Indiana 27-23 in overtime, led by Amritraj doubles sets with Dürr and Drysdale. Two nights later in Phoenix, the last-place Racquets throttled 'em 28-15. It was easy to see Anaheim's issue: with Casals out and Austin's cameo over, they had no women's game.

July 30 in Anaheim, the Oranges overcame the visiting Gaters, 26-25. Anaheim played every day that week, including tweaking the Strings at home 29-25 and fileting the Friars in San Diego, 28-23. August 6 at Boston U.'s Brown Arena, Dale "The Animal" Collings proved to live or die by his murderous serve, as he tied a WTT record with 11 aces in one set to crush Mark Cox, and lift his Lobsters over the Oranges, 30-27. Two nights later, Dürr-Amritraj shredded the Nets' John Lucas-Pat Bostrom 6-2 to rally the Oranges 28-25. The victory placed the two squads into another third-place tie.

Sunday, August 13, the last-place Loves ended their dismal season by picking off the visiting Oranges 28-23. But two nights prior in New Haven, Anaheim beat New Orleans—to back into the final playoff spot, against the two-time defending champion Apples.

Anaheim (20-24) began their opening round bid back at Madison Square Garden. In Game One, the Apples blasted the Oranges, 29-16. Facing elimination, coach Drysdale expressed optimism: "I definitely think we can come back. This is not a team that will quit."

The Oranges could not secure a home playoff date at the A.C.C., so they tried other Orange County facilities from Newport Beach Club to Fountain Valley High Gym before opting for the 11,250-seat L.A. Forum. The *Los Angeles Times* (10/12/78) reported "the Oranges had only gotten about 200 of their nearly 1,500 season ticket holders to buy playoff seats." The Forum crowd of 1,043—the smallest of 1978 in Anaheim or L.A.—saw the Gerulaitis-fueled Apples race to a 24-11 advantage after the first three sets and then held on 27-20.

> ## "There was no excuse for this team's performance. We were complacent and simply did not play well. We didn't deserve to go on."
> ### —NANCY RICHEY, Anaheim Oranges, 1978

The Oranges ceased to exist on January 4, 1979. Hall said operations would stop as soon as all eight hundred ticketholders for 1979 got reimbursed. The team had maintained limited administrative office functions at 800 West Katella Avenue as they studied the rebuilding efforts of WTT, reduced to two franchises. Hall conceded: "We were faced with decisions that required substantial expenditures, and it is in our opinion that there are too many unanswered questions about the future of WTT to go ahead."

After WTT folded, Mariani-Buss Associates paid off the contracts of Cliff Drysdale, Rosie Casals, and Françoise Dürr. In the summer of 1979, the Oranges-originated men's doubles tandem of Drysdale-Cox ranked #4 in the world.

1974

EASTERN DIVISION
ATLANTIC SECTION
Philadelphia Freedoms 39-5
Boston Lobsters....................19-25
Baltimore Banners................16-28
New York Sets 15-29
CENTRAL SECTION
Detroit Loves..........................30-14
Pittsburgh Triangles.............30-14
Cleveland Nets......................21-23
Toronto-Buffalo Royals.........13-31

WESTERN DIVISION
GULF PLAINS SECTION
Minnesota Buckskins 27-17
Houston E-Z Riders...............25-19
Florida Flamingos.................19-25
Chicago Aces 15-29
PACIFIC SECTION
Denver Racquets...................30-14
Golden Gaters 23-21
Los Angeles Strings..............16-28
Hawaii Leis 14-30

Champions: Denver Racquets d. Philadelphia Freedoms 27-21, 28-24 (55-45 total)
Coach of the Year: Tony Roche, Denver Racquets
Most Valuable Player: Billie Jean King, Philadelphia Freedoms

1975

EASTERN DIVISION
Pittsburgh Triangles...............36-8
New York Sets 34-10
Boston Lobsters....................20-26
Indiana Loves........................18-26
Cleveland Nets......................16-28

WESTERN DIVISION
Golden Gaters 29-15
Phoenix Racquets.................22-22
Los Angeles Strings..............20-24
Hawaii Leis 14-30
San Diego Friars 14-30

Champions: Pittsburgh Triangles d. Golden Gaters 25-26, 28-25, 21-14 (74-65 total)
Coach of the Year: Frew McMillan, Golden Gaters
Female MVP: Evonne Goolagong, Pittsburgh Triangles
Male MVP: Tom Okker, Golden Gaters
Female Rookie of the Year: Greer Stevens, Boston Lobsters
Male Rookie of the Year: Marty Riessen, Cleveland Nets

1976

EASTERN DIVISION
New York Sets 33-10
Pittsburgh Triangles.............24-20
Cleveland Nets......................20-24
Indiana Loves........................19-25
Boston Lobsters....................18-25

WESTERN DIVISION
Phoenix Racquets.................30-14
Golden Gaters 28-16
Los Angeles Strings..............22-22
San Diego Friars 13-31
Hawaii Leis 12-32

Champions: New York Sets d. Golden Gaters 31-23, 29-21, 31-13 (91-57 total)
Coach of the Year: Fred Stolle, New York Sets
Female MVP: Chris Evert, Phoenix Racquets
Male MVP: Sandy Mayer, New York Sets
Female Rookie of the Year: Chris Evert, Phoenix Racquets
Male Rookie of the Year: Rod Laver, San Diego Friars

Eastern Division All-Stars, WTT All-Star Match, San Diego Sports Arena, 1977
L-R: Tony Roche, Marty Riessen, Vitas Gerulaitis, Björn Borg, Fred Stolle,
Billie Jean King, Sue Barker, Olga Morozova, Roy Emerson, Martina Navratilova

1977

EASTERN DIVISION		WESTERN DIVISION	
Boston Lobsters	35-9	Phoenix Racquets	28-16
New York Apples	33-11	Golden Gaters	25-19
Indiana Loves	21-23	San Diego Friars	21-23
Cleveland Nets	16-28	Sea-Port Cascades	18-26
The Soviets	12-32	L.A. Strings	11-33

Champions: New York Apples d. Phoenix Racquets 27-22, 28-17 (55-39 total)
Coach of the Year: Fred Stolle, New York Apples
Female MVP: Chris Evert, Phoenix Racquets
Male MVP: Frew McMillan, Golden Gaters
Female Rookie of the Year: Sue Barker, Indiana Loves
Male Rookie of the Year: Björn Borg, Cleveland-Pittsburgh Nets

1978

EASTERN DIVISION		WESTERN DIVISION	
Boston Lobsters	33-11	San Diego Friars	30-14
New York Apples	22-22	L.A. Strings	27-17
Anaheim Oranges	20-24	Golden Gaters	21-23
New Orleans Nets	20-24	Seattle Cascades	20-24
Indiana Loves	13-31	Phoenix Racquets	14-30

Champions: L.A. Strings d. Boston Lobsters 24-21, 30-20, 26-27, 28-25 (108-93 total)
Coach of the Year: Ilie Năstase, Los Angeles Strings
Female MVP: Martina Navratilova, Boston Lobsters
Male MVP: Frew McMillan, Golden Gaters
Rookie of the Year: Sherwood Stewart, Seattle Cascades

WTT HISTORY 1974-1978

The Art of World Team Tennis, by Greg Hoffman, 1977 (all 1974-1976 statistics)

Anchorage Daily News, "Love To Be A Forbidden Word In Tennis," AP, October 5, 1972

Observer-Reporter, "National Tennis League Begun by Pittsburghers," AP, October 5, 1972

Star-News, "Inter City Tennis League Formed," UPI, October 5, 1972

Tampa Tribune, "White Out Love Forbidden," Tribune Wire Service, October 5, 1972

Daily Times, "National Tennis League Visionary," by Rick Cullen, October 19, 1977

Sarasota Herald-Tribune, "Pro Tennis League in '74," H-T Wire Report, March 15, 1973

St. Joseph News-Press, "Two Tennis Bodies Merge, Form WTT," AP, April 27, 1973

Anchorage Daily News, "Merger Forms Team Play," by Terry Flynn, April 28, 1973

Evening Independent, "Tennis Nets New Look For The Future," AP, April 28, 1973

Lakeland Ledger, "New Pro Tennis League Being Formed," AP, April 28, 1973

The Sun, "Peace Agreement On Tennis Front," April 28, 1973

Toledo Blade, "Pro Net Leagues Announce Merger," AP, April 28, 1973

Chicago Tribune, "Coed Tennis Finally Has its Day," by Wayne Dunham, April 29, 1974

Daily Chronicle, "French Nasty Over WTT Play," UPI, May 22, 1974

Montreal Gazette, "Toronto Part of 16-Team League," CP, May 22, 1973

Deseret News, "And Now It's Team Tennis For The Pros," UPI, May 23, 1973

Milwaukee Journal, "Team Tennis League Formed," Press Dispatches, May 23, 1973

Modesto Bee, "Pro Tennis League Sets 1974 Opening," AP, May 23, 1973

Montgomery Advertiser, "World Pro Tennis League Formed," AP, May 23, 1973

Schenectady Gazette, "Pro Tennis League To Feature Team Play," AP, May 23, 1973

Spokane Daily Chronicle, "Pro Tennis Loop Slated For 1974," AP, May 23, 1973

Williamson Daily News, "Cincy Group Buy Colonels," by Terry Flynn, June 15, 1973

Montreal Gazette, "Pros Talking To Team League," AP, June 25, 1973

Observer-Reporter, "World Team Tennis Seeking Top Stars," AP, June 25, 1973

The Age, "Tennis League Rethink," AP, June 26, 1973

Pittsburgh Post-Gazette, "Sidelights on Sports," by Al Abrams, June 26, 1973

Spokane Daily Chronicle, "Team Tennis Loop Director Recruits," AP, June 26, 1973

Vancouver Sun, "Team Tennis Makes Its Pitch," AP, June 27, 1973

Herald-Journal, "Net League Interest Reported Increasing," AP, June 29, 1973

Anchorage Daily News, "Tennis Holds Draft," AP, August 4, 1973

Eugene Register-Guard, "Tennis Tour Drafts Stars," AP, August 4, 1973

Free Lance-Star, "King 'Drafted'," AP, August 4, 1973

Herald-Journal, "WTT Draft Gets Newcombe, King First," AP, August 4, 1973

Lodi News-Sentinel, "World Tennis Draft," UPI, August 4, 1973

Milwaukee Sentinel, "King Goes 1st in Draft," Sentinel Wire Service, August 4, 1973

Montreal Gazette, "New Pro Tennis League Drafts Stars, Signs Two," AP, August 4, 1973

Observer-Reporter, "Team Tennis Conducts First Pro Draft," AP, August 4, 1973

The Phoenix, "Tennis Draft Underway," AP, August 4, 1973

Schenectady Gazette, "Team Tennis Signs Billie Jean," by Frank Brown, August 4, 1973

St. Petersburg Times, "Tennis League Nets Queen," AP, August 4, 1973

Victoria Advocate, "Pro Tennis Draft Held," AP, August 4, 1973

The Record (NJ), "Sets Leave Lot To Be Desired," by Mark Ruskie, August 5, 1973

Windsor Star, "Court Joins Team Tennis Organization," AP, October 30, 1973

Arizona Republic, "Team Tennis Threatening Pro Circuit," AP, November 14, 1973

Sports Illustrated, "Scorecard," by Robert Creamer, November 26, 1973

Spokane Daily Chronicle, "Team Tennis Flayed By Canadian Player," UPI, January 9, 1974

New York Times, "Pro Tennis Unites on Pension," January 18, 1974

Chicago Tribune, "Pro Tennis Gets USLTA Nod," UPI, January 19, 1974

New York Times, "Team Tennis Is Offered U.S. Sanction," January 19, 1974

Gettysburg Times, "USLTA To Sanction World Team Tennis," AP, January 19, 1974

Gadsden Times, "Team Tennis Sanctioned," AP, January 20, 1974

Daytona Beach Morning Journal, "Tennis War Erupts," AP, January 25, 1974

New York Times, "The Progress Index," AP, January 26, 1974

Danville Register, "Tennis Wars," AP, January 26, 1974

Palm Beach Post, "Ashe Rejects Team Tennis," AP, January 26, 1974

New York Times, "ILTF Lists Conditions For League," by Fred Tupper, January 27, 1974

New York Times, "WTT Reaches Accord With ILTF," February 15, 1974

Observer-Reporter, "WTT Clears Giant Hurdle," AP, February 15, 1974

Newport Daily News, "Van Allen Considers WTT," by Elliott K. Stein, February 19, 1974

Spokesman-Review, "Billie Jean Bruised Up By Gimmick," AP, February 19, 1974

Pensacola News Journal, "World Team Tennis Banned by Italy," AP, February 26, 1974

Cumberland Evening Times, UPI, March 6, 1974

New York Times, "WTT Set To Bypass Sanctions," April 9, 1974

Sports Illustrated, "Scorecard," by Andrew Crichton, April 22, 1974

Sarasota Herald-Tribune, "Sports In Brief," H-T Wire Services, April 23, 1974

Sports Illustrated, "They Said It," by Andrew Crichton, April 29, 1974

Evening Independent, "WTT: Will It Be A Hit... Or A Miss," by Bob Chick, May 4, 1974

Green Bay Press-Gazette, "World Team Tennis Ready for 1st Year," AP, May 5, 1974

Evening Independent, "Screams, Catcalls On Tennis Scene," AP, May 6, 1974

Miami News, "Unisex Team Concepts Dawn," by Jack Wilkinson, May 6, 1974

Morning News (DE), "Rowdy Crowd King's Hope for Pro Tennis," AP, May 6, 1974

Kentucky New Era, "World Team Tennis Debuts," AP, May 6, 1974

Philadelphia Inquirer, "Freedoms Debut Rain Delayed," by John Dell, May 7, 1974

Portsmouth Times, "Tennis League Moves Into Gear," AP, May 7, 1974

The Tennessean, "WTT Gives Birth Americanized Tennis," by Jeff Hanna, May 7, 1974

Albany Herald, "Long Rough Road Seen Ahead For WTT," AP, May 8, 1974

The Eagle (TX), Houston EZ Riders Win Opening Match, AP, May 8, 1974

Gettysburg Times, "Start Feud To Help Team Tennis At Gate?" AP, May 8, 1974

Watertown Daily Times, "Billie Jean Leads Team To Victory," UPI, May 8, 1974

The Age, "They're Still Calling It Tennis," by Peter Stone, May 9, 1974

European Stars and Bars, "WTT Should Retain Scoring," AP, May 9, 1974

Fort Lauderdale News, "World Team Tennis: A Rude Awakening," UPI, May 9, 1974

Minneapolis Star, "Tennis Becomes Social Commentary," by Chan Keith, May 9, 1974

Newport Daily News (RI), "WTT Jolts Leftist Onlooker," by Elliott K. Stein, May 9, 1974

Boston Globe, "WTT Topples Love and Marriage," May 10, 1974

Waycross Journal, "Evonne Finds Team Tennis Concept Problem," AP, May 10, 1974

Los Angeles Times, European Tennis Opens Attack on WTT," AP, May 15, 1974

Palm Beach Post, "WTT May Change Format," Post Wire Service, May 15, 1974

Washington Post, "Tennis' Changing Times," by Mark Asher, May 15, 1974

The Age, "World Tennis Threat," Reuters, May 16, 1974

Miami News, "WTT Needs Players Who Yell Back," by John Crittenden, May 16, 1974

Star News, "Team Tennis May Shorten Program," AP, May 17, 1974

New York Times, "Program Altered by WTT," by Charles Friedman, May 19, 1974

Sports Illustrated, "A Golden Week For Oldies," by Joe Jures, May 20, 1974

Boston Globe, "Connors Chases Lira, WTT Burns," by Ernie Roberts, May 22, 1974

Leader-Post, "Tennis World Is Stirred Up," AP, May 22, 1974

Palm Beach Post, "Connors, Goolagong Can't Play," UPI, May 22, 1974

Sarasota Herald-Tribune, "Connors Gets Refused," UPI, May 22, 1974

Beaver County Times, "Heckling Hurting WTT," by Andy Nuzzo, May 23, 1974

Statesville Record and Landmark, "WTT Players Are Banned," AP, May 23, 1974

The Telegraph, "Controversy Heating Up In Tennis," AP, May 23, 1974

Palm Beach Post, "Connors Banned in Italy," AP, May 26, 1974

Palm Beach Post, "Pro Tennis The WTT Way," by Ron Smith, May 26, 1974

Herald-Journal, "Tennis Without Love," AP, May 29, 1974

El Paso Herald Post, "WTT Now Streamlined," by Margaret Osbourne, May 30, 1974

El Paso Herald Post, "Golden Gaters Outdraw Oakland A's," May 30, 1974

Michigan Daily, "Polite, Placid Tennis Takes On A New Look," AP, May 31, 1974

Asbury Park Press, "French Turn Down Connors and Goolagong," AP, June 1, 1974

Florence Morning News, "Connors Goolagong Suit Tossed Out," AP, June 1, 1974

Palm Beach Post, "French Open Ban Upheld," AP, June 1, 1974

Courier-Journal (KY), "Barnum & Bailey Tennis," by Will Grimsley, June 2, 1974

Lakeland Ledger, "Fan Participation Could Lead To Bottle Throwing," AP, June 4, 1974

Oakland Tribune, "Ralston Raps WTT Etiquette," AP, June 4, 1974

Des Moines Tribune, "Tennis No. 1 to Bill Cosby," by John Dell, June 7, 1974

Herald-Journal "Noise Will Just Be Part of the Game," by Mike Hembree June 12, 1974

Reading Eagle, "Tiebreaker Decides Three Tennis Matches," AP, June 12, 1974

Pittsburgh Post-Gazette, "Casals Tri's Harder," by Phil Axlerod, June 13, 1974

Chicago Tribune, "WTT Crowds Slim in Key Cities," by Steve Nidetz, June 14, 1974

Danville News, "Austins Don't Sit Around," by Mike Morrow, June 19, 1974

Eugene Register-Guard, "I'll Double Fault You!" by Jim Murray, June 22, 1974

Herald-Journal, "Clash in New War," AP, June 24, 1974

New York Times, "Tennis Ban Spurs Suit By WTT," June 24, 1974

Pittsburgh Post-Gazette, "Fuhrer Slams For Triangles," by Charley Feeney, June 25, 1974

Pittsburgh Press, "Growing Pains For WTT," by Pat Livingston, June 25, 1974

Lebanon Daily-News, "Tennis Doesn't Need Violence," by Jim Murray, June 27, 1974

Baltimore Sun, "Suit Dropped By WTT," July 3, 1974

Christian Science Monitor, "World Team Tennis sketch," July 26, 1974

Pittsburgh Post-Gazette, "Tri's Gunter Downs Nets," by Vince Leonard, July 26, 1974

Dayton Daily News (OH), "WTT Attendance Lags," by Bob Moon, August 11, 1974

Daytona Beach Morning Journal, "WTT Starts With A Pop," AP, August 11, 1974

Beaver County Times, "World Team Tennis Playoff Roundup," August 19, 1974

Spokane Daily Chronicle, "Four Teams Score Win In Net Play," AP, August 21, 1974

Miami News, "Controversial Ban Lifted On WTT Players," AP, August 22, 1974

Gettysburg Times, "Racquets Defeat Freedoms," AP, August 27, 1974

York Daily Record, "WTT Confab Inconclusive," UPI, November 27, 1974

Muncie Evening Press, "Der Fuhrer Isn't Kaput," UPI, August 31, 1974

Times Daily, "Fuhrer President Of New WTT," AP, August 31, 1974

Star-News, "Fuhrer Succeeds Kaiser," UPI, September 1, 1974

Palladium-Item, "Fuhrer Succeeds Kaiser As Leader," UPI, September 1, 1974

Detroit Free Press, "WTT Rejects Rap For Borg's Injury," September 9, 1977

Daytona Beach News-Journal, "King Makes A Point," by Robin Herman, September 11, 1974

Pittsburgh Press, "Triangles To Name Edwards Coach," UPI, October 23, 1974

Bangor Daily News, "Billie Jean Drafts Bobby Riggs," AP, November 27, 1974

Boston Globe, "It Is To Laugh: Carson, Cosby Among WTT Draftees," November 27, 1974

Lewiston Morning Tribune, "Billie Jean Tabs Riggs," AP, November 27, 1974

New York Times, "Tight Money, Bobby Riggs, At Draft," by Neil Amdur, November 27, 1974

Redlands Daily Facts, "Evert, Connors Call Off Marriage Plans," UPI, December 14, 1974

Gadsden Times, "11 Teams In World Tennis," AP, February 2, 1975

New York Times, "WTT Is Reducing To 11 Teams," UPI, February 2, 1975

People, "Tennis' Next Star," February 3, 1975

Los Angeles Times, "WTT Reorganized," by Candace Mayeron, February 5, 1975

Indiana Gazette, "Pro Sports Boom in for Big Fold," by Fred Rothenberg, March 26, 1975

Bangor Daily News, "Pro Expansion Boom Is Now Going Bust," AP, April 1, 1975

Scottsdale Daily Progress, "Froehling On WTT Future," by Judy Frank, April 1, 1975

Toledo Blade, "Sportswhirl," AP, May 1, 1975

Los Angeles Times, "WTT Gives It Another Try," by Cheryl Bentsen, May 5, 1975

News-Dispatch, "Size Of Crowd Disappointing," by Jim McKay, May 6, 1975

Sports Illustrated, "Patching A Tattered Image," by Joe Jares, May 12, 1975

Los Angeles Times, "Melody Lingers On," by Ron Rapoport, May 17, 1975

New York Times, "Star Game in WTT Set Tonight," by Leonard Koppett, July 12, 1975

Detroit Free Press, "Coed Showers in WTT," by Mickey Herskowitz, May 18, 1975

Boston Globe, "Lobsters Lose 2 — It's A Joke," by John Powers. May 25, 1975

Los Angeles Times, "Strings Field WTT Event Here," May 25, 1975

Los Angeles Times, "Strings 'Spectacular' Opening," by Dwight Chapin, June 4, 1975

Indianapolis News, "Loves Love Noisy Fans," by Dick Denny, June 14, 1975

Reading Eagle, "Margaret Court Called Unrecognized Queen," UPI, June 15, 1975

Press-Courier, "Strings Have Knotty Problem," by Bud Tucker, June 20, 1975

Reading Eagle, "Few Owners Bullish On Team Tennis," by Karol Stronger June 29, 1975

Spokesman Review, "Doubts Continue About Team Tennis," AP, July 2, 1975

Press-Courier, "World Team Tennis Sets Stage For All-Star Match," AP, July 11, 1975

Ellensburg Daily Record, "Riessen Paces All-Star Net Victory," UPI, July 14, 1975

Observer-Reporter, "Billie Jean Gets Ovation; Loses All-Star Match," July 14, 1975

Spokesman-Review, "John Lucas Eyes Career In Two Sports," AP, July 19, 1975

Pittsburgh Post-Gazette, "WTT Puts House In Order," by Vince Leonard, July 28, 1975

Tennis Illustrated, "World Team Tennis 1974-1975: Is This the End?" August 1975

Daytona Beach Morning Journal, "Connors' Lawsuits Settled," AP, August 23, 1975

San Mateo Times, "Evonne, Vitas Key Win Over Gaters," UPI, August 26, 1975

San Antonio Express, "WTT Here to Stay Says King," AP, October 28, 1975

San Antonio Light, "Nastase In Finals," AP, December 7, 1975

Danville Register, "WTT Lands Nastase," AP, December 12, 1975

Findlay Republican Courier, "WTT Draft," UPI, December 12, 1975

Spokane Daily Chronicle, "Team Tennis To Survive," AP, December 12, 1975

Herald-Journal, "World Team Tennis Still Grabbing Top Players," AP, February 18, 1976

Youngstown Vindicator, "WTT Has Lock On Most Name Players," AP, February 22, 1976

Los Angeles Times, "Zing They Go," by John Hall, March 11, 1976

Pittsburgh Press, "Draft on Tap Before Bar," by Pat Livingston, March 16, 1976

Sarasota Herald-Tribune, "New Leagues Have Same Names," AP, March 28, 1976

Los Angeles Times, "WTT's Third Season," by Candace Mayeron, April 13, 1976

Salt Lake Tribune, "Racquets Rule In Salt Lake," April 13, 1976

Danville Register, "WTT Opens Third Season," April 25, 1976

Pittsburgh Post-Gazette, "WTT Eyes One Million In Attendance," AP, April 26, 1976

Gettysburg Times, "Fuhrer Seeks To Depose Larry King," AP, April 27, 1976

Arizona Republic, "Chris Evert: Lonely Star," by Penny Butler, May 2, 1976

New York Times, "WTT Slips Into Third Season," by Tony Kornheiser, May 2, 1976

Pittsburgh Post-Gazette, "Ralston Pulls Strings," by Vince Leonard, May 7, 1976

Beaver County Times, "Nastase: WTT Isn't Good Tennis," by Rich Emert, May 13, 1976

Gadsden Times, "Lucas To Turn Pro in Basketball, Tennis," AP, June 9, 1976

Oakland Tribune, "Tennis Gaters After Lucas," by Ed Levitt, June 10, 1976

Beaver County Times, "Evert, Laver Lead WTT West All-Stars," UPI, June 15, 1976

Boca Raton News, "Team Tennis Fighting A Losing Battle," UPI, June 27, 1976

St. Petersburg Times, "Chris, West Big Underdogs," UPI, July 10, 1976

Bangor Daily News "Goolagong Outlasts Evert, Gives West Verdict," AP, July 12, 1976

Bakersfield Californian, "West Wins WTT All-Star Thriller," AP, July 12, 1976

News and Courier, "West Takes All-Star Classics," AP, July 12, 1976

Pittsburgh Post-Gazette, "Triangles In New York After Stars Thriller," July 12, 1976

Observer-Reporter, "Team Tennis To Expand Operation," AP, July 16, 1976

Pittsburgh Post-Gazette, "WTT Puts House In Order," by Vince Leonard, July 28, 1976

Ellensburg Daily Record, "Nastase Blasts Fans," UPI, August 11, 1976

Santa Ana Register, "WTT Attendance Jumps," AP, August 20, 1976

Van Nuys Valley News, "Jerry Buss Pulls The Strings," August 25, 1976

Gettysburg Times, "Pa. Keystones Have Drafted Dr. Richards," AP, January 13, 1977

St. Joseph News-Press, "Richards To Consider Pro Bid," AP, January 13, 1977

St. Petersburg Times, "Draft Of Renee Stirs Controversy," UPI, January 14, 1977

Spokane Daily Chronicle, "Borg Will Join New Net Loop," AP, February 2, 1977

Albuquerque Journal, "World Team Tennis Inks Borg," AP, February 3, 1977

Christian Science Monitor, "WTT Serves A News Smash," by Ross Atkin, February 8, 1977

Daily News, "Team Tennis Holds Its Own," by Will Grimsley, April 26, 1977

Lakeland Ledger, "World Team Tennis In Fourth Season," AP, April 26, 1977

Fairbanks Daily News-Miner, "A Different Game," by Will Grimsley, April 28, 1977

Sports Illustrated, "Roundup of the Week," May 9, 1977

The Times Of Trenton, "Tennis, Everyone?" by Curtis G. Way, May 12, 1977

Lodi News-Sentinel, "Transsexual With Nets," UPI, June 3, 1977

Observer-Reporter, "WTT Nets Sign Dr. Richards," AP, June 3, 1977

Reading Eagle, "Chromosome Test For Renee," AP, June 3, 1977

Star-News, "Ms. Richards Signs With World Team Tennis," UPI, June 3, 1977

Lawrence Journal-World, "Reaction To Renee Proves Frightening," AP, June 4, 1977

Daily Union, "Nets Signing Of Richards Meets Tennis Controversy," AP, June 6, 1977

Press-Courier, "Renee Stirs Up A Fuss," by Will Grimsley, June 8, 1977

Tuscaloosa News, "Richards Test 'Not Available'," AP, June 9, 1977

The Bulletin, "Richards Waits While Evert Wins," AP, June 10, 1977

Oakland Tribune, "War Clouds On Horizon For Tennis," by Jack Rux, June 15, 1977

Oakland Tribune, "Owners Praise Peterson," by Jack Rux, June 15, 1977

Daily News, "Renee Richards To Quit Playing Tennis," Reuters, June 16, 1977

Lakeland Ledger, "Renee Richards To Quit Pro Tennis," AP, June 16, 1977

Sydney Morning Herald, "Brilliant On The Court," by Rod Humphries, June 19, 1977

Montreal Gazette, "WTT Plans European Division In '78," AP, June 28, 1977

New York Times, "Connors Shadow Hangs Over WTT," by Fred Tupper, July 10, 1977

Daily Breeze (CA), "Laver Has Enough," by Mike Braham, July 10, 1977

Los Angeles Times, "Dispute Flares At All-Star Match," July 10, 1977

Star-News, "World Team Tennis Starting To Get Fans," AP, July 16, 1977

Sports Illustrated, "Zing Go The Strings," by Joe Jures, July 25, 1977

Sports Illustrated, "A Sure Cure For Sore Necks," by Joe Jures, August 29, 1977

New York Times, "Sports Notes," September 1, 1977

Bakersfield Californian, "Connors Rejects World Team Tennis," UPI, October 1, 1977

Lakeland Ledger, "Renee's Opponent Walks Off," AP, October 15, 1977

Los Angeles Times, "1978 WTT Roundup, Strings Toughest In West," March 9, 1978

New York Times, "No Music In Nashville," by Dave Anderson, March 19, 1978

Los Angeles Times, "The Women Are No. 1," by Elizabeth Wheeler, April 19, 1978

Galveston Daily News, "Team Owner Says WTT Is Growing Fast," UPI, May 28, 1978

Sports Illustrated, "Roundup Of The Week June 12-18," June 26, 1978

Decatur Herald, "Navratilova Whips Evert Again," AP, July 15, 1978

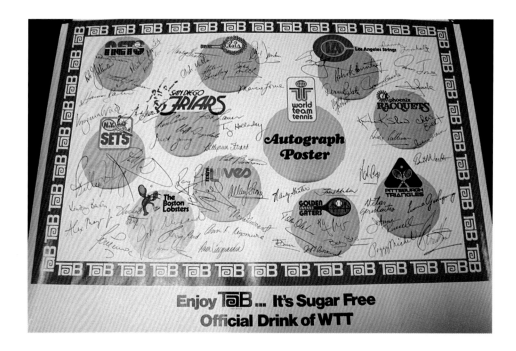

Ellensburg Daily Record, "Navratilova Whips Evert Again," UPI, July 15, 1978

Logansport Pharos-Tribune, "Navratilova Leads East To Victory," UPI, July 16, 1978

Reading Eagle, "Nets Win," AP, July 22, 1978

Reading Eagle, "Dibbs Confident In Louisville," UPI, July 26, 1978

Schenectady Gazette, "WTT's Top Stars Headline Playoffs," AP, August 12, 1978

Youngstown Indicator, "Gerulaitis, Martina Pace Playoff Wins," AP, August 16, 1978

Evening News, "WTT Resumes On Two Fronts," by Christy Barber, August 22, 1978

Philadelphia Inquirer, "Odd Couple," by Bill Livingston, September 7, 1978

Ellensburg Daily Record, "WTT Losing Biggest Teams," UPI, October 24, 1978

Spokane Daily Chronicle, "WTT End Appears Certain," AP, October 24, 1978

Indiana Gazette, "WTT on Verge of Demise," AP, October 25, 1978

Observer-Reporter, "Team Tennis Has Money Woes," AP, October 25, 1978

Winnipeg Free Press, "Sports In Short," UPI, October 26, 1978

Youngstown Vindicator, "2 WTT Teams Fold," UPI, October 27, 1978

Rochester Sentinel, "WTT Hanging On By A String," AP, October 28, 1978

Schenectady Gazette, "Two Teams Fold; WTT Survival Threatening," AP Oct. 28, 1978

Vancouver Sun, "Two Franchises Desert WTT," CP, October 28, 1978

St. Louis Post-Dispatch, "Lobsters, Apples Fold: WTT Shaky," AP, October 29, 1978

Times Daily, "World Team Tennis May Fold," UPI, November 5, 1978

Sports Illustrated, "Scorecard," by Jerry Kirshenbaum, November 6, 1978

Lodi News-Sentinel, "World Team Tennis Is Threatened," UPI, November 7, 1978

Evening Independent, "A Folding Dilemma," AP, November 8, 1978

Kingman Daily Miner, "WTT Folding Over Financial Problems," AP, November 9, 1978

Miami News, "Things Look Dark For World Team Tennis," UPI, November 9, 1978

Evening Independent, "Losing The Loves," AP, November 10, 1978

Lewiston Morning Tribune, "WTT Keeps Losing Teams," AP, November 10, 1978

Lewiston Daily Sun, "Team Tennis Leaguers To Continue," AP, November 10, 1978

Leader-Post, "WTT Will Operate — Buchholz," AP, November 10, 1978

Reading Eagle, "Future In Doubt," AP, November 10, 1978

Sarasota Herald-Tribune, "Loves 5th WTT Franchise To Fold," UPI, November 10, 1978

New York Times, "Now WTT Is Team-less Tennis," by Gerald Eskenazi, November 20, 1978

New York Times, "Match Point Against WTT," by Gerald Eskenazi, November 21, 1978

New York Times, "Now Isn't It A Small World!" by Gerald Eskenazi, November 24, 1978

York Dispatch (PA), "World Team Tennis Fights," NYT Wire Service, November 24, 1978

Eugene Register-Guard, "World Team Tennis Adds 3 Teams," UPI, December 1, 1978

Modesto Bee, "World Team Tennis Folds; Gaters Stay," AP, March 8, 1979

Petaluma Argus-Courier, "Team Tennis Dead for '79," UPI, March 8, 1979

Salina Journal, "World Team Tennis Folds But May Return," UPI, March 8, 1979

Spokesman-Review, "Sports Digest," UPI, March 8, 1979

Sports Illustrated, "More Teletrash, Please," by Curry Kirkpatrick, September 7, 1987

Sports Illustrated, "Is Tennis Dying?" cover story, May 9, 1994

Sunday Courier, "History of World Team Tennis," by Chris Howard, January 16, 1995

Billie Jean King: Tennis Trailblazer, by Joanne Lannin, 1999

Sports Illustrated, "Jimbo," by Alexander Wolff, August 30, 2004

Press Box Online, "Something Was Missing In Translation," by Phil Jackman, July 2007

TennisWarehouse.com, "Team Tennis Salaries 1976-1977" thread, June 29, 2009

Gretzky's Tears, by Stephen Brunt, 2010

Game, Set, Match, by Susan Ware, 2011

ESPN.com, "Original 9 Reunite 40 Years Later," April 7, 2012

Fun While It Lasted, "World Team Tennis," by Andy Crossley, 2011

Tennis.com, "Why is American Tennis Dying?" by Merlisa Corbett, November 21, 2013

ANAHEIM ORANGES (1978)

Los Angeles Times, "Anaheim to Host Five WTT Clubs in 3-Day Event," July 17, 1975

Los Angeles Times, "Anaheim To Host Matches," April 13, 1976

Los Angeles Times, "Anaheim To Get WTT Franchise," by Pete Donovan, December 2, 1977

The Tuscaloosa News, "Anaheim Joins WTT League," AP, December 6, 1977

The Evening Independent, "Juicy New Entry In Team Tennis," AP, December 7, 1977

St. Joseph's News-Press, "New Team In Anaheim," AP, December 7, 1977

Los Angeles Times, "Anaheim Joins WTT, Gets Casals," by Pete Donovan, December 7, 1977

Santa Ana Register, "Oranges Blossom in WTT," by Charles Abair, December 7, 1977

Anaheim Oranges Newsletter #2, "Oranges Assemble Potential Power," March 1978

Los Angeles Times, "Experiment Succeeds: Anaheim Gets WTT Team," March 9, 1978

Los Angeles Times, "Casals Joins Oranges," March 9, 1978

Los Angeles Times, "Makings Of A Balanced Attack," by Pete Donovan, March 17, 1978

Reading Eagle, "Apples-Oranges To Mix Here," by Tony Zonca, March 11, 1978

Los Angeles Times, "Durr, Kiyomura, Tolleson Join Southland Squads," March 23, 1978

Los Angeles Times, "Competition Tough For 1978 WTT Teams," April 7, 1978

Los Angeles Times, "Drysdale: Man of Influence," by Pete Donovan, April 14, 1978

Los Angeles Times, "Oranges Seek Winning Blend," by Pete Donovan, May 1, 1978

Los Angeles Times, "Oranges Red Hot In 31-13 Rout," by Pete Donovan, May 2, 1978

Los Angeles Times, "Oranges Lose Again: Now 4-11," May 3, 1978

Arizona Republic, "Oranges Rip Phoenix, 31-13," May 4, 1978

Los Angeles Times, "Oranges' Amritraj Doubles," by Pete Donovan, May 9, 1978

Daily Breeze (CA), "Casals Misses Her Fans," by Mike Braham, May 14, 1978

Los Angeles Times, "Oranges Losing Numbers Game," May 16, 1978

Los Angeles Times, "Drysdale, Cox Spur Oranges' Comeback," May 23, 1978

Press-Courier, "Strings Host Rival Oranges," May 24, 1978

Press-Courier, "Late Surge Carries Strings Past the Oranges, 28-27," May 25, 1978

The Spokesman-Review, "Casals Leads Anaheim Win," AP, May 27, 1978

Los Angeles Times, "Surging Oranges Beat Apples," by Pete Donovan, May 28, 1978

Taylor Daily Press, "WTT Tennis Back in Austin," by Sports Staff, June 2, 1978

Los Angeles Times, "Oranges Beat The Nets," June 4, 1978

Reading Eagle, "This Fruit Bowl Has Punch," June 4, 1978

Boston Globe, "Oranges Squeeze Lobsters," June 7, 1978

Los Angeles Times, "Oranges Win On Tie-Breaker, 28-27," June 8, 1978

Reading Eagle, "Apples Double Up Oranges," by Doyle Dietz, June 10, 1978

Reading Eagle, "Match Was The Pits For Heller," by Tony Zonca, June 11, 1978

Los Angeles Times, "Oranges Square It With Loves," June 11, 1978

Reading Eagle, "Apples The Pits For Oranges," by Tony Zonca, June 18, 1978

Los Angeles Times, "Oranges Are (3,000 Miles From) Home," June 19, 1978

Arizona Republic, "Knee Surgery Shelves Rosie," AP, June 20, 1978

Miami News, "Casals Gets Cut," AP, June 20, 1978

Schenectady Gazette, "Casals Goes Under Knife," UPI, June 20, 1978

The Star Press, "Casals Out For WTT Season," UPI, June 20, 1978

The Miami News, "Casals Gets Cut," June 20, 1978

Courier News, "Tracy Austin to play for Anaheim in WTT," AP, June 29, 1978

Ellensburg Daily Record, "Oranges Add Tracy Austin," AP, June 29, 1978

Ocala Star-Banner, "Austin Plays For Oranges," AP, June 29, 1978

Ellensburg Daily Record, "Austin Signs No-Pay Contract," UPI, June 30, 1978

Los Angeles Times, "Oranges' New Kid In Town," by Pete Donovan, July 11, 1978

New York Times, "Tracy Austin Triumphs In First WTT Match," July 12, 1978

Indianapolis Star, "Oranges Squeeze Loves in OT," by Bill Pickett, July 26, 1978

Los Angeles Times, "Racquets Romp As Oranges Roll Over," July 28, 1978

Lodi News-Sentinel, "Austin Pulls Out Win," UPI, July 13, 1978

Santa Cruz Sentinel, "Little Tracy, Oranges Top Gaters," AP, July 13, 1978

Reading Eagle, "In The WTT," UPI, July 26, 1978

Reading Eagle, "Oranges Win," AP, July 31, 1978

Los Angeles Times, "Strings Face Oranges," by Elizabeth Wheeler, August 1, 1978

Los Angeles Times, "Oranges Out to Clinch Playoff," by Pete Donovan, August 3, 1978

Los Angeles Times, "Oranges Rally To Beat Nets," August 9, 1978

Los Angeles Times, "Oranges Win Sets Up Match," by Pete Donovan, August 12, 1978

Los Angeles Times, "Apples Make It a Sour Season," by Pete Donovan, August 12, 1978

Arizona Republic, "Defending Apples Squash Oranges," AP, August 16, 1978

Evening Independent, "Picking Up Where They Left Off," AP, August 16, 1978

Los Angeles Times, "Oranges Must Win," by Pete Donovan, August 17, 1978

Los Angeles Times, "2 1/2 Teams in Team Tennis, Anaheim Half In," August 17, 1978

Los Angeles Times, "Oranges Are Dead And Kicking," by Pete Donovan, November 14, 1978

Pittsburgh Press, "Anaheim Struggling in Crumbling WTT," UPI, November 15, 1978

Los Angeles Times, "Anaheim Drops From Pro Tennis League," AP, January 5, 1979

Bangor Daily News, "Another WTT Franchise Folds," AP, January 5, 1979

BALTIMORE BANNERS (1974)

Annapolis Capital, "Baltimore Gets Tennis Team from Phoenix," AP, August 10, 1973

Arizona Daily Star, "Phoenix Net Team Sold," AP, August 10, 1973

Standard-Speaker (PA), "Phoenix Tennis Team Sold to Baltimore," AP, August 10, 1973

Baltimore Sun, "Banners Name Don Candy As Coach," by Bill Free, November 2, 1973

Pittsburgh Post-Gazette, "Brass, Name Set For Netters In Baltimore," AP, November 2, 1973

Salisbury Daily Times, "Candy Selected Baltimore Tennis Coach," November 4, 1974

Baltimore Sun, "Banners Sign Civic Center Pact," by Jim Caffrey, November 16, 1973

Baltimore Sun, "Connors Agrees To Play For Banners in WTT," December 7, 1973

Kentucky New Era, "Connors Signs With World Team Tennis," AP, December 7, 1973

Cumberland Evening Times, "Banners Like Candy," December 12, 1973

Baltimore Sun, "Tickets Anyone?" January 6, 1974

Baltimore Sun, "Connors Signs Banners' Contract," by Jim Caffrey, January 20, 1974

Baltimore Sun, "Banners Open Here vs. Hawaii," February 24, 1974

Salisbury Daily Times, "Banners Season Ticket Drive On," April 2, 1974

Baltimore Sun, "Baltimore Tennis Team Gets Byron Bertram," AP, April 4, 1974

Annapolis Capital, "World Team Tennis Is On The Way," April 6, 1974

Baltimore Sun, "Fred Neil Chosen By Banners," by Jim Caffrey, April 7, 1974

Baltimore Sun, "Banners Establish Tennis Hall of Fame," by Jim Caffrey, April 7, 1974

Baltimore Sun, "Banners Sign Carmichael," April 18, 1974

Hagerstown Daily Mail, "Sports Shorts," April 18, 1974

Baltimore Afro-American, "Banners Net Camp To Open," April 20, 1974

Baltimore Sun, "Freeman Leaves Banners," April 20, 1974

Lakeland Ledger, "Tennis," AP, April 21, 1974

Baltimore Sun, "Banners Complete Roster," by Kent Baker, April 23, 1974

Evening Sun (MD), "Banners Sign Stove," by Michael Janofsky, April 23, 1974

Baltimore Sun, "Banners Acquire Rights to Gerken," AP, April 25, 1974

Glasgow Herald, "Tennis In Baltimore," April 26, 1974

Baltimore Sun, "Refunds Pledged if Connors Can't Play," by Jim Caffrey, May 1, 1974

Hartford Courant, "Baltimore Banners Say Connors Will Play," AP, May 1, 1974

Baltimore Sun, "Banners Trade Pigeon For Kodes Draft Rights," May 3, 1974

New York Times, "WTT Announces Signings," May 5, 1974

Baltimore Sun, "Connors to play when Banners Open," by Jim Caffrey, May 8, 1974

Albany Herald, "Banners Beat Leis," AP, May 9, 1974

Danville Bee, "Baltimore's Opening Crowd Approves," by Gordon Beard, May 9, 1974

Evening Sun, "Banners One Need: People In The Stands," by Bill Tanton, May 9, 1974

Baltimore Afro-American, "Like A Hole In The Head," editorial, May 11, 1974

Baltimore Sun, "Okker-less Royals Defeat Banners," by Jim Caffrey, May 12, 1974

Detroit Free Press, "Okker Sick...Match Called Off," AP, May 12, 1974

Gettysburg Times, "Connors Takes On Philadelphia Crowd," AP, May 14, 1974

Philadelphia Inquirer, "Jim Connors Expletive," by Jack McKinney, May 15, 1974

The Tennessean, "Irate Connors Rushes Stands," Wire Services, May 15, 1974

Baltimore Sun, "12,900-fan Average Ranks 15th," by Jim Caffrey, May 17, 1974

Baltimore Sun, "Freedoms Defeat Banners," by Jim Caffrey, May 18, 1974

Baltimore Sun, "Only 556 See Sets Defeated," May 20, 1974

Baltimore Sun, "Banners Defeat Sets, 24-23, in Tiebreaker," May 21, 1974

Boston Globe, "Banners Ruffle Lobsters, 27-22," by Will McDonough, May 22, 1974

Danville Bee, "WTT Controversy Around Goolagong, Connors," AP, May 22, 1974

Florence Morning News, "Connors Leaves for Europe," UPI, May 22, 1974

Reading Eagle, "WTT Banners Rout Boston," AP, May 22, 1974

Schenectady Gazette, "Connors Set To Resolve Net Problems," AP, May 22, 1974

Baltimore Sun, "Banners Bow to Houston, 29 to 25," by Jim Caffrey, May 23, 1974

Baltimore Sun, "Banners Meet Nets tonight," May 29, 1974

Evening Sun (MD), Hume Tennis Loser Fan Fave, by Michael Janofsky, May 29, 1974

Baltimore Sun, "Nets Rip Banners Before 425," May 30, 1974

Baltimore Sun, "4,000 fans see Triangles top Banners," by Jim Caffrey, June 2, 1974

Baltimore Sun, "Banner Interest is Growing," by Jim Caffrey, June 3, 1974

Baltimore Sun, "Banners Beat Sets, 31 to 23," June 9, 1974

Baltimore Sun, "Mixed Doubles Team Gives Banners Victory," June 13, 1974

Baltimore Sun, "Banners Acquire Help for Women's Competition," June 14, 1974

New York Times, "Match of the Year: Evert and Connors," June 23, 1974

New York Times, "Tennis Roundup World Team Tennis," July 9, 1974

Boca Raton News, "Jimmy Connors Wants To Sleep," July 11, 1974

Evening Sun (MD), "Million Dollar Connors Returns," by Bill Tanton, July 11, 1974

Observer-Reporter (PA), "Jim Connors Enjoys Wimbledon Aftertaste," AP, July 11, 1974

The Times-News, "Connors Beats Rosewall In World Tennis," AP, July 11, 1974

Daily News (PA), "Triangles Nip Banner," UPI, July 12, 1974

Arizona Republic, "Tired Connors, Evert Leaving on Vacation," UPI, July 13, 1974

Evening Independent, "Connors, Evert Taking Break," AP, July 13, 1974

Baltimore Sun, "Banners Limit Appearances of Connors," July 17, 1974

Baltimore Sun, "Banners Beaten," July 23, 1974

Baltimore Sun, "Banners Sign Indian Star," July 7, 1974

Baltimore Sun, "Banners Can Now Claim Best," July 8, 1974

Baltimore Sun, "Banners to Watch Gate," by Jim Caffrey, July 11, 1974

Baltimore Sun, "Banners Snap Losing Streak," by Jim Caffrey, July 15, 1974

Baltimore Sun, "Mixed Doubles Gives Banners Win," by Jim Caffrey, July 21, 1974

People, "Chris & Jimmy: Love Is Grand," July 22, 1974

Boston Globe, "Faltering Lobsters Bow to Banners," July 27, 1974

Lowell Sun, "Banners Defeat Lobsters," UPI, July 27, 1974

Los Angeles Times, "Baltimore Rallies to Defeat Strings," August 1, 1974

Frederick News Post, "Banners Bidding to Make Playoffs," August 2, 1974

Baltimore Afro-American, "Banners Feature Denver Racquets," August 3, 1974

Greeley Daily Tribune, "Racquets Defeat Banners Twice," August 3, 1974

Sports Illustrated, "Lobsters Go To Pot," by Curry Fitzpatrick, August 4, 1974

Frederick News Post, "Tennis Pros Boost Frederick Night," August 5, 1974

Pittsburgh Post-Gazette, "Triangles Edge Banners," by Vince Leonard, August 5, 1974

Baltimore Sun, "Banners Lose to Lobsters by 23-21," by Ken Nigro, August 8, 1974

Frederick News Post, "Frederick Night With the Banners," by Lee Short, August 9, 1974

Baltimore Sun, "Banners Bow to Play-On," by William Lowenberger, August 10, 1974

Salisbury Daily Times, "Carmichael Top Banners Player," August 11, 1974

Los Angeles Strings, "Strings Top Banners In Last Home Stand," August 15, 1974

Baltimore Sun, "Neil Released Banners Win Finale," by Jim Caffrey, August 18 1974

Charleston Gazette, "Screen Tests," August 24, 1974

Baltimore Sun, "Banners Trade Connors," by Alan Goldstein, November 7, 1974

Pittsburgh Post-Gazette, "Tris Deal For Connors," by Charles Feeney, November 7, 1974

Baltimore Sun, "WTT Banners Call It Quits," by Alan Goldstein, February 2, 1975

Baltimore Sun, "Targets Of Opportunity," by Phil Jackman, February 13, 1995

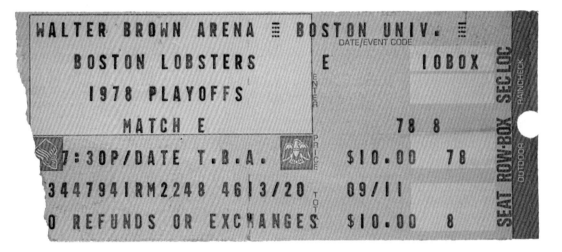

BOSTON LOBSTERS (1974-1978)

St. Joseph News-Press, "Lobsters Latest Net Franchise," AP, December 18, 1973

Lewiston Evening Journal, "The Latest in NE Sports," AP, December 18, 1973

Tri City Herald, "Claw Your Way To Success," AP, December 18, 1973

Boston Globe, "Lobsters Deal Pilic to NY," by John Powers, April 23, 1974

Lawrence Journal-World, "Boston Lands Janet," AP, April 25, 1974

Newport Daily News, "Lobsters Sign Ocean Stater," May 1, 1974

Boston Globe, "Lobsters Sing Hooray For 'Volleywood,'" by Karen Kane, May 5, 1974

Lewiston Daily Sun, "Lobsters Open Wednesday," AP, May 7, 1974

Boston Globe, "Lobsters Let Freedoms Ring," by Bud Collins, May 9, 1974

Boston Globe, "Taylor Defeat of Pilic Spurs Lobsters Over Sets," May 18, 1974

Lewiston Evening Journal, "Lobsters In Win Column," AP, May 18, 1974

The Telegraph, "Lobsters Win," AP, May 18, 1975

Boston Globe, "Galloping Lobsters Whip Chicago," by Will McDonough, May 26, 1974

The Dispatch, "Officials Debate Penalty," UPI, May 29, 1974

Boston Globe, "Lobsters Walk Off, Forfeit," May 30, 1974

Danville Bee, "Lobsters Protest Forfeit," AP, May 30, 1974

Evening Independent, "Lobsters Boil," AP, May 30, 1974

Pittsburgh Press, "Boston Forfeits Tennis Match," UPI, May 30, 1974

Pittsburgh Post-Gazette, "Leg Fractures Sideline Janet," AP, May 30, 1974

Boston Globe, "Lobsters Edged By Nets," by Will McDonough, May 31, 1974

Harvard Crimson, "The Lobsters' Game," by Timothy Carlson, May 31, 1974

Chicago Tribune, "Boston Rallies To Beat Aces," by Steve Nidetz, June 12, 1974

Lewiston Evening Journal, "Lobsters Win Big," AP, June 13, 1974

Boca Raton News, "Jimmy Connors Wants To Sleep," July 11, 1974

Lewiston Evening Journal, "Lobsters Win," AP, July 11, 1974

Boston Globe, "Taylor Finds Player-Coach Duties Tough," July 15, 1974

Lewiston Evening Journal, "Boston Lobsters," AP, July 25, 1974

Boston Globe, "Lobsters Rebound Against Strings," by John Powers, July 31, 1974

Sports Illustrated, "Going To Pot With The Lobsters," by Curry Kirkpatrick, August 5, 1974

Boston Globe, "A Love Season for the Lobsters," by Maria Karagianis, August 22, 1974

Boston Globe, "The Fan's View..." September 8, 1974

Gettysburg Times, "Lobsters Drop Only N.E. Player," AP, September 19, 1974

Rock Hill Herald, "Voikos Dropped," AP, September 19, 1974

Robesonian, "Dropped," AP, October 31, 1974

Lowell Sun, "Lobsters Seek To Save Shells," UPI, February 4, 1975

Bennington Banner, "Lobsters Play Beat The Clock," UPI, February 7, 1975

The Telegraph, "Money Troubled Lobsters Running Out Of Time," UPI, February 7, 1975

Boston Globe, "Lobsters Seeking a Love Set," by Bud Collins, February 14, 1975

Schenectady Gazette, "Freedom Owner Takes Team To Boston," AP, March 11, 1975

Pittsburgh Post-Gazette, "Will The Freedoms Become The Lobsters," March 12, 1975

Bennington Banner, "Lobsters May Be Freedoms," UPI March 14, 1975

Boston Globe, "Lobsters Live! (I think...)," March 14, 1975

The Telegraph, "Lobsters May Be Reborn From Philly," by Gil Peters, March 14, 1975

St. Petersburg Times, "Boston Bidding For Freedoms," UPI, March 15, 1975

Gettysburg Times, "Freedoms Sold To Boston," AP, March 19, 1975

Boston Globe, "Tennis...? He'll Learn," March 26, 1975

Bangor Daily News, "Novices To Head Hub Net Franchise," UPI, March 28, 1975

Ottawa Citizen, "New Tennis Coach," AP, April 9, 1975

Winnipeg Free Press, "Named Coach Boston," AP, April 11, 1975

Boston Globe, "The Lobsters," by Leigh Montville, May 18, 1975

Boston Globe, "WTT 'Festivals' on Shaky Ground," by Will McDonough, May 26, 1975

St. Petersburg Times, "Boston Lobs Upset Leis," AP, May 28, 1975

Boston Globe, "The Sports Log," June 6, 1975

Gadsden Times, "Boston Lobsters Gets Rights To Navratilova," AP, June 13, 1975

Pittsburgh Press, "Triangles Bring Lobsters' Hewitt To A Boil," UPI, June 14, 1975

Daily Dispatch (IL), "Bud Collins on Tennis," by Bud Collins, June 17, 1975

The Times-News, "Sports Shorts," AP, September 13, 1975

Ottawa Herald, "Mades Made GM," AP, September 16, 1975

Bangor Daily News, "Name Gilbertson To Tennis Post," UPI, November 18, 1975

Boston Globe, "Lobsters Top Strings, 25-24," by Francis Rosa, July 21, 1976

Lawrence Journal-World, "Boston Gets Stevens," AP, October 27, 1975

The Evening Independent, "High Goals For Janet," by Anne Hughes, January 24, 1976

The Journal, "Lobsters To Play 4 At Hartford," May 5, 1976

Gadsden Times, "Brogna Is Trainer," AP, May 11, 1976

Boston Globe, "Lobsters Too Much For Leis," by Neil Singelais, August 6, 1976

Lewiston Evening Journal, "Lobsters Win In Tennis Play," AP, August 6, 1976

Boston Globe, "Lobsters Trip Nets in OT," August 12, 1976

Pittsburgh Post-Gazette, "Lobsters Name New GM," AP, October 14, 1976

The Day, "Emerson To Use Power As Coach," AP, November 15, 1976

The Day, "Plans to Buy Lobsters Near Completion," AP, November 19, 1976

Deseret News, "Boston Lobsters Net Navratilova," AP, April 29, 1977

Boston Globe, "Lobsters' TV Schedule Stiff Competition," by Jack Craig, May 12, 1977

Berkshire Eagle, "Lobsters Suddenly WTT's Hottest," by Steve Krause, May 14, 1977

The Day, "Navratilova Leads Lobsters To Victory," AP, May 26, 1977

Pittsburgh Post-Gazette, "Martina Holds Court," by Vince Leonard, May 26, 1977

Boston Globe, "Lobsters shell Cascades, 30-14," AP, June 8, 1977

Argus Press, "Lobster Change," AP, July 2, 1977

Youngstown Vindicator, "Boston Duo Bears Record," AP, July 6, 1977

Lewiston Evening Journal, "Boston Lobsters Topple Soviets," AP, July 12, 1977

Reading Eagle, "Lobsters Move Into 1st Place," AP, July 20, 1977

The Hour, "Boston Lobsters Whip Indiana Loves, 25-22," UPI, July 25, 1977

Spokane Daily Chronicle, "Navratilova Nips Evert," AP, July 27, 1977

Boston Globe, "Lobsters Rip Apart the Nets," August 1, 1977

The Hour, "Navratilova Leads Lobsters," UPI, August 4, 1977

Boston Globe, "Lobsters Chew Up Apples," by John Powers, August 9, 1977

The Telegraph, "Lobsters Tip NY," AP, August 9, 1977

Los Angeles Times, "Bench-Sitting in the WTT," by Sheila Moran, August 10, 1977

Lewiston Evening Journal, "Playoffs Begin For Lobsters," AP, August 16, 1977

Christian Science Monitor, "From Cellar to City Hall," by Ross Atkin, August 19, 1977

Lewiston Evening Journal, "Lobsters Claw Nets, Take On NY," AP, August 20, 1977

The Art of World Team Tennis, by Greg Hoffman, 1977

Boston Globe, "Lobsters' Show Opens on Coast," by Barry Cadigan, April 23, 1978

The Evening News, "Lobsters Triumph," AP, June 8, 1978

Boston Globe, "Lobsters Topple Apples," by Harry Eisenberg, June 18, 1978

Tucson Citizen, "Martina Misses Home, Family," by Jane Gross, July 8, 1978

Boston Globe, "Lobsters Fall in Tiebreaker, 26-25," July 19, 1978

Boston Globe, "Rookie Helps Lobsters Win, 32-26," by Lesley Visser, July 24, 1978

Boston Globe, "Holladay, Lobsters roll, 30-20," by Steve Marantz, July 25, 1978

Boston Globe, "Lowly Loves Hand Lobsters Loss," by Lesley Visser, July 27, 1978

Boston Globe, "Apples Bounce Back, 25-24," by Bob Monahan, August 1, 1978

Boston Globe, "Lobsters Whip NY, 27-19," by Lesley Visser, August 4, 1978

Boston Globe, "Lobsters Ace Oranges, 30-27," by Harry Eisenberg, August 7, 1978

Boston Globe, "Lobsters Polish Off Racquets, 30-24," by Bob Monahan, August 9, 1978

Boston Globe, "Lobsters Open Playoffs on Home Court Tuesday," August 13, 1978

Boston Globe, "Lobsters Begin Playoff Quest Against New Orleans," August 15, 1978

Boston Globe, "Lobsters Open Playoff With Seattle Tuesday," August 20, 1978

Lewiston Evening Journal, "Lobsters Take Lead In Semi-Finals," AP, August 23, 1978

Boston Globe, "Lobster Unstrung In Playoff Opener," by Francis Rosa, September 14, 1978

Los Angeles Times, "Martina Helps Lobsters," by Elizabeth Wheeler, September 20, 1978

Merced Sun, "Lobsters Nip Strings In Super-Tiebreaker," AP, September 20, 1978

Youngstown Vindicator, "Lobsters End Spin In Series," AP, September 20, 1978

Boston Globe, "Injury Burden Bent Lobsters," by Gil Peters, September 23, 1978

Lewiston Morning Tribune, "Lobsters Owner Mum On Dissolution," AP, October 24, 1978

Morning Record and Journal, "Boston To Keep Pro Tennis," UPI, October 24, 1978

Milwaukee Sentinel, "Sports In Brief," October 24, 1978

The Hour, "Lobsters Want Foes To Ink Big Names," UPI, October 26, 1978

Star-News, "Lobsters, Apples Cease To Operate," AP, October 28, 1978

Gainesville Sun, "Ex-Tennis League Owner Buying Pats," AP, September 19, 1985

Tennis Forum, April 2006

Tennis Confidential II, by Paul Fein, 2008

Boston Globe, "Tennis Star Bob Hewitt Accused," by Bob Hohler, August 28, 2011

The Patriot Ledger, "Myra Kraft Served As Inspiration," by Mike Fine, February 3, 2012

CHICAGO ACES (1974)

Chicago Tribune, "Riessen and Riggs Chicago Net Picks," August 4, 1973

Chicago Tribune, "Chicago Aces Sign Sue Stap," by Ralph Leo, January 22, 1974

Chicago Tribune, "Aces Hope to Sign Star Soon," March 18, 1974

Portsmouth Times, "Riessen Signs," March 25, 1974

Chicago Tribune, "Chicago Aces to Sign Riessen," March 26, 1974

Chicago Tribune, "Tickets On Sale to Tennis Aces Home Matches," March 28, 1974

The Phoenix, "Marty Joins Aces," AP, March 29, 1974

Chicago Tribune, "Teaming With Possibilities," April 29, 1974

Chicago Tribune, "Riessen Remains Unsigned," by Steve Nidetz, May 1, 1974

The Daily Illini, "Aces Will Be Banking On Riessen," by Jeff Metcalfe, May 1, 1974

Chicago Tribune, "No Aces in Riessen's Cards," by Steve Nidetz, May 3, 1974

Daily Herald (IL), "Will Marty Riessen Sign," by Art Mugalian, May 3, 1974

New York Times, "WTT Announces Signings," May 5, 1974

Chicago Tribune, "Aces Open Tonight in Denver," by Steve Nidetz, May 7, 1974

Albany Herald, "Aces Edge Racquets in Opener," AP, May 8, 1974

Chicago Tribune, "Aces Arrive Early — For Cocktails!" by John Husar, May 9, 1974

Chicago Tribune, "Houston Trumps Chicago Aces," by Steve Nidetz, May 9, 1974

Albany Herald, "Aces Edge Royals," AP, May 11, 1974

Chicago Tribune, "Sue Charges Net, Aces Win," by Steve Nidetz, May 13, 1974

Albany Herald, "Aces Beat Buckskins," AP, May 13, 1974

Chicago Tribune, "Aces Lower Prices; Play Riders Next," May 15, 1974

Chicago Tribune, "Drysdale, Flamingos Next for Aces," by Steve Nidetz, May 17, 1974

Chicago Tribune, "Flamingos Deal Aces Defeat," by Steve Nidetz, May 18, 1974

Chicago Tribune, "In the Wake of the News," by David Condon, May 19, 1974

Chicago Tribune, "Aces Suffer 2nd Straight Loss 28-18," UPI, May 21, 1974

Atlanta Constitution, "Hustler Riggs Does It Again," May 24, 1974

Chicago Tribune, "Aces Hopes Take to the Road," by Steve Nidetz, May 25, 1975

Boston Globe, "Brother-Sister Act Sparks Nets," May 27, 1974

Chicago Tribune, "276 Watch Aces Beat Buckskins," by Steve Nidetz, June 3, 1974

Chicago Tribune, "Only 310 Watch Aces Win," June 4, 1974

New York Times, "Attendance Fluctuates For WTT," June 4, 1974

Modesto Bee, "Player-Coach Drops Emerson," AP, June 4, 1974

Southern Illinoisan, "Chicago Aces Win 3rd in Row," AP, June 6, 1974

Chicago Tribune, "Aces Bow to Denver 31-24," June 8, 1974

Chicago Tribune, "Boston Rallies to Beat Aces," by Steve Nidetz, June 12, 1974

The Telegraph, "Lobsters Nip Aces," AP, June 12, 1974

Chicago Tribune, "Well, That's World Team Tennis," June 13, 1974

Chicago Tribune, "3,180 See Riggs Play, Aces Lose," by Steve Nidetz, June 14, 1974

Leader-Post, "Aces Lose," AP, June 14, 1974

Chicago Tribune, "Aces' Coach to Play In Monaco," by Steve Nidetz, June 19, 1974

Chicago Tribune, "Fire!" by Clifford Terry, June 20, 1974

Chicago Tribune, "In the Wake of the News," by David Condon, June 20, 1974

Los Angeles Times, "Strings Trump Chicago Aces by 25-21," June 20, 1974

Beaver County Times, "Tiebreaker Wins For Chicago Aces," UPI, July 8, 1974

Chicago Tribune, "Aces Cut Down Strings," July 8, 1974

Chicago Tribune, "Aces Seek Another Upset Against Denver," July 9, 1974

Chicago Tribune, "Denver Wins 5 Events to Beat Aces 32-22," July 10, 1974

Chicago Tribune, "Aces Win Over Strings By 26-21," July 14, 1974

Chicago Tribune, "Kids Try WTT Format and Like It," by Steve Nidetz, July 17, 1974

Chicago Tribune, "4,000 See Aces Bow To Houston," July 20, 1974

Chicago Tribune, "Aces Top S.F. Gaters 32-23," July 22, 1974

Chicago Tribune, "Chicago War of Words Must Cease," by Steve Nidetz, July 24, 1974

Chicago Tribune, "Aces To Stage Benefit Match For Clinic," July 26, 1974

Chicago Tribune, "Aces To Aid Drug Group vs. Denver," July 28, 1974

Chicago Tribune, "Racquets Overwhelm Aces 31-18," July 29, 1974

Chicago Tribune, "Aces To Host Benefit For March of Dimes," August 1, 1974

Chicago Tribune, "Aces Top New York By 25-20," August 3, 1974

Chicago Tribune, "Aces Hold On, Down Flamingos," August 5, 1974

Chicago Tribune, "Aces Close Out Season Tonight vs. Banners," August 18, 1974

Chicago Tribune, "Notes, Quotes, Gloats and Anecdotes," AP, August 18, 1974

Chicago Tribune, "Kaiser Is Upbeat As Aces Close," by Steve Nidetz, August 19, 1974

Chicago Tribune, "WTT Aces Facing Court Battle," by Steve Nidetz, October 24, 1974

Chicago Tribune, "Aces Put Up For Sale," by Steve Nidetz, October 26, 1974

Cincinnati Enquirer, "Chicago's WTT Aces May Go To Atlanta," AP, October 26, 1974

Ottawa Citizen, "Sports In Brief," AP, October 30, 1974

Huntington Daily News, "WTT Chicago Aces Sued by 2 Players," AP, October 30, 1974

Standard-Speaker, "Suit Filed Against World Team Tennis," AP, October 30, 1974

Chicago Tribune, "Aces Grab Orantes and Panetta In Draft," November 27, 1974

Chicago Tribune, "King Sees WTT in Chicago," by Steve Nidetz, January 14, 1975

Chicago Tribune, "Aces Are Dropped by WTT", by Steve Nidetz, February 2, 1975

Chicago Tribune, "The Man Who Made Ball Bounce," by Steve Nidetz, March 13, 1975

CLEVELAND NETS/ NEW ORLEANS NETS (1974-1978)

Observer-Reporter, "Nets Sign Richey," AP, April 10, 1974

Chicago Tribune, "Nets Deal In Wife 'Swapping,'" April 26, 1974

News-Dispatch, "Triangles, Nets Trade," UPI, April 26, 1974

St. Louis Post-Dispatch, "Wife Swapping Tennis Style" by Rick Hummel, April 28, 1974

Lewiston Evening Journal, "Nets Are Feeling Mighty Good," AP, May 31, 1974

Daily Sentinel, "Cleveland Nets Triumph, 29-25," UPI, June 6, 1974

Vancouver Sun, "Baselines," CP, July 16, 1974

Vancouver Sun, "Baselines," CP, July 18, 1974

Pittsburgh Press, "Triangles Face Turbulent Cleveland," by Bill Heufelder, July 23, 1974

Bryan Times, "Signs With Nets," UPI, July 24, 1974

Star-News, "Sports Roundup," July 25, 1974

Bryan Times, "Nets Snared," UPI, July 26, 1974

Observer-Reporter, "Forfeit Helps Triangles Win," AP, July 26, 1974

The Times Recorder (OH), "Bartkowicz Leaves Nets," UPI, July 16, 1974

Leader-Post, "Richey Unhappy," August 6, 1974

Pittsburgh Press, "Freedoms Eliminate Nets," UPI, August 21, 1974

Youngstown Vindicator, "Nets Eliminated By Freedoms," August 21, 1974

Gettysburg Times, "Nets Trade Gunter For Wendy Overton," AP, March 11, 1975

Prescott Courier, "Sports In Brief," AP, March 11, 1975

Gadsden Times, "Nets Acquire Overton," AP, March 12, 1975

Tuscaloosa News, "Nets Sign Reissen," AP, March 23, 1975

Baltimore Afro-American, "Afro Sports," April 29, 1975

Pittsburgh Post-Gazette, "It's the Little Things," by Vince Leonard, May 9, 1975

Youngstown Vindicator, "Newest Member of Nets," AP, May 13, 1975

Baltimore Sun, "Margo Tiff Out-Everts Chris," May 18, 1975

Pittsburgh Press, "Turnbull Paces Nets' Victory," May 21, 1975

Dover Times Reporter, "Nets Rally For Narrow Win," AP, May 23, 1975

Ocala Star-Banner, "Riessen Fines Self, Partner," AP, June 8, 1975

Southeast Missourian, "A New Pro," AP, July 14, 1975

Boca Raton News, "Riessen Tops Team Tennis," UPI, July 17, 1975

Gettysburg Times, "Cleveland Nets Sign Rayni Fox," AP, November 11, 1975

Miami Herald, "Turnbull Gets Herself Angry," by Susan Shackelford, January 15, 1976

Evening Independent, "Nets Sign Rahim," AP, March 30, 1976

Youngstown Vindicator, "Racquets Irk Zingale, May File Suit," AP, August 16, 1976

Mansfield News-Journal, "Nets-Triangles One Team," AP, December 15, 1976

Honolulu Star-Bulletin, "Renee was a Hit," by Rock Rothrock, December 26, 1976

Pittsburgh Post-Gazette, "Nets Lure Borg, Sweetie," by Vince Leonard, January 27, 1977

Deseret News, "Nets Want Borg," UPI, January 28, 1977

Pittsburgh Press, "Zingale Names McGibbeny 'Tri-Nets' GM," UPI, February 1, 1977

Milwaukee Journal, "Borg Leads Big Money Parade," UPI, February 2, 1977

New York Times, "Nets Get Borg and his Fiancée," by Neil Amdur, February 2, 1977

Spokane Daily Chronicle, "Borg Signs Contract With WTT," AP, February 2, 1977

Albuquerque Journal, "World Team Tennis Inks Borg," AP, February 3, 1977

News-Dispatch, "Borg 'Nets' $1.5 Million," UPI, February 3, 1977

St. Joseph Gazette, "Cleveland-Pittsburgh Signs Borg, Fiancée," AP, February 3, 1977

Akron Beacon Journal, "Pollution Too Much for Navratilova," AP, April 29, 1977

Hartford Courant, "Martina Eagerly Anticipates Future," by Ginny Apple, April 29, 1977

Pittsburgh Post-Gazette, "Navratilova: Much Cleveland Pollution," AP, April 29, 1977

Pittsburgh Post-Gazette, "Nets, Starless Sea-Port" by Vince Leonard, April 30, 1977

Pittsburgh Press, "Sounds Of Silence Spur Borg," by Bill Heufelder, May 5, 1977

News-Dispatch, "Nets: Just A Big Nothing In Pittsburgh," by Bob Osborne, May 6, 1977

Boston Globe, "Borg In Lobster Country," by John Powers, May 17, 1977

Pittsburgh Press, "Net Result: Too Few Fans," by Bill Heufelder, May 26, 1977

Arlington Heights Herald (IL), "Renee Richards to play WTT," UPI, June 3, 1977

Morning Record and Journal, "WTT Nets Sign On Dr. Richards," AP, June 3, 1977

Pittsburgh Press-Gazette, "Zingale Coy On Future," by Vince Leonard, June 3, 1977

Times-News, "Nets Sign Renee Richards," by William Grimsley, June 4, 1977

Daily News, "Best Season For Borg," June 7, 1977

Pittsburgh Press-Gazette, "Nets Die Here," by Vince Leonard, June 22, 1977

Morning Record and Journal, "Borg Goes Back To Team Tennis," AP, July 7, 1977

Youngstown Vindicator, "6,118 See Borg Lead Nets Past Lobsters," AP, July 7, 1977

Pittsburgh Press, "Peggy Michel Signs Nets Contract," AP, August 16, 1977

Lewiston Evening Journal, "Lobsters Seek Series Sweep," AP, August 18, 1977

Bangor Daily News, "Borg Quits Team Net Tour," AP, December 30, 1977

Finger Lakes Times, "WTT Return For Borg?" AP, December 31, 1977

Youngstown Vindicator, "La. Shift For Nets," AP, February 15, 1978

Los Angeles Times, "The Newswire," February 25, 1978

Los Angeles Times, "Morning Briefing," February 26, 1978

Los Angeles Times, "WTT Roundup," March 9, 1978

New York Times, "Sports Guide," April 24, 1978

Gettysburg Times, "Sun Belt Nets Return To Ohio," AP, May 5, 1978

Lawrence Journal-World, "Sun Belt Nets Set Games in Old Home," AP, May 5, 1978

New York Times, "Can Peaches Come Back?" May 7, 1978

Los Angeles Times, "Morning Briefing," May 13, 1978

Spokane Daily Chronicle, "On Display," April 25, 1978

Gadsden Times, "Nets Return To Cleveland," AP, May 6, 1978

Ellensburg Daily Record, "Cascades Lose 7 Straight," UPI, May 12, 1978

The Hour, "Sports Brief," UPI, May 13, 1978

Youngstown Vindicator, "Renee Upsets Billie Jean King," AP, May 15, 1978

Lakeland Ledger, "Nets' Lucas Is A Travelin' Man," by Dick Schneider, May 23, 1978

Sports Illustrated, "Rocket With A Racquet," by Melissa Ludtke, May 29, 1978

Rock Hill Herald, "Lucas Tries Two Pro Careers," by Earl Gault, May 30, 1978

Modesto Bee, "Richards Leads Nets Over Gaters," AP, June 10, 1978

Prescott Courier, "Nets Get By Racquets," AP, July 17, 1978

Merced Sun-Star, "Nets Tough On Gaters," AP, July 19, 1978

Reading Eagle, "Nets Win," AP, July 22, 1978

Chicago Tribune, "Tennis' Star Dropout Tries Again," July 28, 1978

Boston Globe, "Key Players Missed By Lobsters, 28-20," July 29, 1978

Sarasota Herald Tribune, "Evert Whips Renee Richards," UPI, July 31, 1978

Ellensburg Daily Record, "Only 126 Fans Show Up For Nets," UPI, August 1, 1978

Kokomo Tribune, "A Tougher Renee Emerges," by Christy Barbee, August 5, 1978

Modesto Bee, "Renee Richards Finds Peace," by Christie Barbee, August 8, 1978

Boston Globe, "Lobsters' Streak Ends As Nets Prevail, 31-25," August 13, 1978

Evening News, "Nets Face Tough Series," AP, August 14, 1978

Boston Globe, "Lobs Open Playoffs With Easy Win," by Harry Eisenberg, August 16, 1978

Reading Eagle, "Lucas and Richards: A Mixed Bag," by Tony Zonca, September 12, 1978

Philadelphia Daily News, "This Is Your Life Lucas," by Phil Jasner, November 3, 1994

Sports In Cleveland, by John J. Grabowski, 1996

Sports Illustrated, "Call Him Coach," by L. Jon Wertheim, July 16, 1997

No Way Renée, by Renée Richards, 2007

Cleveland.com, by Bill Livingston, November 1, 2008

DENVER RACQUETS/PHOENIX RACQUETS (1974-1978)

Playground Daily News, "Denver Signs Durr," UPI, January 17, 1974

Anchorage Daily News, "Returns To Competition," AP, April 20, 1974

New York Times, "Sets Defeated By Denver Team," June 6, 1974

Press-Courier, "Racquets Edge Houston, 29-23," AP, June 10, 1974

Las Cruces Sun-News, "World Tennis Exciting Austins," by Mike Morrow, June 28, 1974

Tampa Bay Times, "WTT: Boos, Beer, Bands, Rowdy," by Eric Lincoln, July 15, 1974

Modesto Bee, "Denver Team Edges Golden Gaters," AP, July 17, 1974

Greeley Daily Tribune, "Denver Clinch Pacific Title," by Steve Bauer, August 14, 1974

Greeley Daily Tribune, "Racquets Clinch Tie For West," by Steve Bauer, August 15, 1974

Modesto Bee, "Golden Gaters Fall To Denver," AP, August 21, 1974

New York Times, "Freedoms Seal Division Crown," August 24, 1974

Spokane Daily Chronicle, "Finals Set Up," AP, August 24, 1974

Ellensburg Daily Record, "Racquets Take Title," AP, August 27, 1974

Las Vegas Optic, "Racquets Win First WTT Title," by Tom Wilt, August 27, 1974

Merced Sun-Star, "Racquets Snare World Net Title," AP, August 27, 1974

New York Times, "Racquets Capture Team Tennis Title," August 27, 1974

Observer-Reporter, "Denver Sweeps WTT Playoffs," AP, August 27, 1974

Pittsburgh Press, "Denver Notches Team Tennis Title," UPI, August 27, 1974

Prescott Courier, "World Tennis Title Is Better Than Expected," AP, August 27, 1974

Star-News, "Racquets Win First World Tennis Title," UPI, August 27, 1974

New Straits Times, "Tony Roche Picked As Coach Of Year," UPI, October 2, 1974

Baltimore Sun, "Denver Racquets For Sale," December 9, 1974

Salt Lake Tribune, "Denver Up For Sale," UPI, December 10, 1974

Arizona Republic, "Phoenix Joins WTT," by Mike Garrett, February 7, 1975

Fort Collins Coloradoan, "A's Jackson Leads Group for Racquets," AP, February 7, 1975

Arizona Republic, "Racquets Clip Gaters," by Penny Butler, May 4, 1975

Arizona Republic, "Racquets Plan Clinic, Sports Briefing," May 31, 1975

Scottsdale Daily Progress, "Rental Payment Made," June 27, 1975

Princeton Daily Clarion (IN), "Kris Kemmer Comes," by Stan Wawer, August 1, 1975

Boston Globe, "Lobsters Trap Phoenix," August 10, 1975

Alton Telegraph, "Money Dangled To Lure Chris," AP, October 29, 1975

Daytona Beach Morning Journal, "Racquets Nab Rights To Chris," AP, October 29, 1975

Lakeland Ledger, "Phoenix Claims Contract Rights To Evert," AP, October 29, 1975

Lewiston Morning Tribune, "Evert Key To Circuit," AP, October 29, 1975

Rome News-Tribune, "Can Lure Of Cash Get Chrissie?" AP, October 29, 1975

Times Daily, "Phoenix Racquets Make Offer To Chrissie," by John Schurr, October 29, 1975

Redlands Daily Facts, "Gaters Assign Evert Rights To Phoenix," October 30, 1975

Prescott Courier, "Chris Evert Signs With Phoenix Club," AP, November 13, 1975

Boston Globe, "Evert Signs With Phoenix of WTT," UPI, November 14, 1975

Free Lance-Star, "Racquets Sign Evert To Two-Year Contract," AP, November 14, 1975

Pensacola News Journal, "Phoenix Racquets Net Chris Evert," AP, November 14, 1975

Salina Journal, "Chris to WTT," UPI, November 14, 1975

Spokesman-Review, "Phoenix Signs Chris," AP, November 14, 1975

Tuscaloosa News, "Chris Evert Joins World Team Tennis," AP, November 14, 1975

Evening Independent, "Evert Shakes Jitters," AP, May 6, 1976

Kingman Daily Miner, "Evert Paces Racquets Over Loves In Opener," AP, May 6, 1976

Beaver County Times, "Racquets Win Fourth In Row," UPI, May 14, 1976

Boston Globe, "Evert-led Racquets Tumble Lobsters," May 24, 1976

Prescott Courier, "Triangles Down Racquets," AP, July 26, 1976

Scottsdale Daily Progress, "Racquets Take On Gaters," August 16, 1976

Sports Illustrated, "the Court Belongs To Chris," by Sarah Pileggi, December 20, 1976

New York Times, "Chris Evert Beaten," April 30, 1977

Press-Courier, "Phoenix Polishes Apples Before 13,675," AP, June 7, 1977

Spokane Daily Chronicle, "Walts Sparks Phoenix Win At Seattle," AP, July 12, 1977

St. Petersburg Times, "Newberry Signs With Racquets," UPI, July 12, 1977

New York Times, "Apples Pin Loss On Racquets," by Thomas Rogers, July 30, 1977

Pittsburgh Press, "Chris Sparks Racquets To Win, Finals Birth," UPI, August 23, 1977

Casa Grande Dispatch, "Evert To Leave Phoenix," AP, December 15, 1977

Herald-Journal, "Phoenix May Lose Evert," AP, December 15, 1977

New York Times, "Miss Barker Joins Racquets," AP, February 9, 1978

Reading Eagle, "Barker Signs," AP, February 9, 1978

Prescott Courier, AP, "Shaw Signs," February 14, 1978

Los Angeles Times, "Competition Tough For 1978 WTT Teams," April 7, 1978

Los Angeles Times, "New-Look Racquets Top Oranges," by Pete Donovan, May 2, 1978

Reading Eagle, "Barker Beats Chris Evert," AP, May 9, 1978

Evening Independent, "Crushing A Complex," AP, May 31, 1978

Yuma Daily Sun, "Phoenix Racquets Name New Officials," AP, May 31, 1978

Los Angeles Times, "Friars Beaten By Racquets," June 6, 1978

Los Angeles Times, "Dean Martin Jr. Does It His Way," by Pete Donovan, June 9, 1978

Boston Globe, "Lobsters Fall In Tiebreaker," July 19, 1978

Prescott Courier, "Men Lead Racquets," AP, July 26, 1978

Spokesman-Review, "Racquets Win," AP, July 26, 1978

Los Angeles Times, "Racquets Beat Oranges, 28-15," July 28, 1978

Kingman Daily Miner, "Racquets Out Of It," AP, August 10, 1978

People, "This Swinger Is Dean Martin's Son," by Martha Smilgis, November 6, 1978

Arizona Republic, "Wetmore Quits Racquets," by Penny Butler, February 17, 1979

St. Petersburg Times, "'Players' Fault Is Mediocrity," by Roy Peter Clark, June 11, 1979

Rome Tribune, "Courtship of Dean-Paul Martin," by Peer Oppenheimer, August 5, 1979

Westworld, "Moments Of Glory," by Bill Gallo, November 18, 1999

DETROIT LOVES/INDIANA LOVES (1974-1978)

Press Telegram, "A Tennis Love Tap," AP, February 18, 1974

Statesman-Journal, "King Hurt By Racket," AP, February 19, 1974

Chicago Tribune, "Dent Signs Pact With Detroit Loves," March 29, 1974

Argus-Press, "Last New Male Love Is Signed," AP, April 22, 1974

Toledo Blade, "Come Meet Detroit Loves Coach Jack Shaw," April 22, 1974

Lawrence Journal-World, "Loves Fill Roster By Signing Two More," AP, April 25, 1974

Argus-Press, "Loves Open Tonight," by Larry Paladino, May 9, 1974

Ludington Daily News, "Team Tennis Makes Debut In Detroit," UPI, May 9, 1974

Miami News, "Love is Dead With a Vengeance," by John Crittenden, May 9, 1974

News-Palladium, "Brode Figures Loves Can Break," by Larry Paladino, May 9, 1974

Windsor Star, "Casals Loves' Margin," AP, May 9, 1974

Argus-Press, "Loves Victorious In Opener," by Larry Paladino, May 10, 1974

Boston Globe, "Detroit Win Brings Forth First Protest," May 10, 1974

Michigan Daily, "Loves Win Debut," by George Hastings, May 10, 1974

Toledo Blade, "Slim Crowd Sees Loves Win," by Tom Loomis, May 10, 1974

Michigan Daily, "Loves Win Debut," by George Hastings, May 11, 1974

Star-News, "Sports Roundup," AP, May 11, 1974

Press-Courier, "Net Loves Win Again," AP, May 13, 1974

Toledo Blade, "Loves Level Lobsters," AP, May 13, 1974

Boston Globe, "Loves Conquer Lobsters Again," May 15, 1974

Michigan Daily, "WTT... Is It Tennis," by George Hastings, May 15, 1974

Argus-Press, "No Triangles For Tennis Loves," AP, May 18, 1974

Pittsburgh Post-Gazette, "Casals Unstrings Fernandez," by Vince Leonard, May 18, 1974

Argus-Press, "No Love..." AP, May 23, 1974

Argus-Press, "Loves Rally For Close Win," AP, May 27, 1974

Pittsburgh Post-Gazette, "Loves Stage Rally, Beat E-Z Riders," AP, May 28, 1974

Detroit Free Press, "Dent Combines Talent," by Howard Erickson, May 31, 1974

Argus-Press, "Love-Leis; Rosie Wins 15th Straight," AP, June 1, 1974

Luddington Daily News, "Loves Get Tagged," UPI, June 4, 1974

Argus-Press, "Casals, Dent Keep Loves In Second," AP, June 11, 1974

Beaver County Times, "Evonne Turns Tables On Rosie," by Andy Nuzzo, June 14, 1974

Boston Globe, "Loves Have Banner Night," AP, June 15, 1974

New York Times, "Pregnancy Has Little Effect On Sports," by Jay Searcy, July 5, 1974

New York Times, "Sets Win 28-27," July 9, 1974

Miami News, "Everything's Just Rosie," by Bob Mack, July 11, 1974

Miami News, "Casals Gets Back At Fans," by Jack Wilkerson, July 11, 1974

Bryan News, "Loves Nip Nets," UPI, July 13, 1974

Reading Eagle, "Loves Keep Winning," AP, July 18, 1974

Windsor Star, "Loves Still Hot At Home," AP, July 22, 1974

Argus-Press, "Loves Make It Five Straight," AP, July 30, 1974

New York Times, "Sets Bow To Loves; Miss Casals Stars," July 31, 1974

Toledo Blade, "Casals Notches Victory No. 34," AP, July 31, 1974

Honolulu Star-Bulletin, "A Little Hot," by Jim Easterwood, August 1, 1974

Boston Globe, "Freedoms, Triangles Win Showdowns," August 20, 1974

Windsor Star, "Loves Still Streaking," AP, August 2, 1974

Leader-Post, "A Little Rest Helps The Loves," AP, August 9, 1974

Pittsburgh Press, "Gamble 'Rosie' Love Potion," by Dan Donovan, August 9, 1974

Philadelphia Daily News, "Detroit Loves Plans," by Bill Fleischman, August 14, 1974

Toledo Blade, "Dent Paces Loves Past Lobs," AP, August 16, 1974

Windsor Star, "Loves On The Spot," AP, August 19, 1974

Boston Globe, "Freedoms, Triangles Win Showdowns," August 20, 1974

Luddington Daily News, "Loves Get Bounced," UPI, August 26, 1974

Argus-Press, "Want To Buy 430,000 Loser? See Loves' Owners," AP, November 2, 1974

Benton Harbor News Palladium, "Loves May Move," AP, November 2, 1974

New York Times, "Loves For Sale In Detroit," November 2, 1974

Benton Harbor News Palladium, "Loves Sold, Moved To Indy," AP, November 19, 1974

Boston Globe, "Indianapolis Gains Loves," November 19, 1974

Evening Independent, "Loves To Indianapolis," AP, November 19, 1974

Evening News, "Detroit Loves Will Be Moved," AP, November 19, 1974

Kokomo Tribune, "Bostrom Signs With Loves," AP, March 26, 1975

New York Times, "Loves Sign Bostrom," March 26, 1975

Beaver County Times, "Sports Of All Sorts," April 11, 1975

Seymour Daily Tribune (IN), "Indiana Loves Tennis Matches Set," May 3, 1975

Indianapolis News, "Loves Wins Sans Stars," Special to the News, May 10, 1975

Corpus Christi Times, "WTT Takes Break For Wimbledon," UPI, June 16, 1975

Indianapolis Star, "Carmel Plans Varied July 4th Activities," Area Report, July 2, 1975

Los Angeles Times, "East Side West Side Gerulaitis," by Candace Mayeron, July 11, 1975

Beaver County Times, "Triangles Capture Seventh Straight Win," UPI, July 16, 1975

Kentucky New Era, "Loves Keep Promise," AP, July 24, 1975

The Journal, "Loves Bow To Gaters," AP, August 5, 1975

Chicago Tribune, "The Other Gerulaitis," by David Condon, January 31, 1976

Indianapolis News, "Loves Seek Tennis Court," Special to the News, April 5, 1976

Beaver County Times, "Loves Knock Off Friars Again," May 14, 1976

Indianapolis News, "WTT, Chris Both Benefit," by Dick Denny, May 26, 1976

Pittsburgh Post-Gazette, "Cleveland Falls To Loves, 30-22" AP, August 11, 1976

Pittsburgh Press, "Indiana's Owner Loves To Talk," by Bill Heufelder, August 11, 1976

Victoria Advocate, "Britain's Barker Nears Loves Pact," AP, February 8, 1977

Indiana Loves Media Guide 1977, March 1977

Spokesman-Review, "Loves Defeat Cascades," AP, May 2, 1977

Pittsburgh Post-Gazette, "Vitas Scorns Nets For KC," by Vince Leonard, May 4, 1977

Pittsburgh Post-Gazette, "Indiana Shows No Love," by Vince Leonard, May 5, 1977

Spokane Daily Chronicle, "World Tennis Opener Features Soviet Team," April 26, 1977

Spokesman-Review, "Gerulaitis Out," AP, July 2, 1977

Sports Illustrated, "It's Veni, Vidi, Vici, Vitas," by Barry McDermott, August 15, 1977

Times Daily, "Loves Count On Fromholtz, Masters," UPI, April 15, 1978

Spokesman-Review, "Loves Tip Anaheim," AP, June 4, 1978

Youngstown Vindicator, "Loves Jar Lobsters," AP, June 10, 1978

Indianapolis Star, "Loves Call It Quits In WTT," by Steve Herman, November 8, 1978

Tri City Herald, "Loves Lost To Indiana," AP, November 9, 1978

Victoria Advocate, "Indiana Joins Dropouts," AP, November 9, 1978

New York Times, "Loves Join The Fold," November 10, 1978

Sarasota Herald-Tribune, "Loves 5th Franchise To Fold," UPI, November 10, 1978

St. Louis Dispatch, "Sexism Was No Handicap For Eisel," February 28, 1988

Detroit News, "Tennis In Detroit? King Would Love It," July 31, 2005

FLORIDA FLAMINGOS (1974)

Miami News, "WTT Florida," December 25, 1973

Sarasota Herald-Tribune, "Froehling A One-Man Team," AP, January 18, 1974

Miami Herald, "WTT Gives Boost to Flamingos," by Jim Martz, February 3, 1974

Miami News, "Miami WTT Entry Counting on Chris," by Gene Williams, February 3, 1974

Palm Beach Post, "Flamingos Sign 2 More Players," April 8, 1974

Miami News, "Former Tomboy Epstein," by Bill Brubaker, April 16, 1974

Lewiston Daily Sun, "Flamingos Set," AP, May 7, 1974

Ocala Star-Banner, "Flamingos Sign Net Comebackers," AP, May 7, 1974

Boca Raton News, "Tennis Opens Tonight," UPI, May 8, 1974

Los Angeles Times, "The Douglas Gang," by John Hall, May 8, 1974

Boca Raton News, "Flamingos Edge Strings, 27-26," UPI, May 9, 1974

Lakeland Ledger, "Flamingos Win Opener, Coach Credits Fans," AP, May 9, 1974

Los Angeles Times, "Strings Lose Opener To Flamingos, 27-26," May 9, 1974

Evening Independent, "Triangles Find Florida Easy," AP, May 11, 1974

Miami Herald, "Flamingos Fall 29-21 Deal for Kuykendall," by Jim Martz, May 12, 1974

Colorado Springs Gazette, "Racquets Meet Flamingos," May 14, 1974

Miami News, "Flamingos Lose Fifth Straight," May 16, 1974

Miami News, "Flamingos Trump Aces," May 18, 1974

Miami News, "Robbie: Flamingos, Toros To Make It," by Jack Wilkinson, May 23, 1974

Miami News, "Embarrassed Flamingos," by Jack Wilkinson, May 23, 1974

New Castle News, "Freedoms Roll By Flamingos," May 23, 1974

Leader-Post, "Tennis Anyone?" AP, May 25, 1974

Miami News, "Ganz Puts Foot Down To Be Flam," by Jack Wilkinson, May 25, 1974

Palm Beach Post, "Pro Tennis The WTT Way," by Ron Smith, May 26, 1974

Boston Globe, "Flamingos Edge EZ Riders, 28-27," June 1, 1974

Palm Beach Post, "Laurie Fleming: I Can't Get Going," by Ron Smith, June 5, 1974

Miami News, "Flamingos Lose On Tie-Breaker," Special to *Miami News*, June 5, 1974

The Argus, "Gaters Capture Tie-Breaker To Trim Flamingos," UPI, June 6, 1974

Los Angeles Times, "Flamingos Hand Strings Third Defeat in Row," June 8, 1974

Star News, "Flamingos Nip Strings," UPI, June 8, 1974

Palm Beach Post, "Flamingo Doesn't Fit Comeback Mold," by Ron Smith, June 13, 1974

Miami News, "Flamingos Belkin Enjoys Bench," by Jack Wilkinson, June 13, 1974

San Mateo Times, "Flamingos Nip Gaters," AP, June 13, 1974

Reading Eagle, "Flamingos Do Well On Home Courts," AP, June 15, 1974

Pacific Stars and Stripes, "Flamingos Triumph Over Royals," UPI, June 17, 1974

Los Angeles Times, "Strings Lose to Flamingos, Play Chicago," July 7, 1974

Miami News, AP, "Fleming Helps Flamingos Rally," July 7, 1974

Naples Daily News, "Maria Bueno Fired," AP, July 15, 1974

Evening Independent, "Tests: Belkin, Bayfront," by Phil Gulick, July 16, 1974

Evening Independent, "Bueno Fired," AP, July 15, 1974

Palm Beach Post, "Flamingos Cut Bueno," AP, July 16, 1974

Miami News, AP, "Fleming Helps Flamingos Rally," July 18, 1974

Miami News, "Flamingos Still In Running," July 31, 1974

Sarasota Herald-Tribune, "WTT's Flamingos In St. Pete," by Bob Ruf, August 4, 1974

St. Petersburg Times, "Flamingos Begin Big Tennis Test," by Jack Ellison, August 4, 1974

Evening Independent, "Flamingos Feather The Nest," by Bob LeNoir, August 9, 1974

St. Petersburg Times, "Flamingos Net Nets," by Jack Flowers, August 10, 1974

Tampa Tribune, "Flamingos Coach Keeping Busy," by Greg Gordon, August 11, 1974

St. Petersburg Times, "Flamingos Lose Bayfront Debut," August 12, 1974

Miami News, "Snow White and the 7 Flams?" by Jack Wilkinson, August 14, 1974

Evening Independent, "It Doesn't Figure," AP, September 3, 1974

Miami News, "Flamingos Send Bills Packing," by Jack Wilkinson, December 4, 1974

Palm Beach Post, "Fleming Returns To Tennis," by Karl Gulbronsen, June 9, 1976

The Art of World Team Tennis, by Greg Hoffman, 1977

GOLDEN GATERS (1974-1978)

San Mateo Times, "Golden Gaters Tennis Signing," November 13, 1973

San Mateo Times, "Gaters Sign Ann Kiyomura," by Jack Bluth, February 27, 1974

Daily Review, "Neutral Corner Tennis Anyone?" by Lowell Hickey, May 8, 1974

Modesto Bee, "Golden Gaters Are Defeated By Minnesota," AP, May 16, 1974

Oakland Tribune, "Gaters Leap Back To The Top," Special to the Tribune, May 21, 1974

Daily Review, "Ilana Kloss of Gaters Learning New Game," May 31, 1974

Daily Review, "E-Z Riders Dump Gaters," UPI, June 3, 1974

Daily Review, "Hunt Ignites Gaters to Win," by Charles Tonelli, June 6, 1974

GO WITH THE GATERS IN '77

world team tennis

1976 WTT All-Star Match
Oakland-Alameda County
Coliseum Arena
Attendance - 12,587

El Paso Herald Post, "Stolle Leads Philly," UPI, June 11, 1974

San Mateo Times, "Billie Jean King Wows Em," by Dick Draper, June 11, 1974

San Francisco Examiner, "Gaters Prevail," by Jim Bainbridge, August 6, 1974

Oakland Tribune, "Win String," Special To The Tribune, August 11, 1974

Tuscaloosa News, "Ouch That Smarts," AP, August 18, 1974

Daily Review, "Gaters Eliminated," August 21, 1974

Modesto Bee, "Golden Gaters Fall To Denver," AP, August 21, 1974

Sacramento Bee, "Racquets Slap Gaters Out of WTT Playoffs," AP, August 21, 1974

Berkeley Gazette, "Hunt Miffed at Gaters Trade," by Steve Kennedy, January 8, 1975

Oakland Tribune, "Gaters Serve More King," by Jack Rux, March 26, 1975

The Journal, "Nets, Gaters End Losses," AP, June 9, 1975

Miami Herald, "Teens Teaming In Doubles Spark Gaters," UPI, June 12, 1975

Oakland Tribune, "A Breeze For The Gaters," Special to the Tribune, June 13, 1975

Kentucky New Era, "Golden Gaters Tops," AP, July 15, 1975

Modesto Bee, "Golden Gaters Nip Loves," AP, August 5, 1975

Daily Review, "Gaters Try To Make It Like the Golden State Warriors," August 19, 1975

San Mateo Times, "Gaters Win Wild West Playoffs," by Dick Draper, August 20, 1975

Redlands Daily Facts, "Triangles Favored Over Gaters," August 21, 1975

Oakland Tribune, "Durr Not Signed To Hard Line," by Jack Rux, January 29, 1976

Oakland Tribune, "Gaters Lose WTT Opener," by Jack Rux, May 2, 1976

Merced Sun-Star, "Gaters Humble Friars," AP, May 6, 1976

Redlands Daily Facts, "Gaters Edge Strings In WTT Action," UPI, May 12, 1976

Berkeley Gazette, "Gaters Win Several Reasons," by Steve Kennedy, June 3, 1976

Merced Sun-Star, "Gaters Blast Leis," AP, June 5, 1976

Oakland Tribune, "Gaters Roll On," by Jack Rux, June 7, 1976

Oakland Tribune, "Tennis Gaters After Lucas," by Ed Levitt, June 10, 1976

Lewiston Morning Tribune, "Lucas Signs In Second Pro Sport," AP, June 11, 1976

Berkeley Gazette, "Smart Gater Gamble on Lucas," by Steve Kennedy, June 12, 1976

Michigan Daily, "Number One Cage Pick Signs Pro Tennis Pact," AP, June 12, 1976

Oakland Tribune, "Gaters Sign Lucas," by Jack Rux, June 12, 1976

Reading Eagle, "Gaters Sign Lucas," AP, June 12, 1976

Modesto Bee, "Gaters Down Strings 22-20," AP, August 12, 1976

Oakland Tribune, "Playoffs Start Tonight," August 16, 1976

Modesto Bee, "Gaters Nip Phoenix in Playoffs," AP, August 18, 1976

Modesto Bee, "Golden Gaters Tumble in Playoffs," AP, August 20, 1976

Oakland Tribune, "Coliseum Crowds," by Robert Stinnett, August 20, 1976

Oakland Tribune, "McMillan Savors Strategy," by Jack Rux, August 21, 1976

Hattiesburg American, "Sets Over Gaters," August 22, 1976

New York Times, "Sets-Gaters Series Continues Tonight," August 23, 1976

San Francisco Examiner, "Sets Fall on Gaters," by Jim Bainbridge, August 24, 1976

Nevada State Journal, "Gaters Lose To Sets," UPI, August 28, 1976

Oakland Tribune, "Gaters Shop For Help," by Jack Rux, September 5, 1976

New York Times, "Diamond Quits Gaters," UPI, December 19, 1976

Evening Independent, "Betsy Right On," UPI, April 29, 1977

San Mateo Times, "Kiyomura Helps Beat Gaters," UPI, May 17, 1977

Fresno Bee, "A Disgusted Ilie Nastase Delays Play After Losing A Call," July 26, 1977

Oakland Tribune, "Loves Sweep Gaters," AP, June 6, 1977

San Francisco Examiner, "Gaters Owner Last Laugh," by Frank Cooney, June 8, 1977

Miami News, "Golden Gaters Defeat Soviets," AP, July 20, 1977

Merced Sun-Star, "Gaters Shade Friars," AP, July 21, 1977

Daily Review, "Peterson Pieces Gaters Together," by Jeff Chapman, July 26, 1977

Reading Eagle, "WTT Gators Success At Gate," by Gordon Sakamoto, August 7, 1977

Rutland Gazette, "Peterson's Principles Successful for Gaters," AP, August 7, 1977

Daily Union Democrat, "Gaters Downed," UPI, August 17, 1977

Daily Union Underground, "Gaters Drop Opener," UPI, April 24, 1978

Daily Union Democrat, "Gaters Squeeze By," UPI, April 27, 1978

Merced Sun-Star, "Gaters Post Narrow Win," AP, June 13, 1978

Press-Courier, "Born Again Tennis Bum," by Bud Tucker, July 25, 1978

Daily Union Democrat, "Gaters Sign Another," UPI, August 10, 1978

Spokane Daily Chronicle, "Owners To Rescue, UPI, January 4, 1979

Modesto Bee, "World Team Tennis Folds, Gaters Stay," AP, March 8, 1979

Philadelphia Daily News, "This Is Your Life Lucas," by Phil Jasner, November 3, 1994

HAWAII LEIS (1974-1976)

Colorado Springs Gazette-Telegraph, "San Diego Netters Swingers," AP, May 30, 1973

Star-News, "San Diego Team Obtains Franchise," UPI, May 31, 1973

Pittsburgh Post-Gazette, "WTT Swings to Hawaii," AP, February 19, 1974

Baltimore Sun, "Hawaii Leis Sign Ann Kiyomura," AP, April 28, 1974

Honolulu Star-Bulletin, "A Primo Sort of Game," by Jerry Tune, May 3, 1974

Morning Herald, "Hawaii Leis Beat Triangles," AP, May 13, 1974

Ellensburg Daily Record, "Trade Made," UPI, June 5, 1974

Merced Sun-Star, "Gaters Blast Leis," AP, June 5, 1974

Reading Eagle, "Freedoms Keep Leis In Net Rut," AP, June 13, 1974

Redlands Daily Facts, "Redlands Resident In WTT," June 13, 1974

Lowell Sun, AP, "Hawaii Loses To Billie Jean," June 13, 1974

Winona Daily News, "Hawaii Trims Buckskins," AP, July 30, 1974

El Paso Herald Post, "Late Rally Saves Leis," UPI, August 3, 1974

Sports Illustrated, "Go To Pot With The Lobsters," by Curry Kirkpatrick, August 9, 1974

San Mateo Times, "Leis Lose To Golden Gaters," by Dick Draper, August 16, 1974

Daily Capital News, "Newcombe To Hawaii," AP, May 7, 1975

The Morning Record, "Newcombe Inks Team Tennis Pact," AP, May 7, 1975

Observer-Reporter (PA), "Newcombe Will Join Hawaii," AP, May 7, 1975

St. Petersburg Times, "Newcombe To Join Hawaii Leis," UPI, May 7, 1975

Honolulu Star-Bulletin, "Butch is Now," by Jim Easterwood, May 17, 1975

Pittsburgh Press, "Triangles Lose In Hawaii," Special to The Press, May 22, 1975

Oakland Tribune, "Streak of Seven On Line For Gaters," June 3, 1975

Sarasota Herald Tribune, "Newk Is Out Of Wimbledon," AP, June 10, 1975

Honolulu Advertiser, "Hawaii Netters Beat Leaders," by Dan McGuire, June 15, 1975

New York Times, "Sets Defeat Ailing Leis By 27 to 17," July 16, 1975

Hattiesburg American, "San Diego Loses Two," AP, August 4, 1975

New York Times, "Sets Down By 15-10, Gain 22-20 Victory," August 6, 1975

New York Times, "Leis Sign Nastase; WTT Sees Profit," by Parton Keese, December 12, 1975

St. Petersburg Times, "Nastase Joins Leis," AP, December 12, 1975

Argus Press, "Nastase Honors Leis," UPI, May 12, 1976

Reading Eagle, "Two Imports Help Gaters," AP, May 19, 1976

New York Times, "Nastase Draws Criticism," May 22, 1976

New York Times, "Nastase Doubts A Return," May 23, 1976

Evening Independent, "You Come Right Home Young Man!" AP, May 28, 1976

Spokane Daily Chronicle, "Nastase Ordered To Return Home," AP, May 28, 1976

The Bulletin, "Leis Win In Portland," AP, May 28, 1976

Reading Eagle, "Nastase Leis Down Racket," AP, May 29, 1976

Sarasota Herald-Tribune, "Nastase Wals Out on Leis," UPI, May 29, 1976

Daytona Beach News-Journal, "Nastase Leaves For Romania," AP, May 30, 1976

St. Petersburg Times, "Nastase Quits Leis," AP, June 5, 1976

Honolulu Star-Bulletin, "The Leis Give up on Nastase," by Rock Rothrock, June 13, 1976

Spokesman Daily Chronicle, "Nastase Slates Hawaii Return," AP, June 23, 1976

The Bulletin, "Hawaii Leis Look At Possible Move," AP, July 3, 1976

San Francisco Chronicle, "Nastase Returns," UPI, June 23, 1976

Prescott Courier, "Racquets Wilt Leis," AP, July 19, 1976

Spokesman-Review, "Leis Lace Strings," AP, August 1, 1976

Honolulu Advertiser, "Ilie Misbehaves and Leis Lose," UPI, August 5, 1976

Los Angeles Times, "Nastase's Not So Nasty After All," by John Weyler, August 19, 1976

New York Times, "Leis Of WTT Moving," AP, September 24, 1976

Spokesman Daily Chronicle, "Leis Move To Coast," AP, September 24, 1976

Spokesman-Review, "Pro Franchises Wilt in Hawaii," by Dave Distel, December 12, 1976

Hawaii Leis Press Release, 1976

The Art of World Team Tennis, by Greg Hoffman, 1977

HOUSTON E-Z RIDERS (1974)

Middlesboro Daily News, "Newcombe Signs Up," UPI, February 12, 1974

San Antonio Light, "World Team Tennis: A New Dimension," February 26, 1974

Seguin Gazette, "World Team Tennis in Texas," February 26, 1974

San Antonio Express, "EZ Riders Tennis in S.A.," March 14, 1974

Seguin Gazette, "World Team Tennis Comes to Texas," by Bob Thaxton, March 21, 1974

Los Angeles Times, "EZ Riders Sign Two," AP, April 10, 1974

Port Arthur News, "Texas Joins World Team Tennis," UPI, May 12, 1974

St. Petersburg Times, "Newcombe Wins — For Houston," AP, May 13, 1974

Beaver County Times, "Newcombe Ace For EZ Riders," UPI, May 14, 1974

Port Arthur News, "Houston Tops Minnesota At Decrepit Sam Houston," May 14, 1974

Panama City Herald, "Cops Stop West," UPI, May 15, 1974

Boston Globe, "Sets Drop Third Home Match," May 16, 1974

St. Petersburg Times, "Sports In Brief," UPI, May 16, 1974

Clovis News Journal, "Houston Wins In 29-25 In WTT Play," UPI, May 23, 1974

Leader-Post, "Tennis Anyone?" AP, May 25, 1974

New York Times, "Newcombe's Commitment," by Dave Anderson, May 26, 1974

Pittsburgh Post-Gazette, "Tris Face EZ Newcombe," by Phil Axelrod, May 28, 1974

Daily Review, "E-Z Riders Dump Gaters," UPI, June 3, 1974

El Paso Herald Post, "Sports Briefs," UPI, June 4, 1974

Los Angeles Times, "Strings Beaten By Houston E-Z Riders," UPI, June 4, 1974

Daily Journal, "EZ Riders Beat Freedoms," AP, June 7, 1974

Boston Globe, "WTT Roundup: Houston Upsets Philly, 23-20," June 7, 1974

Clovis News Journal, "Newcombe Takes Win In WTT," UPI, June 11, 1974

Los Angeles Times, "Strings Lose to EZ Riders; Redondo Wins," UPI, June 11, 1974

Chronicle Telegram, "World Team Tennis," AP, June 14, 1974

Jennings Daily News, "Riders Sign Foster," UPI, July 8, 1974

San Mateo Times, "Newcombe Rips the Idiots," by Dick Draper, July 18, 1974

Corpus Christi Times, "Moody Words Of Advice," AP, July 30, 1974

Del Rio Herald, "E-Z Riders," August 7, 1974

Baytown Sun, "EZ Riders at Sam Houston Coliseum," by Glena Pfenning, August 8, 1974

Daily Review, "Gaters Dump EZ Riders," August 8, 1974

Chicago Tribune, "Houston Rides Past Aces 28-16," AP, August 11, 1974

Bakersfield Californian, "Luckless Leis Lose On Forfeit," August 14, 1974

Star Tribune, "Houston Beats Buckskins," by Joe Soucheray, August 20, 1974

Pittsburgh Press, "EZ Riders Bounced," UPI, August 21, 1974

Sports Illustrated, "Going To Pot With The Lobsters" by Curry Kirkpatrick, August 1974

Sports Illustrated, "Last of the Awesome Aussies," by Frank Deford, August 26, 1974

Sports Illustrated, "19th Hole," September 23, 1974

Galveston Daily News, "EZ Riders Sued," UPI, October 19, 1974

Boston Globe, "Lobsters Live! (I Think...)," March 14, 1975

Corpus Christi Times, "Newcombe Beaten," AP, April 30, 1975

Baltimore Sun, "Houston Drops Out of WTT," AP, May 3, 1975

Des Moines Register, "Houston WTT Entry Drops From League," UPI, May 3, 1975

Big Spring Herald, "Operations Suspended," AP, May 4, 1975

The Art of World Team Tennis, by Greg Hoffman, 1977

Fun While It Lasted, by Andy Crossley, February 12, 2012

LOS ANGELES STRINGS (1974-1978)

Los Angeles Times, "Aussie Alexander Joins L.A. Net Team," AP, October 10, 1973

Nevada Daily Mall, "Sports Roundup," Oct. 10, 1973

Lebanon Daily News, "Sports Brief," UPI, February 28, 1974

Lakeland Ledger, "Sports In Brief," AP, April 16, 1974

Los Angeles Times, "Strings Have Two Signed; Seek Laver," April 16, 1974

Sports Illustrated, "They Said It," April 29, 1974

Los Angeles Times, "There Are Strings Attached," by Ted Green, May 7, 1974

Los Angeles Times, "Strings Sign Fort As Alexander Sub," May 8, 1974

Star News, UPI, "Team Tennis Opens Play," May 8, 1974

Los Angeles Times, "Strings Lose Opener To Flamingos," May 9, 1974

Los Angeles Times, "Strings Defeat Golden Gaters for First Win," May 12, 1974

The Independent, "4,666 See Strings Opener," by Gary Rausch, May 16, 1974

Los Angeles Times, "Strings Opener Draws 4,666," by Ted Green, May 16, 1974

Los Angeles Times, "Strings Win Before Crowd of Only 1,351," May 18, 1974

Los Angeles Times, "Masters-Susman Duo Leads Strings," May 23, 1974

Los Angeles Times, "Strings Score in Doubles to Defeat Royals," May 30, 1974

Los Angeles Times, "Strings Drop Match, 24-23, on Tie-Breaker," June 13, 1974

Los Angeles Times, "Hawaii Beats Strings, Snaps 15-Match Slump," June 16, 1974

Los Angeles Times, "Tennis," by Candace Mayeron, June 19, 1974

Pittsburgh Post-Gazette, "Strings Ink Cramer," AP, July 6, 1974

Los Angeles Times, "Strings Lose For 8th Straight Time, 29-23," July 13, 1974

Los Angeles Times, "Hawaii Hands Strings 10th Straight Loss," July 18, 1974

Los Angeles Times, "Strings Handed 12th Straight Loss," July 21, 1974

Los Angeles Times, "Strings Lose 14th Straight," July 27, 1974

Los Angeles Times, "Strings Losing Now Before Intermission," August 4, 1974

Los Angeles Times, "Strings Defeat Houston, 27-26, on Tiebreaker," Aug. 10, 1974

Los Angeles Times, "Strings Lose To Denver," Aug. 12, 1974

Los Angeles Times, "Strings Lose Home Finale to Golden Gaters," Aug. 18, 1974

Los Angeles Times, "Busy Schedule Looms for Anaheim," by Jack Boettner, December 6, 1974

Los Angeles Times, "L.A. Gets Rosie Casals," March 30, 1975

Los Angeles Times, "Strings, Friars Rosters Set," by Candace Mayeron, April 2, 1975

Progress Bulletin, "Strings to Host Specials," AP, May 5, 1975

San Francisco Examiner, "Tyrant Slackens Strings," by Jim Bainbridge, June 2, 1975

Los Angeles Times, "Casals and the Strings Win," June 13, 1975

Los Angeles Times, "Casals Defeats Court As Strings Top Leis," July 12, 1975

Los Angeles Times, "Indiana Beats Strings, 23-21," August 10, 1975

Los Angeles Times, "Strings Eliminated From Playoffs, 20-8," August 18, 1975

Los Angeles Times, "Strings Look To Successful Year," by Jerry Cohen, January 21, 1976

Los Angeles Times, "Ralston To Coach, Play With Strings," by Ted Green, February 11, 1976

Los Angeles Times, "Rosie Casals Signs With Strings," March 21, 1976

Pittsburgh Post-Gazette, "Strings Obtain Vijay Amritraj," April 12, 1976

Bakersfield Californian, "Dennis Happy With Job," by Larry Press, April 25, 1976

Los Angeles Times, "Strings Have New Coach, Home," by Ted Green, April 30, 1976

Los Angeles Times, "Strings Win Opener, 22-19," May 2, 1976

Los Angeles Times, "Fromholtz Swings Only on Court," by Ted Green, May 12, 1976

Beaver County Times, "Strings Make It Three Straight," UPI, May 24, 1976

Los Angeles Times, "Strings Win Fourth in Row," May 25, 1976

Anchorage Daily News, "A New Racket," by Jim Murray, May 29, 1976

Los Angeles Times, "Strings Defeat Indiana as Lutz Beats Ruffels," June 6, 1976

Los Angeles Times, "Two Strings Named for All-Star Game," June 16, 1976

Los Angeles Times, "Strings Rally and Beat Indiana in Tie-Breaker," July 19, 1976

Lakeland Ledger, "Strings Sign Pasarell, AP, July 21, 1976

Los Angeles Times, "Lobsters Beat Strings," July 21, 1976

New York Times, "Strings Sign Pasarell," AP, July 21, 1976

Los Angeles Times, "Strings Snap Sets, Win Streak," July 22, 1976

Los Angeles Times, "Strings Upset New York, 28-23," July 29, 1976

Los Angeles Times, "Lutz Paces Strings Win, 32-22," July 31, 1976

Lewiston Evening Journal, "WTT Seeking To Corner Connors," AP, August 10, 1976

Eugene Register-Guard, "People In Sports," August 11, 1976

Pittsburgh Post-Gazette, "Strings Flirt With Connors," AP, August 11, 1976

Schenectady Gazette, "Strings Willing To Pay Connors $200G," AP, August 11, 1976

Press-Courier, "Strings Edge Friars," AP, August 13, 1976

Los Angeles Times, "Lutz Beats Nastase and Strings Win Before 7,425," August 14, 1976

New York Times, "Ilie Takes His Act To Hollywood," by Neil Amdur, March 29, 1977

Schenectady Gazette, "Ilie Signs Multi-Year Pact," UPI, March 30, 1977

Los Angeles Times, "Charlie Pasarell Joins Strings As Doubles Player," April 4, 1977

Los Angeles Times, "Strings Open Season With High Aspirations," April 5, 1977

Los Angeles Times, "Capsule Look Offered of WTT Teams," April 4, 1977

Los Angeles Times, "Strings Lose Opener," April 29, 1977

Los Angeles Times, "Strings Lose Home Opener," by Sheila Moran, May 12, 1977

Los Angeles Times, "Strings May Be at End of Theirs," by Sheila Moran, May 23, 1977

Los Angeles Times, "Strings Lose 11th Straight Time," by Sheila Moran, May 26, 1977

Los Angeles Times, "Strings Handed 12th Straight Loss," by Dave Distel, May 28, 1977

Los Angeles Times, "Strings Make Trade, Then Lose Again," June 2, 1977

Los Angeles Times, "Strings Lose 14th Straight," June 3, 1977

Los Angeles Times, "Here Comes Nastase and Strings," by Sheila Moran, July 3, 1977

Los Angeles Times, "Strings Lose Again, Face Friars Tonight at Forum," July 8, 1977

Los Angeles Times, "Strings Use Tracy Austin as Fill-In," by Sheila Moran, July 9, 1977

Los Angeles Times, "Strings Win Fourth in Row," July 18, 1977

Los Angeles Times, "Strings Win Streak Ends," July 21, 1977

Los Angeles Times, "Strings Lose To Friars," July 24, 1977

Van Nuys Valley News, "Focus On Tennis," June 29, 1977

Los Angeles Times, "World Team Tennis Decisions," July 25, 1977

Evening Independent, "Borg Held To Tie In Cellar-Strings Surprise," AP, July 30, 1977

The Argus (CA), "Nastase's Antics Bad for WTT," by Lowell Hickey, August 6, 1977

Los Angeles Times, "Strings Rout Sea-Port," August 15, 1977

Van Nuys Valley News, "Focus On Tennis," August 17, 1977

Los Angeles Times, "Colin Dibley Strings' Top Draft Choice," October 11, 1977

Lakeland Ledger, "Names In Sports," December 16, 1977

Los Angeles Times, "Flamboyant Nastase returns to Strings Lineup," December 29, 1977

Observer-Reporter, "Unattached But With 'Strings'," AP, February 3, 1978

Ellensburg Daily Record, "Strings Sign Best Player," UPI, February 22, 1978

Los Angeles Times, "Nastase, Strings Pay Penalty in Phoenix," April 30, 1978

Los Angeles Times, "Connors, Borg Watch Strings," by Elizabeth Wheeler, May 13, 1978

Boston Globe, "Nastase's Strings Tip Racquets," May 14, 1978

Los Angeles Times, "'Nasty' Can Really Coach," by Elizabeth Wheeler, June 2, 1978

Press-Courier, "Olympic Team Chosen," by Rich Romine, June 7, 1978

Deseret News, "Evert Paces Strings," AP, July 13, 1978

Reading Eagle, "Strings Win," AP, June 17, 1978

Calgary Herald, "A Big Fine For Nastase," AP, July 13, 1978

Milwaukee Journal, "Another Fine For Nastase," AP, July 13, 1978

Evening Independent, "Break-Even Point, Nastase," AP, July 14, 1978

Reading Eagle, "Nastase Tossed," AP, August 7, 1978

Los Angeles Times, "Nastase Tops Laver and Strings Win," August 13, 1978

Los Angeles Times, "Evert To Snap Wade Jinx" by Elizabeth Wheeler, August 17, 1978

Press-Courier, "Near Perfect Evert Sparks Strings Win," AP, August 23, 1978

Youngstown Vindicator, "Evert Sparks Strings Play In Finals," AP, September 14, 1978

Evening Independent, "Springing A Surprise On The Strings," AP, September 20, 1978

Desert Sun, "Chris Nips Martina As Strings Win WTT," AP, September 22, 1978

Evening Independent, "Chasing The Blahs Away," AP, September 22, 1978

Lakeland Ledger, "Strings Win WTT Championship," AP, September 22, 1978

The Hour, "L.A. Strings Annex World Net Crown," UPI, September 22, 1978

San Pedro News-Pilot, "Strings Pull Off Victory," by Mike Braham, September 22, 1978

Christian Science Monitor, "Amritraj in stride with WTT," by Ross Atkin, September 25, 1978

Sports Illustrated, "Roundup Of The Week Sept. 11-17," September 25, 1978

Daytona Beach Morning Journal, "LA Strings Broken," UPI, November 8, 1978

Reading Eagle, "WTT Strings Fold," AP, November 8, 1978

San Bernardino County Sun, "Strings 3rd Squad to Fold," AP, November 8, 1978

Star Tribune, "Los Angeles Strings Fold Franchise in WTT," AP, November 8, 1978

Bangor Daily News, "World Team Tennis Add New Franchise," AP, December 20, 1978

News and Courier, "New L.A. Owner Buss Has Distinctive Ideas," AP, June 17, 1979

Fun While It Lasted, by Andy Crossley, January 11, 2012

MINNESOTA BUCKSKINS (1974)

Winona Daily News, "Buckskins Near First Signing," AP, August 26, 1973

Bemidji Pioneer, "Owners Named For Buckskins," August 25, 1973

Winona Daily News, "Buckskins Sign Jones," AP, April 18, 1974

Anchorage Daily, "Buckskins Sell Stock," UPI, April 27, 1974

Minneapolis Star, "Buckskins Talk Team, City Unity," by Bill Hengen, May 2, 1974

New York Times, "WTT Announced Signings," May 5, 1974

Bemidji Pioneer, "WTT Matches Too Long?" AP, May 8, 1974

Albany Herald, "Buckskins Win," AP, May 11, 1974

Modesto Bee, "Golden Gaters Are Defeated By Minnesota," AP, May 16, 1974

Bemidji Pioneer, "Buckskins Sweep Aces," AP, May 21, 1974

Pittsburgh Post-Gazette, "Bucks Top Sets, 25-17," AP, May 23, 1974

Miami News, "Hewitt Would Double His Pleasure," by Jack Wilkerson, May 27, 1974

Minneapolis Star, "Billie Jean Said No To Million," June 1, 1974

Winona Daily News, "Billie Jean Said No To $2 Million," AP, June 2, 1974

St. Cloud Times, "Buckskins Post Split," UPI, June 3, 1974

Winona Daily News, "Buckskins Upset Freedoms," June 3, 1974

Boston Globe, "Sports Roundup," June 4, 1974

Winona Daily News, "Buckskins move into First Place," AP, June 3, 1974

Star Tribune, "3,614 Watch Buckskins Nip Leis," by Jon Roe, June 8, 1974

Oakland Tribune, "Mother Freedom's Baby," by Jack Rux, June 9, 1974

Winona Daily News, "Buckskins Outlast Hawaii For 11th Win," AP, June 9, 1974

Bemidji Pioneer, "Buckskins Whip Florida To Hold First," AP, June 11, 1974

Beaver County Times, "Minnesota Buckskins Topple LA Strings," UPI, June 12, 1974

Los Angeles Times, "Strings Drop Match, 24-23, on Tie-Breaker," June 13, 1974

Pittsburgh Press, "Triangles Host Minnesota," June 14, 1974

New York Times, "Buckskins Edge Sets' Team, 26-25," July 15, 1974

Winona Daily News, "Buckskins Tops The Nets," AP, July 17, 1974

Los Angeles Times, "Minnesota Plays Strings Tonight," AP, August 3, 1974

Daily Journal, "Buckskins Win," August 8, 1974

Bemidji Pioneer, "Denver Aces Bucks," AP, August 15, 1974

Winona Daily News, "Buckskins Cinch Division Crown AP," August 18, 1974

Winona Daily News, "Houston Tops Buckskins In Playoff Start," AP, August 20, 1974

Bemidji Pioneer, "Buckskins Advance," AP, August 21, 1974

New York Times, "Sports News Brief," AP, August 21, 1974

Pittsburgh Press, "WTT Takes Over 'Skins," UPI, August 21, 1974

European Stars and Bars, "Buckskins Taken Over By WTT," AP, August 22, 1974

Winona Daily News, "Buckskins Tumble To Denver," AP, August 23, 1974

European Stars And Stripes, "Racquets Demolish Buckskins," AP, August 24, 1974

Winona Daily News, "Denver Ousts Buckskins in Semi-Finals," AP, August 25, 1974

El Paso Herald Post, "Buckskins Whip Houston Riders," UPI, August 26, 1974

Bangor Daily News, "Way Cleared For Top Stars," AP, August 29, 1974

Wisconsin State Journal, "Minnesota WTT Team Faces Sale," September 5, 1974

Minneapolis Star, "Indiana Group Fails to use Buckskins Option," September 9, 1974

Vancouver Sun, "Baselines," AP, September 11, 1974

New York Times, "Buckskins In Trouble," UPI, November 7, 1974

The Art of World Team Tennis, by Greg Hoffman, 1977

St. Paul Pioneer Press, "King, 49, Still Big Booster of WTT," May 12, 1993

Minneapolis Star, "Area Pro Tennis Bucked," by John Greenwald, May 19, 1975

Minnesota Sports Almanac, by Joel A. Rippel, 2006

NEW YORK SETS (1974-1976)/NEW YORK APPLES (1977-1978)

New York Times, "Mrs. King Accepts New Group's Pact," August 4, 1973

New York Times, "Nastase Wants To Play For New Yorkers," December 27, 1973

Baltimore Sun, "WTT Expected to Sign Nastase," Reuters, January 21, 1974

Schenectady Gazette, "Ilie Nastase Would Play For NY Sets," AP, February 6, 1974

New York Times, "Sets Expect To Get Nastase," by Neil Amdur, February 15, 1974

New York Times, "Sets Are A Headache For WTT," by Neil Amdur, April 14, 1974

New York Times, "Sets Seeking Pilic, Miss Wade," by Neil Amdur, April 19, 1974

New York Times, "Pilic, Yugoslav Star, Signs New York Sets Contract," April 23, 1974

The Telegraph, "Lobsters Trade Nikki Pilic," UPI, April 23, 1974

Lakeland Ledger, "NY Sets Sign Owens," AP, April 24, 1974

New York Times, "People In Sports," May 1, 1974

New York Times, "The Sets' Schedule," May 5, 1974

NBC-TV, "Revolutionary Team Tennis Concept Makes Debut," May 10, 1974

Boston Globe, "Sets Drop Third Home Match," May 16, 1974

New York Daily News, "Pilic: No Love for Screamers," by Dave Hirshey, May 17, 1974

New York Times, "Pilic Will Play For Sets Tonight," by Neil Amdur, May 17, 1974

New York Times, "Sets Lose For 9th Time As Women Falter Again," May 20, 1974

New York Times, "457 Watch Sets Drop 6th Match," May 23, 1974

New York Times, "Riders, Rain Add To Sets' Gloom," by Robin Herman, May 25, 1974

Pittsburgh Post-Gazette, "Sets Sign Graebner," May 25, 1974

Baltimore Sun, "Unbeaten Freedoms Top New York," AP, May 26, 1974

New York Times, "Sharon Walsh Signed By Sets," by Charles Friedman, May 28, 1974

New York Times, "Sets Lose For 9th Time," by Robin Herman, May 29, 1974

Argus-Press, "Sets Surprise The Loves, 27-26," AP, June 4, 1974

Lakeland Ledger, "Sets Notch First Home Win Ever," AP, June 4, 1974

New York Times, "Sets Beat Banners With Make-Shift Lineup," June 11, 1974

New York Times, "Sets Win Match, Will Lose Coach," June 14, 1974

New York Times, "Pilic Sharp As Sets Post 24-21 Victory," June 16, 1974
Baltimore Sun, "Nikki Pilic Named Sets Player-Coach," AP, June 30, 1974
Herald-Journal, "Pilic Replaces Sets' Santana," AP, June 30, 1974
New York Times, "Sets Lose 25-21 To Lobster Team," July 8, 1974
Lakeland Ledger, "Tennis," AP, July 16, 1974
New York Times, "Sets Win 28-22, From Flamingos," July 19, 1974
New York Times, "5,204 Fans See Sets Win, 26-23," July 24, 1974
New York Times, "7,535 See Sets Bow To Freedoms," by Robin Herman, July 27, 1974
New York Times, "Sets Down Loves, 29-24, In Tennis," August 9, 1974
New York Times, "Sets Win By 28-13 From Flamingos," August 11, 1974
Sarasota Journal, "Weary Wade Savior For Sets," by Alan Lassila, August 13, 1974
New York Times, "Sets Beat Billie Jean, Lose Game," by Michael Strauss, August 17, 1974
New York Times, "Sports Briefs," October 5, 1974
Sarasota Herald-Tribune, "New York Sets Name Kain GM," AP, October 30, 1974
New York Times, "Sets Get Rights To Stan Smith," November 7, 1974

New York Times, "WTT Sees Profit," December 12, 1975
New York Times, "Mrs. King Heading To Sets?" by Neil Amdur, February 5, 1975
Evening Independent, "Don't Need Biggies, The King Declares," AP, February 6, 1975
New York Times, "Mrs. King Will Play For Sets," by Neil Amdur, February 6, 1975
Pittsburgh Post-Gazette, "Billie Jean Traded To Set," AP, February 6, 1975
Pittsburgh Press, "King Wish Fulfilled," UPI, February 6, 1975
Salt Lake Tribune, "Billie Jean Traded To Sets," UPI, February 6, 1975
Daily Press, "WTT Sets Give Post To Stolle," AP, April 4, 1975
Herald-Journal, "Fred Stolle Named Player-Coach," AP, April 4, 1975
Anchorage Daily News, "Schallau Signs With Sets," AP, April 24, 1975
St. Petersburg, "Sets Sign Betsy," UPI, April 29, 1975
New York Times, "Sets Make Loves 6th Victim In Row," May 28, 1975
Village Voice, "Playing Tennis In The Shade," by Fred Misurella, July 7, 1975
New York Times, "Sets Beaten By Lobsters, 33-21," July 9, 1975
The Journal, "Sets Top Triangles To Take Over Lead," AP, August 2, 1975
The Journal, "Sets Beat Triangles," AP, August 9, 1975
New York Times, "Sets Beaten, 27-22," August 12, 1975
New York Times, "Mayer Helps Sets Down Gaters, 29-21," August 14, 1975
New York Times, "Sets Defeat Nets, 26-18, in WTT," August 16, 1975
Arizona Republic, "Lobsters Pinch Sets," AP, August 18, 1975

Sarasota Herald-Tribune, "Sets Trade Mona Schallau," UPI, October 8, 1975

Bakersfield Californian, "Nastase Signs With Leis," December 12, 1975

Boca Raton News, "Sets Sign Dent, Stolle," February 3, 1976

New York Times, "Sets Lose General Manager," February 14, 1976

Lakeland Ledger, "NY Sets Ink Beaven," AP, April 22, 1976

Evening News, "Sets Sting Strings," AP, May 20, 1976

Pittsburgh Press, "Mayer An 'Up' Set," by Bill Heufelder," June 11, 1976

Beaver County Times, "Road Jinx Hits Triangles Again," UPI, July 12, 1976

New York Times, "Sets Easily Triumph Over Friars," July 15, 1976

Spokesman-Review, "Short Cuts," August 11, 1976

Pittsburgh Press, "Unranked JoAnne Rankles NY Sets," by Bill Heufelder, August 17, 1976

Pittsburgh Post-Gazette, "Mayer and King Lead Sets," by Phil Axelrod, August 19, 1976

Evening Independent, "King's Second Chance," AP, August 20, 1976

Youngstown Vindicator, "Sets Oust Triangles," AP, August 20, 1976

Free Lance-Star, "King Serious About WTT Title Series," AP, August 21, 1976

Chicago Tribune, "Sets Take Lead In WTT Final," August 22, 1976

Press-Courier, "NY Sets Crush Gaters," AP, August 22, 1976

Daily Union, "Mayer Optimistic For World Tennis Title," AP, August 23, 1976

St. Petersburg Times, "Sets Looking To Dent," AP, August 23, 1976

New York Times, "Sets Beat Gaters, Lead In Series, 2-0," August 24, 1976

New York Times, "Sets Win Title With 31-13 Rout," by Robin Herman, August 28, 1976

Lodi News-Sentinel, "Sets Sweep Golden Gaters To Win Title," UPI, August 28, 1976

Leader-Post, "Sets Sweep Tennis Title," AP, August 28, 1976

Youngstown Vindicator, "Sets Bag Net Title," AP, August 28, 1976

New York Daily News, "Apples Pluck Vitas in Draft," by Dave Hirshey, January 4, 1977

Spokesman-Review, "Vitas Going To Apples?" AP, January 4, 1977

Spokesman-Review, "Stolle Signs Pact," AP, March 18, 1977

St. Petersburg Times, "Apples Sign Wade," AP, April 1, 1977

New York Times, "Apples Set Tonight," by John S. Radosta, April 28, 1977

New York Times, "Apples Top Cascades At Forum," by Neil Amdur, April 29, 1977

The Bulletin, "Apples Whip Cascades; Friars Win," AP, May 28, 1977

Evening News, "Virginia Wade Rallies Apples," AP, June 5, 1977

New York Times, "Apples Lose; Evert, King Draw 13,675," by Tom Rogers, June 7, 1977

Annapolis Capital, "New York Apples," AP, June 9, 1977

Valley News (CA), "Wimbledon Champ Wade Can Do it Again," UPI, July 13, 1977

Deseret News, "Teams, News Blacked Out," AP, July 14, 1977

Youngstown Vindicator, "Apples Top Nets," AP, July 22, 1977

New York Daily News, "Virginia Acts Like a Hot Dog" by Mike Lupica, July 23, 1977

Los Angeles Times, "Apples Defeat Strings, 29-18," July 31, 1977

Evening Independent, "Wade Loves Apples Diet," AP, August 17, 1977

New York Times, "Apples Conquer Loves In Opener" by Robin Herman, August 17, 1977

Spokane Daily Chronicle, "Apples Take Net Series," AP, August 19, 1977

Youngstown Vindicator, "New York Sets Win In Tennis Playoff," AP, August 19, 1977

New York Times, "Apples Defeat Lobsters 29-26, And Gain WTT Final," August 23, 1977

The Telegraph, "Apples Eliminate Lobsters, 29-26," AP, August 23, 1977

New York Times, "Apples Win To Retain Title," August 28, 1977

Berkshire Eagle, "Apples Unstring Racquets For 2nd Title In Row," UPI, August 29, 1977

New York Daily News, "Virginia's Golden Bagel," by Mike Lupica, August 29, 1977

Daily Union Democrat, "Apples Take Title," UPI, August 29, 1977

Sports Illustrated, "Roundup Of The Week Aug. 22-28," September 5, 1977

Tuscaloosa News, "Stolle Is Top Coach," November 17, 1977

Great Falls Tribune, "Abe Saperstein's Boy Jerry," by Red Smith, February 3, 1978

New York Times, "Gerulaitis Joins Apples In Trade," February 14, 1978

Pittsburgh Press, "Apples Acquire Vitas Gerulaitis," UPI, February 14, 1978

Evening Independent, "Free Swinger Picks Apples," AP, February 15, 1978

Spokane Daily Chronicle, "Gerulaitis Set To Help Needy," AP, February 15, 1978

St. Joseph Gazette, "Gerulaitis Brings Playboy Rep To Apples," AP, February 15, 1978

Free Lance-Star, "Apples Sign 2," AP, March 28, 1978

New York Times, "Apples 28, Oranges 25," by John S. Radosta, April 22, 1978

New York Times, "Nets Crush Apples As Vitas Loses," by Neil Amdur, April 26, 1978

New York Times, "Apples Trounce Loves, 33-19," by Tony Kornheiser, April 28, 1978

Youngstown Vindicator, "Apples Continue Streak," AP, May 6, 1978

New York Times, "Mrs. King Excels As Apples Triumph," May 10, 1978

New York Times, "Stolle Fills In, Leads Apples To Victory," May 19, 1978

New York Times, "Vitas and 'Those Three Guys,'" by Dave Anderson, May 19, 1978

New York Daily News, "Gerulaitis King Missing," by Jack Wilkinson, May 24, 1978

Times-Union, "Billie Jean Undoes Loves," UPI, June 5, 1978

New York Daily News, "Oranges Fall to N.Y. in OT," by Jack Wilkinson, June 6, 1978

New York Times, "Mrs. King Is The Star As Apples Rout Oranges," June 6, 1978

Prescott Courier, "Apples Rout Racquets As Barker Loses 14th," AP, June 13, 1978

People, "Gerulaitis Is A Hustling Tennis Player," by Martha Smilgis, July 3, 1978

The Hour, "Sports Probe," by Steve K. Walz, July 6, 1978

New York Times, "Gerulaitis Sparks Apples 27-25 Win," by Parton Keese, July 25, 1978

Evening News, "Apples Triumph," AP, August 1, 1978

New York Times, "Apples Defeat Lobsters In WTT Match, 25-24," August 1, 1978

New York Times, "Apples Losing Tempers and Polish," by Parton Keese, August 9, 1978

Evening Independent, "Apples Hang By A String," AP, August 24, 1978

Youngstown Vindicator, "Apples Ousted," AP, August 25, 1978

Tuscaloosa News, "Owens Not King But Future Bright," by Chris Welch, June 27, 1979

BarryPopik.com, by Barry Popik, February 19, 2006

PHILADELPHIA FREEDOMS (1974)

Sarasota Journal, "King To Provide Winner For Philly," UPI, November 27, 1973

Gettysburg Times, "Will Ehlinger Be Able To Do For Tennis What He Did For Soccer in Philadelphia?"
by Ralph Bernstein, January 18, 1974

Chicago Tribune, "Fairlie Signs with Philadelphia WTT," UPI, January 24, 1974

Reading Eagle, "Freedoms Sign Fairlie," AP, January 24, 1974

Gettysburg Times, "Philly Freedoms Sign Fred Stolle," AP, March 7, 1974

Palm Beach Post, "Fretz Signs With Freedoms," AP, April 17, 1974

Reading Eagle, "Freedoms Exhibition," April 30, 1974

Morning News, "Billie Jean the Coach Readies Freedoms," AP, May 2, 1974

Bucks County Courier Times, "Freedoms Capture Opener," by Ted Haider, May 7, 1974

Capital Times, "Hoopla Marks WTT Start," by Ralph Bernstein, May 7, 1974

Observer-Reporter, "Freedoms Win Bizarre Opener," AP, May 7, 1974

Courier-Express, "Billie Jean King's Freedoms Ring," AP, May 8, 1974

Tucson Daily Citizen, "Freedoms On Newest Streak," AP, May 8, 1974

Delaware County Daily Times, "Freedoms in Hawaii," UPI, May 9, 1974

Reading Eagle, "Billie Jean Rallies Freedom," AP, May 9, 1974

New York Times, "Players Dig Cadillacs, Bank Accounts," by Neil Amdur, May 12, 1974

Delaware County Daily Times, "Banners Lose To Freedoms," AP, May 14, 1974

Gettysburg Times, "Freedoms In 5th Straight Tennis Way," AP, May 14, 1974

Reading Eagle, "Freedoms Sole Unbeaten Club," AP, May 16, 1974

News Journal, "Freedoms Continue Undefeated," AP, May 18, 1974

Edwardsville Intelligencer, "Unbeaten Philly Freedoms Win Again," AP, May 21, 1974

Bakersfield Californian, "Freedoms May Give Philly Another Title," AP, May 21, 1974

The Age, "Freedoms Sole Unbeaten Club," AP, May 22, 1974

Boca Raton News, "Freedoms Trounce Flamingos," UPI, May 23, 1974

Reading Eagle, "Freedoms Win Ninth," AP, May 23, 1974

Reading Eagle, "Freedoms Now 10-0," AP, May 24, 1974

New York Times, "Freedoms Beat Sets To Win 11th," May 26, 1974

Reading Eagle, "Freedoms Make It 12-0," AP, May 30, 1974

Star Tribune, 10,658 Watch Mrs. King Do Her Thing," by John Croft, June 2, 1974

Winona Daily News, "Buckskins Upset Freedoms," June 3, 1974

Boston Globe, "Oops... Freedoms Lose 2nd Straight," June 3, 1974

Reading Eagle, "Sad Weekend for Freedoms," AP, June 3, 1974

Orlando Sentinel, "Freedoms Get Part-Owner Bill Cosby," Sentinel Services, June 9, 1974

Daily Review, "Billie Jean Is King," by Lowell Hickey, June 12, 1974

Ocala Star-Banner, "Kuykendall Loses Freedom," AP, June 14, 1974

Courier-Post, "Freedoms Cut Ticket Prices, Start at 50¢" by Craig Evans, June 26, 1974

Bradford Era, "Freedoms Cut Ticket Prices," AP, June 26, 1974

Chicago Tribune, "Freedom Too Much For Aces," July 19, 1974

Philadelphia Daily News, "Billie Jean Raps Support," by Bill Fleischman, July 23, 1974

PHILADELPHIA

FREEDOMS

ATLANTIC SECTION
CHAMPIONS

Staff
Directory

T. Richard Butera
President

H. Kenneth Butera
General Counsel

Billie Jean King
Player-Coach

Merrill Reese
Director of Communications

Philadelphia Daily News, "Valley of the Doll," by Larry McMullen, July 23, 1974

Gettysburg Times, "Billie Jean Ticked Off By Attendance," AP, July 24, 1974

Pittsburgh Post-Gazette, "Billie Jean Wins Again," AP, July 24, 1974

Winona Daily News, "Freedoms Can't Win At Gate," AP, July 24, 1974

Bangor Daily News, "Billie Jean King Facing 2 Flyers," AP, July 25, 1974

Gettysburg Times, "Billie Jean To Play Two Philly Flyers," AP, July 25, 1974

Morning News, "Ms. King's at it Again," AP, July 25, 1974

Philadelphia Daily News, "Freedoms Now Serving Cosby, Elton," July 25, 1974

Philadelphia Inquirer, "9,746 See Freedoms, Bill Cosby," by Dave Sims, July 26, 1974

Philadelphia Daily News, "Billie Jean Destroys Dornhoefer, MacLeish," July 26, 1974

Philadelphia Daily News, "Freedoms Raucous Fans," by Bill Fleischman, July 26, 1974

New York Times, "Billie Jean Scales Another Pique," by Dave Anderson, July 27, 1974

Albuquerque Journal, "Billy Jean Meets Brutes on Court," AP, July 28, 1974

Arizona Daily Star, "Billy Jean King Just Might Be Coach of Year," AP, July 29, 1974

Delaware County Daily News, "Philadelphia Freedoms Play Ball," AP, July 30, 1974

Reading Eagle, "Freedoms Get Easy Victory," AP, July 30, 1974

Ellensburg Daily Record, "Philadelphia Wins 16th," UPI, July 30, 1974

Philadelphia Daily News, "Some Freedom Advice," by Phil Jasner, July 30, 1974

Gettysburg Times, "Freedoms Win 17th In Row," AP, July 31, 1974

Pittsburgh Post-Gazette, "Drill Instructor Billie Jean," by Vince Leonard, August 3, 1974

Star-News, "WTT Has First Dynasty," UPI, August 14, 1974

Gettysburg Times, "Perfect Year For Freedoms At Spectrum," AP, August 15, 1974

Delaware County Daily Times, "Freedoms Capture 39th," AP, August 15, 1974

Philadelphia Daily News, "Billie Jean Has No Mind," by Julie Anthony, August 19, 1974

Boston Globe, "Freedoms, Triangles Win Showdowns," August 20, 1974

Elyria Chronicle Telegram, "Freedoms Beat The Street Fighters," AP, August 21, 1974

Observer-Reporter, "Freedoms Beat Nets In Playoff," AP, August 21, 1974

Kittanning Simpson Leader Times, "Freedoms Odds On Favorite," August 22, 1974

Star-News, "Freedoms Picked To Top Triangles," UPI, August 22, 1974

Huntington Daily News, "Freedoms Top Pittsburgh in East Final," UPI, August 24, 1974

New York Times, "Freedoms Seal Division Crown," August 24, 1974

Pittsburgh Press, "Freedoms Downed In Title Opener," UPI, August 25, 1974

Morning News, "Freedoms Lose in WTT," AP, August 26, 1974

Spokane Daily Chronicle, "Billie Jean's Losses Help Denver," AP, August 26, 1974

Boston Globe, "Racquets Beat Freedoms For Title," AP, August 27, 1974

Courier-News (NJ), "Buster and Billie," by Leroy Samuels, August 27, 1974

Newport Daily News, "Racquets Crowned WTT Champs," AP, August 27, 1974

Port Arthur News, "Denver Best WTT Team," UPI, August 27, 1974

Reno Gazette-Journal, "Billie Jean King Praises Racquets Balance," AP, August 27, 1974

St. Petersburg Times, "Betsy Again Drafted By Freedoms," November 27, 1974

Spokane Daily Chronicle, "Billie Jean Is Traded," AP, February 5, 1975

Los Angeles Times, "Billie Jean Traded to New York Team," UPI, February 6, 1975

Pittsburgh Press, "King Wish Fulfilled," UPI, February 6, 1975

Tonawanda News, "Freedoms Give Billie Jean Hers," UPI, February 6, 1975

Pittsburgh Press, "Sports Notes," by Glenn Sheeley, March 13, 1975

The Art of World Team Tennis, by Greg Hoffman, 1977

Philadelphia Inquirer, "The Philadelphia Freedoms Are Back," May 7, 2002

PITTSBURGH TRIANGLES (1974-1977)

Pittsburgh Post-Gazette, "Playing Games," by Bill Christine, November 29, 1973

Pittsburgh Press, "City To Field Team In Pro Tennis Loop," May 23, 1973

Pittsburgh Post-Gazette, "Net Loop Begins Play Next May," May 23, 1973

Pittsburgh Press, "Triangles Hope To Land Names," by Bill Heufelder, July 21, 1973

Pittsburgh Press, "Triangles Draft Rosewall First," August 3, 1973

Pittsburgh Post-Gazette, "Triangles Optimistic," by Vince Leonard, August 4, 1973

Beaver County Times, "Triangles First Serve A Smash," by Andy Nuzzo, September 17, 1973

Asbury Park Press (NJ), "Goolagong Signed by Triangles," AP, September 18, 1973

Gettysburg Times, "Goolagong Signs With Pittsburgh," AP, September 18, 1973

Pittsburgh Press, "Evonne Squared Away With Tris," by Bill Heufelder, September 18, 1973

Pittsburgh Press, "Triangles Sign Isabel Fernandez," October 10, 1973

Beaver County Times, "Rosewall Says Maybe Yes," by Rich Emert, December 3, 1973

Lakeland Ledger, "Rosewall Signs With Triangles," AP, December 13, 1973

Pittsburgh Press, "Triangles Trade For Michel," December 23, 1973

Observer-Reporter, "Triangles Trade For Stan Smith," AP, February 7, 1974

Gettysburg Times, "Is Tennis Too Sissy For Tough Pittsburgh Fans?" AP, May 1, 1974

Beaver County Times, "Hawaii Leis One On Triangles," by Andy Nuzzo, May 13, 1974

Beaver County Times, "Triangles Lose Fourth Straight," by Andy Nuzzo, May 20, 1974

Pittsburgh Press, "Royals Breeze Past Triangles," by Bill Heufelder, May 20, 1974

Observer-Reporter, "Triangles Slash Strings 28-16," by Fred Sigler, May 22, 1974

Pittsburgh Press, "Evonne Provides Winning Touch," by Bill Heufelder, May 22, 1974

Pittsburgh Press, "Triangles Set Hawaii, 24-16," UPI, May 25, 1974

Charleston Daily Mail, "In On Court," May 31, 1974

Herald-Journal, "Triangles Beat Flamingos," AP, May 31, 1974

Pittsburgh Post-Gazette, "Tris Try Harder, 25 to 21," by Phil Axelrod, May 31, 1974

Pittsburgh Post-Gazette, "Nets Top Tris," June 3, 1974

Pittsburgh Post-Gazette, "Tris Hope To Shell Lobsters," AP, June 4, 1974

News-Dispatch, "Triangles Win Again," UPI, June 7, 1974

Pittsburgh Post-Gazette, "Dutchman Okker Flying," by Vince Leonard, June 8, 1974

Beaver County Times, "Evonne Turns Tables on Rosie," by Andy Nuzzo, June 14, 1974

Pittsburgh Post-Gazette, "Gals Stumble," by Tom Bunevich, July 10, 1974

Beaver County Times, "Tris Win On Tiebreaker," by Andy Nuzzo, July 22, 1974

Beaver County Times, "Triangles Get Past Nets," by Andy Nuzzo, July 25, 1974

Pittsburgh Post-Gazette, "Nets Protest Arena's Roof," July 26, 1974

Beaver County Times, "Triangles Roll Past Cleveland Nets," UPI, July 29, 1974

Bryan Times, "Nets Knotted," UPI, July 29, 1974

Pittsburgh Post-Gazette, "Triangles Trip Nets, Stay Alive," UPI, August 14, 1974

Michigan Daily, "Pittsburgh Ransacks Loves," AP, August 21, 1974

Pittsburgh Post-Gazette, "Freedoms Survive Rally," by Vince Leonard, August 24, 1974

Spokesman-Review, "Reichblum Quits," AP, September 4, 1974

Pittsburgh Press, "Edwards Joins Fuhrer," by Bill Heufelder, October 4, 1974

Observer-Reporter, "Triangles Score Ace With Connors Trade," AP, November 7, 1974

Pittsburgh Post-Gazette, "Tris Trade For Connors," by Charley Feeney, November 7, 1974

Sarasota Herald-Tribune, "Triangles, Connors Negotiate," UPI, January 26, 1975

Pittsburgh Press, "Peggy Michel Finds Her Love Match," by Ann Butler, February 8, 1975

Pittsburgh Press, "Connors, Triangles Fail To Agree," February 20, 1975

Pittsburgh Press, "Rayni Forecast Shines On," by Bill Heufelder, February 21, 1975

Leader-Post, "Connors Shunning Lavers Request?" AP, February 22, 1975

Pittsburgh Post-Gazette, "Triangles Sign Two For Part-Time Duty," April 23, 1975

Pittsburgh Post-Gazette, "Reichblum Back With Triangles," April 24, 1975

Pittsburgh Post-Gazette, "Evonne Nets Ace: Roger" by Vince Leonard, April 30, 1975

Pittsburgh Press, "Triangles Open With Mark," May 1, 1975

Pittsburgh Post-Gazette, "Triangles Love It As Evonne Stars," May 2, 1975

Pittsburgh Post-Gazette, "Tris Lobster Trick Tonight," by Vince Leonard, May 3, 1975

Beaver County Times, "Tris Minus Evonne At Arena Tonight," UPI, May 5, 1975

Observer-Reporter, "Vitas Lit Spark In Triangles Win," AP, May 5, 1975

Pittsburgh Post-Gazette, "Gunter Triangle Debut," by Vince Leonard, May 5, 1975

Beaver County Times, "Strings Pull Out Win," by Andy Nuzzo, May 6, 1975

Pittsburgh Press, "Strings Rein Over Tris," by Bill Heufelder, May 6, 1975

Beaver County Times, "Triangles Latest Troubled Tenant," by Andy Nuzzo, May 9, 1975

Beaver County Times, "Tris Out-Fox Nets," by Andy Nuzzo, May 10, 1975

Pittsburgh Post-Gazette "Foxy Triangles Edge Nets," by Vince Leonard May 10, 1975

Pittsburgh Post-Gazette, "Triangles Pull Right Strings," by Vince Leonard, May 20, 1975

Pittsburgh Post-Gazette, "Triangles Cook Up Promotion," by Vince Leonard, May 29, 1975

Pittsburgh Post-Gazette, "Cox Leads Triangles Against New Lobsters," May 31, 1975

Pittsburgh Press, "Triangles Broil Lobsters," by Bill Heufelder, June 1, 1975

News-Dispatch, "Triangles Host Leis Saturday," UPI, June 6, 1975

Beaver County Times, "Triangles Rout Loves," by William Branigin, June 11, 1975

Pittsburgh Press, "Short Love Affair Fun For Tris," by Glenn Sheeley, June 11, 1975

Press-Courier, "Triangles Quickly Triumph," AP, June 11, 1975

Beaver County Times, "Triangles Smash Boston Lobsters," UPI, June 14, 1975

Pittsburgh Press, "Triangles Lasso Love," June 14, 1975

Beaver County Times, "Triangles Defeat Hawaii, Increase Lead," UPI, July 17, 1975

Beaver County Times, "Triangles Knock Off Defending Champs," UPI, July 21, 1975

News-Dispatch, "Triangles' Win Skein Up To Ten," UPI, July 22, 1975

Pittsburgh Post-Gazette, "Triangles Top Attendance," July 28, 1976

Pittsburgh Post-Gazette, "Triangles Try Nets," by Vince Leonard, July 29, 1975

Pittsburgh Post-Gazette, "Triangles On Guard," by Vince Leonard, July 31, 1975

Pittsburgh Press, "Triangles' Music Sour To Gaters," by Bill Heufelder, August 1, 1975

Pittsburgh Post-Gazette, "King or Wade?" by Vince Leonard, August 7, 1975

Pittsburgh Press, "Tris Set To Avoid A Fuhrer?" by Pat Livingston, August 15, 1975

Pittsburgh Press, "Triangles Settle For Lobsters," August 18, 1975

Pittsburgh Press, "Tris Must Beat Gaters Today," by Glenn Sheeley, August 23, 1975

The Dispatch, "Triangles Capture World Tennis Crown," August 25, 1975

Milwaukee Journal, "TV Covers For Tennis Spectators," UPI, August 25, 1975

New York Times, "Triangles Tie WTT Finals," AP, August 25, 1975

Titusville Herald, "Triangles Tie Net Title Playoffs," UPI, August 25, 1975

Daily American (PA), "Pittsburgh Cops WTT Championship," AP, August 26, 1975

Ellensburg Daily Record, "Pittsburgh Wins Team Tennis Title," UPI, August 26, 1975

Pittsburgh Press, "Bubbling Triangles Pop Gaters," by Glenn Sheeley, August 26, 1975

Portsmouth Times, "Triangles Capture Net Championship," AP, August 26, 1975

Pittsburgh Press, "Tris Acquire Nets' Sue Stap," August 27, 1975

Southeast Missourian, "Sue Stap Signs," AP, September 3, 1975

Beaver County Times, "Fuhrer Fires Edwards," by Dan Hicks, September 10, 1975

Bangor Daily News, "Champion Tennis Coach Unexpectedly Fired," AP, September 10, 1975

Beaver County Times "Tris Owner In Fuhrer Over Arena," by Dan Hicks September 26, 1975

New Castle News, "Tris Possible Scheduling Conflict," UPI, September 26, 1975

Pittsburgh Post-Gazette, "Arena Dates Irk Fuhrer," by Phil Axelrod, September 26, 1975

Beaver County Press, "Triangles, Arena Reach Agreement," UPI, September 29, 1975

Pittsburgh Press, "Tris, Arena Net Agreement," Sept. 29, 1975

Pittsburgh Press, "Mark Cox Player-Coach of Triangles in '76," March 17, 1976

Beaver County Times "Triangles Boss Already In Furor," by Rich Emert, April 27, 1976

Pittsburgh Post-Gazette, "King or Fuhrer?" by Marino Parascenzo, April 30, 1976

Beaver County Times, "Vitas And Mitton: Quite A Pair," by Rich Emert, May 6, 1976

Beaver County Times "Triangles Triumph, Evonne Injured," by Rich Emert, May 8, 1976

The Record (NJ), "Marriage Increases Evonne Net Worth," by Mike Farber, May 13, 1976

Beaver County Times, "Fuhrer To Shake Up Tris," by Rich Emert, May 24, 1976

Toledo Blade, "Triangles Sign Gunter For Sub," AP, May 15, 1976

Boston Globe, "Goolagong-less Triangles Visit Lobsters Tonight," May 17, 1976

Pittsburgh Post-Gazette, "Triangles Trump Sets," by Vince Leonard, June 3, 1976

Pittsburgh Post-Gazette, "Triangles' Girls Rest Easy," by Vince Leonard, June 4, 1976

Pittsburgh Post-Gazette, "Peg Michel 'Disabled,'" by Russ Brown, June 8, 1976

Pittsburgh Press, "Triangles Double Up Boston," by Bill Heufelder, June 13, 1976

Observer-Reporter, "Frank Fuhrer Raising Furor With Triangles," AP, June 16, 1976

Sports Illustrated, "Not Nearly As Sweet As He Looks," by Myron Cope, June 28, 1976

Observer-Reporter, "Triangles' New Coach Is Jack Of All Trades," AP, July 17, 1976

Pittsburgh Post-Gazette, "Triangles Upset Racquets," by Vince Leonard, July 9, 1976

Pittsburgh Press, "Triangles Play Giveaway," by Bill Heufelder, July 15, 1976

Observer-Reporter, "Triangles Coach Enjoys First Win," AP, July 19, 1976

Beaver County Times, "Tris Losers At Cleveland," UPI, July 28, 1976

Pittsburgh Press, "McGibbeny Provides Lift," by John Clayton, July 28, 1976

News-Dispatch, "Triangles Back Home," UPI, July 30, 1976

Pittsburgh Post-Gazette, "Triangles Stars Rising In Bid For Playoffs," August 2, 1976

Pittsburgh Post-Gazette, "Triangles Lose McGibbeny," August 3, 1976

Monessen Valley Independent, "Nastase Nasty In Loss To Triangles," UPI, August 5, 1976

Schenectady Gazette, "Team Doctor Picked WTT Head Coach," AP, August 5, 1976

Pittsburgh Post-Gazette, "Tris in Stretch Run," by Frank Ramsden, August 11, 1976

Pittsburgh Post-Gazette, "Tris Near WTT Playoffs," by Vince Leonard, August 12, 1976

Pittsburgh Press, "Tris In Playoffs With Super Win," by Bill Heufelder, August 14, 1976

Uniontown Evening Standard, "Triangles Eye WTT Playoffs," August 16, 1976

The Derrick, "Triangles Squeeze Into Playoffs," UPI, August 17, 1976

Danville Bee, "Triangles Edge Sets In Opener," AP, August 18, 1976

Abilene Reporter-News, "Goolagong Gets Roasted," AP, August 21, 1976

Pittsburgh Press, "Pregnancy Devalues Tris, To Idle Evonne," October 14, 1976

Weirton Daily Times, "Triangles To Announce Future Plans," UPI, December 14, 1976

Derrick Times, "Fuhrer Dumps Triangles For At Least A Year," December 15, 1976

New York Times, "Triangles Withdrawn From Team Tennis," AP, December 15, 1976

Pittsburgh Post-Gazette, "It May Be 'Trinets,'" by Vince Leonard, December 15, 1976

Gettysburg Times, "Losing Millions, Owner Of Triangles Sits It Out," AP, December 15, 1976

Pittsburgh Post-Gazette, "Tris' Ex-Coach Dan McGibbeny Is Dead At 26," September 7, 1977

The Art of World Team Tennis, by Greg Hoffman, 1977

Pittsburgh Post-Gazette, "Why Is Vic Still In Pittsburgh?" by Steve Hecht, July 20, 1978

Pittsburgh Post-Gazette, "Love Triangles," by Rick Shrum, September 10, 2000

The Duquesne Duke, "When Tennis Ruled The A'Burgh," by Robert Healy, December 7, 2006

The Best Pittsburgh Sports Arguments, by Joe Mehno, 2007

Pittsburgh Magazine, "Home Sweet Dome," by Craig McConnell, July 2010

Were You There? by Stephen Milligan, 2011

Pittsburgh Post-Gazette, "Ugly Pittsburghers, 1974," by Joseph Adler, March 30, 2012

Wikipedia, "Pittsburgh Triangles," December 29, 2011

SAN DIEGO FRIARS (1975-1978)

Los Angeles Times, "Strings, Friars Rosters Set," by Candace Mayeron, April 2, 1975

Honolulu Star-Bulletin, "Kingston Takes Job with Friars," S-B Staff, June 18, 1975

Boston Globe, "Lobsters Bow To Friars," by Dan Shaughnessy, July 21, 1975

Herald-Journal (SC), "Just Friends and Relatives at this Match," AP, August 12, 1975

Los Angeles Times, "Player-Coach," by Candace Mayeron, August 13, 1975

Herald-Journal, "Rod Laver Joins Friars," AP, January 16, 1976

Boston Globe, "Friars Expected To Sign Laver," February 12, 1976

Lodi News-Sentinel, "Laver Signs For Richest Contract," UPI, February 17, 1976

Leader-Post, "Laver Signs Hefty Pact," AP, February 17, 1976

New York Times, "Laver: A New Face In Team Tennis," February 17, 1976

San Mateo Times, "Rod's Rich WTT Pact," February 17, 1976

Los Angeles Times, "Zing They Go," by John Hall, March 11, 1976

New York Times, "People In Sports," April 13, 1976

Times-Advocate, "Laver's Talents Surviving Age," by Dave Hoff, April 22, 1976

New York Times, "WTT Faces Draft Suit," by Tony Kornheiser, May 19, 1976

Pittsburgh Press, "Friars Ride Rocket, 28-26," by Bill Heufelder, June 6, 1976

Pittsburgh Post-Gazette, "San Diego Halts Tris At 9," by Vince Leonard, June 13, 1975

Pittsburgh Post-Gazette, "Laver Off Friars Again," AP, July 7, 1976

Indiana Gazette (PA), "No Holladay for Terry," by Bob Fulton, July 23, 1976

Los Angeles Times, "Strings Lose to Friars," AP, July 26, 1976

Press Telegram, "Friars Interested," August 12, 1976

Los Angeles Times, "Capsule Look Offered of WTT Teams," April 4, 1977

Boston Globe, "WTT '77," April 24, 1977

New York Times, "Apples Beat Friars In Tiebreaker," by Robin Herman, May 18, 1977

Los Angeles Times, "Laver to Lead Friars Against L.A. In Anaheim," May 27, 1977

Los Angeles Times, "Strings Lose to Friars, 32-21," July 24, 1977

Los Angeles Times, "Friars, Gaters Vie Tonight," July 28, 1977

Annapolis Capital, "World Team Tennis Spotlight," July 30, 1977

Spokesman-Review, "Friars Win Without Rod," AP, August 1, 1977

Merced Sun-Star, "San Diego Beats Gaters," AP, August 17, 1977

Sarasota Herald-Tribune, "Laver Is Player-Coach of Friars," UPI, March 9, 1978

Los Angeles Times, "Friars Expect 2,000 Season Tickets," April 7, 1978

Los Angeles Times, "Competition Tough For 1978 WTT Teams," April 7, 1978

Los Angeles Times, "Laver Looks Ahead To Coaching Career," April 8, 1978

Los Angeles Times, "Friars' Reid Plays Navratilova," April 27, 1978

Los Angeles Times, "Lobsters Beat Friars On Final Win," April 28, 1978

Los Angeles Times, "Reid Helps Friars Win Another," by Pete Donovan, May 1, 1978

Los Angeles Times, "Kerry Reid Starting 2nd Career at 30," by Dave Distel, May 5, 1978

Los Angeles Times, "San Diego Beats Strings With a Final Set Victory," May 12, 1978

Los Angeles Times, "Women Lead Friars to Victory," May 14, 1978

Prescott Courier, "Friars Upend Racquets," AP, May 14, 1978

Los Angeles Times, "Friars Defeat Apples for 7th Straight Win," AP, May 17, 1978

Los Angeles Times, "Friars Win 8th Straight," May 18, 1978

Los Angeles Times, "Friars Stay Hot, Beat Racquets," AP, May 23, 1978

Reading Eagle, "Friars Beat Racquets," AP, May 23, 1978

Boston Globe, "Navratilova Scores, Lobsters Win, 26-24," May 27, 1978

Los Angeles Times, "Kerry Reid Rallies and Sparks Friars," June 1, 1978

Los Angeles Times, "Guerrant Offers Double Trouble," by Dave Distel, June 2, 1978

Los Angeles Times, "Friars' Guerrant a VIP in WTT", by Elizabeth Wheeler, June 2, 1978

Los Angeles Times, "Gerulaitis Hits Chicken, Friars Win," by Dave Distel, June 3, 1978

Los Angeles Times, "Friars Beaten By Racquets," June 6, 1978

Los Angeles Times, "Friars Defeat Cascades, 28-24," June 9, 1978

Los Angeles Times, "Friars Host Nets and Renee," June 14, 1978

Los Angeles Times, "Case-Guerrant Duo Leads Friars' Win," June 15, 1978

Boston Globe, "WTT At The Break," by Lesley Visser, June 25, 1978

Los Angeles Times, "Friars Play Racquets Tonight," July 19, 1978

Los Angeles Times, "Friars Win Again, Move Near Spot In Playoffs," July 20, 1978

Los Angeles Times, "Friars Beat Loves in Overtime," July 22, 1978

Los Angeles Times, "Friars Seek To Set Mark Against Loves," August 10, 1978

Prescott Courier, "Last Goal Of Net Star Laver a WTT Crown," AP, August 10, 1978

Windsor Star, "Friars Cooking," AP, August 16, 1978

Evening Independent, "Top Ten," October 30, 1978

Baltimore Sun, "Friars Became Fourth WTT Team To Fold," AP, November 9, 1978

Los Angeles Times, "Friars Follow Strings Into Oblivion," Elizabeth Wheeler, November 9 1978

SEA-PORT CASCADES/SEATTLE CASCADES (1978)

Walla Walla Union Bulletin, "World Team Tennis Eyes NW," AP, July 4, 1976

Eugene Register-Guard, "New Pro Team In Portland," UPI, August 25, 1976

The Bulletin, "Seattle, Portland Gets Leis," AP, September 24, 1976

Anchorage Daily News, "Sea-Port Cascades Sign First Player," UPI, January 28, 1977

Spokane Daily Chronicle, "Spokane Loses Pro Tourney," by Sue English, February 22, 1977

The Bulletin, "Sea-Port Team Signs Gorman," AP, March 8, 1977

Ellensburg Daily Record, "Gorman Needs Woman," by John Engstrom, March 8, 1977

Galveston Daily News, "Gorman Signs As WTT Coach," UPI, March 8, 1977

Walla Walla Union Bulletin, "Gorman As Coach," AP, March 8, 1977

Spokane Daily Chronicle, "Cascades Sign Players," AP, March 16, 1977

Tri City Herald, AP, "Cascades Draft Stove," AP, March 17, 1977

Walla Walla Union Bulletin, "Cascades Make Stove Top Pick," AP, March 17, 1977

Spokane Daily Chronicle, "Cascades Sign Dillen," March 21, 1977

Anchorage Daily News, "Seattle Cascades Must Win At Gate," AP, March 26, 1977

Gettysburg Times, "Betty Stove May Sign With Seattle," AP, April 12, 1977

San Mateo Times, "Erik Van Dillen He's Sold On WTT," by Dick Draper, May 10, 1977

Ellensburg Daily Record, "Cascades Dramatic Win," by John Engstrom, May 18, 1977

Los Angeles Times, "Strings Play Cascades Tonight," May 18, 1977

Ellensburg Daily Record, "Fans Wild About Sea-Port," by John Engstrom, May 23, 1977

Eugene Register-Guard, "Only 1,588 See Cascades Beaten," UPI, June 2, 1977

Longview Daily News (WA), "Cascades Front Office Shakeup Near," AP, June 15, 1977

Spokesman-Review, "JoAnne Russell: Unknown Champ," by Bob Payne, July 6, 1977

The Bulletin, "Sea-Port Cascades Crack Losing Streak," AP, June 11, 1977

Port Angeles Daily News, "PR Man Out In Sea-Port Tennis Shakeup," AP, June 15, 1977

Pittsburgh Press, "Sea-Port Franchise Sinking In Seattle," UPI, June 19, 1977

Spokesman-Review, "Stove Leads Net Stars To Town," by Bob Payne, July 2, 1977

Eugene Register-Guard, "Cascades Pluck Strings As Stove Takes Pair," AP, July 8, 1977

Spokesman-Review, "Cascades, Local Foe, Both Lose," AP, July 8, 1977

Eugene Register-Guard, "Cascades Rip Soviets," UPI, July 11, 1977

Eugene Register-Guard, "Gorman Sparks Sea-Port Win," AP, July 14, 1977

Spokane Daily Chronicle, "Russell Paces Cascades' Win," AP, July 15, 1977

Spokesman-Review, "Cascades Win Again," AP, July 15, 1977

Eugene Register-Guard, "Loving It In Seattle," UPI, July 19, 1977

Spokane Daily Chronicle, "Estep Trims Tom Gorman," AP, July 20, 1977

New York Daily News, "Apples Bomb SeaPort Cascades," by Mike Lupica, July 24, 1977

New York Times, "Cascades Defeat Apples in Overtime," by Parton Keese, August 2, 1978

Eugene Register-Guard, "Strings Finish Year By Beating Sea-Port," UPI, Aug. 15, 1977

Ellensburg Daily Record, "Cascades Smothered," UPI, August 17, 1977

Eugene Register-Guard, "Cascades Lose Season's Final," AP, August 18, 1977

Lewiston Morning Tribune, "Cascades Draw Only 700," AP, August 19, 1977

Eugene Register-Guard, "Cascades To Move Next Year," AP, August 19, 1977

Lewiston Morning Tribune, "Sea-Port Owner Favors Seattle," AP, September 10, 1977

The Bulletin, "It'll Be Seattle Cascades Next Season," AP, September 13, 1977

Spokane Daily Chronicle, "Seattle Wins," by Sue English, September 15, 1977

Spokane Daily Chronicle, "Cascades Get Seattle Money," AP, February 2, 1978

Eugene Register-Guard, "Cascades Involved In Three-Way Trade," UPI, March 4, 1978

Ellensburg Daily Record, "Cascades Serve Up Season," March 21, 1978

Ellensburg Daily Record, "Seattle Pro Tennis Team Ready For Opener," April 6, 1978

Ellensburg Daily Record, "Cascades Open Season Friday," UPI, April 19, 1978

New York Daily News, "Seattle All Right For Slew," by Jack Wilkinson, May 9, 1978

Spokesman-Review, AP, "Cascades Win One," May 12, 1978

Ellensburg Daily Record, "Cascades Rip Loves," UPI, May 17, 1978

Spokesman-Review, "Ruling Beats Seattle Team," AP, June 16, 1978

Ellensburg Daily Record, "Cascades Win Third Straight," UPI, July 18, 1978

Ellensburg Daily Record, "Cascades Lose To Friars," UPI, July 28, 1978

Spokesman-Review, "Cascades Clobber Racquets," AP, July 31, 1978

Ellensburg Daily Record, "Cascades Are In Playoffs," UPI, August 5, 1978

Ellensburg Daily Record, "Cascades Dunk Apples," UPI, August 8, 1978

Prescott Courier, "Cascades Top Racquet Squad," August 11, 1978

Ellensburg Daily Record, "Cascades Win Playoff," UPI, August 19, 1978

Ellensburg Daily Record, "Boston Eliminates Cascades," UPI, August 25, 1978

Spokane Daily Chronicle, "Cascades Sale Eyed," AP, September 21, 1978

Evening Independent, "Cascades Seeking New Home," AP, September 29, 1978

Spokane Daily Chronicle, "Seattle Team Will Leave," AP, September 29, 1978

Eugene Register-Guard, "People In Sports," October 15, 1978

Sportspress Northwest, by David Eskenazi, July 19, 2008

The Great Book Of Seattle Sports Lists, by Mike Gastineau, 2010

The Oregonian, "The Rise and Fall Of The Cascades," by Douglas Perry, October 26, 2012

THE SOVIETS (1977)

Scottsdale Daily Progress, "Casals To Lead Americans vs. Russia," AP, January 20, 1976

Philadelphia Daily News, "Faults Aside WTT," by Michael Knight, March 15, 1976

The Modesto Bee, "Billie Jean Helps U.S. Netters Complete Sweep," AP, March 16, 1976

Sports Illustrated, "Court Case For Détente," by Marsh Clark, March 22, 1976

Pittsburgh Press, "Keystones To Play Here," December 15, 1976

Beaver County Times, "Pittsburgh To Share A Team," UPI, December 15, 1976

Pittsburgh Press, "By Other Names, Its Tri, Tri Again," by Bill Heufelder, December 16, 1976
News-Dispatch, "Richards Keystones' Top Choice," UPI, January 13, 1977
Reading Eagle, "Renee Has To Think," AP, January 13, 1977
Pittsburgh Post-Gazette, "The Mark of Zingale," by Vince Leonard, January 21, 1977
New York Times, "WTT Pact Near For Soviet Entry," by Neil Amdur, February 1, 1977
Montreal Gazette, "Soviet Netters Turning Pro," AP, February 2, 1977
Observer-Reporter, "The Russians Are Coming, The Russians Are Coming," February 2, 1977
Pittsburgh Post-Gazette, "Tennis," AP, February 2, 1977
Pittsburgh Press, "WTT Signs Borg, Soviets," UPI, February 3, 1977
Bangor Daily News, "Soviets Enter Tennis Loop," AP, February 4, 1977
Playground Daily News, "Soviets to Join WTT," UPI, February 4, 1977

New York Times, "Six-Player Soviet Squad Joins WTT," by Tony Kornheiser, February 4, 1977
Observer-Reporter (PA), "USSR Joins Team Tennis," UPI, February 4, 1977
Rome News-Tribune, "Soviets Join Team Tennis," UPI, February 4, 1977
Salina Journal, "Soviet Team Joins WTT Loop," UPI, February 4, 1977
Spokesman-Review, "Few Games Scheduled in Philly," AP, February 4, 1977
Sunday Times-Sentinel, "Soviets Team Joins Team Tennis," UPI, February 4, 1977
Windsor Star, "World Team Tennis Now Really Is," AP, February 4, 1977
Sports Illustrated, "Scorecard," by Robert W. Creamer, February 7, 1977
Calgary Herald, "Top Soviet Trio Take Over Team," AP, February 15, 1977
Leavenworth Times, "No Hammer and Sickle," AP, February 15, 1977
Modesto Bee, "Russians Are Ready For WTT," by Will Grimsley, February 15, 1977
Sarasota Journal, "Soviet Stars Don't Wear Black Hats," AP, February 15, 1977
Washington C.H. Record-Herald, "Stars Replace Sickles," AP, February 15, 1977
Press-Courier, "Russ Team In U.S. Hockey," by Wil Grimsley, February 18, 1977
Daytona Beach Morning Journal, "WTT To Play In Plains?" AP, February 24, 1977
Sarasota Herald-Tribune, "Soviets To Play In Plains," UPI, February 25, 1977
Bangor Daily News, "Plains Plans Peanut Classic," UPI, March 18, 1977
Spokesman-Review, "Soviets, Seattle Slate Net Event," March 26, 1977
Los Angeles Times, "Russian Team Slated To Play In WTT season," April 4, 1977
The Morning Call, "Soviets to Visit Reading," by Marc Markowitz, April 7, 1977
Los Angeles Times, "Team Tennis Acquires a Big Red Machine," April 9, 1977

Philadelphia Daily News, "Our Soviets Hit Road," by Mary Flannery, April 12, 1977

Modesto Bee, "Soviets, Gaters Win," AP, April 22, 1977

Milwaukee Sentinel, "Soviet Netters To Play Game In Green Bay," April 23, 1977

New York Times, "Soviet Union Joins Team Tennis This Week," April 24, 1977

Palm Beach Post, "Soviets Get Acid Test in World Team Tennis," AP, April 24, 1977

Tuscaloosa News, "Russians, King-Led Apples, in Birmingham Friday," April 24, 1977

Spokane Daily Chronicle, "Cascades Tip Soviets," AP, April 25, 1977

Hagerstown Morning Herald, "Soviets Join WTT Competition," AP, April 26, 1977

The Independent, "Soviets Ushered into WTT," by Bob Martin, April 26, 1977

Indianapolis Star, "Loves Start Soviets Tour Tonight," by Bill Benner, April 26, 1977

Call-Leader, "Loves Whip USSR," AP, April 27, 1977

Corpus Christi Times, "Soviets Impress In Defeat," AP, April 27, 1977

New York Times, "Soviets Bow To Loves In Debut" by Paul Montgomery, April 27, 1977

Los Angeles Times, "Soviets Lose Their WTT Opener," April 28, 1977

Times Daily, "Russians Defeat New York Apples," UPI, April 28, 1977

Arizona Republic, "Racquets Face Russians in Peanut Match," AP, April 30, 1977

Gadsden Times, "Plains 'Peanut Tennis' Classic Starts Today," AP, April 30, 1977

Albany Herald, "Racquets Save Plains From Soviets," by Paul McCorvey, May 1, 1977

Arizona Republic, "Racquets Reign Mainly in Plains," by Penny Butler, May 1, 1977

New York Times, "Plains, Ga. Bestirred By Soviets," by Tony Kornheiser, May 1, 1977

Reading Eagle, "Billy Carter Tennis 'Hit'," AP, May 1, 1977

Danville Bee, "Teenager Helps Soviets Beat Strings, 26-25," AP, May 5, 1977

New York Times "Soviets Fall To Apples, See Mini Protest," by Neil Amdur, May 6, 1977

Reading Eagle, "Soviets Programmed," May 8, 1977

Indiana (Pa.) Gazette, "Soviets Short Stay Nets Victory," by Bob Fulton, May 9, 1977

Sports Illustrated, "The WTT Reigns In Plains," by Barry McDermott, May 9, 1977

Reading Eagle, "Soviets Tired," AP, May 11, 1977

Gettysburg Times, "Boston Lobsters Defeat Soviets," AP, May 12, 1977

Manitowoc Herald Times, "Arena Hosts WTT Match," by Steve Poellmann, May 12, 1977

Anchorage Daily News, "To Russia With Love," AP, May 18, 1977

Daily Union Democrat, "Soviets Visit," May 19, 1977

Daily Press (VA), "Russian WTT Star Power Chmyreva," by Tom Foster, May 25, 1977

Tri City Herald, "Soviets Battered By Lobsters," AP, May 26, 1977

Boston Globe, "Navratilova Leads As Lobsters Sock Soviets," May 27, 1977

Albany Herald, "King's Win Lifts Apples," UPI, May 31, 1977

The Californian, "WTT Drowning Soviets," UPI, June 3, 1977

Salina Journal, "Traveling A Headache For Soviet Tennis Team," UPI, June 3, 1977

Milwaukee Sentinel, "Russians Love It Here," by Dale Hofmann, June 4, 1977

Spokesman-Review, "Clinic Scheduled By Soviet Netters," June 30, 1977

Chicago Tribune, "Pair Joins WTT Soviets," AP, July 7, 1977

Spokane Daily Chronicle, "Soviets Arrive For Pro Tennis Confrontation," July 9, 1977

Spokesman-Review, "WTT Opens Test On Fans," by Bob Payne, July 10, 1977

Spokane Daily Chronicle, "Slim Crowd Sees Tennis Stars," by Sue English, July 11, 1977

Spokane Daily Chronicle, "Courtside," by Sue English, July 14, 1977

Deseret News, "Hard Times For Soviet Net Team," by Ray Gross, July 16, 1977

Reading Eagle, "Soviets Triumph," AP, July 19, 1977

Merced Sun-Star, "Gaters Thrash Soviets," AP, July 20, 1977

Miami News, "Golden Gaters Defeat Soviets," AP, July 20, 1977

Pacific Stars and Stripes, "Call Em The Arky Soviets," AP, July 21, 1977

Courier-Journal, "Nomadic Russians Drift to Louisville," by Gary Schultz, July 22, 1977

Spokane Daily Chronicle, "Soviet Netters Top Cleveland," AP, July 23, 1977

Salt Lake Tribune, "Soviets in Salt Lake," by Lex Hemphill, July 24, 1977

Deseret News, "Soviets Are Comin' On Strong," by Ray Grass, July 26, 1977

Miami News, "Soviets Would Rather Be in Philadelphia," July 26, 1977

New York Times, "Soviets Beat Nets, 21-19, In World Team Tennis," July 26, 1977

Los Angeles Times, "Nastase Upset As Soviets Beat Strings," July 27, 1977

Milwaukee Sentinel, "Northwestern Gets The OK," UPI, July 27, 1977

Chicago Tribune, "Soviets Wander Through WTT Loss," by Bill Jauss, July 28, 1977

St. Joseph News-Press, "Soviets Stop Racquets," AP, July 29, 1977

Los Angeles Times, "Détente Is Alive and Well in World Team Tennis," July 30, 1977

Clovis News Journal, "Tennis and Natasha," by Mike Braham, August 28, 1977

TORONTO-BUFFALO ROYALS (1974)

Leader-Post, "Toronto Part of 16-City Tennis League," CP, November 17, 1973

El Paso Herald Post, "Okker to Toronto," UPI, March 19, 1974

Baltimore Sun, "Okker Signs Net Pact With Toronto-Buffalo," AP, March 20, 1974

Calgary Herald, "Hockey to Football to Tennis for Bassett," by Mic Huber, April 1, 1974

Montreal Gazette, "Okker Set to Play Tonight," CP, May 7, 1974

Red Deer Advocate, "Northmen to Become Memphis Southmen," CP, May 7, 1974

Star-Phoenix, "Okker Heads Toronto Team," CP, May 7, 1974

Canandaigua Daily Messenger, "Toronto Against Cleveland," UPI, May 8, 1974

The Evening Independent, "Sports Clippings," AP, May 8, 1974

Windsor Star, "Okker Kingpin in Toronto Edge," CP, May 8, 1974

Benton Harbor News Palladium, "Crowd Disappoints In Opener," AP, May 10, 1975

Michigan Daily, "Loves Win Debut," by George Hastings, May 10, 1974

Leader-Post, "Toronto Team Loses Tennis," Canadian Press, May 11, 1974

Baltimore Sun, "Banners Beaten by Royals, 31-28," May 12, 1974

Baltimore Sun, "Okker-less Royals Defeat Banners," by Jim Caffrey, May 12, 1974

Lakeland Ledger, "Tennis," AP, May 12, 1974

Sunday Gazette-Mail, "Okker Sick, Cancels," AP, May 12, 1974

New York Times, "Tennis Team is Not Fond of Okker's Absence," May 13, 1974

Democrat and Chronicle, "Buffalo Debut Success for 2-City Team," AP, May 14, 1974

Boston Globe, "Sets Drop Third Home Match," May 16, 1974

Leader-Post, "Sets Broken By The Royals," AP, May 16, 1974

Boston Globe, "Lobsters Demolish Toronto," May 17, 1974

Pittsburgh Press, "Royals Breeze Past Triangles," by Bill Heufelder, May 20, 1974

News-Dispatch, "Lose 4th In A Row," UPI, May 20, 1974

Leader-Post, "Royals Whip Riders," CP, May 21, 1974

Democrat and Chronicle, "Royals Fall to Ms. King," AP, May 14, 1974

Vallejo Times-Herald, "8,329 See WTT," UPI, May 24, 1974

York Daily Record, "Billie Jean King Shows Form, Voice," UPI, May 24, 1974

Fort Worth Telegram, "Estep Says Worst Male Could Beat Top Woman," May 31, 1974

Ottawa Citizen, "Women's Lib?" CP, May 31, 1974

Canandaigua Daily Messenger, "Sports Clippings," UPI, June 4, 1974

Boston Globe, "Goolagong Rallies Triangles Over Royals," AP, June 10, 1974

Miami News, "The Man Who Stole Dolphins," by Jack Wilkinson, June 14, 1974

Argus-Press, "Loves Edge Toronto-Buffalo," AP, June 17, 1974

Canandaigua Daily Messenger, "Royals In Tailspin," UPI, July 9, 1974

Evening Independent, "Royals Win 23-20 Over Cleveland Nets," AP, July 19, 1974

El Paso Herald Post, "Okker Estep Pace Royals," UPI, July 20, 1974

Town Talk, "Okker's Effort Leads to Victory," AP, July 20, 1974

Christian Science Monitor, "Nine-Tenths of Woe," by Dave Langworthy, July 22, 1974

Canandaigua Daily Messenger, "Royals Back in Losing Column," UPI, July 23, 1974

Canandaigua Daily Messenger, "Royals Back to Losing," UPI, July 23, 1974

San Mateo Times, "Gaters Edge Royals," AP, July 23, 1974

El Paso Herald Post, "Doubles Give NY Sets Edge," UPI, July 30, 1974

Beaver County Times, "Tiebreaker Proves Triangles Downfall," UPI, July 31, 1974

Detroit Free Press, "983 See Loves Win in Toronto," Sports Editors, August 3, 1974

San Mateo Times, "Gaters Host Royals," Sports Staff, August 5, 1974

Daily Review, "Royals Lose to Gaters," by Charles Slyngstad, August 6, 1974

Honolulu Star-Bulletin, "Leis Rally Nips Royals," by Dave Koga, August 10, 1974

Pittsburgh Press, "Okker Finding Schedule Hectic," UPI, August 13, 1974

Windsor Star, "Okker Earns Short Rest," by Ron Sudlow, August 13, 1974

Calgary Herald, "Toronto, Buffalo Tied For Cellar," Canadian Press, August 19, 1974

Sydney Morning Herald, "Quieter for Jan, Bowreys," by Rod Humphries, October 1, 1974

Playground Daily News, "WTT Toronto Franchise To Hartford," UPI, October 17, 1974

Montreal Gazette, "Toronto Sports Status Cooling," Canadian Press, February 6, 1975

Oakland Tribune, "Toronto Folded," Special to the Tribune, April 3, 1975

Los Angeles Times, Morning Brief, April 28, 1977

The Art of World Team Tennis, by Greg Hoffman, 1977

The Tribune (IN), "John Bassett Dies of Cancer," AP, May 15, 1986

Buffalo News, "The Aud Had It All," by Robert J. Summers, March 30, 1996

About the Cover

WTT co-founder Billie Jean King served as player-coach of the 1974 Philadelphia Freedoms, owned by her real estate developer friend Dick Butera. In a 2018 phone conversation with Butera, I described a Billie Jean/Freedoms TV spot on YouTube that looked like some '70s high-art video installation. To cut a long story short, my partner-in-crime Tony Mann contacted legendary ad man Elliott Curson, who provided two incredible print ads, one based around the Julie Anthony image on this book's cover, the other reproduced on page 64.

Curson explains: "Well, you know, to do good advertising, you need a good client. And that was Billie Jean and Dick Butera of the Philadelphia Freedoms. So I met at a photography studio with players Fred Stolle and Julie Anthony. I got a racquet and cut the strings and smashed it over Fred's head. He was a good sport about it. And then Julie really put her hand through it. So these things are organic. If you don't plan these things out, you're gonna draw it out too long. Let's just do it, right? The idea was to call attention to the team and to the league—and to get some people out there with some special deals. I'm flattered by the cover."

313

Author's Note
Balls to the Wall

Billie Jean King, Philadelphia Freedoms, 1974
Inspiration for a generation of athletic activism

314

"WTT was LGBTQ in an X-Y world; a 'woke' sports league back when all others slept."

It was almost ten years ago when I was channel-surfing late-night cable TV and came upon an interview with Billie Jean King on MSG Network. She was speaking about some recently unearthed World Team Tennis match footage of her 1978 New York Apples against the Seattle Cascades at Madison Square Garden. Of course, I was thoroughly stunned by the extreme '70s-ness of this strange team sport. Ms. King spoke—about her league's battle for on-court gender equality; her vision of social change through pro sports; her WTT fan friend Elton John's hit "Philadelphia Freedom" and her teammate Vitas Gerulaitis' late-night shenanigans at Studio 54—and not one word about tennis.

If you know of my 2001 Feral House book *American Hardcore* or the accompanying documentary film, it was a detailed punk rock history that told a larger story of Reagan-era radicalism. So as I watched Billie Jean, I instinctively understood the socio-political parallels of brash World Team Tennis to both the concurrent '70s Dogtown skateboarding scene and late 20th-century rock subculture (albeit with no musical commonalities).

Understand World Team Tennis as one of those bold ideas too ahead of its time—so forward-thinking it only now makes sense. WTT was LGBTQ in an X-Y world; a "woke" sports league back when all others slept. The players did not

Mark Ein, WTT owner 2017-2019, with Billie Jean King and D.C. mayor Adrian Fenty

behave, and they did not wear white. The audiences of blue-collar sports fans were encouraged to get drunk and loud in support of their "home team" and to heckle the opposition between serves. In its final season, the league's top mixed doubles team was an African-American NBA star and a trans woman. European global tennis elites detested this American incursion and did everything to destroy such corrosion of conformity.

BUSTIN' BALLS: Pro Sports, Pop Culture, Progressive Politics is the final result of my quest to make sense of this strange but true history involving the crossover of sex, drugs, rock n roll, and tennis equality. I am particularly proud of the 20 individual franchise histories, and how their stories connected to—or failed to connect with—local tribal flavor. Such a bold vision could never happen again—if for no other reason that the anything-goes '70s has little in common with today's realpolitik. Consider this a modern sports book, for renegades and anti-social activists of all forms!

Very few of the key participants of this 1974-1978 era that I engaged with early on in this process shared my enthusiastic, forward-leaning viewpoint. Most of them are too old and upper-lipped to understand or to appreciate any association with punk rock or rebel sports (ABA, WHA, USFL), and are spooked by someone embracing their WTT daze. So, as a tennis outsider—who sees a mighty physical pursuit obscured by an elitist culture—the more tennis-insider pushback I encountered, the more I knew that I was onto something. So here's to 320 pages of unrelenting anti-tennis attitude!

Lastly, after five seasons of failed social or financial progress, King's star-power led to attempts to rebrand WTT over the past 40 years, each downsized from the previous incarnation, and each decreasingly edgy, exciting, and lucrative. The league has reiterated itself as a corporate-sponsor-funded artificial construct, be it through funding by a chemical company like DuPont WTT, a "lending servicer" like Advanta WTT, or the EpiPen scandal pharmaceutical firm Mylan WTT. Then came the 2016 debut of King's New York Empire team of a revamped "World TeamTennis" (spelled as such), attended by this author along with 150 or so other holders of free tickets, who cleared out by halftime. None of that is part of this great story of a unique place and time.

Bustin' Balls would not have been possible were it not for the effort and vision of Jessica Parfrey, Christina Ward, Ron Kretsch, and the late great Adam Parfrey. I am proud to return to the Feral House family.

I dedicate this book to my most loyal and loving fans, Alyssa Fisher Blush and Jackie Fisher Blush. Special shout-outs go to the Blush, Fisher, Radick, and Goldstein families.

A massive thank-you to everyone who helped propel this project, in various orders of magnitude: George Petros, Tony Mann, John Reis, Ray Ciccolo, Dick Butera, Elliott Curson, Alexander Patsos, Jennifer Maldonado, Jeff Jones, John Vondracek, Mark Brian Levine, Jimi Bones, Louie Gasparro, RJ Baker, Wade St. Germaine, Richard Johnson, Rusty Sullivan, Anthony Perrone, Kevin Vonesper, John Law, Toby Poser, Stephen Masucci, Gass Wilde, Anne Slowey, Virginia Joe Jones, Boris Wright, Elle Sunman, Percy Wise, Frank Froehling, John Korff, Howard Freeman, Jim Martz, Marty Appel, and of course Ilana Kloss, Larry King, and Billie Jean King.

STEVEN BLUSH is the author of *American Hardcore*, *American Hair Metal*, *Lost Rockers*, *.45 Dangerous Minds*, and *New York Rock*. He wrote and co-produced the documentary film *American Hardcore* (Sundance Film Festival, Sony Pictures Classics), based on his Feral House book. Blush was the editor and publisher of the award-winning *Seconds Magazine*, and for years was a New York City club DJ/promoter, noted for his sound design for fashion designer Stephen Sprouse. He writes for music-oriented publications, hosts a series of podcasts on the Blush Media Network, and blogs about New York Jets football. *Bustin' Balls* is the first title by Blush Books, hopefully the first of many through Feral House.